# Authentically Orthodox

# AUTHENTICALLY ORTHODOX

## A TRADITION-BOUND FAITH IN AMERICAN LIFE

### ZEV ELEFF

WAYNE STATE UNIVERSITY PRESS

*Detroit*

ISBN 978-0-8143-4481-1 (paperback); ISBN 978-0-8143-4480-4 (hardback);
ISBN 978-0-8143-4482-8 (ebook)

Library of Congress Control Number: 2019948756

Wayne State University Press
Leonard N. Simons Building
4809 Woodward Avenue
Detroit, Michigan 48201–1309

Visit us online at wsupress.wayne.edu

For Adir
Lovable and original.
Authentic, by any standard,
just like his siblings, Meital and Jack.

# CONTENTS

## PART 3. PROTECTING ORTHODOX MALE SPACE

# ACKNOWLEDGMENTS

I AM VERY FORTUNATE that my research and writing is not a lonely experience. In preparing this book, I benefited from the support and counsel of a wide and variegated circle of teachers, students, friends, and family. They bear none of the culpability but ought to claim an ample share of credit for the original ideas and the new knowledge contained in these pages.

I owe much to the mentors in whose classrooms and offices I sat, and for their continued commitment to my work. First to Jonathan Sarna and Jacob J. Schacter, for their wisdom and endless devotion. Rabbi Schacter's class on Jewish autobiography was the toughest and most enriching course of my undergraduate career at Yeshiva College. He revealed to me the complexities and possibilities of historical research. Simply put, Rabbi Schacter taught me to love history. His close reading of every page of this book betokens his enduring influence on my life. Since welcoming me to Brandeis University in 2011, Dr. Sarna has served as an unfailing model of kindness, scholarship, and teaching. Certainly, this book's central argument—that Judaism must be understood in its American religious context, and the orientation of "lived religion"—is influenced by Dr. Sarna's approach to American Jewish history. For this and so much else, I am in his debt. In addition I have studied with outstanding people whose training and writing inform this project. The guidance of scholars like David Hackett Fischer, Sylvia Fishman, Jeffrey Gurock, David Hall, Jane Kamensky, and Eugene Sheppard have encouraged me to deepen my analysis and get the most out of research and writing.

Likewise, my own students have offered fresh insights and helped organize my thoughts on a number of subjects. The students in my undergraduate seminar on Orthodox Judaism tested hypotheses, challenged historical paradigms, and engaged in lively, thought-provoking conversation. In particular, I single out Daniel Gutstein, David Isenberg, Velvel Loeb, Yehuda Dov Reiss, Edward Sandler, and Adeev Segal for arriving to class each day, prepared to reject flimsy theses and ready to comb through the sources in search of better arguments.

Of course historians cannot set their projects into motion without primary sources to interrogate. A bounty of materials is available online. But a lot of the scholarly building blocks that fortify this work are kept in the traditional storehouses of archives, libraries, and private collections. Owing to this, I hasten to offer gratitude to Shulamith Z. Berger of the Yeshiva University Archives. For more than a dozen years, Shuli has fielded my many requests, scanned documents, and helped navigate through historical quagmires. Her friendship and graciousness form the bedrock of a number of these chapters. Likewise, I am a better historian because of my friend and colleague Menachem Butler. I have gained a lot from his keen wit and wisdom. He has also directed me toward many of the essential texts used in the present work. Moreover, I am very heartened that Menachem has happily agreed to allow me to publish a revised version of our study of bat mitzvah, originally published for a symposium at the *Torah Musings* online journal.

Archivists and librarians generously mined materials and proved eager to help. Thanks are dutifully due to Dana Herman, Elisa Ho, Kevin Proffitt, and Gary Zola of the Jacob Rader Marcus Center of the American Jewish Archives; staff members of the American Jewish Historical Society; Jill Aizenstein and Shira London of Beth Tfiloh Dahan Community School; Patrick Robbins of Bob Jones University; Chloe Morse-Harding of the Robert D. Farber University Archives and Special Collections of Brandeis University; Sarah Goss of the Gordon College Archives; Jennifer Duplaga of the Duggan Library Archives at Hanover College; Vardit Samuels of Harvard University's Widener Library; Joanna Church of the Jewish Museum of Maryland; Marikit Schwartz Fain of John Brown University; Moshe Kolodny of Agudath Israel of America's Orthodox Jewish Archives; Doug Denne of the University of the Ozarks; Kathy Bloch and Gail Goldberg of Spertus Institute; and David Osielski of the Buswell Library at Wheaton College.

Several individuals provided materials from personal and family collections or guided me to those hard-to-find repositories. I am grateful to Shlomo Appel, Freda Birnbaum, Laura Shaw Frank, Roz Goldberg, Becky Gordon, Cheryl Haut, Ittai Hershman, Harry Kozlovsky, David Levitt, Aryeh Lieberman, Shalom Menora, Shaul Robinson, Freda Rosenfeld, Marc Shapiro, Rita Shloush, David Selis, Shimon Steinmetz, Tamara Weissman, Marvin Wiener,

Shmuel Winiarz, and Daniel Yolkut. I also benefited from several clues and ideas shared via social media forums like Facebook. This is a relatively new resource for scholars, and, for me anyway, "crowd sourcing" has confirmed that PhD-credentialed scholars don't hold a monopoly on historical research. As well, the Saul Silber Memorial Library of the Hebrew Theological College, my home institution, holds countless scholarly treasures that aided this research. For other books and periodicals, I am all too appreciative for the efforts of the interlibrary loan staffs at Brandeis University and the Skokie Public Library for fielding repeated requests.

Colleagues and friends read parts of this manuscript, listened to sections delivered at conferences, and sat with me to discuss work-in-progress. I am so very grateful to Gavriel Bachrach, Dovid Bashevkin, Kimmy Caplan, Mike Cohen, Hillel Davis, Yitzi Ehrenberg, Jonathan Engel, Seth Farber, Adam Ferziger, Joshua Furman, Rachel Gordan, Avi Helfand, Jerold Isenberg, Yoel Kelman, Leslie Ginsparg Klein, Laura Leibman, Abraham Lieberman, Leonard Matanky, Adam Mendelssohn, Adam Mintz, Lincoln Mullen, Shari Rabin, Jeffrey Saks, Shmuel Schuman, Moshe Schapiro, Marc Shapiro, Gil Student, Shimon Unterman, and Chaim Waxman.

This volume is a testament to the benefits of working within the scholarly establishment and the process of peer review. I delivered sections of this book at academic conferences. In addition, universities, synagogues, and other institutions invited me as a guest lecturer and scholar-in-residence to present my work, and I am grateful for those invitations and the discussions that ensued after those dozens of talks. Most of these chapters are brand new, except for Chapters 2 and 4. I dutifully acknowledge the graciousness of Johns Hopkins University Press and the editors of *American Jewish History* for authorizing the use of my December 2010 article on the College Bowl, and of Gil Student of *Torah Musings* for permitting the reuse of an article I coauthored with Menachem Butler that appeared in a May 2016 symposium. I have reconsidered and augmented both chapters, and the iterations presented here should be considered my most up-to-date thinking on those subjects. In addition I published several shorter and popular-style essays that appeared on *The Lehrhaus* website. This catalyzed and helped crystalize the ideas that form the basis of Chapter 5, on Orthodox consumerism and children's culture. *The Lehrhaus* is an online journal that I cofounded with Ari Lamm and Shlomo Zuckier, and coedited from 2016 to 2018. I am thankful to the coeditors of this scholarly initiative for their collaboration and leadership. At Wayne State University Press, Annie Martin, Kathryn Wildfong, Kristin Harpster, Emily Nowak, and Mindy Brown expertly offered judicious doses of encouragement and constructive criticism to improve this project. Along with the anonymous peer reviewers, the staff at Wayne State were the perfect partners to produce this book. In addition, I am most grateful to colleagues at Hebrew Theological College and Touro College for their friendships and commitment to my work and scholarship. I hope this book meets the high standards both schools have come to expect under the leadership of Alan Kadish, Moshe Krupka, Brian Levinson, Patricia Salkin, Shmuel Schuman, Chani Tessler, and Shabsai Wolfe.

Finally, my family. My grandparents, Annette and Morton Eleff, read each word of every iteration of this manuscript. As an undergraduate at Case Western in the 1940s, my grandfather at one point considered pursuing graduate studies in Jewish history. He went on to become a phenomenal and beloved pediatrician but never abandoned his appreciation for history and scholarship. Grandma and Zayde, my love and admiration for you is boundless; your legacy and integrity inspired these pages. I owe much to my parents, Susan and Scott Eleff. In fact my father was probably the first to push me to consider the intersection of lived religion and Jewish law, the topic of the first section of this book. After encountering the position and reaction of Rabbi Moshe Feinstein regarding the use of peanut oil on Passover, my father immediately called me and urged me to explore the topic. Upon detecting a certain incredulousness on my part, he challenged me to investigate the episode. The result is this book. More than anyone else, my mother taught me how to write and always takes an avid interest in my research. My parents were also part of a circle of ambitious young families who founded Yeshivat Rambam in Baltimore, the subject of Chapter 6. My brothers—David, Ben, and Joey—and I attended the school in its most formative period, though none of us at that time could have imagined that it would become a valuable lesson in the chronicles of American religious history. A decade ago I claimed membership to another family. My in-laws, Marcy and Paul Stieglitz, and siblings-in-law welcomed me and have, in their own wonderful way, participated in the conversations that developed into this work. I trust that my father-in-law will appreciate the sports history contained in Chapter 3.

Melissa and our children are the core of this and everything else I do. Melissa is my best friend, most helpful critic, and beloved partner in our most charmed life together. Far better than I, she can trace the genesis of every idea and word of this book, explaining just what it was at a dinnertime conversation or car-ride discussion that animated this research. I was just fortunate to be there and to be inspired by her. Meital, Jack, and Adir are our young children who make each moment purposeful and incalculably wonderful. Aspiring readers and eager story-time listeners, Meital and Jack, I trust, will welcome this book to our bedtime rotation. Adir is the precocious and relative newcomer to our family, born during the final stages of writing. He and I still have much to talk about. For our kids, I am most thankful.

# INTRODUCTION

In April 1961, Rabbi Leonard Gewirtz of Adas Kodesch Shel Emeth Congregation in Wilmington, Delaware, completed a manual for Orthodox Jews. But he did not describe it like that. Instead he addressed it to "Authentic Jews." Understood in its American Protestant context, the use of "Orthodox" gave some credibility to non-Orthodox denominations, that each branch was legitimate based on a common creed and a valid reading of the Bible and other sacred texts.[1] Gewirtz did not believe this. To the contrary, the writer claimed that there was only one Jewish movement that was bound by "Jewish memories and Jewish tradition."[2] Others might have provided a history lesson to prove an allegiance to a religious tradition, tracing a line from earlier epochs in Jewish life to the current iteration of Orthodox faith. Gewirtz, however, argued that traditionalism could be tested in the present. It was born out of genuine religious experiences. He therefore described his tradition-bound creed as Authentic Judaism: obeyed as a peerless brand of Jewish faith, practiced "as naturally as the air he breathes."[3] The Authentic Jew punctiliously observed the Sabbath and holidays; engaged in regular and pious prayer; abided by the kosher dietary laws and the rules governing family purity. Most of all "Authentic Judaism" called for its adherents to "open our hearts and souls authentically to God in Jewish prayer and worship, [so that] a change will come over us too."[4] Orthodox Judaism, or Authentic Judaism, was a feeling, possessed of a palpable religious energy.

"Authenticity" is a word used like an anchor to moor a ship amid shifting waters. It's needed because religion is never static. Its purpose is to stabilize a society or community amid change. The notion therefore emerged as a popular virtue in the European Enlightenment era of the eighteenth century, much to the credit of Jean-Jacques Rousseau.[5] The French philosopher called for living an "authentic life," one that was sincere and removed from the dangers of rootless fashions and opinions.[6] Even back then authenticity was an attribute hard to pin down. But it could be associated with feelings of devotion to a tradition, heartfelt earnestness, virtue, and, for religious people, piety. The claim to authenticity was perhaps Orthodox Judaism's most compelling trait. In 1950 Hermann Schwab, a descendant of Rabbi Samson Raphael Hirsch's Frankfurt enclave, declared that "German-Jewish Orthodoxy was Sinai Judaism."[7] To separate themselves from religious reformers, Schwab's parents and grandparents in Frankfurt might have described themselves as *Urjudentum*, or followers of "Original Judaism." These were extreme historical formulations provoked by a perceived need to stabilize a religious world amid rapid social, cultural, and religious change. They were also uniquely German ideas, possibly prompted by a circle of philosophers led by Martin Heidegger, who understood authenticity as a state of being uninfluenced by external conditions.[8] Most German Orthodox Jews, even Heidegger devotees like the theologian Rabbi Eliezer Berkovits, would have conceded that their religious practices differed from Mosaic forms.[9] Still, many Orthodox Jews imagined a historical line that connected their behaviors and rituals to the kinds practiced by Jews two or three centuries earlier.[10]

True or not, this is the sort of conception of bindingness and traditionalism that suited "orthodox" faiths, groups alleging the "correct belief." The sociologist Shmuel Eisenstadt described orthodox religions as proffering perpetual "common symbols of tradition."[11] Similarly, the historian Eric Hobsbawm described a "set of practices, normally governed by overtly or tacitly accepted rules and of a ritual or symbolic nature, which seek to inculcate certain values and norms of behavior by repetition, which automatically implies continuity with the past."[12] As Clifford Geertz argued, the desire of traditional communities to connect rituals to the practices of the past was particularly important in the United States, where religion was decoupled from state-sponsored faiths and Old World traditions.[13] This is probably the most conventional understanding of authenticity and how it is envisaged by religious leaders.[14] More than just obedience to Jewish law, American Orthodox Judaism—like Catholicism, Lutheranism, and other tradition-bound faiths—used symbols like rituals, resistance to ecumenism, and proscribed gender roles to claim fidelity to religion.[15] These religiously conservative features complemented the common characteristics of orthodox faiths. Contrast this with more liberal enclaves like those of Conservative and Reform Jews—consistent with mainline Protestant groups—that engaged more openly in debates on how to negotiate "tradition" and "innovation."[16]

Yet there is something less definitional about authenticity, that fervor articulated by Rabbi Gewirtz to describe the experiences of Orthodox Jews and their lived religion. The anthropologist Regina Bendix described authenticity as a "quality of experience": in her words, like the "chills running down one's spine during musical performances, for instance, moments that may stir one to tears, laughter, elation—which on reflection crystalize into categories and in the process lose the immediacy that characterizes authenticity."[17] These sensations endow experiences with significant meaning and legitimize interactions and occasions. For Bendix, authenticity is "experiential"—the composite of cultural forces engaging one another—and not something "static and lasting."[18] Orthodox Jews also claimed that the authenticity they ascribed to their variety of faith could be experienced and verified. It wasn't just that this brand of creed, so they submitted, most closely resembled the faith of their forefathers, as Eisenstadt and Hobsbawm would have probably described religion's relationship to authenticity. Orthodox Judaism, claimed Leonard Gewirtz, for example, could be confirmed by less tangible—but no less meaningful—means: by how it "naturally" summoned Jews to Torah study and prayer.[19] The correctness of Orthodox Judaism was proven by the "soul-stirring cry of repentance" on Yom Kippur.[20] The parallel to Bendix's imagery is unmistakable.

How can historians tasked with proffering frameworks and methods of analysis measure this experiential expression of authenticity? I define authenticity as a web of experiences mediated by any number of cultural forces, similar to historian Robert Orsi's articulation of religion as a "web of relationships."[21] To steady themselves in a raging sea of change, tradition-bound faith communities—those which outwardly claimed a fidelity to a useable past and inherited rites and customs—calibrate their religious positions in realms like religious law, youth culture, education, and gender by considering a host of internal and external factors and calculating the result by some approximate measure of authenticity. They desperately required this, as generations of Americans unmoored themselves from denominationalism to seek out a more individualistic and "holistic, all-encompassing vision of life."[22] Moreover, it is the experience—the context of time and place—that endows an action or moment with authentic feeling. The chapters that follow aim to prove that the unceasing search for religious experiences is authenticated by surrounding forces. Without that, actions and rituals stop being authentic. While also acknowledging some of the other factors that determine religious authenticity, my labor in this book is to show the influence of American religious culture as a determining force in moderating "authenticity" in Orthodox Judaism—and other tradition-bound faiths.

The other key focus of this book is on "lived religion": that is, how faith is manifested and practiced beyond the doctrines pronounced in synagogues by clergymen and other religious "elites." In the United States that authentic religious experience was informed by a myriad of cultural forces. Sometimes it could be found in the mundane parts of life. In the United States, in contrast to Europe, contended theologian Reinhold Niebuhr, there stood no ancient churches or other such evidence of formalized religious influences and tradition. Instead, wrote Niebuhr, "we Americans have somehow combined good plumbing with religious faith in the 'American way of life.' "[23] Technology, music, and foodways have also shared in this New World phenomenon. Ever since Alexis de Tocqueville wrote his treatise on American life in the 1830s, foreign observers have marveled at the ways religion manifested itself in American climes. The Scottish scholar D. W. Brogan, for instance, was puzzled by the way Americans inserted religious lyrics into popular music and how they embroidered grace into the tablecloths in dining cars of the New Haven Railroad.[24] But Americans understood that these were fine and authentic expressions of their faith. The same was the case within American Judaism and other tradition-bound religions that claim authenticity as a compelling characteristic of their faith.

Most histories have tracked religious change in Orthodox Judaism as its adherents move between the two supposedly oppositional poles of "tradition" and "modernity."[25] Scholars have plotted this linear movement to explain changes in education, religious and ritual observance, and interaction with outside culture. But for Orthodox Judaism, authentic religion was far more than a negotiation with modern life; not merely obedience to Jewish law and a set of behaviors and rituals that project toward Old World traditionalism. That's just the start. Just as important are the religious sensibilities that help decide, above and beyond the dictates of Jewish law, what is authentic and what is not. These pages investigate Orthodox Judaism in the culturally complex and quick-changing twentieth century, and the emergent American factors that developed the attitudes and sensibilities that helped decide what was religiously authentic or not. Before I get to that, however, it makes good sense to understand the too-often-overlooked beginnings of American Orthodox Judaism and how it formed within a particularly New World religious clime.

## The Beginning of American Orthodox Judaism

In January 1826 Jacob Mordecai penned a lengthy dissertation on Judaism. The Virginian and noted Jewish scholar was compelled to write it, distressed as he was by Isaac Harby and his plot to bring about "schism" in South Carolina. One year earlier Harby and his Charleston circle had established the Reformed Society of Israelites.[26] These young people—no more than fifty in all—broke from South Carolina's Sephardic congregation to form a group that prayed without "every thing that might excite the disgust of the well informed Israelite."[27] In a discourse marking the occasion of the split, Harby explained that his worship meant to add more English, "to throw away Rabbinical interpolations," and to "avoid useless repetitions."[28] Jacob Mordecai was deeply disturbed by Harby's remarks, but at first decided to ignore them. Then he changed his mind. Harby's forty-page essay had achieved an impressive circulation, reaching many of America's six thousand Jews and US dignitaries such as Thomas Jefferson and John C. Calhoun.[29] The public conversation surrounding the "Reform" discourse impelled Mordecai to respond to Harby, to "examine the principles he advocated and test their solidity and their orthodoxy by the translations of Holy writ."[30]

Jacob Mordecai, then, introduced Orthodox Judaism to the United States. Before that time, all religiously engaged Jews belonged to a handful of synagogue communities that had no need to sort themselves or construct identities as specific types of Judaism. Mordecai and likeminded Jews would have described the basics of their Orthodox Judaism as loyal to the essentials of Jewish law and the tenets of its faith. Orthodox Jews observed the Sabbath by refraining from what the sages and their later interpreters defined as "work." The same went for the many Jewish holidays that dot the calendar. The Sabbath and festivals summoned Orthodox Jews to acquire and use religious objects and partake in specific rituals, like the palm and citron on Sukkot and eating matzah and bitter herbs on Passover. There were some clear-cut rules governing the kosher dietary laws and a consensus opinion on family purity and the liturgy. Jewish law specified requirements for minors and adults and differing religious obligations for women and men. Mordecai also believed in the oneness of God, messianism, Mosaic prophecy, the divinity of the Bible, and the authority of the Talmud. For the next several decades, their opponents would reconsider each of these religious planks.[31]

Mordecai's response established the foundation of an American form of Orthodox Judaism. The refutation of Harby and his "Reform" brand of Judaism drew from typical sources: the Talmud, Maimonides, and, most prominently, the Bible. He utilized these texts to rebuff Harby's "belief that America truly is the land of promise spoken of in our ancient Scriptures; that this is the region to which the children of Israel, if they are wise, will hasten to come."[32] His own daughter described Mordecai's rebuke as "harsh," but most traditional-minded Jews were happy he wrote it.[33] Mordecai was not about to let Harby and his reformers "destroy the ancient fabrick of Israelite worship and to gradually undermine all confidence in their religion under the pretext of divesting it of Rabbinical impurities and interpretations."[34] Mordecai expressed gratitude for his religious freedoms in the United States. He was rather convinced that his authentic Judaism fit well in American environs.

American Judaism was not at all unique among New World faith groups. The 1820s and 1830s were a period of religious schism in the United States. A number of Christian denominations splintered over questions of how to express religious authenticity in American life. Elias Hicks's enlightened and populist-focused Quakers broke away from Orthodox Friends, whom the former group considered too traditional and out of step with American forms of individualism.[35] Barton Stone and Alexander Campbell led two friction-filled factions of the Disciples of Christ, each claiming that their group was a better and more authentic fit in their American climes.[36] And a rising group of Irish Catholics distanced itself from the established American Catholics and their lay-driven religious "republicanism."[37] Each rift revealed the challenges faced by faith communities to prove their American bona fides in the early republic, usually by marshalling citations from the Bible. Jacob Mordecai's and Isaac Harby's debate over New World Judaism was linked to that very same struggle to claim standing as the authentic American brand of the Jewish faith. Harby, like other religious liberals, felt compelled to radically reshape his faith to fit American values. Mordecai, on the other hand, stressed fidelity to the plain meaning of the Bible and the American right to religious freedom as the best reasons to maintain traditional rites and observances. As the century unfolded the Harby-Mordecai dispute anticipated many future battles between Orthodox and Reform exponents in the nineteenth century and the role that America would play in shaping these religious debates.

The multireligious confrontation over authenticity and Americanism had many causes. More than anything else America's lack of authoritative order provoked the widespread religious dissent. Despite attempts to create a shared political and cultural tradition, American national identity suffered from a lack of rootedness, leaving all sorts of leaders and ideologues trying to fill the void. The result was a religious marketplace full of options and interpretations of American religion. The American religious historian Nathan Hatch put it this way:

> The flexibility and innovation of religious organizations made it possible for an American to find an amenable group no matter what his or her preference in belief, practice, or institutional structure. Churches ranged from egalitarian to autocratic and included all degrees of organizational complexity. One could be a Presbyterian who favored or opposed the freedom of the will, a Methodist who promoted or denounced democracy in the church, a Baptist who advocated or condemned foreign missions, and a member of virtually any denomination that upheld or opposed slavery. . . . Religious options in the early republic seemed unlimited: one could worship on Saturday, practice foot washing, ordain women, advocate pacifism, prohibit alcohol, or toy with spiritualism, phrenology, or health reform.[38]

The debates among opposing religious groups took on many forms but usually circled back to principles and values connected to the young nation: freedom and liberty.[39] Successful faith groups argued how their dogma best suited—was the most authentic expression of—American environs and explained why others did not. Once again American Judaism was no different. Like his European reforming counterparts, Harby had read the works of the enlightened philosopher Moses Mendelssohn of Berlin. Yet Harby recruited followers best by linking his cause for "progress" with those of "this happy land." In response public personalities like the Jewish diplomat and playwright

Mordecai Noah accused Harby and his friends of being "unacquainted with the essential forms of the religion," guilty of "retrograde instead of advancing," and therefore unpatriotic.[40] Like so many other faith communities, American Judaism—both its Orthodox and Reform factions—debated the limits of American republicanism in a religious context. It was not so much a question of tradition and fidelity to the past as what was most authentic in the New World.

The origins of Orthodox Judaism in the United States offer a different model compared to its European counterpart. Historians Jacob Katz, Rachel Manekin, Moshe Samet, and Michael Silber all subscribed to a theory that European Orthodox Judaism emerged in response to modernity and secularization.[41] For Katz, the pathbreaker of this research, these were important concepts in his doctoral training in sociology.[42] Focusing mostly on the Jewish experience in Germany and Hungary, these historians proposed that religious elites—rabbis, mostly—cultivated a religious culture that could protect their constituencies and their traditions from the dangers of outside forces. This meant heavy doses of separatism to shield from non-Jewish and non-Orthodox forces, instituting more stringent interpretations of Jewish law and careful monitoring of the communities' access to liberal Western learning. In so doing historians of Orthodox Judaism documented the many ways Orthodox Jews grappled with notions of change along a continuum between tradition and modernity.

There has been some attempt to parse out the differences among various Orthodox Jewish locales. Mordechai Breuer, one of Katz's students, argued that German Orthodoxy was a post-emancipationist invention, blending innovation, religious consolidation, elitism, and strong rabbinic authority to create a compelling idea for traditional religionists.[43] More recently, Yosef Salmon contended that Orthodox Judaism in Lithuania developed in three stages during the final decades of the nineteenth century: ideological responses to reform, halakhic method and the use of metahalakhic considerations, and reaction to Jewish nationalism.[44] However, none of the many researches into the beginnings of Orthodox Judaism sought to situate it in its local religious context.

Orthodox Judaism in the United States was at its core an American religious phenomenon. Jews in this country had grappled with a deep exposure to modernity and secularization before their counterparts on the Continent.

It chronologically paralleled the Orthodox Judaisms of other places, but it was catalyzed by forces not considered by scholars of modern Jewish history. In fact the American origins of Orthodox Judaism suggest that much can be gained through a more thorough understanding of the religious milieu in which British, Galician, German, Hungarian, Lithuanian, Polish, and Russian Orthodox Judaism developed. I take this cue from the Oxford-based comparative religionist Max Müller who, a century ago, was wont to suggest that it is essential to know two religions in order to fully understand just one.[45] At Harvard the religion scholar Diana Eck often tells her students that "if you know one religion . . . you don't know any."[46] There is much truth in the view that modern and secular forces shaped Orthodox Judaism. I suggest, however, that the labors of social historians would be enhanced with the lenses employed by scholars of religion.

## The Rise of an American Orthodox Judaism

American Orthodoxy developed specific religious characteristics in the mid-nineteenth century. Long ago, historian Moshe Davis wrote that America's Orthodox Jews were those who adopted the traditional "medieval" Jewish view on the authority of the Talmud and codes, the mission of Israel, the messiah, reward and punishment, and Zion.[47] Yet it was more than this. In an earlier book I made the case that "Orthodox" and "Reform" were religious labels that emerged out of the rabbinic conquest of the lay-driven form of American Judaism that dominated the eighteenth and first half of the nineteenth century. Rabbis gained a stronger foothold in congregational life once determinants of change—increased affluence leading to new and impressive synagogues, nationwide reevaluation of authority structures, and the strained relations between Jews in Europe and the United States—in the 1860s forced a wave of ecclesiasticism to wash over all American Jewish life.[48] All the while, the formation of definite religious monikers like "Orthodox" and "Reform" was deliberate and enabled rabbis to assert their brand of Judaism on an increasingly bolixed and less engaged laity.

Orthodox Jews believed that their faith was the form of Judaism that best aligned with Protestant biblicism and, therefore, with America. To Christians the United States was a "biblical nation" whose republican values and national narrative could be found in the Bible's many messages.[49] The study habits of

Orthodox and Reform exponents, as well as their theological points of departure, were the same. Both Orthodox and Reform leaders took to the Bible, certainly more often than the Talmud or other rabbinic texts. They enjoyed their status as "Israelites" whom other faiths counted on to help navigate the New World wilderness and to be the most biblically literate.[50] Most therefore likely agreed with Mordecai Noah, who in 1845 recommended that his coreligionists "shut the Talmud and open the Bible."[51] The rank and file by and large rebuffed efforts by men like Max Lilienthal, Isaac Leeser, or Isaac Mayer Wise to translate medieval and modern Jewish texts into English and to suggest changes to communal life based on those treatises. This contrasts with rabbis of all stripes in Europe who drew from philosophical works and Jewish codes to establish religious identities, whether as Orthodox, Reform, or anything else in between.[52] In the words of one historian, for example, the Orthodox German Jew looked to "German philosophy and searched for lines of connection leading, say, from Immanuel Kant, Max Scheler, and Hans Driesch to the old Jewish teachings."[53]

In the United States sermonizers and rabbinic editorialists were just as opinionated about Judaism but assembled prooftexts from the Bible, in line with other contemporaneous New World religious leaders. There were, of course, fundamental differences between Orthodox and Reform Judaism. Perhaps the most pronounced was Reform's inclination to modify the traditional prayer book and to adopt mixed pews in the synagogues.[54] Reform also tended to prefer a looser definition of the messiah, resurrection, and heaven. The Orthodox, as indicated by Moshe Davis, upheld a much more traditional—the so-called medieval—point of view.

Given their choice of texts, America's Orthodox Jews defended their beliefs and observances differently from their traditional-leaning counterparts in Europe, including Frankfurt rabbi Samson Raphael Hirsch or Moses Sofer, the "Hatam Sofer," in Hungary. Most often, Orthodox leaders in the United States did not quote verses from the Talmud or the teachings of Maimonides to oppose Reform rivals and quell the concerns of their adherents. The Orthodox castigated their religious opponents for their infidelities toward the Bible, the most American-wise authentic sacred text, more than any other Jewish texts. For instance, Isaac Leeser of Philadelphia, a staunchly Orthodox man, appealed to the Bible as he defended the strict dietary laws. The Jew who observed these restrictions was the *"true orthodox,* who thinks with the

Bible, and is willing to live by it."[55] Reform, in this polemical point of view, was anti-Bible. An Orthodox layman wrote to one Reform rabbi, informing him of the "great dissatisfaction evinced by the Israelites of America in regard to *your views* of construction on certain points of our Holy Scriptures."[56] Similarly, Samuel Myer Isaacs of New York deflected Reform innovations in the United States because, to his mind, they misunderstood the Bible, or resorted to "liberal interpretations of plain biblical commands."[57] Sometimes Isaacs faulted Reform for misappropriated values rather than shoddy scholarship. On another occasion, for example, the New York clergyman accused Reformers of worshipping modernity rather than the Bible. In contrast it was the Orthodox who believed in the "faith in the Bible as the revealed word of God."[58]

Likewise, Orthodox Jews maintained their focus on Zion by focusing on Scripture's promises of a return to the Holy Land. Reform's wholesale denial of this theological plank reinforced the importance of Israel in the Orthodox mind. Beginning with Isaac Harby, Reform Jews had adopted the United States as their promised land. This messianism was informed by a religious devotion to American ideas. Almost twenty years later in Charleston, Rev. Gustavus Poznanski announced, at a dedication ceremony for a new synagogue site, that "this synagogue is our *temple*, this city our *Jerusalem*, this happy land our *Palestine*, and our fathers defended with their lives *that* temple, *that* city, and *that* land, so will our sons defend *this* temple, *this* city, and *this* land."[59] In response, Rev. Jacob Rosenfeld told his Orthodox flock in Charleston that "we are bereft of our country, and we must sing praises in a strange land; we have now no Jerusalem, no temple, no high priest, and no burnt offering for thy worship."[60] In Philadelphia the well-known Orthodox philanthropist Rebecca Gratz found Poznanski's heresies against Zion most galling. Word of mouth about his pronouncements had reached her in Pennsylvania, and Gratz quickly responded to the contents of the Charlestonian's speech, chalking up the remarks as part of Reform Judaism's systemic misguidedness toward the Bible and religious principles:

> I have not seen the paper you sent containing an account of the Charleston congregation but have heard some passages quoted that are certainly unorthodox. "This is our temple, this our city, this is our Palestine." Is it possible a Jew can write or speak so? Then where is the truth of prophesy? Where the fulfillment of promises? What is the hope of Israel? Of what

does the scattered people bear witness? Alas we may hang our harps on the willow and weep for the spiritual destruction of Jerusalem when her own children are content to sing the songs of Zion in a strange land and deny the words of God so often repeated by the prophets. I am afraid the good people of Charleston are paying too much for their organ and allow more important objects to be sacrificed.[61]

For Rosenfeld, Gratz, and many other Orthodox Jews, there was never a question of conflicting national loyalties to the United States and the Holy Land. As they read it, and anticipating later Zionist advocates like Louis Brandeis, the Bible offered a place to both lands. The Orthodox rejected Reform's Americanized messianism out of respect for a more literal reading of the Bible that squarely pointed to the Holy Land as the authentic site of the messianic idea. They figured that no pious American could disagree with the Bible, the most sacred book in the United States.

All this was meant to unhinge Reform from American biblicism. In the United States, Protestant denominations shared a common faith in America that far outweighed their theological differences. From the moment they touched down on New World soil, Christians read themselves into the Bible. For example, religious leaders saw the adventures and prophesies of Moses, Deborah, Jeremiah, David, Peter, and Paul in the events leading up to and including the Revolutionary War.[62] To most American Christians all citizens and their families were God's Chosen People. Of course denominational leaders competed with one another for members.[63] Yet they all believed as a matter of principle that each denomination provided just one of multiple pathways to a singular Truth.[64] American Protestants acted with hostility toward Catholicism and Mormonism in large part because those religious groups read different holy texts or variant translations of the Bible.[65] Their faith, Protestants reckoned, was less authentic. What is more, the religious schisms of the early nineteenth century were often centered on how to understand the Bible on, say, matters of heavenly interference and baptism. Jews did not subscribe to these rituals or the fundamental dogma of Christian faith. But they did read the same Bible. Orthodox Jews touted themselves as the most authentic interpreters of the Bible, suggesting that their faith was more American than Reform Judaism. The American religious context, then, mediated the forms of Judaism and their positioning against one another.

Orthodoxy searched in other ways for authentic expressions of American-style religion. It adopted, for instance, a nationally linked rhetoric to describe its values and aims. Consider a speech delivered at the dedication of the Cincinnati Jewish Hospital. There, in March 1866, Rabbi Bernard Illowy delivered an oration in which he stated: "Religious liberty and freedom of conscience are sacred and inalienable rights, which the Israelite always strongly claimed for himself wherever he lived, and he therefore willingly grants it to others, for thus pronounced our divine teacher, Moses, the first President of the first Republic in the world, the fundamental principle of the Jewish constitution."[66] Reform Jewish leaders, contended another Orthodox advocate, confused anarchy for modern democracy. Invoking words and symbols with considerable political and religious currency, Rabbi Morris Raphall mocked reformers for over-exercising their "inalienable rights."[67]

This was more than rabbinic imagination and rhetorical creativity. Orthodox Jews like Isaac Leeser claimed that their group possessed the quotients of refinement and education befitting an American religion.[68] Leeser had been the first to introduce regular sermons into the American synagogue. His preaching focused on topics like messianism, restoration, and heaven, particularly from the Bible's perspective.[69] Likewise, Leeser's successor at Mikveh Israel, Sabato Morais, credited his success to the "study of the Hebrew Bible [which] was deemed in days gone by the imperative duty of every Israelite."[70]

Other synagogue changes boded well for the Orthodox. In 1838 Leeser helped open the first Jewish Sunday school. Leeser asserted that the institution was not novel and not at all out of place, since "Sunday schools are nothing new among our Christian neighbours."[71] The rank and file were all for the "external order and decorum" that Leeser worked to install in American synagogue life. According to one account of that time, many laypeople recognized that a "choir and sermon can be introduced in the service without giving up an iota of Orthodoxy," even if those practices were learned from Protestant sources.[72]

Changes in Orthodox life increased the importance of the rabbinate. Like Isaac Mayer Wise and other Reform leaders, Leeser supported the elevation of the ministry, but he did so in universally agreeable fashion. "There is hardly any Christian society," wrote Leeser in 1844, "which does not strain every nerve to have an intelligent and virtuous ministry, composed of men who would honour any calling by their acquisition and general conduct."[73] In contrast the Reform rabbinate, he later contended, lacked order and substance. In Leeser's words, "True friends of freedom, the true bearers of enlightenment, and Israelites will discover this whenever they come to the clear understanding of the fact that modern reforms are mostly calculated to elevate a priesthood above the heads of the people."[74] In other words, it was Orthodox Judaism that was the "truer" American faith.

Finally, Orthodox Judaism in the United States abided by a strong sense of religious pluralism, an all-important feature of American religious life. Tolerance, if not acceptance, was crucial when it came to most mainline Protestant and Evangelical Christians. Entry into the ranks of America's enlightened was contingent on accepting religious pluralism.[75] Despite Orthodox Jews' contempt for Reform, they got along with their religiously liberal counterparts. European-born and trained extracts like Rabbi Abraham Rice warned Isaac Leeser to stay away from "wolves clothed in sheeps-cover"—but Leeser did not abide.[76] Particularly as Jews moved southward and westward, as historian Shari Rabin has argued, it was critical that they found communities and establish social centers that could provide for all varieties of Jewish creed and deed.[77] Orthodox and Reform leaders contributed articles to the same newspapers, and laypeople of all religious types formed the Board of Delegates of American Israelites in the 1850s to represent American Jewish interests on the national and international scenes.[78] They also joined forces on religious causes like promoting Sabbath observance. In October 1867 Orthodox and Reform rabbis in Richmond, Virginia, signed a broadside declaration that called for ending Sabbath desecration, and appealed to "our Brethren, without distinction of congregation or nationality, to aid our efforts in so good a cause, for the sake of our past glories and future hopes."[79] Both groups cooperated in the development of benevolent societies, orphanages, and other welfare agencies.

The ease with which Orthodox participated with Reform—despite their oft-cantankerous debates—is perhaps the best indicator of how differently America's version of Orthodox Judaism emerged compared to its European counterparts. In Prussia and Hungary, Orthodox Jews, most notably the Frankfurt community led by Samson Raphael Hirsch, furnished separatist groups that sought to insulate themselves from Reform Jews and their influence. In other parts of Europe, Orthodox Jews maintained political and economic ties to Reform but at the very least raised the question of whether that was proper. In the United States, to my knowledge, that was not a concern for most Orthodox Jews in the nineteenth century. All this does not mean that

America and Europe had no contact. To the contrary, Orthodox Jews read and corresponded with traditional-minded Jews across the Atlantic. They published their polemics and considered their points of view. More fundamentally, though, Orthodox Judaism in the United States developed in step with the indigenous religious culture—which promoted biblicism, republicanism, and pluralism—that surrounded it. To them this was the finest and most authentic expression of their faith.

## The Decline of American Orthodox Judaism?

In November 1885 Rabbi Isaac Mayer Wise declared that he and his colleagues were the "orthodox Jews in America." Wise was not Orthodox. Indeed he was the foremost architect of Reform Judaism in the United States and a longstanding, leading critic of Orthodox Jews who, in his words, "attempt to maintain the innovations of the middle ages, in idea or form."[80] By assuming the mantle of "Orthodox Judaism," Wise meant to close the door on the previous iteration of American Orthodoxy and claim for Reform the status of America's most authentic form of Judaism. "You do not represent the ideas and sentiments of the American Jews," he told the old guard. In "this phase upon which Judaism entered in this country, you are an anachronism, strangers in this country, and to your own brethren."[81]

Wise's prognosis of the state of Orthodox Jewish life was right, to an extent. By the final decades of the century, it was clear that Orthodox Judaism had lost significant ground to Reform. Wise tabulated that among three hundred synagogues in 1886, no more than fifty of them would have identified as Orthodox.[82] The figure might have been less than generous. By the close of the 1870s, the Reform-endorsed Union of American Hebrew Congregations claimed one hundred congregations as members.[83] Still, the imbalance was more than a little noticeable. The formation of this congregational body, as well as a rabbinical organization and a rabbinical seminary, ensured that Reform Judaism possessed an infrastructure to raise future generations of adherents. Their Orthodox rivals possessed no such network.

In truth Reform rabbis had steadily seized control of American Judaism throughout the second half of the nineteenth century. Part of the explanation was that the Bible alone proved insufficient to stymie the Reform agenda. In November 1859, for instance, Benjamin Peixotto of Cleveland wrote to Isaac

Leeser to defend his inclination to join with Reform, so long as all parties could agree to maintain "enlightened Orthodoxy." Peixotto was a lay leader of the Orthodox congregation in that city which was at that time considering a merger with the Reform community. "I believe that neither the Pentateuch nor Prophets speak advisably on this point," wrote Peixotto.[84] In Central Europe Orthodox rabbis would have pointed to the Talmud and rabbinic codes to direct this questioner. In Ohio, however, he wanted to see proof in the Bible itself.

As time went on some among the Orthodox continued to try and drive a wedge between the Bible and Reform. One opined that if the Reform rabbi "believes anything at all, he believes that the Bible with all that is therein, is a mere human invention, and that nothing in it commends itself to our respect unless it does so from its intrinsic value."[85] Yet the Bible no longer held the same supreme station in American life—not after the Civil War, when Scripture failed to help determine which side God favored when it came to the issue of slavery. "Both read the same Bible and pray to the same God," said Abraham Lincoln about the Union and the Confederacy in his second inaugural address, "and each invokes His aid against the other." Theologically exhausting as it was bloody, the Civil War called into question America's chosenness and whether the Bible truly spoke to its citizens as the people of God.[86] Instead a new generation of intellectuals emerged, with new sources of truth like philosophy and science.[87] Owing to this turn in perspective, even Orthodox Jews at the outset of the 1870s admitted that it was Reform "to which properly belongs the future."[88]

All things considered, it is not astonishing that in 1885 Rabbi Kaufmann Kohler wondered aloud before Reform congregants: "How many Jews today care to read the Bible, or take interest in that piece of antiquity?" Equally unsurprising, Kohler did not turn to Scripture for the duration of that sermon.[89] Kohler and his Reform clerical colleagues recognized that, at this juncture, it was "progress" and "liberalism" that spoke best to America's Jews, and to Americans in general. They probably concurred with the editor of a Baptist periodical that "no one Jew in ten, it is said, possesses even the Pentateuch for his private perusal."[90] Their religious focus was elsewhere. With English-language prayer books and an openness to in-vogue concepts like evolution, Reform offered much more of American culture than did Orthodox Judaism and its traditionalism.[91]

It was not just that the Orthodox could not keep pace. There were, after all, still some "American" advantages to Orthodox life. For example, a Protestant observer sat in on an Orthodox service during the 1870s and noticed a more democratic system, that "people largely shared the service, as they ought. This alone must attach the Orthodox Hebrews to their rites more than the Reformed, who leave the service more to the minister."[92] Nonetheless, much of the problem for Orthodox Judaism was a paucity of leadership. In earlier decades Orthodox champions had responded to Wise's vituperations with gusto. Now there were hardly any to take up the cause.

By the 1880s these men were gone, and without worthy "Orthodox" successors. Morris Raphall died in 1868, replaced at New York's Bnai Jeshurun by a rabbi who quickly moved the congregation away from its tradition-bound foundations.[93] Around that time, Illowy and Leeser passed away. In recognition of his efforts, the latter's Philadelphia congregation tried to maintain itself, despite declining numbers, believing that "Leeser's pulpit should not be silent."[94] Yet the overall diminished interests in Leeser's legacy reflected the declension of American Orthodox Judaism. In 1878 Samuel Myer Isaacs died and was mourned as the "leading representative of orthodox Judaism in this country."[95] Like Raphall before him, Isaacs was succeeded by a pastor at Congregation Shaarey Tefila who embraced religious reformers. Two years later Orthodox Jews understood that the religious reforms instituted at the synagogue would have been adopted much earlier had it not been for Isaacs's staunch Orthodox creed: "We all regret that the name of the late S. M. Isaacs should have to be coupled with a synagogue which has so violently swerved from the beaten path of orthodox, but we must in all just remember that the storm must have been brewing even in his time, for it is altogether too overwhelming to be of recent origin."[96]

Among the old guard Sabato Morais survived and battled with Reform and its growing number of rabbinic champions and adherents. However, Morais often dueled while waving vaguer banners like "Conservative" or "Historical" Judaism. Younger scholars like Rabbi Henry Schneeberger sometimes liked to promote "Positive Judaism."[97] Some congregations were equivocal about their Orthodox identities as well. For instance, traditional Jews in Pittsfield, Massachusetts, established Anshe Amunim in 1872 and designated their community as "Orthodox or according to the ritual of Polish Jews."[98] In earlier American synagogue constitutions, it was standard for the congregation's founders to indicate in one article that it was Orthodox and then—usually in the very next section—identify which ritual format (usually English, German, or Polish) was preferred in the synagogue's worship. The deliberate conflation between religious orientation (Orthodox) and ritual (Polish) explains just how uncertain traditional-minded Jews were about the "authentic" bona fides of what was commonly called Orthodox Judaism. All in all the multiplicity of monikers and visions obstructed attempts to maintain the banner of Orthodox Judaism in this epoch of American Jewish life.

## This Book

The experience of Orthodox Judaism during the formative 1800s offers crucial insight into this tradition-bound community's development in the subsequent century. The rapid decline of a uniquely American type of Orthodox Judaism unfolded just as hundreds of thousands of Eastern European Jews migrated to the United States. In 1880 there were 250,000 Jews living in the United States. By 1900 that figure spiked to more than a million Jewish women, men, and children.[99] Most left Europe due to rising antisemitism and in search of better economic situations. These émigrés brought with them orthodoxies and religious cultures cultivated in distinct environments and under specific circumstances. What they counted as religiously authentic Judaism differed from the republican biblicism of Jacob Mordecai, Isaac Leeser, and other by that time relatively forgotten American Orthodox champions. For this reason scholars of Orthodox Judaism have tended to impose Jacob Katz's Eurocentric paradigm on the post-1880 American Jewish experience. Adam Ferziger, Jeffrey Gurock, Samuel Heilman, and Chaim Waxman all presume that American Orthodoxy was imported from Europe, dismissing the indigenous American origins of Orthodox Judaism and the efforts of this community to form an identity that did not exactly match the Orthodox conditions in Europe.[100] Most recently, Waxman has written about the "absence of rabbinic leadership" in this early period. "Rabbis did not begin to appear significantly on the American scene until well into the nineteenth century, and the traditional rabbinic scholarly elite did not exist until the twentieth century."[101] The prior period was discontinuous, in these historians' judgments.

The standard Katz-influenced interpretations of religious change in Orthodox life presume a continuous and one-dimensional or linear path, particularly after millions of Eastern European émigrés departed their homes for safer and better lives in the New World. From this point forward Orthodox Judaism grappled with the forces of modernity and secularization, then Americanized, and then, most recently, stepped away from this process of acculturation in favor of a course of isolationism and rigidification. This is what is fashionably known as the "slide to the right" of American Orthodox Judaism.[102] Historians writing this narrative place "modernity" as Orthodox Judaism's foil, just as it is according to scholars of European Orthodoxy.

This, I contend, is shortsighted. And, in some cases, unsubstantiated. For instance, American religion surely played a much larger role than, say, Hatam Sofer and his religious conservativism in shaping Orthodox Judaism in the past 150 years. His students by and large did not settle in the United States, and American rabbinic writers did not concentrate on his teachings. One of the rare Sofer-trained rabbis to settle in the New World was Bernard Illowy, who maintained good relations with Reform rabbis in Baltimore and Cincinnati, a trademark transgression, according to the Pressburg sage.[103] Nonetheless the same theories of Hungarian Orthodox Judaism that are forthcoming from researches into Rabbi Moses Sofer and his circle are so often applied to the scholarship on American Orthodoxy.[104] Others have also posed challenges to the Katz paradigm. For example, Menachem Keren-Kratz has questioned the utility of the tradition-modernity, right-left measuring stick to account for notions of Zionism, spirituality, and political influence in Orthodox religious life. He introduced more variables to compare Orthodox communities in different times and places.[105]

My present call for reconsideration stems from a different point of view. The "Europeanization" argument ignores the "American" foundations that persisted in Orthodox Jewish life despite its downward turn in the final decades of the nineteenth century. This has something to do with an overemphasis on the rabbinic elites who sometimes offered pronouncements that mirrored the rhetoric of their European predecessors. More attention paid to "lived religion," as Robert Orsi termed it, provides a different understanding of Orthodox life.[106] In addition, prior studies do not account for the scholarship on twentieth-century American religion. New developments and changes in this period impacted Orthodox Judaism, just as it played a pivotal role in the prior century. Most fundamentally, historians ought to pay more attention to the major lesson of the nineteenth-century Orthodox Jewish experience in the

United States: the quest for authenticity. Unlike most other historians, I argue that the latter half of the nineteenth century did not create a blank slate.[107] Despite the upheavals and rapid migration from Europe, the elusive search for authentic expressions of religion remained the most significant determinant of change in the subsequent century in these American environs.

Most acutely, authenticity emerged as an important commodity in twentieth-century American life. To be sure, scholars in the field of American studies have pointed out the long-held anxieties over colonialism, race, and class, and the influence these have had on the formation of an authentic and native national identity.[108] Nevertheless Americans of all kinds started around the turn of the century—amid significant cultural, social, and technological change—to search for what they deemed authentic expressions of life and culture. It was a means to stabilize a shifting world. This was the case for those in the realm of literature, like Ernest Hemingway and members of the Harlem Renaissance.[109] It was further propelled by the rise of modern consumerism and new technologies, changes that disrupted the norms of erstwhile American society.[110] American tradition-bound religious groups also grappled with notions of authenticity.[111] Take the Catholic encounter with contraception during the long haul of the twentieth century. This historical episode involved massive changes in medicine and the social dynamics of the American Catholic family. In response priests and the rest of the ecclesiastical hierarchy struggled to convince the Catholic laity of the "sinfulness" of birth control and its deleterious impact on domestic life. Most of the rank and file did not adhere to the prohibition. In the final decades of the 1900s, explained historian Leslie Tentler, the two sides stopped engaging this critical question. Apropos of all the above, Tentler concluded her book on the subject invoking both authenticity and tradition: "The laity need answers to these questions—authentically Christian answers, grounded in Catholic tradition."[112] The Catholic conundrum over contraception therefore linked the challenge of a tradition-bound faith to articulate a religious attitude in line with American modern mores.

The same general challenge was certainly the case for Orthodox Judaism, a faith community that tended to define and shape itself around different conceptions of authenticity. This was the reason that some Orthodox Jews censored and revised their history to form a more usable past for their present religious conditions.[113] For America's Orthodox Jews authenticity played an important role in determining their lukewarm embrace of Hirsch's Frankfurt

Orthodoxy and their more welcoming attitude toward Lithuanian rabbinic culture.[114] Similarly, currents in American culture were viewed as more acceptable than others and at different times based on changing conceptions of religious authenticity. In the 1960s, for example, Rabbi Emanuel Rackman wrote about "authentic" Judaism and its ability to speak to forces of contemporary culture.[115] Sometimes reconciliation was deemed impossible. Along these lines some Orthodox Jews cautioned that authenticity was something to be preserved. In December 1964 the head of the Orthodox Union struggled with working with Conservative and Reform leaders, fearing that it would indicate the "ipso facto recognition of non-Orthodox philosophies as legitimate alternatives to the historic and authentic Judaism of Orthodoxy."[116] Others supported Orthodox Judaism's rhetorical posturing. The non-Orthodox and non-Jews sometimes encouraged the belief that "Orthodoxy is the voice of Jewish authenticity."[117]

Among themselves Orthodox Jews did not always agree on what was authentic. They drew lines and sometimes splintered over questions of authenticity. In December 1965 the editors of the Agudath Israel monthly magazine referred to the "authentic Jewish thinking" of their rabbinic leaders, who rejected the non-Orthodox as well as more moderate Orthodox rabbis of the Rabbinical Council of America (RCA). The RCA rabbis held much more positive views on Zionism, liberal education, and ecumenical matters.[118] To the more rigid Agudath Israel, these features rendered other Orthodox camps—they were not prepared to disqualify them as non-Orthodox—less than fully authentic. On the other hand, Rabbi Norman Lamm, one of the RCA's leading lights at that time, was more sanguine about his group of so-called Modern Orthodox Jews, who sought out theological tensions: "those Jews who sincerely are groping for direction and meaningfulness, for a way to live their lives in the framework of the *authentic* Jewish tradition."[119] Despite the infighting, Orthodox Judaism continued to wave the banner of "Authentic Judaism." In July 1987 a newly arrived Orthodox rabbi in Boca Raton, Florida, counted on much success because "young people are looking for something that's real. People intuitively sense that which is authentic and I think there's a desperate yearning for authenticity."[120] All this calls for a more thorough understanding of American Orthodox Judaism's encounter with authenticity.

The purpose of this book is to use historical episodes and case studies to explore what is "American" about the history of Orthodox Judaism in the

United States, and how sensitivities to the more indigenous religious culture shaped conceptions of authenticity, the defining characteristic, I argue, of Orthodox Judaism in this location. To some degree or another, historians of Conservative and Reform Judaism have already made the point about American religious history, as have scholars of Jewish identity in the latter portions of the twentieth century.[121] I do not contend that past researches of American Orthodox Judaism are wrong. Studies that draw from Jacob Katz's model offer terrific perspective and information. The scope of study of Orthodox Judaism in America, I maintain, needs to be widened to fit other scholarly perspectives.

The case studies in this book are divided into three sections. Each represents an area in the lived experience of Orthodox Judaism during the twentieth century. In every instance Orthodox Jews evaluated cultural cues and measured their Jewish "web of experiences" against the backdrop of mediating American religious sensibilities. The result of this historical arithmetic yielded "authenticity." Part 1 examines three chapters in the history of American Halakhah, or Jewish law. The most crucial aspect of religious behavior in Orthodox life, Halakhah in the United States was decided by more than just careful readings of traditional rabbinic legal codes. Jewish law was shaped by how "elite religion" and "folk religion" migrated from Europe and interacted in their new American locale. Enlarging the scholarly lens to view America as part of the broader Atlantic region is less "Katzian" than it is drawing from Americanists like Bernard Bailyn and Daniel Rodgers.[122] The massive migration from Europe to the United States around the turn of the twentieth century set off a complex set of cultural clashes between migrants equipped with customs and rituals they brought with them to the New World. The condition of religious observance and the competing allegiances to Old World practices were unlike those of previous epochs in American Orthodox life, or anywhere else: It brought into focus the interaction between Orthodox Judaism and various streams of twentieth-century American culture. These chapters argue that changing attitudes in American forms of pluralism, egalitarianism, frontierism, and civic life helped determine and modify kosher standards and acceptable Passover cuisines, normative bat mitzvah rites for young girls, and the male requirement to don a yarmulke in private and public spaces. In no small way, prevailing American sensibilities enabled or hindered halakhic folkways from taking root in New World soil.

These episodes also complicate our understanding of the easy-to-plot trajectory of Orthodox religious practices in the United States. Others have suggested that American interpretations of Halakhah have moved from a "left-leaning" liberal attitude to a "right-pulling" conservatism and rigidness. This narrow view of history seems too simple when we account for the variety of forces weighing on Orthodox observance. The history of Halakhah in the United States is not binary. Its movements and changes represent unconscious reactions to indigenous extratextual conditions. This is especially true for the gray areas of Jewish jurisprudence, and these chapters demonstrate just how critical American religious culture was to the collective decision-making of Orthodox rabbis and laypeople. These "external" variables played important roles in determining what was religiously authentic in everyday Orthodox life.

Part 2 of this book examines Orthodox childhood and youth culture. In some cases, as with Yeshiva University (YU) undergraduates' success on a nationally televised quiz show, young people's efforts helped authenticate new cultural expressions and religious revivals. Like other tradition-bound religious groups, Orthodox Judaism emphasized the importance of education to help transition youngsters to adulthood. This includes the formal teaching of the laws and behaviors of religious observance and the customs of daily life. However, Orthodoxy has also developed a culture around childhood to inculcate, preserve, and sometimes empower a spirit of religious authenticity.[123] The chapters in this second section zero in on religious change in the arena of Orthodox youth culture, particularly in the postwar period. Here the indigenous American religious ethos as well as popular culture played a pivotal role. In the 1960s the Orthodox underwent a process of rejuvenation, spearheaded in large measure by young people. In one case study a band of Yeshiva University undergraduates proved to countless numbers of coreligionists that their success on a widely watched television gameshow was a testament to their devotion to Orthodox Jewish life and undaunted confidence in their place alongside other American peers. At this juncture, then, a dutiful embrace of American cultural norms was viewed as authentically Orthodox.

This changed along American cultural lines. The two other chapters in this section illuminate a conscious policing of cultural boundaries. Within this faith community, a more powerful and aggressive Orthodox Right—my term, borrowing upon the American Protestant equivalent rather than saying anything about movements to the "left" or "right"—promoted a youth culture that was far less positive about earlier and more open forms of Orthodox childhood. Growing less and less comfortable with modern culture, this group of Orthodox Jews furnished parallel childhood commodities like toys and collectibles. For example, some Orthodox Jews peddled and traded rabbi cards instead of baseball cards. Rather than take part in spelling bees, the Orthodox designed the "Brochos Bee"—blessing bees—to ensure that their children had access to the youthful notions of competition but did so apart from their non-Jewish neighbors. These initiatives and enterprises did much to help Orthodox Judaism—like other American tradition-bound faiths no longer so comfortable with their surrounding milieu—benefit from its outside environs and culture of consumerism while allowing it to maintain the requisite levels of religious authenticity. When this sort of thinking proved ineffective, Orthodox Jews in the final decades of the century retreated, choosing to look inward, to behave in ways they considered to be more authentic, like other conservative faith communities. That Orthodox Jewish life resembled other webs of experiences and quests for authenticity among American religions is incredibly instructive.

Part 3 tackles the competing conceptions of gendered spaces—masculine spaces, in particular—among Orthodox Jews and other Americans. Gender emerged as the major theme of twentieth-century American Judaism. Riv-Ellen Prell once argued that "gender has served to symbolize Jews' relationships to nation, family, and work."[124] Similarly, Pamela Nadell posited that women's long struggle to enter the rabbinate represented American Judaism's "encounter with modernity."[125] This and other gender-related decisions served as dividing lines (and when crossed, symbols of "progress") among Conservative, Orthodox, Reconstructionist, and Reform Judaism. This was not yet the case in the earlier epochs of the American Jewish experience. Karla Goldman and Jonathan Sarna have shown that nineteenth-century reforms like mixed seating and female choirs were instituted much more out of convenience than for ideological reasons.[126] Often congregations introduced "family pews" after acquiring and refurbishing a church with this sort of seating configuration. Mixed choirs and genderless seating were also ways for rabbis and lay leaders to fill seats and assign ritual responsibilities on the Sabbath. Overall, however, congregational life in American Judaism remained, like its European counterparts, a male-dominated sphere.

This changed in the decades surrounding the turn of the twentieth century.[127] Congregations established sisterhoods. Some synagogues opened general membership to women. Outside of the synagogue America's Jews formed the National Council of Jewish Women in 1893 and the first Young Women's Hebrew Associations in the first decade of the 1900s.[128] The appearance of more and more women in traditionally male-dominated leadership spaces in Jewish life challenged this religious community to reconsider both femininity and masculinity. It is therefore at this historical moment that historian Ann Braude's important call to link gender and American religion becomes most relevant.[129] In the twentieth century, especially, gender and egalitarianism had a way of animating the anxieties of religious groups in the United States. The appearance of women in positions of leadership (religious, political, etc.), women's suffrage, and advances in women's education and employment on all levels changed the landscapes of American religious life. In turn historians have studied Orthodox Judaism's response to feminism. Of course feminism played an important role in Orthodox Judaism's interaction with gender. Yet just a few scholars have called attention to masculinity and male space.[130] In Europe and the United States, Orthodox Judaism was viewed as a patriarchal faith. Its most visible symbols of prayer and learning were all conjured up with men in view and women more or less out of sight. Traditional Jewish law demands that its male adherents attend synagogue several times daily for prayer and study. Women are exempt from this obligation. The results are the longstanding images of the scholarly, pale, and long-fingered rabbinic man and the domestic woman detached from the dominant and more visible male Orthodox culture. Tethered as they were to specific communal sites, these archetypes were defended in a kind of socio-religious turf war.

Masculinity is an important subject beyond the small circle of Orthodox historians. In the first decades of the twentieth century, growing numbers of Americans started to subscribe to Theodore Roosevelt's idea of a rugged "strenuous life" and the so-called muscular Christianity that took hold of church activities, as historian Clifford Putney explained.[131] Both Putney and sociologist Michael Kimmel are in agreement that the first part of the century placed acute pressure on American men to seize on their increasingly more elusive form of masculinity, even if it meant drastic attempts to exclude "others," including women.[132]

Orthodox Judaism paralleled other American religious groups but also paved its own unique path on this score. Sarah Imhoff's recent monograph demonstrates that American Judaism did not feel all that compelled to follow the masculine-forming direction of its Protestant alternative.[133] Orthodox Judaism even more so. Long ago the sages of the Talmud (Sanhedrin 26b) warned that those who study its weighty rabbinic tomes would become "weakened" by it. The bookish and brainy male ideal loomed large in Orthodox circles, no matter how the local American attitude toward gender and manliness tried to teach them otherwise. This played out most visibly in "male sacred spaces," like the yeshiva and synagogue. More than any other section of American Jewish life, Orthodoxy fought vigorously to hold on to traditionally masculine spaces. This battle compounded many Orthodox Jews' opposition to feminism. Their struggle can be contextualized within the collective anxieties of many American religious groups. Various indigenous American forces mediated the Orthodox Jewish experience, pushing this faith community to reconsider gender roles and spaces. The chapters on dating practices, women's Talmud study, and women's prayer groups focus on how Orthodox Jews recalibrated their outlook on male space and sought to preserve masculine religious authenticity along a specifically conservative and tradition-bound line of American religious sensibilities while remaining open to some changes in traditional practices.

This book offers something new to our understanding of Orthodox Judaism, as well as American religion and modern Jewish history. The path traversed by Orthodox Judaism in the United States should not be retraced as "slides to the right" or "leftward shifts."[134] That appears far too simple, given the complicated forces at play. Faith communities like Orthodox Judaism have encountered change by measuring its religious experiences against various expressions of Americanism. The result of this interaction is an articulation of "authenticity." What counts for authentic differs in all places and times and is usually a composite of varied forces that surround it.

# PART 1

# HALAKHAH AND CHANGE

# CHAPTER 1

# BATTLING FOODWAYS AND HALAKHIC FOLKWAYS

## The Case of Passover Peanut Oil

In Sidney Roth's home on Manhattan's Lower East Side, Passover preparation began months in advance. His mother planned for the springtime holiday, recalled Roth, just as the winter season commenced. As she shopped for her family's Sabbath meals, Mrs. Roth made sure to purchase the fattiest chickens "because now was the time to start saving 'Schmaltz for Pesach.'" At the turn of the twentieth century, chicken fat was a critical ingredient for most Passover recipes: Jews used *schmaltz* for potato fritters, fried matzah, and "even just to put on a slice of Matzo with a little bit of salt." For the Roths and so many other Jews, Passover dining had to be basic; available foods and ingredients were quite limited. As late as the 1920s, kosher food producers did not yet offer much beyond matzah and "kosher soap for washing dishes." Recalling the limited culinary situation many years later, Roth put it this way:

> There were no "Heshgochos" [certifications] for canned foods. Choco-
> late candy was "Avada Chomitz" [definitely leavened bread] and even
> butter was "better not," according to my father. So there was very little
> you could have with matzo except the schmaltz.[1]

On any other occasion households like Roth's would have relied on Crisco and other vegetable shortenings. A replacement for other "heavy fats and oils," Crisco became a household item as "Jewish women quickly appreciated its merits."[2] On Passover, however, most Ashkenazic Jews withheld from consuming oils extracted from legumes, *kitniyot*, that might contain grain particles. They therefore resorted to chicken fat to grease their pans and moisten their Passover desserts. That changed in the 1930s. By then most American chefs had discovered peanut oil. Jews certainly noticed. Recalling their memories of Eastern Europe, America's Jews had never heard of a Passover ban on peanuts in association with the Ashkenazic proscription against *kitniyot*.

It is also important to recall the dynamics of Jewish migration to the United States. Lithuanian Jews were overrepresented among the millions of Eastern European Jews who settled in the United States around the turn of the twentieth century.[3] The so-called Litvaks brought with them a rationalist intellectual bent and a relative openness to modern ideas—so long as they did not compromise their devotion to tradition. Their rabbinic leaders tended to issue lenient halakhic rulings, although they were unafraid to revert to the stringent position if other considerations were at stake.[4] It is therefore unsurprising that Lithuanian-trained rabbis permitted peanuts and peanut oil on Passover in the United States. Accordingly, American Jews began using that more appealing product in their kitchens rather than less appetizing *schmaltz*.

However, by the 1990s the Orthodox Union's Passover guide reported that "it is questionable if peanuts are kitniyos and it is questionable in general if oils are kitniyos. Please note that peanut oil is not used in any OU-P products."[5] The statement was a bold reversal from the organization's longstanding stance on the matter, one that dated back to the 1940s. It is tempting to explain this later rightward move toward stringency as a function of what historian Haym Soloveitchik described as the "disappearance of a way of life and the mimetic tradition" and the emergence of "text-based religiosity."[6] This outlook suggests that, due to the Holocaust, there was "little chance that the old ways would be preserved."[7] As a result Orthodox Jews turned to more rigid texts to decide religious practice while doing their best to suppress the opaque memories of their parents' and grandparents' conflicting religious norms. Perhaps, then, American Jews looked to rabbinic literature and interpreted that peanuts should also be part of the *kitniyot* ban, despite the decades-long tradition to the contrary.

This explanation played a role. But there is a more cogent explanation, one having to do with rabbinic folkways competing for the right to determine Orthodox authenticity in the United States. In his studies of European cultural migration to the United States, historian David Hackett Fischer understood folkways in the broadest sense as the culture and customs of specific communities that complicated the exchange of ideas and attitudes within the

Atlantic region.[8] Folkways, a salient feature of American history, help explore how immigrant cultures moved to the culturally malleable climes in the New World. In contrast to less permeable cultures in Europe, the porous American ethos has provided space for these transplanted folkways to interact and shape the surrounding environment. This was certainly the case for religion. For instance, large-scale migration from southern German areas and then Ireland in the nineteenth century "Romanized" American Catholicism, an effort to render Catholic faith in America more authentic to its practitioners.[9]

The same was true for Orthodox Judaism in the United States. Arriving at different historical junctures, various European Orthodox folkways encountered one another on American soil. The results of these interactions modified religious experiences and attitudes. By midcentury large numbers of Jews from the Ukraine and Hungary settled in the United States and oftentimes chose to live in homes and apartments near coreligionists from their specific European regions.[10] Even before noticing this, one rabbinic observer noted the "new kinds of creatures with peculiar hyphenated names, such as, German-Jews, Russian-Jews, [and] Polish-Israelites," suggesting that Jewish immigrants had found it difficult to relinquish their European identities, at least at this juncture.[11]

This sorting process helped to fortify cultural folkways and, reasonably so, foodways as well. Food preferences often divided Jews from different European enclaves. But there was something much deeper to the friction between the American Orthodox communities led by Lithuanian-trained rabbis and these newer migrants.[12] Hungarian Jews arrived with luggage filled with a traditional culture known for its rigidness and stringency.[13] For example, the Hungarian extracts did not by and large eat machine-made matzah on Passover. They balked for halakhic reasons and because mass-produced matzah looked different—for one thing, they were produced square, not round—from handmade matzah.[14] On the peanut oil score, Hungarian Jews prepared for Passover with *schmaltz* rather than peanut oil. They considered the latter an inauthentic Passover ingredient, part of the centuries-old ban on *kitniyot*.[15] With the help of other native American religious forces, the Hungarian folkway eventually toppled the "old system," despite the steady footing that the Lithuanian folkway had achieved.[16] The rise and fall of Passover peanut oil, then, was a protracted bout for the claim of authenticity. One of the major determining forces in this battle was an American culture that encouraged competition among migrating folkways and ultimately made space for a stricter and more "authentic" kind of religious observance in the postwar period.

## The American Jewish Kitchen and Peanut Oil

Peanuts came to the New World aboard slave ships from Africa. It remained mostly a "slave food" until the Civil War, when Union and Confederate troops encamped in the South made use of peanuts as a substitute for less-abundant snack items. In the 1870s the upper classes of American society regarded peanut consumption as "ungenteel," but peanuts were "almost universally liked" and spread throughout the country and into kitchen pantries.[17] Peanut oil, though, did not gain a sturdy foothold until much later. Most Americans discovered peanut oil, like other peanut products, during the Civil War. In response to Union blockades, Confederate forces and industrialists found peanut oil a satisfactory substitute for the whale oil used to lubricate machinery. Also short on supplies and funds, Northerners tried peanut oil. But after the war peanut oil was dropped for other types.[18] It finally emerged as a major domestic product during World War II. In 1942 the United States restricted the commercial availability of most lards, oils, and butters. To the great fortune of Planters Edible Oil Company—established in 1933—the federal government did not place limits on the sale of peanut oil. From then on peanut oil was a staple in millions of American homes.[19]

One of the first groups to embrace peanut oil was the Jewish community. A marketing specialist for the US Department of Agriculture reported in 1941 that a "white form of refined peanut oil enjoys much popularity among the Jewish trade in several eastern cities."[20] Peanut oil had become a particularly precious item—recall, the alternative was chicken fat—for the Eastern European immigrants and their first-generation American children. Much of the Jewish consumption of peanut oil had to do with Passover. In March 1936 Planters Peanuts announced a line of "kosher peanut-oil as well by retaining rabbis to inspect production."[21] Anticipating high volumes in sales, Jewish newspapers and magazines around springtime featured advertisements for Planters' brand as well as a peanut oil produced by Rokeach and Sons, a Brooklyn-based Jewish food manufacturer.[22] Two reasons account for this. First, Jewish cooks happily greased their pans with peanut oil rather than

One of the very first ads for Passover-approved Planters peanut oil appeared in the April 1936 issue of *Hapardes*, a rabbinical journal published in Chicago, IL. The Planters ad boasted the oil as the ideal ingredient for cooking, frying, and general healthfulness. (Kraft Heinz Foods Company)

chicken fat during the holiday. Second, Orthodox Jews did not view peanut oil, in contrast to vegetable oils, as falling under the rabbinic prohibition against eating *kitniyot* on Passover.

## *Kitniyot* and Its Extratalmudic History

The question of Passover peanut oil was not based on any sort of rereading of sacred rabbinic texts. The Bible (Deuteronomy 16:3) proscribes consumption of "leavened bread" during the seven days of Passover. In accord with the plain meaning of Scripture, the Talmud (Pesahim 35a) enumerates five specific grains that count as leavened bread once they come into close contact with water. The debate over the halakhic status of *kitniyot* on Passover postdates the Talmud, within the Ashkenazic fold. Sephardic Jews, therefore, have never refrained from eating foods like beans and rice on Passover. Writing at the end of the twelfth century, for example, Maimonides maintained the same list of proscribed items without any emendations. He also explicitly permitted eating *kitniyot*: "legumes such as rice, millet, beans, lentils and the like do not become leavened."[23] Subsequently, Sephardic Jews have followed Maimonides's ruling.

Whence *kitniyot*? It emerged in Ashkenaz, probably a century or two before the tradition made its way into rabbinic writing in the thirteenth century.[24] The thirteenth-century scholar Yitzhak ben Yosef of Corbeil was one of the first to record the stringent tradition that forbade *kitniyot*.[25] In subsequent centuries rabbinic writers offered two primary explanations for the stringency: First, the consumption of *kitniyot* products on Passover could confuse the most pious Jews and lead them to inadvertently eat bread on the holiday. Second, forbidden grains might be found in the same containers that held *kitniyot* foods.[26] Despite the Talmud's ruling to the contrary, by the sixteenth century virtually all Ashkenazic Jews abstained from eating legumes on Passover.[27] Leading halakhic authority Moses Isserles of Krakow codified the stringent position and decreed that it was "impermissible to deviate from it."[28]

Since then Ashkenazic Jews encountered new foods like corn, potatoes, peanuts, and most recently quinoa with the same penetrating question: Is it permitted on Passover? Throughout the centuries rabbinic writers developed tools to decide whether to broaden the Passover menu: They have considered how the food grows, determined whether it develops in isolation or in bunches, and researched how the food is baked or cooked.[29] Halakhists borrowed several of these lines of inquiry from alternate realms of Jewish law and justified others based on common sense. Their solutions were creative but fully removed from any learned reading of the Talmud. In all cases, therefore, authorities understood that their decisions were products of what we might describe as religious intuition rather than anything directly derived from rabbinic sources.[30]

The stringent custom persisted undisturbed for hundreds of years. Despite lacking any textual evidence, the established rabbinic intuition accrued considerable religious currency. However, amid radicalism and religious upheaval in Europe, *kitniyot* became a major area of religious conflict in the nineteenth century. Since *kitniyot* stood out as an extratalmudic prohibition, its wide-spread observance reflected Orthodox Jewry's fidelity to a traditional way of life rather than narrower devotion to the corpus of laws included in Judaism's most sacred texts. For these Jews *kitniyot* represented Jewish commitment to an Orthodox attitude, a religious practice above and beyond what could be deduced from text-learning or logic.

Not everyone agreed. New conditions challenged the role of rabbinic intuition in determining Orthodox observance. Owing to the financial bur-dens of their coreligionists, moderate reformers sought to suspend the *kitniyot* prohibition and allow European Jews to purchase more affordable foodstuff for Passover. In 1810 reformers in Westphalia attempted to abolish the custom, and thought they could because it lacked any basis in the Talmud. In turn religiously conservative leaders responded, arguing that there was much more to traditional religion than what was explicitly handed down in the Talmud.[31] This second, more powerful group prevailed. In 1843 Samuel Adler's first reform as district rabbi of Alzey was to eliminate the Passover ban on legumes, but his effort was defeated.[32] Similar episodes took place decades later in Lith-uania. Each side offered arguments that echoed those voiced during the earlier Westphalia affair. On most occasions those advancing the stricter argument presented the more compelling case for Europe's Jews.[33]

A final noteworthy incident took place in Palestine in 1909. In his rabbin-ical post in Jaffa, Rabbi Avraham Yitzhak Kook permitted his community to use sesame-seed oil on Passover. Unquestionably Orthodox, Kook knew well that traditional Jews considered sesame oil a form of *kitniyot* and therefore refrained from using it during Passover. A member of the Jaffa community who had opened a factory that produced sesame oil asked Kook to authorize his product for Passover use. The businessman explained that his oil was man-ufactured by machines that obviated the concerns linked to *kitniyot*. This was sufficient for Kook to offer a lenient ruling. But his decision was adamantly opposed by the leading rabbinic court in Jerusalem. One of the Jerusalem rab-bis' primary concerns was that Kook's position appeared in accord with the well-known viewpoint of European reformers and therefore was unacceptable from an Orthodox point of view. Ultimately Kook retreated in the face of the strong stand of the Hungarian-trained Jerusalem court, a decision that would do much to solidify the strict stance maintained by Orthodox Jews in Israel in subsequent decades.[34]

In 1948 Planters Edible Oil Company published a Yiddish
recipe book that included forty-six Passover meals, each
featuring peanut oil as an integral ingredient. (Kraft Heinz
Foods Company)

Meanwhile, in the United States peanut oil emerged as Passover's primary
culinary conundrum. It was a preferred oil; its high smoke point made it a
good oil for stovetop frying, and its mild-taste made it suitable for all other
forms of greasing and baking. In 1941 Mildred Bellin published a popular
kosher cookbook with an expanded Passover chapter to make room for new
oil-based recipes that cut down on the "heaviness" of the holiday cuisine.[35]
American manufacturers also took notice of increased Jewish consumption
of peanut oil. For instance, Planters Peanut Company published a Yiddish-
language cookbook of forty-six Passover recipes that all utilized peanut oil.
"Planters Hi Hat Peanut Oil," the cookbook's editors boasted, "is the ideal
oil for all your Passover cooking, baking, frying, salads and gravies."[36] It did

not last, however. By the 1960s another Jewish folkway, this one from Hungary, had reached America and established itself as a formidable rival to the lenience-granting Lithuanian brand of Orthodox authenticity that had existed in the United States for nearly a century.[37]

## A Lithuanian Folkway

Peanuts did not enter the European diet until the very end of the nineteenth century, so none of the vociferous *kitniyot* debates involved the crop or foods made from it.[38] When peanuts finally reached Eastern Europe, Jews freely ate them on Passover without concern that they might be *kitniyot*.[39] Even if there was any nervousness over peanuts, Jews in that region no doubt would still use peanut oil. In a nineteenth-century responsum that permitted Jews to consume products made from buckwheat, Lithuanian Jewry's leading authority, Rabbi Yitzhak Elhanan Spektor of Kovno, ruled that in most cases oils extracted from *kitniyot* could also be used on Passover, so long as the product was checked for grain prior to production.[40]

The Lithuanian rabbinate and most Eastern European Jews followed Spektor's lenient decision. In fact they took his ruling with them to the United States.[41] Early on just a few American Jews raised questions about the veracity of Passover-certified peanut oil. Several highly respected North American rabbis put those skeptics' fears to rest. Rabbi Yosef Eliyahu Henkin of New York cited Spektor's ruling for good measure. Ergo, he maintained that there was no reason to count peanuts under the rubric of *kitniyot*.[42] Henkin's position carried tremendous weight.[43] In 1935 Toronto's Rabbi Yehudah Leib Graubart—his followers called Graubart the "Stashever Rebbe"—was more cautious about peanuts but agreed with Henkin about the permissibility of peanut oil. Graubart relied on Spektor's lenient ruling.[44] In addition Rabbi Shmuel Pardes of Chicago guaranteed the readers of his monthly journal that he could vouch for the dependability of the few manufacturers that produced Passover-approved peanut oil.[45] Pardes reaffirmed his position the following year, this time according specific mention of Rokeach's brand of peanut oil, a line that he personally supervised.[46]

For decades American Jews relied on peanut oil to get them through the gastronomically restrictive Passover holiday. They were thankful for the Lithuanian rabbinic intuition that sanctioned it. In 1948 the traditionalist rabbis who ran the Rabbinical Council of America and the Orthodox Union formally offered their approval of peanut oil for Passover.[47] From that point forward the Orthodox Union routinely listed peanut oil among the approved "consumer products" for Passover.[48] The OU and other Orthodox institutions felt comfortable with that decision, since they had the backing of a Lithuanian rabbinic tradition that so often sought out leniency wherever possible to make Jewish living easier. Some didn't even think that level of oversight was needed. The Chicago Rabbinical Council, for instance, determined that "pure peanut oil does not need special rabbinic certification for Passover use."[49] In addition the usually more stringent Union of Chassidic Rabbis of the United States and Canada gave peanut oil a pass. In the late 1950s, its journal told consumers:

It is customary not to use rice, millet, beans or peas on Passover; not saffron, cloves or mustard; nor dried fruits, figs, dates or prunes, unless they are dried and packed by responsible Jewish concerns under Rabbinical supervision. Many do not use salted mackerel or herring on Passover but others do, after soaking it in "three waters" before Passover.[50]

Peanuts escaped unscathed. The Orthodox laypeople were certainly appreciative of all this. Well into the 1960s no one could object when a food columnist for Boston's Jewish weekly opined that "Jewish housewives . . . depend on Planters Peanut Oil for so much of their cooking and baking."[51] Planters advertised its oil each year in the spring as the solution to "better tasting Passover meals."[52] Often the company offered consumers a complimentary copy of its Passover recipe book.[53] By the end of the decade, the leading peanut-product manufacturer published a new English-language cookbook that reinforced its product as an approved alternative for a holiday when "everyday foods [are] forbidden."[54] Peanut oil, Planters once again claimed, was a key ingredient to "feather-light matzo balls."[55] Orthodox Jews were meant to believe that, branded this way, peanut oil could enhance the traditional Passover menu. This rhetoric of American consumerism purchased more than a modicum of religious authenticity and helped peanut oil secure its foothold in Orthodox homes.

# A Hungarian Folkway

The Hungarian rabbinic folkway challenged earlier conceptions of rabbinic intuition and competed to determine the scope of religious authenticity for America's Orthodox Jews. In 1966 Rabbi Yaakov Goldman wrote to Rabbi Moshe Feinstein about a "new custom" he had observed in the Orthodox community. Goldman had recently moved from Manhattan's Lower East Side to Brooklyn.[56] As a Hebrew book publisher, Goldman maintained strong ties to leading Lithuanian rabbis like Feinstein in Lower Manhattan as well as Hungarian scholars who inhabited various neighborhoods in Brooklyn.[57] Despite his familiarity with the Hungarian element, Goldman was taken aback to find that his new neighbors did not use peanut oil on Passover. He therefore wrote to Feinstein seeking clarification.

Goldman's question indicated his sense of confusion. Feinstein's response revealed his utter frustration. As Feinstein understood it, the *kitniyot* prohibition was a ban that had always been governed by popular practice rather than any rabbinic ruling decided in a rabbinic synod or court. Were it initiated by learned scholars, presumed Feinstein, there would have been a set of rules transmitted throughout generations to decide which foods were and were not to be considered *kitniyot* on Passover. In stride with his Lithuanian-born colleagues, Feinstein argued that the absence of such a guide tacitly implied that only those foods like rice, millet, and beans, which were known to earlier Jews, were off limits for Passover. Further, he recalled, Jews had snacked on peanuts during Passover when he was a child in Belarus. Feinstein therefore saw absolutely no reason to refrain from peanuts and its oil during Passover.[58]

At the time Goldman submitted his peanut query, Feinstein was recognized as an important rabbinic authority in the United States. Orthodox Jews hailed him as a "Torah giant," and more religiously liberal coreligionists at the very least acknowledged Feinstein as an undisputable "genius."[59] More than anything else Feinstein was highly regarded for his role as a halakhist. The publication of his responsa was considered by many to be a "major halachic event" in America, by much of the Orthodox Right and the more moderate Orthodox alike.[60] In addition Feinstein held prominent positions within the Agudath Israel, Agudath Ha-Rabbonim, and other institutions that made up the Orthodox Right. His peerless reputation as a master of Jewish jurisprudence helped him extend past the religious barriers that boxed in most other

Orthodox leaders. Nevertheless a Hungarian folkway proved to be a formidable rival for Feinstein and likeminded Eastern European immigrants.

The Hungarian rabbinate, composed of both erudite Hasidim and so-called Mitnagdim (those "against" Hasidim), could amply match Feinstein's childhood recollections with its own memories of a far more rigid but no less traditional halakhic culture.[61] In the mid-nineteenth century, Rabbi Yekusiel Yehuda Teitelbaum, the Grand Rebbe of Sighet, prohibited all oils on Passover. In an undated letter to a rabbinic colleague, Teitelbaum refused to permit anything other than chicken fat, lest Jews accidentally use prohibited *kitniyot* oils on the holiday.[62] Probably, though, the Grand Rebbe never came across peanuts in his lifetime. The task of banning that food fell to his son and heir, Rabbi Hananya Yom Tov Lipa Teitelbaum. The son prohibited peanuts in a *Shabbat ha-Gadol* discourse delivered around the turn of the twentieth century. The ruling was predicated on concern that Teitelbaum's followers would mix up permitted and prohibited ingredients and a predilection that Passover foods should taste a certain way. Cooking with peanut oil rendered food smoother and lighter. As an arbiter of Hungarian Orthodox culture and lived experience, Teitelbaum deemed this inherently inauthentic.[63] The decision held its own in the face of rabbinic opposition to Teitelbaum's restrictive ruling.[64] In one instance a leading Hungarian scholar offered initial support for Passover peanut oil in 1922 but quickly backpedaled after the leading rabbis in that region disagreed with his conclusion.[65] That same year Rabbi Yehuda Leib Tsirelson in nearby Romania permitted his community to consume peanuts on Passover. Deemed religiously inauthentic, Tsirelson's opinion was promptly challenged by neighboring rabbis.[66]

The Hungarian culture of halakhic stringency eventually migrated to the United States, challenging earlier assumptions of which attitudes were best suited to direct Orthodox Jews toward religiously authentic practices and behaviors. The Hungarians gained steady traction in 1947 with the arrival of Rabbi Yoel Teitelbaum, the scion of the Sighet Hasidic dynasty.[67] In the aftermath of the Holocaust, Teitelbaum, known as the Satmar Rebbe, restarted his family's Hasidic court in the Williamsburg section of Brooklyn.[68] For Teitelbaum, Williamsburg was fertile soil and, according to one observer, "already the center of the more religious Hungarian Jews in America."[69] Agreeable followers empowered the charismatic leader to offer ideas and positions that were at odds with Feinstein and other Eastern European halakhists. Use of peanut oil on Passover was one of many points of disagreement between Teitelbaum and Feinstein.[70] After Teitelbaum's passing in 1979, his followers continued to adhere to his position despite the arguments put forward by Eastern European Jews.[71]

The Hungarian inclination toward stringency manifested itself in areas beyond the Satmar community. In the 1950s Rabbi Yonatan Steif of Williamsburg held firm to the stance on peanut oil that he had articulated earlier as a leading authority in Budapest.[72] Stationed in England, Rabbi Yitzhak Yaakov Weiss refused to budge from his stringent ruling on cottonseed oil. No matter how many reasons others offered him to be lenient, Weiss, by then a leading international authority on Jewish law, believed that "the custom throughout the Diaspora was to rule stringently on all cases of oil that they be considered *kitniyot* on Passover."[73] Similarly a Brooklyn-based rabbinic journal published several essays in the 1950s that called into question American Orthodoxy's longstanding tradition to consume products made from buckwheat and honey on Passover.[74] These rulings also wordlessly told the followers of these Hungarian leaders that peanut oil was off limits as well.

The conflict left American Orthodoxy without a unified position. For a while the Orthodox Union of the old Lithuanian guard continued to certify peanut oil, but few others were of one mind.[75] In his popular 1977 English guidebook, Rabbi Shimon Eider acknowledged "various opinions" and that "one should conduct himself according to his minhag" or "consult" a rabbinic authority.[76] Another publication declared, under the heading "Please Read This Important Notice," that "there are Rabbis who permit the use of oils and syrups that are derived from *kitniyos* [while] there are other Rabbis who are more stringent concerning this and do not allow the use of these products on Pesach."[77]

The emergent equivocation frustrated the Orthodox establishment that grew up with peanut oil in their Passover pantries. Evidently Planters Peanuts also felt a need to push the issue. In the 1970s the snack and oil manufacturer rebranded its peanut oil as the "Passover Oil."[78] As the decade drew to a close, fewer Jewish consumers believed in that slogan. Instead Orthodox Jews contacted *kashrut* organizations to confirm that the "OK" symbol that appeared on the Planters label was indeed legitimate.[79] The rabbinic certifier of Planters' peanut oil lamented the "many inquiries" he received about peanut oil. To assure confused constituents Rabbi Bernard Levy thought it best to print a

For over thirty-five years, families have been relying on Planters Oil for all their Kosher cooking. On Passover and all year through. They like it because it's pure, light and polyunsaturated. So the true taste of the food comes through. Try this traditional Passover recipe and see what we mean. Cook it with Kosher and Parve Planters Oil. And Happy Passover.

# A Passover Recipe from the Passover Oil

COQ AU VIN FOR PASSOVER
Makes 6 servings

1 (3-pound) frying chicken, cut up
2 tablespoons Planters Peanut Oil
8 small white onions, peeled
4 carrots, peeled and cut into thirds
4 scallions, sliced crosswise
1 teaspoon salt
¼ teaspoon pepper
2 cups dry white wine
½ pound small mushroom caps
2 tablespoons potato starch
2 tablespoons water
Chopped parsley

Wash chicken pieces; blot dry with paper towels. Heat Planters Peanut Oil in Dutch oven over moderate heat. Add chicken pieces in a single layer and brown well on all sides. Set chicken aside. Pour off all but 2 tablespoons fat from Dutch oven. Add onions, carrots and scallions. Sauté until onions begin to brown. Return chicken to pot. Sprinkle in salt and pepper. Pour in wine. Simmer covered for 25 minutes. Mix in mushroom caps. Simmer covered for an additional 20 minutes. Blend together potato starch and water. Quickly stir into hot liquid. Cook 1 minute longer.
Serve garnished with chopped parsley.

Certified Kosher and Parve for Passover by Rabbi Bernard Levy.

Another fine product of Standard Brands.

A 1978 advertisement campaign trumpeted peanut oil as the "Passover oil" for American Jewish homes during the springtime holiday. (Kraft Heinz Foods Company)

personal correspondence with Moshe Feinstein in *The Jewish Homemaker*. In the letter, which the *kashrut* administrator republished almost yearly, Feinstein assured both Levy and his readers that "you may give certification for peanuts and the oil derived from them."[80] But for a growing number, Feinstein's approval was no longer sufficient against the Hungarian brand of Orthodox Judaism.

What was it about the Hungarian folkway that enabled it to compete—and eventually overwhelm—the Eastern European establishment in America? Part of the answer is timing. In the 1970s American Protestantism underwent a conservative upsurge, a reaction to the radical politics and social agendas of Christian denominations during the previous decades.[81] Much like evangelical leaders, Hungarian Jewish exponents offered their followers a more insular form of religious instruction that stressed piety of conduct rather than social responsibility and tolerance.[82] As well, the Hungarian Orthodoxy paralleled historian George Marsden's definition of Christian fundamentalism: "militantly anti-modernist Protestant evangelicalism."[83] Both religious groups vigorously opposed all things "modern," a trend that tended to resonate with segments of American Christians who no longer recognized religious ideologies in the politicized statements of their "centrist" and "liberal" leaders.[84] Instead these disenchanted Protestants of the 1970s were taken by the "Right's ability to balance biblical rigidity, pietism, and separatism."[85]

Concurrently Americans were expanding their definitions of pluralism to smaller "group identities," encouraging them to embrace specific ethnic and religious consciousnesses.[86] Hungarian Jews gained a level of authenticity through their separatism. Unlike many Eastern European immigrants who happily took over existing Jewish schools and organizations when they arrived in the United States, the Hungarians preferred to start new institutions.[87] Moreover Hungarian Jews in Brooklyn prided themselves on their unique dress. Men sported long beards and sidelocks. Some wore fur hats, even in sweltering New York summers. Hungarian women were easily identifiable, dressed in plain and modest dresses, hair fully concealed by small hats atop wigs.[88] These features lent Hungarian Orthodoxy authenticity that could not be matched by most Eastern European elements. As a result, to measure their own punctiliousness and levels of observance, Orthodox Jews who did not necessarily dress like or identify with Hungarian Orthodoxy nevertheless sought out this community's guidance and, ultimately, its approval. Orthodox Jews therefore started to purchase meat and other foods produced by Satmar-owned Meal Mart, a company that guaranteed the strictest and restrictive—"glatt" kosher—supervision.[89] This was the same phenomenon that concomitantly attracted and piqued the interest of Protestants to the "New Christian Right." Both ruptured expectations of religious experience. Questioning the halakhic veracity of peanut oil on Passover was just one small way Orthodox Jews broke the status quo.

# An Israeli Folkway

In time the stringent Hungarian folkway overpowered the Eastern European culture that had for so long served as the establishment within American Orthodox Judaism. At the outset of the 1980s, a shrinking but sizable number of households continued to keep peanut oil in their cooking repertoire.[90] This may have had as much to do with the high costs of other approved Passover oils as it did with maintaining older halakhic traditions. Heavily burdened by the cost of Passover foods, Jewish homemakers looked wherever they could to reduce their grocery costs. In fact in 1981 the president of the Rabbinical Alliance of America issued a statement deploring the high costs of Passover foods, which benefitted "money hungry store keepers and distributors."[91]

Eventually the vast majority of Orthodox Jews abandoned peanut oil. One woman in 1985 was clearly unaware of a more lenient tradition when she wrote matter-of-factly that "Sephardim traditionally use rice, corn, peanuts and pulse and the Ashkenazim do not."[92] According to another observer who wrote about *kitniyot* at the end of the decade, "Items in that category include corn, rice and peanuts."[93] The disappearance of peanut oil from Orthodox Jewish life was apparent in other ways, too. For example, in an Orthodox children's song, "Found Some Peanuts," a verse that specifically detailed the various uses of peanut oil listed its utility for lighting Hanukkah candles but failed to mention its place in the Passover kitchen. Whereas Planters had convinced so many Jewish consumers of its product's status as the premier "Passover Oil," the image of peanut oil was apparently no longer bound up with Passover when this lyricist composed his peanut song by 1982.[94]

The transition toward strictness as a more acceptable and authentic--deemed rabbinic attitude was helped along by a likeminded Israeli folkway. Traditionalists in Israel did not eat peanuts or use peanut oil on Passover. Back in 1926 Rabbi David Zvi Hoffman of Berlin reported that the custom in Jerusalem was to rule stringently.[95] That incorrigible culture emanated from Jerusalem and carried influence throughout the Holy Land, as Rabbi Avraham Yitzhak Kook had learned well in 1909. Rabbi Zvi Pesah Frank, a leading judge in Jerusalem, could not change the trend at midcentury.[96] In 1966 Rabbi Yehoshua Moshe Aaronson of Petah Tikva refused to budge from the established practice.[97] Just two years later in nearby Tel Aviv, the local rabbinic establishment was met with great reservation by other rabbis and laypeople.[98]

Eventually the Chief Rabbinate of Israel officially proscribed peanut oil.[99] More recently the late Rabbi Yosef Shalom Elyashiv reaffirmed the stringent practice for Jews living in Israel.[100]

An explanation for the successful transplant of the Israeli folkway is far less complex than the earlier Hungarian one. It had much to do with the death of Moshe Feinstein in 1986. In addition to Feinstein, other leading scholars— Rabbi Yaakov Kamenetsky and Yaakov Yitzchok Ruderman—also passed away that year. But even before that date, Feinstein's health prohibited him from maintaining his station as American Orthodoxy's leading halakhist.[101] With no one in the United States deemed worthy of replacing Feinstein, his non-Hungarian followers looked to Israel to fill the vacuum.[102] This was certainly true for the Orthodox Right and, to some degree or another, the more acculturated and moderate Modern Orthodox Jews who attended OU-affiliated synagogues and whose congregations hired RCA-affiliated rabbis. This transition could only hurt the case of those who supported Passover peanut oil, a dwindling group that for more than a decade had been pushed to the periphery. Sure enough, Planters discontinued its line of peanut oil in the early 1990s.[103] The Rokeach brand stayed in circulation longer but with vanishing consumer interest. Rokeach finally dropped its brand in 2002. Since then the Orthodox Union's "Kosher for Passover" division has not certified peanut oil.[104] The extraordinary turnabout reflected the hard-to-describe forces that weigh on Jewish law and observance. The competing religious folkways and rabbinic intuitions that battled with one another in the United States over Passover peanut oil demonstrate the plasticity of American religious groups. They reflect the enduring importance of crucial notions like "authenticity" and the role of American culture in animating and empowering folkways once transplanted in the United States.

# CHAPTER 2

# HOW BAT MITZVAH
# BECAME ORTHODOX

In December 1972 Kehilath Jeshurun in New York City announced the debut of a new synagogue ritual. The Upper East Side congregation held a program on a Saturday afternoon to "honor four young ladies from our congregational family who have recently reached their twelfth birthday and who are, therefore, recognized by the Jewish community as responsible members of the Jewish people." On this weekend the *Se'udah Shlishit*—the "third" Sabbath meal—was reoriented to observe what was "commonly referred to as Bat Mitzvah." The addition of bat mitzvah to the Jewish lifecycle was a relatively recent feature intended, if only in nomenclature, to match the boys' bar mitzvah ritual. For traditional Jews the two rites of passage could never be exactly the same. Unlike a bar mitzvah celebration, which usually called on the thirteen-year-old boy to chant from the Torah on the Sabbath and lay *tefillin* on the weekday, the bat mitzvah lacked any firm ceremonial structure or liturgical formulation. The traditional Jewish worship does not afford women an active role. The amorphousness of bat mitzvah boded well for Orthodox congregations that would not compromise the integrity of Jewish law; a celebratory sermon and a smattering of songs, figured Upper East Side advocates, did not violate any section of Jewish law. At Kehilath Jeshurun, Rabbi Haskel Lookstein addressed the group of girls to acknowledge that "much more is expected of women in religious performance." Songs were also dedicated in their honor.[1] Soon after, the Looksteins celebrated their own daughter's bat mitzvah at Kehilath Jeshurun:

> We are pleased to announce that the Bat Mitzvah celebration for Mindy
> Lookstein, daughter of Rabbi and Mrs. Haskel Lookstein, will be held on

Shabbat Hagadol afternoon, April 14th, in the Main Synagogue and in the Kamber Auditorium.

Mindy, a student in Grade 6 in Ramaz, will deliver a brief talk at a Seudah Shlishit in her honor. Mincha services will begin that afternoon at 5:45. The entire congregation is invited to join with the Looksteins in celebration of this happy milestone in their family's life.[2]

The Orthodox contingent of the Upper West Side also introduced bat mitzvah around this time. In June 1973 Lincoln Square Synagogue organized a modest ritual for Miss Elana Kagan.[3] In the ensuing years, a number of other Lincoln Square families—but not all—elected to celebrate some form of bat mitzvah ceremony, at the encouragement of Rabbi Shlomo Riskin.[4] In 1974 Rabbi Norman Lamm showed some caution as he reported to the congregants at the Jewish Center that he would "accept" bat mitzvah under certain circumstances ("provided the young lay recites divrei Torah so as to distinguish it from an ordinary birthday party"). While he "neither encouraged nor discouraged

The 1973 graduating class of the Lincoln Square Synagogue Feldman Hebrew School included (front row, right to left) Judi Riskin and Elena Kagan. Pictured in the top row (center) is Rabbi Shlomo Riskin, Judi's father. (Lincoln Square Synagogue)

it," Lamm anticipated that in time he would stand alongside Lookstein and Riskin as a supporter of the new Orthodox practice. He confessed, "Some day in the near future, I suspect, I may actively encourage young ladies to celebrate Bat Mitzvah."[5]

In New York these were some of the rare and exceptional instances of Orthodox Judaism's embrace of bat mitzvah. In the 1970s one rabbinic writer observed that bat mitzvah rituals were "virtually ignored by most segments of Orthodox Judaism."[6] That a thousand Orthodox congregations in New York and nearby New Jersey, as a rule, disregarded bat mitzvah rites is important. After all this represented 63 percent of all Orthodox synagogues (1,600 total) in the United States.[7] Certainly New Yorkers like Lookstein and Riskin recognized this. Neither was in favor of initiating a bat mitzvah that looked exactly like the male equivalent. Both, however, felt that some sort of marker of a girl's ascendance to Jewish adulthood was a necessary modern accommodation. To quell potential resistance Lookstein explained to his constituents that the introduction of a bat mitzvah ritual was unconnected to religious egalitarianism. He was clear that his intention was not to "duplicate the corresponding ceremony for boys" but to establish a religious mechanism for young women to acknowledge their transition to maturity.[8] Riskin did not offer a defense for the ritual but did take political measures to avoid controversy. The announcement for the inaugural Lincoln Square bat mitzvah was broadcast as an understated bulletin notice, listed among eighteen other "Congratulations and Mazel Tov" wishes: "Mr. and Mrs. Robert Kagan on the Bat Mitzvah of their daughter Elana."[9]

Lamm's ambivalence at the Jewish Center bespoke a sense of trepidation among Orthodox rabbis that inhibited the girls' ceremony from gaining a substantial foothold in this community. Their thirteen-year-old brothers celebrated bar mitzvah rites. Twelve-year-old girls also moved into adulthood, but without fanfare and outside of rabbinic space. To many the bat mitzvah was a "heterodox" ritual. Many Conservative and Reform congregations held bat mitzvah and confirmation rites for girls that aimed to parallel bar mitzvah. This troubled the Orthodox observers in New York who, on Jewish legal grounds, resisted any attempt to move toward religious egalitarianism and on principle stood in cautious opposition to this ritual innovation, particularly in the synagogue. Most of all, Orthodox rabbinic opponents challenged any religious innovation that lacked a firm connection to earlier customs.[10]

However, the situation outside that Gotham nucleus of Orthodox Judaism was markedly different. Along the Jewish frontier beyond the Tri-State, Orthodox rabbis and laypeople around midcentury started to embrace bat mitzvah as an appropriate ritual to recruit members to their communities. The frontier in the Southern and Western regions of the United States was an important crucible for religious experimentation. In these small pockets of Jewish life, women and men of varied religious points of view cooperated with one another by dint of "cohesion and togetherness," as Shari Rabin has put it.[11] In the nineteenth century the hybrid rituals created on the Jewish frontier were oftentimes inconsistent with the most formalized varieties of Orthodox or Reform Judaism. In some cases that was more compelling than static religious styles. Such "frontierism" was a unique feature of American culture. Long ago, historian Frederick Jackson Turner theorized that the pioneers along the American frontier were the primary developers of "American social development."[12] It was a particularly profitable scene for Evangelicals, who popularized their rank-and-file "folk religion" beyond the reach of mainline Protestant ministers and their "stuffy" forms of "elite religion" in larger cities.[13]

The spread of bat mitzvah along that same frontier reflected the dynamism and development of an Orthodox Jewish spirit in the United States that was willing to take halakhic risks to gain a sturdier foothold in the suburban hinterland. There Conservative Judaism had conquered the bulk of the crabgrass terrain.[14] This branch of American Judaism boasted a spirit of traditionalism while also embracing "change" and "modernity." By the 1950s Conservative Judaism had adopted family pews and other religious alterations to incorporate women into the worship, updated the prayer book, and permitted riding in an automobile on the Sabbath under certain circumstances—among other changes—to attract a younger and more Americanized generation of Jews.[15] In response Orthodox Jews broke from the New York–centric rabbinic "elite religion" and fashioned their own kind of malleable "folk religion." The sociologist Charles Liebman presumed that Orthodox "folk religion" of the rank-and-file people and rabbis detached from the major Orthodox centers would invariably bow to "elite" and "rightward" forms. Yet the case of bat mitzvah, examined in its American context, proves otherwise.[16]

Orthodox leaders on the frontier, out of reach of the larger East Coast hubs, felt compelled to seek out creative rituals and programs to compete with their Conservative rivals. For example, Orthodox Jews advocated

"Friday-night forums." In the winter months, when the Sabbath started during workday hours, many Jews did not end business early to attend synagogue. To accommodate, Conservative congregations hosted late-evening prayer services. This was unacceptable to many Orthodox rabbis who could not countenance "religious miscreants." In their congregations prayers were scheduled "on time." To remain in line with traditional synagogue service times and offer creative religious activities for suburban Jews, a number of Orthodox congregations hosted on-time Sabbath-eve worship and additional late "Friday-night forums." These nonritualized evenings were designed to assuage the unease of Orthodox adherents and attract other Jews by featuring lectures and songs. Configured this way the late Friday-night program did not change the prayer schedule but did offer a portal of entry for suburban Jews into the Orthodox synagogue.[17]

The same was the case for bat mitzvah rituals. In the modest-sized, non–New York Jewish communities of Chicago and Los Angeles, and in the boondocks in states like Georgia, Maryland, Nebraska, and Ohio, the momentum for bat mitzvah grew subtly and stealthily. Outside New York, Orthodox communities adopted bat mitzvah as a necessary means to ensure Orthodox social stability. Along the way they proved that certain forms of bat mitzvah rituals did not pose a threat to Orthodox life; in fact bat mitzvah helped the Orthodox compete with other forms of American Judaism.[18] Most of all the popularization of bat mitzvah in these locales proved that the girls' rite of passage could become an authentic ritual in Orthodox Judaism. In time New York Orthodoxy also incorporated bat mitzvah into its lifecycles. The "folk religion" of the periphery, then, heavily influenced the Orthodox geographic center. Furthermore, by the close of the twentieth century, the battle lines of Orthodox and Conservative Judaism had moved so substantially that bat mitzvah no longer represented the same threat to rabbinic leaders that it had around midcentury. Among other factors the religious dynamics of American frontierism helps to explain how—despite early accusations of "heresy"—bat mitzvah emerged as a bona-fide Orthodox ritual.

## Bat Mitzvah and the (New York) Rabbinic Mind

In November 1958 Rabbi Pinchas Teitz of Elizabeth, New Jersey, addressed his colleagues of the Agudath Ha-Rabbonim. His subject was the threat of

Conservative Judaism to Orthodox life in the United States. Teitz spoke at length on the Conservative's blurring of the gender roles, which was evidenced in the installation of mixed pews and the introduction of bat mitzvah ceremonies.[19] In later addresses this leading member of the rabbinical group's presidium spared no opportunity to discourage bat mitzvah ceremonies among the Orthodox.[20] No doubt bat mitzvah was most closely associated with Conservative Judaism.[21] In 1922 the liberal-Conservative (later, Reconstructionist) rabbi Mordecai Kaplan arranged for his daughter, Judith, to pronounce the blessing over the Torah and read from it in Hebrew and English as well. To many writers and scholars, this event represented the introduction of bat mitzvah to American Judaism.[22] By and large Reform Judaism in this period ignored bat mitzvah, dismissing it as a form of "orientalism," out of touch with Western culture. Besides, Reform congregations much preferred confirmation ceremonies, a public religious examination of sixteen- to eighteen-year-old boys and girls typically held on the Shavuot holiday that dated back to nineteenth-century Europe. By 1950 virtually all Reform congregations hosted such confirmation ceremonies, while just a quarter observed some form of bat mitzvah. During the interwar years many Conservative congregations also adopted confirmation and refused bat mitzvah on grounds similar to those of their Reform counterparts.

After much debate bat mitzvah emerged as a staple within the Conservative synagogue by the 1950s and 1960s.[23] The actual ritual differed and depended on the preferences of the rabbis and laypeople of the respective Conservative congregations. In some synagogues young women were formally called up to the Torah. This, of course, more closely paralleled the boys' bar mitzvah than rituals that resembled mere birthday parties. In others an actual *aliyah*—the honor of being called up and reading from a Torah scroll—was too drastic a departure from traditional Jewish law. Instead these more moderate Conservative congregations settled for Friday-night or Saturday-afternoon ceremonies that featured sermons and festivities. In these varieties congregations were still free to compose liturgies and furnish new rituals.

No matter the variety of bat mitzvah celebration, it was still deemed inauthentic for Orthodox use. Teitz was joined by many other respected Orthodox leaders, and not just those in the United States. Rabbi Aharon Walkin of Pinsk categorized bat mitzvah with other traditional synagogue infractions, like the use of an organ in the service, as he called on his rabbinical colleagues to "guard the borders" of Judaism.[24] In Brooklyn Rabbi Meir Amsel blamed Orthodox bat mitzvah organizers for "ignoring the grave sins that cause others to stumble." These included "abuse of holy religion, imitating gentiles, mingling of the sexes and moving them toward sexual illicitness, profaning the holiness of the Torah and the sacredness of the synagogue, and much more that cannot be listed here."[25] Nearby in Williamsburg the Hungarian-trained rabbi Hananiah Yom Tov Lipa Deutsch dubbed bat mitzvah an "abomination."[26] Similarly Rabbi Eliezer Silver of Cincinnati described bat mitzvah as a "reform" that "should not be observed by the Orthodox."[27] For these prominent and learned rabbis, it was of no consequence how the bat mitzvah ritual was structured and whether or not they could pinpoint which sections of the Jewish law code were violated in the process. What mattered was that bat mitzvah was a religious reform disconnected from "tradition" and too closely associated with other forms and movements within Judaism.[28]

Against this abrasive stance toward bat mitzvah, Rabbis Moshe Feinstein and Yehiel Yaakov Weinberg emerged as the lone "supporters" of the girls' ritual for Orthodox Jews in the United States in the immediate post–World War II period.[29] In 1957 Rabbi Bernard Poupko of Pittsburgh queried Feinstein on the parameters of bat mitzvah celebration. Feinstein described bat mitzvah as "meaningless" (*hevel be'alma*) and of no greater halakhic significance than a birthday party. Feinstein forbade bat mitzvah in the synagogue and only with considerable reluctance tolerated it in homes.[30] Feinstein's position essentially downgraded it to a nonreligious lifecycle event. In a later responsum Feinstein permitted a post–prayer service kiddush in honor of the bat mitzvah girl, but only because "it is the custom in this country to host a kiddush for any kind of commemoration."[31] Still this ruling rendered him vulnerable to the condemnations of those who perceived the bat mitzvah— endowed with religious significance or not—as a threat to their traditionalism. Feinstein's opponents seized the opportunity to censure him for his "lenient" stance toward bat mitzvah. They accused him of accommodating a "gentile" practice and parting ways with the elder rabbis in the United States who sought to "defend themselves against reforms of this kind."[32] Owing to this, most Orthodox rabbis in New York could not risk introducing bat mitzvah to their communities.

In 1963 Rabbi Yehiel Yaakov Weinberg, then of Switzerland, submitted a three-part article on bat mitzvah to a leading rabbinic journal in the United

States. He justified bat mitzvah on the grounds that it did not fall into the pro-hibition of imitating gentiles. Offering great encouragement, Weinberg ruled that bat mitzvah celebrations should be observed in homes; he decided against ritualizing it in the synagogue out of respect for the sensitivities of those who opposed the practice. This compromise, he claimed, was in accordance with Feinstein's recent ruling. Weinberg marshalled many proofs to support his claim. It was clear, though, as Weinberg's biographer has pointed out, that the rabbinic scholar "had made up his mind that the bat mitzvah celebration was a positive manifestation, and he then set out to find the means of justifying it halakhically."[33] This was all too apparent in the final paragraphs of the respon-sum. There Weinberg addressed the claim that bat mitzvah could never be tethered to traditional Jewish practice:

> In truth, however, this is no argument. In previous generations it was unnecessary to be preoccupied with the education of girls for every Jewish person was filled with Torah and fear of Heaven. Moreover, the atmosphere in each and every city in Israel was filled to capacity with the flavor and spirit of Judaism. Girls who were raised in a Jewish home imbibed the spirit of Judaism without doing anything and practically absorbed Judaism from their mothers' breast. Now the generations have become radically transformed. The atmosphere of the street removed any spark of Judaism from the heart of every boy and girl. Girls are edu-cated in non-Jewish schools or in secular schools that do not take pains to implant love of the Torah of Israel and of the holy customs of authentic Judaism in the heart of their students.[34]

In truth Weinberg was far keener on bat mitzvah than Feinstein, a point raised by at least one Orthodox rabbinic scholar.[35] Weinberg's essays did not elicit response, perhaps because the rabbinate in the United States had already decided on the halakhic impropriety of the bat mitzvah ritual and was uneager to reopen the matter to further consideration. Some opposed bat mitzvah on technical halakhic grounds: Primarily they questioned whether the blessing formulated for bar mitzvah boys and the celebratory meal in the child-turned-adult's honor were just as applicable for a young girl.[36] However, the main objection to bat mitzvah centered on its affront to traditional Jewish practice—or a blatant incorporation of a non-Orthodox ritual.

# Orthodox Frontierism

In 1944 a congregant in Brooklyn's Congregation Anshe Emes asked her rabbi about the propriety of bat mitzvah in an Orthodox synagogue. "Rabbi, I liked the Bar Mitzvah ceremony very much," she began. "But, tell me, Rabbi, why don't you do something for the girls?" Jerome Tov Feinstein (no known relation to Rabbi Moshe Feinstein) concurred. The reason Orthodox Judaism had not formulated a public ceremony for young women, explained Feinstein, was that it was new. In the past he—like most other Orthodox rabbis—was aware of the hostility toward bat mitzvah. However, in light of the revelatory conversation with his female congregant, Feinstein was now unconvinced by the arguments. "I believe," he told her, "that you are absolutely right in suggesting that some public ceremony be introduced for the girl when she becomes a Bas Mitzvah." Within the next few weeks and with the support of the local sisterhood, Feinstein organized a "Bas Mitzvah class" and prepared his first student for the makeshift ritual:

> In order to obviate any possible criticism, I decided to conduct the cer-
> emony at our Late Friday Evening Oneg Shabbat. With a bit of publicity
> in our Bulletin and special Post Cards, we had a record crowd for the
> Friday of the first Bas Mitzvah and for every other Friday on which we
> had a Bas Mitzvah. People from neighboring congregations came to see
> what it was all about. Relatives appeared in large numbers. The parents of
> the Bas Mitzvah were hosts for the evening and served refreshments. The
> girls began receiving Bas Mitzvah gifts from their relatives. Occasionally
> we had a Bas Mitzvah in the evening and a Bar Mitzvah in the morning.
> Both were treated equally and our girls and women began to feel that
> they were given a "square deal." Remarks were uniformly enthusiastic
> and complimentary.[37]

Particularly in this period the success of the Brooklyn-based bat mitzvah was an aberration. Most potential support for bat mitzvah was inhibited by the fierce rabbinic opposition to it that emanated from the synagogues and *yeshivot* of Orthodox-dense New York. Instead bat mitzvah obtained its initial reception along the Jewish frontier. Out there Orthodox behavior and its overall position were far from fortified. Orthodox leaders were all too aware of this. Leading Orthodox centers, like Yeshiva Torah Vodaath in Brooklyn, warned their students about the dangers of venturing out of New York. "American Jews," wrote one Torah Vodaath graduate in his 1955 yearbook, "have and still are spreading out in remote cities and villages, thereby losing contact with the core of Jewish life which had been established in New York."[38] Still, many did not follow this sort of advice. In the post–World War II era, Orthodox Jews ventured into the suburbs and competed with the other religious movements for adherents. Often suburban Jews invited representatives of Orthodox, Reform, and Conservative Judaism to publicly debate the merits of their respective religious movements. In most cases audiences found the middle-of-the-road Conservative rabbi most appealing.[39] Chagrined by these outcomes, Orthodox suburbanites—typically young married couples with small children nearing bar and bat mitzvah ages—saw innovations such as bat mitzvah as a way to compete on the open-minded frontier. In so doing, suburban clergymen relied on their judgment rather than the harsh declarations of New York rabbis. It helped that there was no set formula for the bat mitzvah ceremony. Orthodox rabbis were free to arrange the girls' ritual on a Friday night after services or toward the close of the Sabbath on Saturday afternoon. Some preferred to host bat mitzvah ceremonies on Sunday mornings, when many family members were more easily able to attend. The common denominator of all these settings and times was that the bat mitzvah would not appear in the context of the Orthodox prayer service.

Bat mitzvah also helped Orthodox Jews cooperate with other religious movements to foster Jewish communal unity. This was far less important to those in New York, who did not require the Jewish infrastructure provided by Reform and Conservative institutions. Take, for instance, the 1956 rabbinic ban on interdenominational dialogue.[40] The "prohibition" was endorsed by leading New York–based scholars such as Rabbis Moshe Feinstein and Aharon Kotler. In fact nine of the eleven rabbinic signatories of the well-circulated censure hailed from New York. The whole matter was a highly disputed issue among and within Tri-State Orthodox communities. In many small "out-of-town" locales, it was nearly impossible to adhere to this policy.[41] In large measure bat mitzvah was a similar feature of suburban Jewish life that the Orthodox could ill afford to reject. In the second half of the twentieth century, bat mitzvah emerged as a popular lifecycle event that invited Jews from all sectors of their community. For Orthodox congregations it was a mechanism to recruit the religiously uninitiated and a ritual that became all-too-standard in close-knit suburban Jewish communities. True, it was also quite a statement that girls had a place in the synagogue. Even if bat mitzvah was not usually woven into the worship, it still penetrated that male-dominated synagogue space. For Orthodox Jews there was more than just a little something to this. But faced with questions of survival, the masculine hegemony made room.

A survey of several suburban Orthodox communities is instructive. In the postwar era few Orthodox Jews in Baltimore could fathom that others considered bat mitzvah a controversial ritual. By this time it was well entrenched in that city. In the 1930s Rabbi Samuel Rosenblatt initiated the bat mitzvah ritual at Beth Tfiloh. At first he was opposed by male lay leaders who, claimed Rabbi Rosenblatt, suffered from a "lack of imagination." Then he was opposed by his rabbinic elders. In March 1936 Rosenblatt wrote Rabbi Moses Hyamson of New York's Congregation Orach Chaim to inquire about this leading sage's position on bat mitzvah. Hyamson responded that such an innovation would be "very objectionable and contrary to the spirit of Orthodox Judaism as universally understood." At all costs, Hyamson urged, no girls' rites should take place within the synagogue.[42] The young rabbi persisted with his plan anyway and recruited an inaugural class of five girls to prepare for their bat mitzvah programs. According to Rosenblatt, that first group of young ladies made quite an impression. The number of bat mitzvah students continued to rise. Moreover, the positive outcome of the Beth Tfiloh innovation compelled "all Orthodox congregations in Baltimore, led by English-speaking rabbis [to] follow suit."[43] He was right. For example, Rabbi Uri Miller of Baltimore's Beth Jacob wrote in 1958 about the bat mitzvah ceremonies in his congregation without any sense that it was off-limits in New York.[44] In the 1950s the reach of bat mitzvah extended even to the rightward-leaning local Bais Yaakov school. At that time the Ladies' Auxiliary urged the school's principal to offer a program to prepare and celebrate bat mitzvah girls. A relative newcomer to Maryland, the Brooklyn-educated Rabbi Hirsch Diskind was surprised by the request and turned to his revered father-in-law, Rabbi Yaakov Kamenetsky, for guidance. The latter's response—in contrast to other Eastern European extracts at this time—surprised the young principal:

Much to Rabbi Diskind's surprise, Reb Yaakov thought it was a terrific idea to impress upon the girls that they were no longer *ketanos* but *gedolos.* Doing so in a school setting was a great way to accomplish this, he said. As a matter of fact, Reb Yaakov told his son-in-law that he himself had held a family *melava malka* in honor of his two daughters' bat mitzvas—for the eldest while he was a rav in Lithuania, and for the youngest, Rabbi Diskind's wife, while he was a rav in Toronto.[45]

Chicago's Orthodox Jews were also quick to embrace the bat mitzvah ritual. In 1940 Oscar Fasman, the thirty-two-year-old president of the Rabbinical Association of the Hebrew Theological College (HTC) in Chicago, announced that his group was "discussing the possibility of framing a dignified 'Bas-Mitzvah' ritual for girls."[46] Four years later Rabbi Fasman published an article in an Orthodox Union periodical in which he urged that the "modern scene necessitates the creation of a ceremony by which the girl who becomes twelve years of age will be impressed with the importance of her status and will feel that Judaism does not ignore her." Similar to Rabbi Jerome Tov Feinstein of Brooklyn, the Chicago-trained rabbi strongly recommended that Orthodox congregations take a "wise step by instituting some form of Bat Mitzvah procedure."[47] A well-read and savvy religious leader, Fasman assuredly was seeking to reject the claims of the anti–bat mitzvah rabbinate while not engaging in a full-fledged halakhic disputation.[48]

Fasman and other HTC graduates were responsible for much of the grassroots spread of bat mitzvah and other accommodations in Jewish suburbia. Yeshiva University in New York held a firm grasp on the placement of rabbis in the far more Orthodox-dense East Coast. Well aware of this, HTC rabbis more often found work in Orthodox congregations in the Midwest and West Coast of the United States. They also populated the pulpits of "Traditional synagogues" that made several—ostensibly temporary—concessions to recruit women and men and to introduce them to a traditional (i.e., non-Conservative) prayer service. To accomplish this these congregations often featured mixed seating and used a microphone on the Sabbath.[49] And in the same spirit—but far less religiously problematic—the rabbis of Traditional synagogues also sanctioned and encouraged bat mitzvah rituals.[50] In 1963 the Council of Traditional Synagogues of Greater Chicago recommended to all constituent congregations "that the Bas Mitzvah ceremony could be conducted for the family and friends."[51]

Rabbis were not the only ones who promoted bat mitzvah. The Yeshiva Women of the Hebrew Theological College produced a Mother's Day play for its Midwestern sisterhoods to perform in their congregations. Describing the lifecycle of the "Orthodox" or "Traditional" Jewess, the script included the following benchmark: "Millie is a young lady now. She has just had her Bas Mitzvah at the shul, and has more fountain pens than the Waterman Co."[52] These efforts on behalf of bat mitzvah achieved considerable success. The local Jewish newspaper in Chicago recorded a number of bat mitzvah ceremonies conducted at Traditional Synagogues:

> Cong. KINS of West Rogers Park will celebrate its first Bat Mitzva Sabbath night service on Saturday, March 14. This special Melaveh Malka service will begin at 7:30 p.m. in the sanctuary of the congregation, 2800 W. North Shore.[53]
>
> Mr. and Mrs. Harry Warshausky of Lincolnwood announce the Bat Mitzva of their daughter Merle Debra, Friday Oct. 9, 8:30 p.m.
>
> Merle Debra's Bat Mitzva will take place at the Lincolnwood Jewish Cong., 7117 N. Crawford, Skokie.[54]
>
> Sharon Joy Greese, daughter of Mr. and Mrs. William Greese, will become Bat Mitzva, Nov. 27, 8 p.m. at the Skokie Valley Traditional Synagog [sic], 8840 N. Monticello, Skokie.
>
> Sharon is an honor student at the Skokie Valley Traditional Synagog Hebrew School and attends Old Orchard Junior High School in Skokie.[55]

HTC men also propagated bat mitzvah beyond Chicago.[56] Rabbi Joseph Krickstein brought the girls' ceremony to Beth Israel in Hamilton, Ohio. Rabbi Isaac Nadoff found it a home in Omaha, Nebraska, as did Rabbi Bernard Schwab in Lexington, Kentucky.[57] In Los Angeles, Rabbi Simon Dolgin introduced bat mitzvah as a late Friday-night "Oneg Shabbat" program to the well-heeled Beth Jacob Congregation in 1955.[58] Chicago-trained rabbis also gained positions in Philadelphia, where in the 1950s a third of the Orthodox synagogues held bat mitzvah celebrations. That figure grew steadily in subsequent decades.[59]

To be sure HTC was far from alone in its support of bat mitzvah. In the 1940s European-born rabbi Henry Goldberger started bat mitzvah classes at Adas Yeshurun Synagogue in Augusta, Georgia.[60] In 1956 B'nai Emunah in Tulsa, Oklahoma, inaugurated bat mitzvah. On this occasion the YU-trained rabbi Arthur Kahn arranged a Friday-evening program for Miss Ronnie Faye

Kahan.[61] Like so many other Orthodox pioneers along the American frontier, Kahn recognized the importance of bat mitzvah to accommodate postwar sensibilities. Rabbi Walter Wurzburger was another YU man who embraced bat mitzvah. In the 1950s Toronto's Shaarei Shomayim under his leadership started a bat mitzvah tradition, "though in keeping with orthodox practice."[62] Nevertheless New York–based Orthodox organizations, such as National Council of Young Israel, the Rabbinical Council of America, and Yeshiva University, remained ambivalent toward the "ceremonial innovation" for young girls. Simply put the ritual raised far too many questions and challenges from the old-guard Orthodox establishment. In fact the annual RCA sermon manuals published from the 1940s to the 1980s contain many entries for "occasional bar mitzvah" celebrations but none in observance of bat mitzvah. Likewise a 1952 bar mitzvah anthology boasted about the boys' rite as the "crucial and dramatic episode in the life of every Jewish youth" without giving any thought to their female counterparts.[63] In locales such as New York and Boston in the 1960s, therefore, it was still very much the perception that "Bas Mitzvah is only a recent custom and that usually orthodox Jews do not practice this ceremony."[64] In fact in the 1970s one member of the Young Israel of Brookline complained that her Mirrer Yeshiva–educated rabbi did not permit the celebration in the synagogue. Instead the girl and her family held a "conventional birthday party."[65]

## Authenticating Bat Mitzvah

By the 1980s it became increasingly clear that bat mitzvah did not present a challenge to the spirit of Orthodox Judaism. That several rabbinic scholars in Israel—where Conservative and Reform Judaism did not pose a threat—agreed certainly helped assuage earlier concerns about the ritual.[66] The most important ruling was that of Rabbi Ovadia Yosef.[67] On several occasions the Sephardic chief rabbi of Israel ruled in favor of bat mitzvah celebrations. In 1982 a popular New York Jewish weekly reported on Yosef's view to interested Orthodox Jews in the United States:

> Yosef conceded that Bat Mitzva celebration was not formerly common among Jewish communities, but he explained that this was perhaps because Jewish girls in olden days "absorbed religious values in the home."

Nowadays, in the much more open society around us, it was essential "from a pedagogic point of view" to encourage girls by giving them Bat Mitzva parties and not causing feelings of resentment among girls by "discriminating" between them and boys, the Chief Rabbi stated.[68]

Still the primary reason for the emergence of bat mitzvah in Orthodox Jewish life had far more to do with the religious negotiation in which Orthodox Jews had engaged along the American Jewish frontier. By the 1980s no one reported that the ritual was a hackneyed version of Conservative Judaism. In this later epoch many Jews raised in frontier communities could testify to this.[69] One New York Jewish writer opined with more than a modicum of exuberance that "in the last decade . . . the Orthodox [had] begun to integrate Bat Mitzvah celebration as part of community norms."[70] Another commented that "these celebrations have become commonplace in many Orthodox circles, with families sometimes traveling great distances to be at a Bat Mitzvah, just as they would for a Bar Mitzvah."[71] In the most ardent Orthodox sectors, bat mitzvah was still not celebrated; but it was not denigrated as it had been in the immediate postwar period. Further, each community performed the bat mitzvah ritual in a manner that reflected a deliberate balance of tradition and innovation. Of course this had much to do with the sanction of a new generation of American-born Orthodox rabbis who did not share their European-trained predecessors' view of bat mitzvah.[72] The new rabbinic outlook was informed by decades of Orthodox bat mitzvah rituals that conformed to Orthodox standards and emphasized traditional piety.[73]

All this lent bat mitzvah quasi-official Orthodox standing. In 1995 the RCA published a rabbi's manual for lifecycle events. In it the editor, Rabbi Reuven Bulka, included an entry for bat mitzvah, as "there are many who celebrate this entry into Judaic responsibility with a meaningful ceremony reinforcing the significance of the Bat-Mitzvah." The leading Orthodox national rabbinical organization's ritual guide acknowledged that "there are a number of potential ingredients which can combine for a meaningful ceremony" and offered "one suggested format from among a host of possibilities" that included a sermon and a carefully worded liturgy.[74] This represented a major departure from the RCA's long-held ambivalent stance. Of course not all varieties of bat mitzvah were universally accepted among the Orthodox. In 1986 Rabbi Pinchas Stolper of the Orthodox Union wrote to Shaarie Torah of Portland,

Oregon, to complain that the bat mitzvah of Miss Stacey Lebenzon had been too egalitarian—the "fine young lady" had "conducted services"—and represented a "deviation of the congregation from orthodoxy." He threatened Rabbi Yonah Geller that the "Orthodox Union can hardly justify maintaining the membership of a congregation in light of the type of service the congregation is prepared to tolerate for a bat-mitzvah."[75] Yet by this time bat mitzvah—performed in an "acceptable" manner and with a few stellar rabbinic approbations—had proven to be an important rite of passage.

The acceptance of bat mitzvah celebrations within the Orthodox fold took significant time, and came only after Orthodox rabbis and laypeople fashioned rituals that distinguished it from the Conservative and Reform bat mitzvah ceremonies that called young girls to the Torah and encouraged them to chant from it. Most of all, Orthodox Jews had to give bat mitzvah a chance. Unsurprisingly, therefore, the ritual was a product of the more subtle, out-of-town Orthodox pioneers who dared to take risks along the American frontier. Decades later it was long forgotten that bat mitzvah was ever a controversial concept, a battle between Orthodox "folk" and "elite" religions. Bat mitzvah had become authentically Orthodox. It had found a space within tradition in the same manner other American faiths had done in the New World.

# CHAPTER 3

# BASKETBALL POLITICS, YARMULKE WARS, AND THE DYNAMICS OF HALAKHIC CHANGE

In February 1981 Sheldon Schaffel grew worried about his basketball team's chances in the upcoming Illinois Class A Regional Basketball Tournament. The Yeshiva High School varsity team started the season with much promise, defeating archrival Ida Crown Jewish Academy for the very first time in that lopsided rivalry. Students from both schools hailed from the same Chicago northside neighborhoods, and their games were highly anticipated events.[1] For the Yeshiva, however, the balance of the season was uneven, and in the students' own words, the team's "playing didn't fulfill its potential."[2] Still the Yeshiva qualified for the Illinois High School Association's (IHSA) postseason tournament, a feat unaccomplished during the school's first two years as a member of the Metropolitan Prep Conference. The team was slated to compete against top-seeded Harvard High School.[3] But the imposing contest against a playoff powerhouse was not Schaffel's major concern. Shortly before the contest the coach had heard a rumor that the referees were instructed to ban his students from donning yarmulkes while playing in the IHSA match. It was considered a possible safety hazard. Fallen skullcaps might cause other players to slip and incur injuries. The option to play bareheaded was unacceptable to the Yeshiva and its brand of Orthodox Judaism.

The Harvard coach assured Schaffel that he would not protest. Besides, no one had ever heard of yarmulke-related basketball injuries. Still Harvard's coach recommended that the Yeshiva contact IHSA headquarters in Bloomington, Illinois.[4] Sure enough the interscholastic league confirmed that yarmulkes were prohibited under its understanding of the organization's guidelines. IHSA reported the same disappointing decision to the Academy coach before its first postseason contest.[5] The decision touched off a two-year First Amendment legal battle. More than just a case study in American legal history, *Menora v. Illinois High School Association* also teaches something very important about the development of Halakhah in the United States and the extratextual forces that impact its interpretation.

The hardwood yarmulke conundrum was a relatively new challenge. Back in the 1920s most Orthodox young men in Chicago did not don yarmulkes in public. One old-timer testified that when he and his friends studied at local universities, "nobody dared to put on a kipah," the Hebrew word for the religious headgear. "The only time we put on a kipah in the university in those days," recalled Rabbi Leonard Mishkin, "was when we had our lunches."[6] Mishkin confirmed that the same was true of theaters, parks, and other public venues. According to the plain meaning of Jewish law, affixing a yarmulke was only a requirement when Jewish men prayed or recited a blessing over food. In all other scenarios Orthodox males did not feel compelled to stand out among other Americans.[7] They therefore wore a hat or appeared bareheaded. Sixty years later the importance of the yarmulke for Orthodox Jews had significantly changed. It represented a sense of belonging in the public sphere, even if only 50 percent of the Orthodox population placed a covering atop their heads. (Many Orthodox married women covered their hair too, but this practice has never assumed the same heightened public symbolism.) The headgear was an icon of Orthodox religious identity, as it was for some Conservative Jews.[8] In fact it was the Yeshiva, Mishkin's very own alma mater, that was involved in this court case, fighting for the right to wear yarmulkes in all venues.

The yarmulke was not merely elevated in stature. Its entire meaning was transformed. In the basketball lawsuit and in other forums by this time, Orthodox leaders described the head covering as a tenet of their faith. They swore under oath that a yarmulke was a requirement at all times. Anything less than that, they charged, would be religiously inauthentic. Other Jews deemed the yarmulke a "nonessential custom" and worried about these "disingenuous" readings of Jewish law.[9] The majority of Jewish legal codes supported this second view. However, yarmulke proponents were not lying. Theirs was a position informed by considerations of Orthodox Jewish life and identity politics.[10] Furthermore the extratextual elevation of the yarmulke's status in

Jewish law was not due to any source-based evidence or rationale. Rather, Orthodox Jews in the final decades of the twentieth century interpreted the yarmulke as a symbol of their community's right to participate in the public sphere in identifiably religious terms. Orthodox males wore their yarmulkes as a requirement, part of a larger responsibility to maintain their community's place within the arena of American civics. The changed status of the yarmulke as evidenced in the commotion surrounding *Menora v. Illinois High School Association* betokened the new expectations for the Orthodox Jewish experience in everyday American life.

## Finding Meaning for the Yarmulke

In January 1950 Brenda Putnam wrote to Rabbi Saul Lieberman about her latest project. The Architect of the US Capitol had commissioned Putnam to furnish a sculpture of Moses Maimonides to be included among the *Portraits of Lawgivers* on display in the House Chamber in Washington, DC. Putnam wished to place a "head-covering, or small cap such as you and your colleagues wear." Lieberman had already informed the master sculptor that neither Maimonides nor any other Jew in the twelfth century wore a yarmulke. Contrary to the artist's impressions, Jewish law, explained Lieberman, did not require men to ubiquitously cover their heads. Still Putnam felt that the anachronism could be excused "because it would make him the more readily identifiable to the thousands of visitors to the galleries."[11] Though she ultimately did not furnish a yarmulke for the Maimonides statue, Putnam's plea represented a major shift in the evolving image of traditional Jewish life in the United States.

A decade earlier most Orthodox and Conservative Jewish men had appeared in public bareheaded, unless they were part of the shrinking "old-fashioned" population that donned a hat in public.[12] They had relied on the rabbinic authorities, who required head coverings for prayer, religious study, and when reciting a blessing over food.[13] A minority of rabbinic writers required covered heads at all times. These authorities pointed to the Talmud's statement, "Cover your head so that the fear of heaven may be upon you" (Shabbat 156b), and an additional saying attributed to the third-century scholar Rav Huna (Kiddushin 31a). They also argued that head coverings helped distinguish Jews from their male Christian counterparts, who appeared bareheaded as a sign of respect. The nineteenth-century Hungarian scholar Rabbi Shlomo Ganzfried suggested in his *Kitzur Shulhan Arukh* (3:6) that young boys should wear yarmulkes to ingrain within them a "fear of heaven." Yet the Orthodox rank and file in the United States abided by the lenient point of view, at least before the mid-1900s. This was the majority position, and it was reinforced, albeit circuitously, by Rabbi Moshe Feinstein, probably the leading Orthodox rabbinic authority in twentieth-century America.[14]

In the 1950s and 1960s, the yarmulke entered the Orthodox mainstream, owing to a variety of changes in Jewish life. One Orthodox Jew in Brooklyn attributed the spike in yarmulkes to the influence of migrants toting a more stringent Hungarian folkway, to "Jews who came [to Borough Park] in the '40s and the '50s."[15] These post-Holocaust émigrés welcomed stringency, even when their positions were among the minority viewpoints within the corpus of Jewish codes.[16] Writing in the pages of an Orthodox Union publication, Rabbi Joseph Weiss of Yeshiva University credited it to a return to "faithfulness" and traditionalism. In anticipating an epoch of Orthodox triumphalism, Weiss noticed a turning away from "elements aiming to reform the Jewish religion [by moving] to discard this symbol" to a recognition, according to him, that "bareheadedness symbolizes unguided freethinking which can bring harm and ruin, individually and collectively."[17]

Others credited the trend to American multiculturalism and Orthodox pride in the wake of the Six-Day War. In June 1967 Rabbi Norman Lamm of Manhattan sermonized about the euphoric young people celebrating and contributing to Israel's cause.[18] Many Jews in the United States understood Israel's astonishing victory over its Arab neighbors as nothing short of miraculous. It propelled a religious revival, tightly linking Jewish identity to Zionism. The sentiment was particularly acute among the Orthodox. Hundreds packed their bags and settled in Israel. Most, though, stayed in the United States and demonstrated their devotion to Judaism and Zionism through outward expressions of pride and symbols. (Israelis had donned yarmulkes with regularity decades before.)[19] In time one rabbi in Los Angeles noticed how Religious Zionists had outfitted themselves with colorful crocheted head coverings that could demarcate their ideological sensibilities from more fundamentalist Orthodox groups who opposed Zionism and stood out for their black hats and velvet yarmulkes.[20] The yarmulke, then, became one such icon for Jewish men, and competed for space alongside other religious, ethnic, and nationalistic images. Several years later Lamm reflected on the change, asserting that the new practice had much more to do with Jewish identity than a stricter Hungarian-style interpretation of Jewish law:

> In my generation, even the most pious did not wear the kippah in museums or libraries, in theatres or universities or public places. . . . [T]oday's youth, not necessarily for religious reasons at all, insists upon wearing the kippah every place—places public and private, streets or home, museum or library or movies, or whatever it might be. They are saying: this is my identity, whether you like it or not. I am who I am, and I shall not be someone else in order to please you.[21]

By the late 1970s the Jewish press announced that the yarmulke was "here to stay." A reporter in Philadelphia opined that the yarmulke denoted American Jews' return to traditionalism. Even among Reform rabbinical students, it was observed, there were many "seen wearing yarmulkes while eating in the dining room."[22]

For the Orthodox, wearing the yarmulke in public fulfilled a need to merge their religious and American identities rather than compartmentalize them, as their fathers and grandfathers had done. The new crop of Orthodox men felt a renewed excitement and responsibility to participate in public activities and gatherings, taking advantage of American culture—but to engage in full religious uniform. Though she was not a yarmulke-wearer, one Orthodox Jewish woman reported in 1978 that in the United States "there's so much greater tolerance for difference that you're no longer considered an oddball if you have particular dietary restrictions, or if you wear a kippah."[23] Without it an Orthodox male appeared as someone much less than religiously authentic, and his participation in the public sphere felt less meaningful. To reinforce this behavior Orthodox day school students in several American locales could be suspended or expelled for appearing on campus bareheaded on the grounds that it violated Jewish law.[24] In certain professions and among an older demographic, the bulk of Orthodox men still did not affix yarmulkes to their heads. However, observers noticed how a newfound "Kippa Culture" was "producing young doctors, lawyers, engineers, social scientists and practitioners who are openly identifying as Orthodox Jews."[25] In the company of other Jews and non-Jews, these up-and-coming professionals fastened their work lives to their religious identities. Public image, therefore, served as an important consideration in halakhic decision-making.

## Orthodox Jews and Free Exercise

Similar sentiments informed the legal complaint filed by the Chicago Jews and their young ballplayers for the right to don yarmulkes on the hardwood court. At no point in the proceedings did the plaintiffs—for the Yeshiva team, Shalom Menora, Ronald Allswang, and Ronald Bruckenstein; for the Academy squad, Michael Weiner and Mitchell Sered—embark on a thorough discussion of the yarmulke in Jewish law. Instead the formal complaint against IHSA claimed that wearing a head covering was one of the "traditional tenets of their religion."[26] The basketball league did not challenge the statement, so no further elaboration was ever required in this section of the litigation. Under those terms, the Yeshiva and the Academy alleged, the basketball league "cannot bar persons wearing yarmulkes from participating in basketball games played under its authority."[27]

The reason had to do with the First Amendment to the US Constitution: "Congress shall make no law respecting an establishment of religion, or prohibiting the free exercise thereof." Ratified in December 1791, the amendment intended to accomplish two things insofar as religion was concerned. First, the so-called Establishment Clause meant to prevent an official, established religion in the United States. Members of all faiths—and atheists, as well—have invoked the Establishment Clause to uphold a separation of church and state in the federal government and, more lately after a landmark 1940 US Supreme Court decision, on the state level. In most instances they have taken to court to halt the efforts of the overwhelming population of Protestants from imposing their religious creeds on government institutions and policies. US Supreme Court cases taking up this matter challenged allowing prayer in public schools (1963), directing funding for religious causes (1971), and placing religious displays on public grounds (1984).[28]

The second section of the First Amendment aimed to protect "Free Exercise," to ensure religious liberties; to allow American citizens to uphold their religious beliefs and rituals without impediment. For instance, the court considered whether public schools could force Jehovah's Witnesses to salute and pledge to symbols like the American flag even though their faith forbade it (1943). In 1972 the judiciary took up an Amish family's refusal to continue their children's public schooling on religious grounds. Similarly, the Supreme Court considered the constitutionality of firing Native Americans for using a state-banned drug (peyote) that was part of their ritual (1990). In March 1999 the Third Circuit Court of Appeals ruled that the Newark police department could not require Muslim officers to work clean-shaven due to freedom of religion.[29]

The Chicago basketball lawsuit centered on the second part of the First Amendment. The ballplayers' lawyers argued that preventing the student athletes from donning yarmulkes during interscholastic competitions "solely because of their adherence to the requirements of the Orthodox Jewish faith" was an infringement on the "fundamental right of free exercise of their religion guaranteed by the First Amendment of the United States Constitution."[30] The plaintiffs claimed that there was something inherently "normal" and "Americanizing" about basketball. This was particularly the case in Chicago and other Midwestern areas in which high school basketball seemed to captivate athletes and fans more than football, the high school sport that claimed supremacy in most other regions.[31] Truth to tell, Jews on Chicago's West Side had dominated Illinois basketball up until the 1950s.[32] While Jewish neighborhoods were no longer hardwood powerhouses in the 1980s, there was still a lot of excitement surrounding competitive basketball, whether a team stood much of a chance to compete for the championship on the University of Illinois campus or not.

The main thing was that the teenagers and their teams could tap into some of the popular sports culture. For Americans sports served as an important rite of passage for adolescents, indoctrinating a competitive spirit that would translate, so the plaintiffs said, to other social and economic realms.[33] In the 1980–81 IHSA season, 835 high schools participated in the statewide basketball league: 703 public schools and 132 private schools. According to league officials, every high school but one in the Chicago area (Lake Forest Academy) was a dues-paying member of the interscholastic league.[34] IHSA-sanctioned basketball was ubiquitous and a pivotal part of extracurricular activities throughout Illinois. Educators and parents tended to think of it as a low-risk-of-injury sport that taught discipline and sportsmanship. The Orthodox young men therefore found wholly unacceptable the suggestion that they could take up another sport that did not regulate headgear.

Yeshiva High School and Ida Crown Jewish Academy varsity basketball teams compete during the 1981 season with yarmulkes fastened on top of their heads. (Hebrew Theological College)

The Chicago Orthodox high schools' angst over Free Exercise matched similar concerns among other coreligionists. In the United States Jews had a long history of invoking the First Amendment to protect their civil liberties. Most Jewish energies, though, were devoted to the Establishment Clause rather than Free Exercise. In their minds it was the Establishment Clause that thwarted a Christian hegemony from behaving toward Jews and against Jewish interests as it had so often done in Europe.[35] The Establishment Clause preserved a certain guarantee of religious tolerance. Free Exercise, for all that it ensured about ritual and conduct in public spaces, was not viewed as the key to American exceptionalism. At times, as the earlier history of the yarmulke indicates, Jews felt pressure to suppress the need to exercise religious expressions in the public sector to emphasize their ability to acculturate to American norms. Jews therefore directed more resources and energies to protect the former instead of the latter constitutional plank.

American Jewish affection for church-state separation commenced early on in the nation's history. In fact Jewish concern over federal- and state-sponsored religion dated back to the initial 1787 meetings of the Constitutional Convention in Philadelphia. At least one Jew wrote a letter to that assembly, pleading with them to look out for their Jewish constituency, "faithful Whigs" who had "bravely fought and bled for liberty."[36] Just before the Bill of Rights was ratified, Jews in Rhode Island traded letters with President George Washington about the importance of establishing a government that tolerated more than just the Christian creed.[37] Decades later likeminded coreligionists in Baltimore urged the Maryland legislature to defeat a bill that would have prevented Jews from holding public office.[38] Jews remained transfixed by the Establishment Clause. It loomed large in the Jewish press during the 1860s to help thwart the Christian Amendment movement's attempts to alter the Constitution so that the Almighty (Protestant) God would be acknowledged as the source of all authority and power in civil government.[39] Several decades later one editorialist commented that "if there is one feature of the American Constitution of which the Jews are more jealous than of all others it is the barrier that has been erected between Church and State; and any infringement upon the domain of either they will always vigorously oppose."[40] Likewise Jews of all types railed against the inclusion of Christmas as a federal holiday.[41] In sum Jews clung to the Establishment Clause to prove their American entitlement.

Orthodox Jews also looked to the Establishment Clause for civic cover. For instance, they campaigned in the early twentieth century to eliminate "blue laws" that restricted retail shopping on Sundays, when Christians were expected to be worshiping in churches. Tradition-abiding Jews did not work on Saturday, when gentile shops and retailers remained open for business. Rabbi Bernard Drachman and other self-appointed Orthodox diplomats preached to Jews and Christians that this was an obvious "establishment of religion" and therefore "incompatible with both the spirit and letter of our government system."[42]

The situation eventually changed. In the 1960s some Orthodox leaders parted ways with other Jewish groups, motivated by their quest to lobby for government aid to religious day schools.[43] In 1962 Rabbi Moshe Sherer of the Agudath Israel expressed the reportedly "prevailing sentiment of Orthodox Jews" in favor of directing federal aid to Jewish private schools. The view was certainly at odds with the straightforward church-state separation doctrine that Jews had supported until then. It hewed much closer to the politics of Catholic groups seeking government funds for their parochial schools. In addition, the National Council of Young Israel and Torah Umesorah endorsed the position, in opposition to the "majority Jewish opinion" aligned with more popular interpretations of the First Amendment.[44] Yet the mainstream Orthodox Union upheld the more traditional view and looked for other ways—like federally funded bussing programs—to ease the burden of tuition and funding for Orthodox day schools.[45] In the words of the moderate Rabbi Joseph Lookstein, "it would be a godsend if the Government would help us, but I would not accept such aid."[46]

In the ensuing decades Orthodox Jews continued to tussle over day school aid and the propriety of public displays of religious objects—such as Chabad menorahs—in public spaces.[47] Observing the increased confusion over the Orthodox position on the First Amendment, one leading Modern Orthodox rabbi commented that he would "prefer a total separation of church and state. I don't think it's in the cards." On a pragmatic level, reasoned Rabbi Walter Wurzburger, "I think it is better to have the Jewish community as viable as possible."[48] Around the same time Wurzburger also urged his coreligionists to cease their "obsessive preoccupation with the Establishment Clause." He claimed that the long-held hardline position on church-state matters was an example of how the "Jewish community went overboard in opposing measures which would have actually advanced their own religious interests." The former president of the Rabbinical Council of America believed it was far too late to find common ground on Establishment Clause issues within the Jewish fold. Instead he urged greater attention be paid to "Free Exercise" matters, an area of constitutional policy about which all Jews were still very much in agreement. In truth religious groups had become far more conscious about religious liberties in the postwar era of enlarged government welfare systems and organizations. That Wurzburger and other Jewish leaders became more cognizant of Free Exercise paralleled a growing trend in America among faith communities. In the 1980s an increasing number of minorities and smaller groups no longer looked to Americanize at the cost of toning down ethnic and religious identities. Jews, figured Wurzburger, ought to do the same. It was time, he believed, to focus on how Orthodox Jews could celebrate and observe their religion openly and freely in public spaces rather than concentrate on hiding all other kinds of religious symbols from public places and policies.

The basketball case was therefore part of a larger shift to protect Jewish religious rights in the public sector rather than to shield American Judaism from perceived attempts to establish a Christian America. The legal maneuvering of the two Chicago high schools was also in line with the times. In the 1980s the Christian Right defended itself against, in the words of historian Martin Marty, the "most modest governmental regulations," depicting federal encroachment of religious expression on television and in the media as a "totalitarian intrusion of their religious rights."[49] In June 1985 this same scholar of American religion told a large gathering of rabbis about the common desire among all American faiths to reinforce their "public image."[50] For Orthodox Jews especially, the yarmulke represented this desire to maintain a public image while behaving like everyone else in the public sphere.

In fact the Chicago case was one of three noteworthy yarmulke lawsuits in the early 1980s. In the others Sergeant Murray Bitterman and Dr. S. Simcha Goldman—both ordained Orthodox rabbis—filed separate suits against the Air Force to be permitted to wear yarmulkes inside their work facilities, against military policy that prohibited headgear indoors. The armed forces argued that uniformity was essential in military settings and helped advance national security. In both cases the courts sided with the Air Force on the grounds that the First Amendment must be subordinate to the military on matters of national security. In the Goldman case the decision in favor of military policy was upheld in the US Supreme Court in a 5–4 decision.[51] Absent the issue of military policy and deference to it, the Chicago case most plainly addresses the role and interpretation of the yarmulke in the American civilian life.

The courts and onlookers in the media took the Chicago case very seriously. In its many legal stages, *Menora v. Illinois High School Association* made its way into the Jewish media and captured headlines in the *Chicago Tribune* and *New York Times*.[52] The appearance of the yarmulke on the basketball court was no small thing, especially for this tradition-bound faith community. By the 1980s Orthodox day schools had embraced the right to compete in basketball games and participate in American sports culture. In New York teenage boys competed in the Metropolitan Yeshiva High School Athletic Association (the so-called Yeshiva League). There, schools formed fierce rivalries, evoking the adrenalin levels typical of other storied athletic battles.[53] In Los Angeles a local Orthodox high school rallied to convince a basketball phenom to remain at athletically average Yeshiva University Los Angeles (YULA) instead of transferring to a nearby public school with more visibility to collegiate scouts and boosters. Teachers and teammates prevailed on young Jeff Remer to remain at the Orthodox school despite its limitations because of the positive impact his play had on the broader religious community's self-confidence and public image. This argument proved good enough for Remer to stay at YULA until graduation.[54] Basketball at their schools represented much of the same for the Yeshiva and the Academy. It was inauthentic and un-American, they argued, that Orthodox young men could not simultaneously dress as Orthodox Jews and use the yarmulke as a public symbol as they competed like any other teenage basketball squad. That was the purpose of the yarmulke, they reckoned, and their right as Orthodox Jews in the United States. The Free Exercise argument helped frame and concretize these religious attitudes in a very public legal proceeding.

## Competing as Authentic Orthodox Jews

On February 23, 1981, the Yeshiva High School was scheduled to face off in an opening-round playoff match against Harvard High School. The prospects looked quite grim a week prior, after a school official wrote to the tournament organizers to explain that "wearing skull caps by male students of the Jewish faith is a fundamental policy of our religion." Rabbi Jerold Isenberg assured IHSA that the boys' yarmulkes were "securely fastened and should not cause any problems."[55] Nonetheless IHSA's Donald Robinson would not relent.[56] In his determination yarmulkes violated the Rule 2–2 of the National Federation of State High School Associations (NFSHSA):

> The referee shall not permit any player to wear equipment which, in his or her judgment, is dangerous to other players. Elbow, hand, finger, wrist or forearm guard, cast or brace made of hard and unyielding leather, plaster, pliable (soft) plastic, metal or any other hard substance, even though covered with soft padding, shall always be declared illegal. Head decorations, headwear, or jewelry are illegal. Barrettes made of soft metal

are legal. Head bands no wider than two inches made of nonabrasive unadorned, single color cloth, fiber, soft leather, pliable plastic or rubber are legal.[57]

School administrators did not read the rules the same way. Their religious headgear was safe, just like the other usable attire permitted under this regulation. The Yeshiva argued that yarmulkes were analogous to the approved "barrettes made of soft metal," but to no avail. Ida Crown's Rabbi Tsvi Blanchard submitted a similar argument about the dependability of flimsy suede- and yarn-based yarmulkes "secured properly with hairpins." He too was rebuffed by IHSA's Robinson.[58] Underlying both petitions, as the Academy head of school asserted, was the conviction that it was a "religious requirement that the students wear a skullcap at all times and during all activities." The yarmulke had a way of sanctifying participation in all activities, rendering them worthwhile. Without it basketball appeared less purposeful for their Orthodox faith.

But basketball was important, at least what it represented to the Chicago Orthodox community. The undeterred Orthodox youngsters and school officials turned to the courts, applying for an emergency restraining order on the day of the Harvard match. Supported by the American Jewish Congress, the Orthodox plaintiffs' complaint centered on the IHSA's "ad hoc" interpretation of the rule that prevented them from exercising the "basic tenets of their religion." The complaint was bolstered by testimonies from both varsity coaches. Each swore under oath that falling yarmulkes was not a safety problem, and that these clothing articles were far more analogous to IHSA-permissible soft barrettes. Fastened to the athletes' hair by three or four bobby pins, a player's yarmulke had never caused an accident or mishap, they alleged. The plaintiffs also solicited the support of the chairman of New York's Metropolitan Yeshiva High School Athletic Association and an IHSA referee of thirty-three years who asserted much of the same.[59]

The core of the Orthodox Jews' argument was that yarmulkes were not a safety hazard, and the IHSA's policy was groundless and discriminated against a religious class. The lawyers alleged that their teenage clients were "required by their religion to keep their heads covered at all times." In all instances the "ban on head coverings," they contended, represented a "blanket exclusion of all Orthodox Jewish boys from a situation otherwise open to all boys." The claim imbued the yarmulke with far more meaning than traditional Jewish law prescribed. Again, most rabbinic codes called on Jews to perform rituals with covered heads, but not necessarily to don yarmulkes at all times. In any case the yarmulke or any other head covering did not represent, according to traditional sources, a "basic tenet" of Jewish faith. The seventeenth-century scholar Rabbi David Halevi wrote that the yarmulke was essential to distinguish between Jews and bareheaded Christians.[60] He in no wise, however, implied that covered heads betokened a creedal plank of Jewish faith.

By the 1980s the yarmulke had become freighted with unprecedented significance. It was for Orthodox Jews a symbol of religious identity. Appearing in public without it would have seemed inauthentic and patently "unorthodox." Several years before *Menora* the Ida Crown team had forfeited a basketball contest for that very cause. In that instance the head referee had refused to permit yarmulkes on the court. In response the Academy coach instructed his players that it was their duty to wear their religious symbols and actively represent their faith in the public scene. The Academy team withdrew from the competition rather than uncouple their public participation from the students' religious identities. In February 1981 the Orthodox youngsters were similarly unyielding in their position on the yarmulke. On this occasion, though, the student athletes were unprepared to forfeit the game. Much more, they believed, was at stake.

The athletes triumphed, at least for the moment. Judge Milton Shadur issued the order, vowing to summon all sides to a hearing if either the Yeshiva or the Academy team advanced to the next round of the tournament. As it happened, later that evening Harvard trounced Yeshiva, 99–54. Likewise St. Gregory overwhelmed the Academy a few days later by a score of 79 to 51.[61] But the unceremonious end to the basketball season did not detract from the courtroom win. In Chicago one Orthodox rabbi sermonized about the "victory for the Jewish players in Jewish pride." The local media reported the event on television, paying much more attention to Judge Shadur's order than the losses to Harvard and St. Gregory. "The incident," preached Rabbi Raphael Schwartzman to his congregants at Congregation Ezras Israel, "reaffirmed that the Jewish student is free to practice his Judaism" and to perform his faith in front of his "fellow Americans."[62] This was, then, an essential religious purpose of the yarmulke and a reason to require Orthodox males to wear it at all times.

The judge's ruling did not end the legal confrontation. To the contrary, Chicago's Orthodox Jews tried at first to resolve the matter outside the

After years of losing to its archrival, Yeshiva finally defeated the Academy in the 1981 season. This, though, was not the most dramatic part of that basketball campaign. (Hebrew Theological College)

courtroom, still clinging to the outsized theological implications of the yarmulke. For example, Rabbi Oscar Fasman prevailed upon IHSA to make an exception for future contests and permit the Orthodox student athletes to don their yarmulkes, which were in his words a "symbol of reverence." Fasman explained that there was a theological basis that underpinned the head covering. "The Orthodox Jew, at all times, acknowledges that he bears the yoke of the Almighty," said the president of the local Associated Talmud Torahs. "The skullcap is that declaration of being servants unto the Lord."[63] To appear without it and in front of others would be a misrepresentation of religious conviction.

Still the basketball league would not desist. Before moving to litigation, IHSA sought to help themselves in two ways. First, the league called on Shadur to recuse himself because of the judge's own Jewish faith and his prior relationship with the American Jewish Congress. Second, in April 1981, the NFSHSA and IHSA changed the rule, eliminating soft barrettes from competition. Now this headwear and all its derivatives were deemed unsafe, too.

Under the revision the yarmulke, no matter the analog, was an illegal apparel. The change was curious, especially given the timing. The ban on both soft and hard barrettes stood in contrast to the opinion of most high school coaches, who found the earlier version of the rule satisfactory. Both strategies backfired. Judge Shadur was irked by the attempts at political jostling. He dismissed the first as an unfair untempt to undermine his integrity. As for the rule change, Shadur acknowledged that he found the change "most troublesome," but promised that the maneuver would not factor into his decision.[64]

In November 1981 Shadur once again ruled in favor of the Orthodox basketball players. He was unmoved by the league's position. He did not accept the defense's argument that it was a private, nonprofit organization and should not be expected to uphold the high standard of Free Exercise in the way government institutions would be. If the Orthodox schools did not feel comfortable competing with the league's guidelines, submitted IHSA, then they need not play basketball. The judge dismissed these arguments, seeing as the IHSA was the only statewide basketball league in Illinois, and that most of its games were played on public school courts. Shadur concluded that the yarmulke reflected Orthodox Jews' "respect to God, in whose presence they believe themselves to be at all times. Those beliefs," the judge had been led to believe, "stem from the ancient Talmud."[65] This concern deserved more credence than the basketball league's safety policies, which the judge did not deem credible. In his opinion the IHSA offered no rational distinction between soft barrettes and yarmulkes affixed by bobby pins, nor did it offer evidence of player slippage due to falling yarmulkes. "In basketball terms," quipped Shadur, "IHSA loses by too many points to make keeping score worthwhile." Finally, wrote Shadur in his decision:

> IHSA's argument involves an impermissible sleight of hand: It falsely equates basketball safety with prohibiting yarmulkes. Basketball safety is of course a legitimate IHSA goal, but this Court need not even consider whether that legitimacy represents a "compelling state interest" in constitutional terms. For what this lawsuit is about is not the abstract question whether IHSA can decree basketball safety, but rather the specific question whether it can prohibit the wearing of yarmulkes and override the exercise of First Amendment rights.

Most important, Shadur was convinced of the power that basketball had on Orthodox Jewish life and the need to emboss that experience with the public donning of yarmulkes. In the press and in the courtroom, the plaintiffs had worked hard to impress this point on the judge. It worked. In Shadur's mind the ban on yarmulkes during basketball contests signified an injustice, impairing a religious group from engaging in the rights of basic American life and culture. "Any prohibition on Yeshiva's and Academy's ability to participate in IHSA interscholastic basketball would have a material negative impact on the schools and upon their students generally," determined Shadur, "both apart from and in addition to the negative impact on members of plaintiff class." The reason was that high school athletics symbolized a great opportunity for this minority group to engage in a national pastime. "Playing of interscholastic basketball by Yeshiva and Academy represents to the community at large that those schools are real schools that participate in the mainstream of American life," concluded Shadur. "Such interscholastic play gives the schools and their student body a sense of normality, self-worth and achievement and provides a special outlet for the students' physical and mental needs."[66] Competitive basketball authenticated the American Jewish experience.

Shadur's was not the final word. In June 1982 the US Court of Appeals for the Seventh Circuit vacated Shadur's decision.[67] The subsequent turn in the litigation also informs much about the yarmulke and public optics. In his majority decision for the Seventh Circuit, Judge Richard Posner did not disagree about the value of the yarmulke in Orthodox life, nor did he separate religious skullcaps from Free Exercise. Posner's paramount concern was safety; he did not dismiss the hazards of falling yarmulkes during competition. Weighing the pros and cons of the two sides—patently in line with his self-styled "economic analysis of law"—Posner ultimately did not agree that players' safety should be dismissed at the expense of the First Amendment.[68] The judge ruled that the Orthodox schools needed to find the best way to fasten their yarmulkes to their heads. After all, reasoned Posner, that Orthodox Jews tend to clip their yarmulkes with bobby pins is an "acknowledgement of the yarmulke's instability on a bobbing head."[69] Further, concluded Posner: "While we are not Talmudic scholars, we are reasonably confident . . . that the precise nature of the head covering and the method by which it is kept on the head are not specified by Jewish law."[70] His rationale was that the Orthodox rabbis, students, and their lawyers were in the best and most efficient position to remedy the matter, a legal position that he had proffered on numerous occasions.[71] In the judge's own words, "We put the burden of proposing an alternative, more secure method of covering the head on the plaintiffs rather than on the defendants because the plaintiffs know so much about Jewish law." This ruling was good enough for the nation's superior court. In January 1983 the US Supreme Court denied a petition to consider the yarmulke suit.[72]

The Court of Appeals' turnabout was not a total loss for the Orthodox schools. By calling on the Yeshiva and the Academy to identify a method to ensure yarmulke safety, Posner's decision changed IHSA's posture from absolute prohibition of headgear to considering alternate forms of safe headwear. Neither school would accept a situation in which the boys would be "forced to wear bizarre head-coverings while playing basketball."[73] In fact their lawyers related to the IHSA side that, "according to our clients, Jewish law mandates the covering of the head for purposes of showing respect to God. It is our clients' sincerely held religious belief that requiring the students to wear bizarre headwear would violate Jewish law."[74] Truth to tell Jewish law did not proscribe absurd-appearing headgear. Still, the role of the yarmulke had moved far beyond the textual definitions of Halakhah. It was very much tethered to the public image of Orthodox Judaism and that community's responsibility to wear its religious symbols outside formal religious spaces and at times beyond the strictures of rites and rituals. From this point of view, therefore, Orthodox leaders demanded that religious head coverings conform to the established images of Orthodox Judaism. A skullcap fabricated for basketball safety might not look like the standard religious symbol. Absent this the head covering— and the young man wearing it—could be lacking in the religious implications of the modern conventional yarmulke.

The schools hired a physicist to conduct a series of experiments, taking into consideration oil, dampness of hair, and yarmulkes made of yarn, silk, and wool. Most important, the scientist found that compared to a bobby pin, the aluminum so-called contour clip was far more durable. A yarmulke was far less likely to become dislodged. There was nothing irregular about this fastening device, which was already an acceptable substitute for the bobby pin. The two sides therefore reached an amenable settlement, and Judge Shadur signed an order that finally ended the suit in June 1983.[75]

The Jewish public celebrated the settlement as a major victory for Free Exercise. The American Jewish Congress trumpeted how its legal team "successfully ensured that these boys will not be forced to stop playing inter-scholastic basketball because of their religious beliefs."[76] Others also chimed in from climes well beyond Chicago. "It is comforting to know," opined one Bay Area Jewish pundit, "that in this specialized arena our national Jewish agencies are constantly watching our flanks."[77]

The Orthodox response to the legal settlement differed. In the autumn of 1983, the Yeshiva's varsity basketball team returned to campus and commenced the usual regimen of preseason practice. On one occasion a player lost his yarmulke. The youngster kicked his small suede skullcap to the sidelines, figuring that more prudent than pausing the scrimmage to replace the yarmulke on his head. To the young man's surprise, Coach Schaffel ordered the player to pause the practice and reaffix the yarmulke to his head with the approved contour clips. The high schooler was somewhat aware of the court case that had transpired during his underclassman years. He also knew the basics of his school's role in its satisfactory resolution. Still he did not fully appreciate the meaning of the ordeal:

"Put your yarmulke on," barked the coach.

The player dutifully dropped the basketball and retrieved his yarmulke.

"If you only knew the trouble we went through to make sure you could play basketball with your head covered," Schaffel admonished.[78]

For the Orthodox Jews the end of the legal episode confirmed the non-negotiable role of the yarmulke in representing religious identity in the American public sphere. Throughout the *Menora* lawsuit the Orthodox plaintiffs proffered a strict halakhic guideline for wearing a yarmulke that was unprecedented in rabbinic codes but in complete concert with civic sentiments born out of indigenous forces. Owing to this, the Jewish high schools' response to the affair was to redouble their efforts, further assigning religious meaning to the yarmulke in uniquely American terms.

# PART 2

# YOUTH, EDUCATION, AND PRESERVATION

# CHAPTER 4

# THE MIGHTY MITES AND THE BOTTOM-UP SECRET BEHIND MODERN ORTHODOXY

IN THE 1960s Jonathan Sacks traveled to the United States to seek some guidance. The impressionable and precocious young man arranged for meetings with the leading lights of Orthodox Judaism at a moment the future chief rabbi of Great Britain described as the "high point of modern orthodoxy in America."[1] Sacks came of age during that decade, modeling his scholarly and rabbinic profile after Rabbi Norman Lamm, one of the most renowned American Orthodox rabbis at that time. Lamm served at Manhattan's Jewish Center, where his sermons and articles elevated him to the stature of one of American Jewry's most promising young scholars.[2] When still a "religiously perplexed" undergraduate, Sacks traveled to New York to seek out Lamm, who was "already famous as one of the most articulate and sophisticated of a new generation of Orthodox thinkers."[3]

There was much to Sacks's itinerary. Lamm and other scholars certainly paved a road for Modern Orthodoxy. By the late 1960s the moniker was no longer recalled with "severe connotations."[4] It had lain fallow long enough for most to forget its confused meaning as used by both Orthodox and Conservative Judaism.[5] The new Modern Orthodoxy was far from elastic; it represented a small but growing cohort of enlightened and educated Orthodox Jews. Yet some of the rabbinic elites preferred not to use it. In December 1966 Rabbi Irving "Yitz" Greenberg explained that he "detested" it.[6] Three years later Rabbi Emanuel Rackman turned down calls to take up the mantle of a new "Modern Orthodox Movement."[7] Instead it was Lamm who assumed the challenge of solving "Modern Orthodoxy's Identity Crisis."[8]

Like the others, the Jewish Center rabbi had confessed to some "discomfort" with the nomenclature.[9] But by the close of the decade and into the 1970s, Lamm embraced his role as head of a "Modern Orthodox" religious enclave and brought many other likeminded—though still somewhat unsure—leaders into the fold. His goal was to remain a part of the broader Orthodox Jewish fold but concentrate his energies on this religious subgroup. Lamm's dynamism and embrace of Western culture and liberal education did a lot to authenticate a more culturally updated form of Orthodoxy. Yet while these rabbinic and academic elites certainly injected excitement and creativity into Orthodox Jewish life, the Orthodox reawakening in the 1960s did not just descend from the top downward. A grassroots youth movement that was quickly spreading throughout the country made this new wave accessible and genuine to Orthodox Jews. Like their Christian counterparts, Orthodox youngsters leveraged new forms of technology and media to spread their word.[10] In turn the increasing interest from the Orthodox rank and file promoted new expressions of a Modern Orthodoxy more willing to embrace American life and culture.

## The Making of a Modern Orthodox Movement

For some, Modern Orthodox Judaism's renaissance could not have come at a more unlikely moment.[11] As the 1950s progressed many predicted the movement's demise in the United States. The sociologist Marshall Sklare wrote in 1955 about Orthodox Jews that "the history of their movement in this country can be written in terms of a case study of institutional decay."[12] Another social scientist, Nathan Glazer, explained the decision to omit a discussion of Orthodox life from his 1957 treatment of American Judaism because "there is little to say. It has survived—barely."[13] Even Orthodox insiders held dim hope for a movement whose crop of intellectuals was "of doubtful description and dubious distinction."[14] But probably no one could detect a broader revival of American religion. From 1950 to 1960 the percentage of Americans worshipping on a weekly basis in church jumped from 55 to nearly 70 percent. The most sizable increase in churchgoers occurred in Catholic and conservative, tradition-bound Protestant settings.[15]

In large measure the new Orthodox leadership that came into view in the following decade proved the naysayers wrong. Lamm was not alone in forming the firmament for Orthodox life. Many within this new group of thinkers published important essays in *Tradition*, the periodical founded by Lamm in 1958. During its heyday in the 1960s, this official organ of the Rabbinical Council of America printed articles by Lamm as well as by Emanuel Feldman, Irving Greenberg, Immanuel Jakobovits, Haskel Lookstein, Shubert Spero, Maurice Wohlgelernter, Walter Wurzburger, and Michael Wyschogrod. *Tradition* also provided a comfortable intellectual venue where established, more senior theologians like Rabbis Eliezer Berkovits, Emanuel Rackman, and Joseph B. Soloveitchik could reach more Orthodox readers. Soloveitchik's essays "Confrontation" and "The Lonely Man of Faith" became two of the most important articles on Jewish theology produced in America during the past century.[16] Each of these men planted the seeds of Modern Orthodoxy that came into full bloom after 1967, when the Arab-Israeli Six-Day War washed a renewed religious spirit over many of America's Jews.

Insiders understood, though, that the top-down leadership was important—but insufficient to inspire an Orthodox awakening. In January 1968 the prominent lay leader Moses Feuerstein credited young people with inspiring a "religious renaissance." He told thousands who gathered in Jerusalem for an international conference of Orthodox Jews that, in his estimation, the "talented," "committed academically," and "religiously committed" youth were igniting a "revival that has inspired us." Their faith and integrity, moreover, signified an "authentic Judaism," an oft-repeated phrase in those proceedings.[17] Lamm, too, understood that the "students of Yeshiva University and other *yeshivot*, young people who had Day School background," were pivotal in this grassroots movement.[18] Their participation authenticated a move toward a more culturally attuned American Orthodox Judaism. Actually, in contrast to America's Christian revivals that were typically invigorated by elites within the mainstream, awakenings captured within the annals of American Jewish history were catalyzed by "young people and others alienated from the religious establishment."[19] In the 1820s young people in Charleston had opposed the heads of Congregation Beth Elohim and founded the Reformed Society of Israelites.[20] A half-century later and amid a significant period of religious declension in American Judaism, teenagers and twenty-somethings had been chiefly responsible for reigniting Jewish religion and culture.[21] The earlier breed of "Modern Orthodox" exponents in the interwar years were also made up of young, newly minted rabbis—an important attribute, although their cause never fully ripened.[22] The young people in the 1960s were destined for a different fate.

## A Modern Orthodox Youth Movement

In truth the arrival of American Orthodoxy's youth movement occurred later than similar developments within American Judaism's other religious groups. Conservative Judaism experienced the 1950s as a golden decade. In those years Conservative Judaism's Camp Ramah, in the words of one scholar, had solidified itself as "a movement."[23] There, at its various sites, the Conservative community's most committed young people underwent training and empowerment in preparation for later becoming leaders in their movement. When camp was not in session, many of these young men and women rehearsed their activism and leadership as members and officers in the hugely popular United Synagogue Youth. The National Federation of Temple Youth's leadership institutes did much the same for Reform Jews. More secular organizations, like the Zionists' Young Judaea and the B'nai B'rith Youth Organization, also reached many Jewish young people in the 1950s. Only the Orthodox lacked a major denominational youth movement.[24]

Postwar patriotism, social activism, interfaith dialogue, and other hot-button national issues worked well for youth organizations in the 1950s. In contrast Jewish pundits recommended that educators "lay off the religious stuff." Statistics indicated that young people wanted it this way. One study found that while only 42 percent of Catholic students and 15 percent of Protestant students believed it important to live by Christianity's traditional teachings, Jewish youths scored even lower; just 8 percent of Jewish children valued their religious education.[25] Conservative and Reform youth programs incorporated, through provocative curricula and popular speakers, all that was culturally and politically in vogue at that time. Conversely, many Orthodox rabbis and educators would only be satisfied with a youth program free of political and social fanfare—emphasizing that "religious stuff." Lack of faith in Orthodox young people to engage the cultural moment contributed to the religious flatness and Orthodox malaise of the 1950s, a period that one writer has described as the "lean years" of American Orthodoxy.[26]

The subsequent 1960s emerged as the pivotal decade for American Orthodoxy, as fresh personalities and ideologies helped to narrow the gap between traditionally observant Jewish youth and more religiously liberal young Jewish leaders. If we widen the scope, the 1960s proved an important decade for American youth. It was the age of counter-culture and unrest, of youth rebellion against the "establishment" and the "church."[27] Orthodox youngsters also took an active role in this period, but with far less irreverence. They drew from a youth culture in the early 1960s that aspired to replicate John F. Kennedy's "image as a charismatic man of revolutionary action and high principle."[28] This attitude empowered American youth and convinced an older generation to make room for younger leaders.

The Orthodox day schools also imparted a "democratic" spirit that inspired bottom-up leadership. "A good Jew," explained an Orthodox pulpit rabbi and principal in those days, "is one who is committed to democracy."[29] The Modern Orthodox schools and its other educational programs were therefore preservational—interested in maintaining the continuity of Jewish observance—and incubators of religious empowerment. More and more Orthodox youngsters started to receive that dual-purpose education. By the 1960s the number of children in Orthodox day schools grew tenfold from its total of 7,700 in 1940.[30] By the 1960s Orthodox Jews claimed hundreds of teenagers and young adults with far greater Jewish knowledge than their parents.

As day schools rapidly emerged as fixtures in Orthodox communities, so too did youth organizations. The three movements leading the youth charge were the Orthodox Union's National Conference of Synagogue Youth (NCSY), Yeshiva University's Torah Leadership Seminar, and the national intercollegiate organization, Yavneh. Its leaders now understood that young people were best energized and attracted to programming that blended Jewish and American culture. After several false starts in the 1950s, NCSY established itself. Although NCSY claimed only a handful of loosely affiliated regional Orthodox youth groups in 1960, six years later it counted fourteen regions sporting three hundred chapters and supported by salaried professional staffs.[31] Torah Leadership Seminar, founded in 1955, attracted thousands of high school students from across the country to participate in biannual conferences and informal Jewish educational experiences. At these meetings hundreds of Jewish youths sat excitedly at the feet of some of the most innovative and intellectually stimulating (and hip) Orthodox rabbis, such as Irving Greenberg, David Hartman, and Shlomo Riskin.[32] Not long after, in February 1960, the same young rabbinic leaders were instrumental in helping eighty collegians from thirteen university campuses establish the education-minded Yavneh.[33] Together these young people stood in support of Modern Orthodoxy, especially in the face of scolding critics who doubted the authenticity of its Americanized form: "the 'Modern Orthodox' type in its American edition and its 'made in Israel' equivalent are equally wrong from the Torah viewpoint."[34]

## The Tale of the Mighty Mites

The effects of newly popular youth groups on the overall life of Orthodoxy could be seen immediately. The combination of renewed vigor in Orthodox scholarship and genuine excitement among the community's youth inspired Orthodoxy to display, from a social perspective, its pride to the non-Orthodox and non-Jewish worlds. From wearing yarmulkes and other distinctive Orthodox clothing in public to establishing restaurants that served exclusively kosher cuisine, Orthodox Jews of the 1960s showed "greater confidence in American pluralism" and an impulse to "combine the best of the Jewish and outside world."[35]

That is exactly what took place in the spring of 1963, when a team of Yeshiva University undergraduates appeared on the *General Electric College Bowl* television program. Yeshiva's Mighty Mites quiz squad—they borrowed the name from the school's basketball team—fell short of a championship and never again competed on national television. Yet the team's unprecedented ability to rally its community around its success reflected a social and intellectual sea change in the history of Modern Orthodox Judaism. While its focus may have been limited to just a few weeks in the spring of 1963, the episode typified the rebirth of Orthodox Judaism being generated through the community's youth.

The television medium was something relatively new for all sectors of American religion. In the 1950s Protestant leaders worried about the emergence of television in American life. By this time most American households owned at least one television. In the post–World War II period, many ministers and commentators did their very best to denounce television as lewd and perverse—they were none too happy about Elvis Pressley's rotating pelvic dance moves, televised in September 1956—and as an affront to the domestic piety that betokened a valued Christian ethic. In the minds of Protestant critics, television also threatened to introduce the worst of "un-American"

Catholicism and secularism into the minds of impressionable and ill-informed young people. Television, it was averred, was an uncontrollable source of antireligious propaganda.[36]

Orthodox Jews also debated the "TV problem," fearing for their many coreligionists who resided in major broadcasting centers and were therefore "in the first line of fire."[37] Doing due diligence to dissuade Orthodox Jews from television, the National Association of Hebrew Day Schools published learned articles by university professors to get the word out to Orthodox parents and teachers.[38] Others recognized that television was there to stay and embraced the opportunity to reach larger audiences—Jewish and non-Jewish—through this made-sacred box. Within Jewish circles no one did this better than Rabbi Louis Finkelstein. In the late-1940s the chancellor of the Jewish Theological Seminary (JTS) made sure that his Conservative brand of Judaism was on full display—visually and audibly—to mass audiences. The seminary's Radio and Television department coordinated with prominent New York churches to produce episodes and broadcasts that appeared regularly on networks like CBS and NBC.[39] Others picked up on the idea. In Chicago the local rabbinical council formed the Jewish Broadcasting Commission. The commission provided space for rabbinic leaders of all major movements to represent their faith to the public.[40] Even before that commission was established in 1957, Chicago's Orthodox exponents, like Rabbi Oscar Fasman of the Hebrew Theological College, understood the value of television in modern American life.[41] So when the YU squad appeared on the much-beloved trivia program, the fiercest battles over the propriety of television in the religious home had already been waged and, from the perspective of the opposition, lost.

Quiz shows first gained considerable popularity as radio broadcasts during the 1940s. Executives finally brought quiz shows to television audiences in the 1950s, when they recognized that such programs "proved cheap to produce, sponsors liked their simplicity"; most important, "no one seemed to grow tired of them."[42] Shows like *The $64,000 Question, What's My Line?* and *You Bet Your Life* offered large cash prizes that thrilled viewers, and they often generated higher ratings than *I Love Lucy* and other powerhouse programs. The *College Bowl*, which emerged in this cultural climate, was sponsored by General Electric and, at that time, hosted by Robert Earle. It first aired on CBS TV on January 4, 1959, and ran on that network until it was moved to NBC-TV on September 22, 1963. The *College Bowl* immediately found a large audience, especially among families and younger viewers, until the program finally stopped production in 1970.[43] Anne Fadiman—the daughter of literary personalities Clifton and Annalee Jacoby Fadiman—recalled that the *College Bowl* "was an article of faith" in her childhood home. Like many other American families, the Fadimans watched the show every Sunday to "compete" against the onscreen contestants. "Fadiman U. could beat any other U., and indeed, in five or six years of competition, we lost only to Brandeis and Colorado College."[44] The Yeshiva team's appearance on the show put the school on a national stage.

In each half-hour trivia competition, two four-member teams representing undergraduate schools from across the country competed for a $1,500 scholarship prize for their school and for the right to defend themselves against another college team on the following week's episode. The game began with a "toss-up" question worth ten points. The team that sounded its buzzer fastest and answered that question correctly earned the right to answer a bonus question, ranging from twenty to forty points in value. After that the show's host posed another "toss-up" question, and the procedure repeated until the end of the program. The team with the highest score when time ran out won.

Millions of viewers tuned in to watch undergraduates rack their brains to answer difficult trivia questions on a very broad range of topics. Fiercely competitive, the teams were fighting for more than just scholarships for their respective colleges. In the minds of the collegians, they were playing for school pride and to prove that theirs was the brightest and brainiest liberal arts program in the nation.[45]

Yeshiva's foray into the *College Bowl* competition was announced in the pages of the Yeshiva College (YC) student newspaper, nearly three months before the team's scheduled television debut. The newspaper reported that Dr. Irving Linn, professor of English at Yeshiva College, would serve as coach. Linn noted that he would select from a large applicant pool from the all-male Yeshiva College and Yeshiva's all-female Stern College in hopes of "discovering the encyclopedia readers" from among the student body.[46] An op-ed in the student newspaper optimistically declared that the *College Bowl* was just the place for YU to promulgate its Orthodox brand of "Coast to Coast Judaism" and reach beyond their standard, Gotham-centered Jewish circle. "Once and for all," wrote the collegiate editorialist, "the world will sit up and gape at Yeshiva's brilliance, thus proving that mother was right."[47]

Captain Shifrah Jungreis and her three teammates compete on the *College Bowl* in 1963. The quiz show undergraduate quartet ably represented Yeshiva University and Orthodox Judaism on national television. (Shifrah Jungreis)

After several rounds of tryouts, the four-member team took shape two weeks before Yeshiva's scheduled May 12, 1963, appearance on the quiz show. The date was significant, since it coincided with the festive Jewish holiday of Lag B'Omer, an occasion that many Orthodox Jews observe with picnics and sports. Many modified their practice that year, spending a little more time in front of their television sets. Shifrah Jungreis, the lone female on the team, was selected as team captain. Although Jungreis fit the common stereotype of a Stern College student in those days—a young bride of a rabbi in Canarsie who wished to teach immediately after graduation—Coach Linn livened up her profile when he described her as "brilliant, mercury-like and vivacious."[48] Yeshiva collegians Sheldon Fink, Lawrence Kaplan, and Asher Reiss completed the team.

All four students held broad extracurricular interests as members of the student newspaper, the debate team, and social clubs, and they also enjoyed music. The men on the team were history majors, while Jungreis focused her studies on English literature. Despite their strengths, Yeshiva University's president, Dr. Samuel Belkin, worried about the school's Orthodox image on national television. He implored the students to consider the implication of the broadcast. "I am certain that you appreciate," Belkin wrote to each member, "the distinctive honor for which you have been chosen."[49]

## Icons of Religious Revival

Although pressured to succeed while maintaining appropriate Orthodox comportment, the Mighty Mites were in all likelihood far more concerned about facing their first heavyweight opponent. The Cardinals of the University of Louisville in Kentucky had been one of the most dominant teams during the *College Bowl*'s brief history. They defeated teams from Kenyon College, the University of Idaho, the University of Delaware, and Iona College. In their previous match, "the high-flying Cardinals" showed America their intellectual prowess by "whipping" Iona by a score of 285–115.[50] By vanquishing Yeshiva, the Louisville team could score its fifth win and retire from the *College Bowl* undefeated. Prior to Louisville's campaign, just one team had been able to survive so many matches without suffering a loss. One piqued observer considered Louisville a "50 point favorite" for its next match, dismissing Yeshiva as a "breather" for the veteran players from Louisville.[51]

That columnist could not have been more wrong. Yeshiva trounced Louisville, 335–140. The Yeshiva onslaught turned out to be the most lopsided affair in an episode of *College Bowl* to date. The New York papers hailed the "Canarsie housewife" and her male sidekicks. "Never underestimate the power of a woman," one Brooklyn daily declared. "Particularly if she is a Canarsie lass."[52] Yet, the incumbents—and the rest of the show's followers—had done more than merely underestimate their challengers. The Cardinals were utterly unprepared for the atmosphere generated by the hundreds of Mighty Mite fans who had accompanied their team to the CBS studios. Accordingly, a local Louisville columnist wrote that he was "sure [that] the Yeshiva quartet which decisioned U.L. in that science quiz on *College Bowl* were [sic] inspired by heavy backing in the audience." The journalist surmised that "athletes, too, react to inspiration. So do actors and actresses and public speakers."[53]

Their efforts validated Orthodox Judaism's ability to be a part of the broader American scene. In addition to the faithful fans who rode the bus down to Midtown Manhattan, the *College Bowl* team soon discovered that thousands of America's Jews had taken an interest in their appearance on the quiz show. One Jewish weekly reported that "interest in the contest was so widespread that portable television sets were set up at dozens of Lag B'Omer affairs and at organization dinners and other functions."[54] Yeshiva administrators basked in the glowing letters of praise that poured into the school's mailroom "from far and wide."[55] Rabbi Gilbert Klaperman of Long Island wrote to Linn to extend his "congratulations on the magnificent performance of your team last Sunday on College Bowl. I believe that all American Jewry, not only Orthodoxy, was transfixed by the mighty accomplishment." A proud alumnus, Klaperman graciously extolled the Yeshiva team for doing "more for improving the image of Yeshiva in half an hour than was done in years of devoted service by all of us."[56]

President Belkin also received many letters. One alumnus viewed the victory over Louisville as a symbol of YU's mission to achieve synthesis in the realms of Torah and secular knowledge. The "College Bowl victory," wrote Rabbi Yaakov Homnick of Philadelphia, served as an "eloquent tribute to [Belkin's] life's work."[57] Rabbi Samuel Adelman of Denver voiced similar sentiments. He called Yeshiva's performance "no small credit" to Belkin, "who, from the very outset, saw how possible it was to evolve a Torah true Jewish youth that would be Jewish, not only in name, but in fact."[58] In another letter addressed to YU's leader, an alumnus supposed that he was just one of "thousands of other Yeshiva men throughout the world" who had "watched with pride and glory the splendid showings of our team on [the] College Bowl." That letter writer asked Belkin to kindly pass along his congratulations to the student competitors and prayed that "they go from strength to greater strength and from glory to greater glory."[59]

Perhaps one of the most important letters from a recruitment standpoint came from Rabbi J. Leonard Azneer of Anshe Emeth Temple in Youngstown, Ohio. He wrote to Yeshiva College's dean of admissions to inform him that his entire congregation was "excited and thrilled at the showing the kids made on the College Bowl." The writer informed the Yeshiva official that a "number of kids of both sexes" from his community "have indicated some interest in attending the university." Azneer requested that Yeshiva send him some catalogs to encourage them.[60] Likewise a prospective student from Virginia wrote to Yeshiva about how impressed he was "by the performance of your scholars on the G.E. College Bowl," and how, as a result, he became "very interested in [the] institution's curriculum." No doubt admissions personnel happily accommodated the youth's request to "please send me one of your catalogs as soon as possible."[61]

Orthodox day school students—exactly the constituency Yeshiva hoped its newfound fame would attract—also praised the Mighty Mites. Members of the Student Government Organization of the Yeshivah of Flatbush "extend[ed] their heartiest congratulations on your decisive victory in yesterday's *College Bowl*." The high schoolers viewed the victory as one that could be shared by all Orthodox youth. "Your fine effort will enhance the image of not only Yeshiva University, but also the entire Yeshiva movement and Jewish Community," wrote the students of the Brooklyn school. "You have made all of us proud to be Yeshiva students."[62] Hoping that his kind words would result in some free tickets to the upcoming competition, the president of Yeshiva University High School's student government reported that his fellow students had "taken a great interest" in the team's *College Bowl* victory over Louisville and "many [students] have expressed a desire to attend the [university]."[63]

Several politicians also took time out to write and congratulate the Yeshiva students. Senator Kenneth Keating of New York—later the US ambassador to Israel—applauded Belkin and his students. "Congratulations on your outstanding victory on the *G.E. College Quiz Bowl*. All of our state can be justly proud of your distinguished scholarship," wrote Keating.[64] More locally President B. S. Gottlieb of the Chamber of Commerce of Washington Heights spoke on behalf of the entire Manhattan neighborhood, which had reportedly beamed with pride over "the wonderful erudition displayed by the Yeshiva team on the *College Bowl*."[65] In addition a politician from Scranton, Pennsylvania, told newly minted hometown hero Sheldon Fink, "It is always good to hear the name Scranton, especially to have one of our native sons so prominent on the *College Bowl* program."[66]

The Jewish press, with much triumphalism, made the most of Orthodoxy's sudden ascendance onto the American scene. "Not only was this a victory for YU but a victory for the Torah world as well, for it is the study of the Torah that sharpens the mind," declared a newspaper editor from New Jersey. "Yeshiva University and yeshivas everywhere may be justly proud of the terrific accomplishment of the YU college bowl team."[67] A Jewish paper from Detroit estimated that its mailbox had been inundated with approximately fifty letters of comments regarding Yeshiva's *College Bowl* victory. However, its editors noted that fewer than half of the letters, from Jews and non-Jews, lauded the team's accomplishments. "[T]he others rebuked Yeshiva for possessing 'smart Jews' and for resenting the emergence of a 'show off' of superiority," reported the newspaper about the negative notes it had received. "Stop displaying your knowledge," some of the deluded bigots advised. The editors theorized that this sort of logic originated from earlier in the century, when antisemitism kept Jews out of many universities and when Jews "were hated because they were successful."[68] The Chicago Jewish press echoed the sentiments: "The old Jewish feeling of insecurity can be noted now among many New York Jews who are hoping that the great Yeshiva University team winning big on TV's *G.E. College Bowl* is beaten so the 'goyim' won't be hurt."[69] The *Detroit Jewish News* defended the Yeshiva team:

> Of course, the People of the Book never heeded such advice. Nor is there any intention of our ever abandoning the craving for knowledge, the training of our children to be steeped in learning, to uphold the principle that Torah is *die beste sekhora*—that Torah is the greatest possession.[70]

The crestfallen members of the Louisville squad returned to their campus to receive a hero's welcome for their part in raising the prestige and intellectual bar of their institution. Feted by hundreds, the student scholars were driven through campus "in an open convertible" as the school's band played "Hail, Hail, the Gang's All Here." Louisville president Philip Davidson told the crowd that he had "never seen anything that captured the imagination of the community and endeared the university to the people more than this team." Kentucky governor Bert Combs flew in to join city officials to personally greet the team. The well-wishers presented the group with gold trophies, and one presenter at the lavish ceremony, in jest, offered the team's coach a "one-year sabbatical for advanced study in Yeshiva."[71]

## Negotiating Orthodox Triumphalism

The Louisville homecoming also taught Yeshiva about the costs of maintaining an image in the public sphere. Despite Belkin's warnings, the YU scholars were accused of not being sufficiently circumspect in their dealings with their Louisville counterparts. For all the school pride in the team's achievement, the

Louisville students returned home with some bitter feelings for their Yeshiva opponents. One Orthodox student at Louisville wrote to Linn, informing him of the "rather awkward situation" in which he found himself upon taking his seat in a graduate seminar several days after the competition. The bulk of his graduate seminar, he wrote, "was taken up with airing the rather acrimonious complaints of the U. of L. team." Members of the Louisville squad had made it known around campus that they were "shocked and taken aback by the unfriendliness of the Yeshiva team." Only one member of the YU group, Lawrence Kaplan, it was alleged, had deigned to socialize with the competitors. As he explained it to Linn, the Orthodox Louisville student attempted to allay the concerns of his classmates by rationalizing that the Yeshiva students' smug behavior had more to do with their New Yorker mentalities than their Jewishness. Nevertheless, the writer found it unfortunate that such behavior had stirred "some latent antisemitism."[72]

Linn responded, informing his correspondent that his "friendly letter" had "provoked a good deal of thoughtful self-examination." He personally vowed to redouble his efforts to achieve camaraderie with the Mighty Mites' upcoming opponent, the University of Nevada team, and to preach to his students about the value of sportsmanship. The Yeshiva coach also related that he had sent a telegram to the Louisville team on the occasion of its homecoming event. The letter on behalf of the Yeshiva *College Bowl* team expressed its admiration for Louisville's numerous victories and "sterling example of good sportsmanship."[73]

Linn might not have felt so compelled to reach out to the slighted students from Kentucky had he read an editorial published in a local Louisville paper. Apparently the gossip surrounding the Yeshiva bout was still circulating a week after the competition. And at least one Louisville native interpreted the complaints about unsportsmanlike conduct, unfair play, and "noisy" YU fans as nonsense. "Let's not be sore losers. Let's agree that the U. of L. Bowlers lost to a team that fairly out-pointed them, just as other teams lost previously," the writer pleaded. "Whatever happened helped or hurt each team equally. We can say that without subtracting one bit of glory from our team."[74]

Aside from the antisemitic murmurings, Yeshiva's administrators delighted in the students' performance on national television, despite some subtle missteps. During a break in the contest, Sheldon Fink had deviated from the script when asked to introduce his teammates and school. Believing himself responsible for showing the Jewishness of Yeshiva, Fink referred to YU's president as "Rabbi Belkin" instead of "Dr. Belkin," as was written before him. Apparently Yeshiva officials much preferred the use of Belkin's more innocuous academic degree, a credential he had in common with most university leaders, over his rabbinic title, which they believed somewhat threatened the academic integrity of the school.

This minor glitch did not mar a very successful day for Yeshiva's public relations. Perhaps just as important as their victory was the fact that the Mighty Mites made their television debut looking dignified and handsome. The three male contestants had donned suits and ties (a spiffy bowtie, in the case of Asher Reiss), and Shifrah Jungreis appeared on the show with a modest but fashionable dress. Interestingly, apparently "very few people knew" that the "attractive" Jungreis "was wearing a *'shaitel,'* " or wig, on the television program. (She also wore a "flimsy" hat.)[75] Most important, the men wore yarmulkes in clear view of the television cameras at a time, as we have come to learn, when many Orthodox Jews still appeared bareheaded in public. It therefore must have been gratifying to Sam Hartstein, Yeshiva's public relations director, when he received a letter from a fellow media-relations expert congratulating him on the students' decision to appear on the show with their heads covered, anticipating a new Orthodox norm, as we have already seen. "While I should have known better, I thought that the boys might have decided to abandon skull caps," wrote Arthur Raybin, the head of media relations at Wheaton College in Massachusetts. "Glad that they didn't. Frankly, this one appearance will do more for the Faith than a whole pile of sermons, clips, and the like."[76]

At the very same time, YU officials were considerably dismayed that Linn, a non-observant Jew, appeared bareheaded. According to one account it "provoked a storm of controversy" on Yeshiva's campus. Students and faculty openly clashed, but the consensus was that "the kipah had become a hallmark of American Orthodoxy."[77] Alumni noticed Linn's infraction, too. Jay Friedman, a Yeshiva College alumnus and a ranking administrator in the Religious Zionist Mizrachi organization, was taken aback by Linn's unwillingness to wear a yarmulke onscreen. "I must say that I was quite amazed to see Dr. Irving Linn appear on the program bereft of a kipah," wrote Friedman. "I cannot view this disregard of tradition as a mere oversight nor as a concession to Dr. Linn's personal level of observance. In this case Dr. Linn represented

Yeshiva and should have done so properly."[78] In response to Friedman's concern, Hartstein profusely and apologetically defended the school and revealed his own frustration with Linn's iconoclasm. Hartstein reminded the concerned alumnus that "in higher education there is such a thing as 'academic freedom.' This covers a broad framework of experiences. Dr. Linn is a big boy. We can only suggest or recommend a procedure."[79]

In preparing for the next week's match, Yeshiva was no underdog. One paper voiced high expectations when it announced: "Triumphant Yeshiva Putting *College Bowl* Laurels on the Line."[80] Once again busloads of rowdy fans escorted the squad to the television studio. Hundreds of members of the local Jewish community stood outside the CBS-TV studio on West 54th Street, vying for a seat indoors or just to cheer on their beloved foursome. Those fans in the studio "cheered every right answer like a crowd at a football game." What is more, all kinds of Orthodox Jews came to lend emotional support. "Peachy-faced youths" sat next to "bearded scholars," and "yarmoulka [*sic*] wearing students" perched themselves alongside "bare-headed graduates." In spite of "their differences, they all cheered for Yeshiva University."[81]

Before the contest the Mighty Mites impressed the studio audience by answering nearly all of their difficult warmup questions. But when it counted the Yeshiva quartet suddenly hit a dry spell. Just a few minutes into the bout, the team found itself on the short end of a 40–0 score.[82] Just as quickly the Nevadans widened that margin to 70–20. Fortunately for YU it gained back the momentum when Reiss correctly knew the names of the last Tudor monarchs in England—Queens Mary and Elizabeth.[83] Moments later Yeshiva pulled away for good when Jungreis identified actor DeWolf Hopper as the individual mainly responsible for popularizing the poem "Casey at the Bat." (Asked later how she knew the answer, Jungreis explained that she "grew up an avid Dodger [*sic*] fan.") The Yeshiva team cruised to a convincing 285–185 victory.

Praise for Yeshiva's second romp came quickly. Los Angeles's Jewish press proclaimed, "Viva Yeshiva!" The editors of that newspaper applauded the students who had gained recognition on a "nationwide scale" after two landslide victories:

It is indeed a tribute to Yeshiva U. that its students, who must be steeped in Jewish education, should show such a wide knowledge of all subjects. Their skills and vast scope of learning has [*sic*], perhaps, surprised the average listener. Perhaps least surprised, however, are those connected with Yeshiva University. After all, they knew all along that they produce an amazing breed of students.[84]

Many Jewish and non-Jewish papers were fascinated that Yeshiva, an institution that reflected the traditional Jewish viewpoint, had selected a woman—a rabbi's wife, no less—to serve as team captain. "That lady mental whiz from Canarsie," a Brooklyn daily wrote about Jungreis, "has done it again! She piloted her three-man YU team to their second victory in a row on CBS-TV last Sunday, upping their winnings to $3,000."[85] Yet the team surprised reporters, who expected its members to affirm progressive views. During an interview break in the match with Nevada, the College Bowl host asked Jungreis about her career ambitions. "As you know," she answered with a smile, "I am the wife of a rabbi and I feel responsible to him and to the community in which we live. I hope to be a teacher of young children and should like to teach in the Canarsie area."[86] Jungreis's dual commitment to intellectual excellence and to a traditional career for an Orthodox Jewish woman matched the impression that Yeshiva wished her to convey to the viewing audience.

This is evident from a letter Linn wrote to a friend several years after the competition. "Our young lady, who announced so proudly to the world at large that her first duty was to be at her rabbi husband's side, has done precisely that," Linn wrote with satisfaction.[87]

Yeshiva received dozens more letters after the win against Nevada. Jewish students seemed especially enthusiastic. Letters addressed to "Shifrah, Asher, Larry and Sheldon"—now household names—from a cohort of Jewish students at Asbury Park High School in New Jersey voiced support for the College Bowl cause. Students from the Hebrew Institute of Long Island's student council wrote to the members of the team, sending their "congratulations on past success and sincerest wishes for future victories."[88] It was not just the Orthodox youngsters. Fifth-grade students of the Conservative-affiliated Hillel Day School in Oak Park, Michigan, likely received help from their teacher when they crafted the following remarks addressed to the Mighty Mites:

We have been watching you on College Bowl with great enthusiasm and excitement. We are writing to tell you we are all rooting for you and that we want to convey our best wishes and encouragement. We would like to see you continue for the full five weeks and bring victory to Yeshiva University.[89]

The youngsters at Hillel Day School spoke for young people throughout the country who saw the Mighty Mites' journey as an inspiration to all American Jews.

Yeshiva's opponents understood the school's goals. Writing to Linn, the defeated Nevada coach saw much in common between his team and Yeshiva's. "I suppose there is a natural parallel in our ideas," wrote Coach Harold Kirkpatrick. "You and your wonderful team trying to show to the layman the true meaning and the real essence of orthodox Judaism, and we from the often misunderstood West trying to show the same layman the academic achievements of which we too are capable."[90]

As for the young Mighty Mites, they had become true media darlings and celebrities on New York's Orthodox scene. After recognizing one of the Yeshiva competitors as an occasional frequenter of his restaurant, the owner of a New York delicatessen invited the entire team for a free meal. "Since Mr. Kaplan, one of the panelists, was a customer of mine," he wrote, "I would be very happy if he and the rest of the members of the *College Bowl* team will be my guests for dinner, at my delicatessen store."[91] The hype surrounding the team "converted a sedate, scholarly atmosphere at the University's campus . . . into areas electric with excitement." One report compared the pandemonium on the uptown Manhattan campus to "the antics of the Mets fans."[92] A YU press release related that when Lawrence Kaplan returned to campus after the team's victory over Nevada, he received a standing ovation in the campus dining hall.[93] At least one College Bowler made the most of his temporary celebrity status. Sheldon Fink told a reporter from the *New York Post* that he had noticed the special attention he was suddenly receiving. "They finally recognize my true worth," he said. Nevertheless, Fink insisted that the fame had not changed him. "I'm still as nice a guy today as I was three weeks ago."[94]

## The End of the Road and a Lasting Legacy

Next up for Yeshiva were the Owls of Temple University. Before the competition with Temple, students blanketed Yeshiva's Washington Heights campus with signs and posters reading "Win With Linn."[95] Once again throngs of fans accompanied the Mighty Mites to the CBS-TV facilities. But during this third match on May 26, exhaustion started to show on the brows of the Orthodox whiz kids. The "wise young Owls" of Temple moved fast out of the gate. The Mighty Mites trailed their opponents in the closing minutes, 240–165. The Yeshiva students fought back at a furious clip, showing their dominance in the areas of music, art, and Civil War trivia. The team pulled to within fifteen points of the leading Owls, 250–235, with thirty seconds to play. It was Temple's team captain, Leonard Goldstein, a Jew like so many other Temple students, who was the first to buzz in on the next and final question: "Who in literature killed his father and later married his mother?" Before the moderator finished with his question, Goldstein buzzed in. His answer, Oedipus, added to Temple's lead as time expired.[96]

The loss surely stung, for the Mighty Mites as well as for their thousands of dedicated fans. Perhaps there was some consolation in the fact that the Philadelphians would eventually become one of *College Bowl*'s historic champions. After competing with Yeshiva, the Owls rattled off another four victories to earn "a place in the *College Bowl* Hall of Fame."[97] The encouragement the YU students received as they transitioned back to their "civilian" lives no doubt soothed and consoled them. The campus newspaper congratulated the "*College Bowl* quiz kids for their fine showing on nation-wide television." Satirically hinting at the great yarmulke debate, the collegiate newsmen publicly thanked the "boisterous supporting cast" of fans and Linn "for his great work in coaching the team and helping to spread Yeshiva's image."[98]

A Brooklyn journalist theorized "that almost the entire Jewish community took it as a personal loss." However, "any sense of disappointment must surely give way to a sense of pride when one considers not only what these young people did and can do, but what they are." The editorialist encouraged the student scholars and their supporters to take pride in having successfully transmitted an improved image of America's Orthodox Jew to the rest of the world:

> It is in this sense that we salute the four young people who did so much to earn the admiration not only of our own people but of the Christian world as well. We are proud of you Shifra [*sic*] Jungreis, Larry Kaplan, Asher Reiss and Sheldon Fink. Sunday night was not the end—it was only the beginning for you have that all too rare combination of brilliance and true religious spirit from which only great things can come.[99]

The opponents also graciously admired Yeshiva's accomplishment. Temple's President Millard Gladfelter spoke for his entire university when he told Yeshiva's Belkin that the Temple team's "first listening to the Yeshiva Bowl team several weeks ago left us with grave doubts for our future prospects." Consequently Temple's top official explained that his students' success against YU was "enthusiastically received because the competition was so formidable."[100] Importantly Gladfelter's comment bespoke just how far Yeshiva had climbed in the minds of those at secular universities. John Clearly, the executive producer of the television program, relayed similar thoughts, thanking Yeshiva for the "fine team which represented Yeshiva University on the *G.E. College Bowl* and for all the cooperation and enthusiasm we received."[101] A newspaper columnist praised Yeshiva's run before he quipped that Temple's victory derailed a highly anticipated showdown of American faiths between Yeshiva and St. Mary's College.[102]

It is impossible to quantify the impact the Mighty Mites had in raising the level of self-confidence of American Jewish Orthodoxy. Yeshiva's *College Bowl* adventure was no watershed moment, but it did signify a changing religious attitude within the Orthodox community. That much is clear from the fanfare and fetes in recognition of the team's accomplishments.[103] Moreover, despite the brevity of their stardom, the Mighty Mites remained the topic of many conversations, even after their third-round loss. For example, in the weeks after the Yeshiva team appeared on national television, Rabbi Sheldon Freedman of Shenandoah, Pennsylvania, published a sermon encouraging his congregants to dispense with the "deep-rooted image" of a "white bearded," "sloppy looking," "shabbily dressed" Orthodox Jew. By way of example Freedman cited the *College Bowl* squad. "Recently there have been many opportunities to point out the error of the Orthodox Jew 'stereotype.' *The College Bowl* . . . has had a team representing Yeshiva University. The students are personable, intelligent, 'modern' Americans, and the boys wear Yarlmulkas. They evidenced a magnificent grasp of secular subjects. They are Orthodox Jewish youngsters."[104] The Mighty Mites helped authenticate a new Americanized image for Modern Orthodox Judaism.

As Linn testified several years after, it did not stop when he and his college bowlers had retired their buzzers and placards. "In the four years that have elapsed since Yeshiva University's appearance on the *College Bowl*," Linn wrote to a colleague, "Not a month goes by without some visitor asking us about the progress of the young people on our team since then."[105] Not even the heartbreaking loss to Temple could erase those Yeshiva whiz kids from popular memory. Although its opponents from Philadelphia made sure the thrill did not last for long—just a footnote in the history of American pop culture—Yeshiva's *College Bowl* team meant a great deal to the new generation of self-described Modern Orthodox Jews that was hitherto rather unsure of its new Americanized identity. The Mighty Mites helped energize a rather listless community, one that an older generation overall struggled to reach. They authenticated an Orthodox youth-led revival, justifying their cause in fashionable American style. The YU quiz show quartet called on fellow Orthodox young people to seize their day.

# CHAPTER 5

# MITZVAH MERCHANTS AND THE CREATION OF AN ORTHODOX CHILDREN'S CULTURE

In March 1971 Torah Umesorah held the inaugural Brochos Bee for Orthodox day schools in New York. It was Rabbi Dovid Price's idea, and the national Orthodox day school organization was eager to bring it to fruition. Four years earlier Price, the principal of Yeshiva of Prospect Park, had concocted the blessing bee for his Brooklyn-based school. It had worked. The Prospect Park youngsters had embraced the game. Thinking much more broadly, Price recruited about a hundred Orthodox elementary and middle schools to quiz their students on the proper blessings to recite on all kinds of foods and other miscellanea, like seeing rainbows and oceans. Local competitions narrowed the field. Pupils hailing from fourteen schools who managed to memorize blessings for the tougher items like peaches and cream, ice cream sandwiches, and roasted chestnuts moved on to the finals at Torah Umesorah's headquarters on Fifth Avenue in Manhattan. There Price and his team of judges led a series of written and oral exams before crowning male and female champions in three age brackets.[1]

Price and Torah Umesorah patterned their competition after the popular spelling bee. The Brochos Bee was therefore a clever expression of acculturation or "coalescence," as sociologists Sylvia Fishman and Yoel Finkelman have termed it.[2] The Brochos Bee drew from American forms of competition— historians long ago documented America's disavowal of Britain's "gentlemanly sport" culture.[3] These aspects of the Brochos Bee ensured that Orthodox enclaves could absorb American culture while remaining apart from it, a value deemed essential by Orthodox educators in the final decades of the twentieth century. Unlike Modern Orthodox educators who oftentimes encouraged their young pupils to participate in American popular culture, proponents of the Orthodox Right eschewed direct interaction with the world beyond their close-knit religious circle.[4] The production of a faith-based youth culture was catalyzed by a desire to coalesce religion and the American ethos. Cognizant of the importance and formativeness of childhood, the Orthodox Right invested considerable resources to manufacture a religious culture marketed to acculturated American children and their families. This chapter explores how the Orthodox Right created a youth culture of day school contests, trading cards, and toys that paralleled popular American ideas and images but remained, however idiosyncratically, patently Orthodox.

## Raising the Orthodox Right

The Orthodox Right's youth revival occurred concomitant with the Modern Orthodox resurgence, albeit with far less fanfare than was displayed during the Mighty Mites episode. This form of Orthodox Judaism was helped along by the religiously rigid postwar Hungarian folkway that migrated after World War II and by the throngs of *ba'alei teshuva*, or "returnees": Jews who craved a more "authentic" Jewish life.[5] By the 1960s the Orthodox Right represented a "visible presence" of the 500,000 Orthodox Jews in the United States.[6] The rise of the Orthodox Right, like its Modern Orthodox equivalent, owed much to the attention paid to young people. In this instance, though, adults directed the youngsters instead of taking inspiration from their lead. From 1947 to 1963 the number of girls attending Bais Yaakov schools increased from 1,200 to 5,000 students. For boys Beth Medrash Govoha, Mesivta Chasan Sofer, Mesivta Rabbi Chaim Berlin, Ner Israel, Telshe Yeshiva, Tifereth Jerusalem, Torah Vodaath, and Yeshivas Chofetz Chaim all took significant steps to attract young people to their secondary schools and advanced forms of Jewish learning.[7] In addition, the religiously conservative Agudath Israel developed its own youth initiatives—insiders called its programs for children their "secret weapon"—in the postwar era.[8] The Orthodox Right's educational programs did not empower young people the way Modern Orthodox initiatives did. In their schools "coalescence" was stabilized by top-down order and discipline. Their adult teachers modeled Orthodox behavior and teachings for the pliant and eager youngsters who absorbed those lessons at an early age to preserve Jewish continuity.

This was the essence of religious education. The same was the case for the leaders of conservative churches who demanded "seriousness" and "strictness" from their children to confront a religiously looser American culture.[9] For instance, many fundamentalist Christians pulled their children out of public schools to avoid "hostile" teachings and "problematic" textbooks. From 1965 to 1983 the number of Evangelical private schools in the United States increased sixfold, and many other parents chose homeschooling.[10] In fact many religious groups—conservative and liberal—gained momentum in the face of "secular religion" during the 1950s and 1960s, but conservative faiths, led by charismatic champions, were especially appealing to "average Americans" looking for a simpler stock to "invest their lives with meaning."[11]

In this agreeable religious milieu, the Orthodox Right's insular-minded attitude intensified in the 1970s. Its proponents produced a type of American youth culture that detached children's games and toys from their erstwhile educational purpose. For the bulk of the twentieth century, children's books, films, and merchandise were intended to help girls and boys transition to adulthood. Print culture and media impressed the importance of parent-child bonding. Toy stores sold Lincoln Logs and Tinkertoys to encourage children to relate to and reconstruct the more grownup world that surrounded them. Beginning in the 1970s larger, profit-focused companies transformed the child-focused industry, providing America's youth with toys and films that evoked fantasy, worlds detached from their parents and adult role models. As a result many Orthodox Jews—and members of other tradition-bound groups—no longer viewed their education-focused child-rearing attitudes as so seamlessly aligned with the new American childhood culture.[12] Even ostensibly wholesome rituals like the spelling bee became less trustworthy in this new age of American youth just because it was associated with "unkosher" sectors. But Orthodox Jews did not disengage from American culture. Instead this group furnished educational activities and a material culture that was in vogue in the United States, and promoted a religious behavior that was religiously educational and unmistakably Orthodox.

This was also the case among Evangelicals. Beginning in the 1970s Protestant groups vigorously promoted a "Christian market" that directed interested parties to "Bible-believing proprietors."[13] To some extent the history of "material Christianity" dates back to Colonial America. Protestants had long ago viewed toys and children's books as tools to socialize youngsters and "allow them imaginatively to integrate religion into their play worlds."[14] However, it was not until the final decades of the twentieth century that Christian manufacturers consciously created lines of toys, dolls, and games that paralleled other popular playthings—Peace Pets in lieu of Care Bears, Power Ponies instead of My Little Ponies, and Heroes of the Kingdom rather than GI Joe figurines—and promoted religious morals and teachings. The burgeoning industry represented a sophisticated attempt to offer Christian families an alternative youth culture that provided more "wholesome" and "unsecular" values.[15] It is unlikely that Orthodox Jews monitored these developments within American Protestant culture. However, these very same impulses inspired new and creative strategies to raise a new generation of rigidly Orthodox Jews in the United States.

## From Spelling Bee to Brochos Bee

The spelling bee is an old institution. Americans in the early nineteenth century made use of spelling competitions as a savvy method to drill youngsters—immigrants and first-generation Americans—on English words and pronunciations. With the aid of radio, spelling bees gained renewed popularity in the interwar period. In 1925 the National Spelling Bee began in Louisville, Kentucky, leading educators to herald the "Spelling Bee's Revival."[16] In 1941 the E. W. Scripps Company acquired the sponsorship of the popular contest. In 1953 it became the custom for the National Spelling Bee winner to visit the White House and with FBI Director J. Edgar Hoover. During the 1960s the champions routinely appeared on a segment of the *Ed Sullivan Show*. It was, then, something of a cultural phenomenon. In December 1969, for instance, the National Spelling Bee loomed large in the very first *Peanuts* film, much to the chagrin of runner-up Charlie Brown.[17]

Torah Umesorah looked to claim a version of the successful spelling bee as its own. Whereas the spelling bee was intended to Americanize its young participants, the Brochos Bee aimed to inculcate a baseline of religious observance. After all, Orthodox Jews tend to recite a lot of blessings during their thrice-daily prayers and before eating food. Shalom Auslander's recollection of a schoolwide Brochos Bee match underscores the parallel between the two contests:

> The blessing bees began easily. Dov Becker got tuna (*shehakol*, the every-thing-else blessing), Ari Mashinsky got matzoh (*hamotzei*, the blessing for bread), and Yisroel Tuchman got stuck with kugel, which he thought was *ho-adamah*—food from the earth—but really was *mezonos*—the blessing on wheat. Three other kids got taken out by oatmeal, borscht with sour cream claimed two others, and by the end of the first round, almost a third of the students were already back in their seats.[18]

The competitive spirit characterized the boys' and girls' Brochos Bee competitions. A *New York Times* reporter depicted the following fierce scene among the Junior Girls Division in March 1976:

> Fast and curious the questions came: what is the blessing appropriate to almonds, American cheese, angel food cake, apples. . . . Down went contestants—on buckwheat, chives, éclair, eggplant, grits, kasha, parsley. Finally, Reana Bookson, aged 6, stumbled on rhubarb, leaving Elaine Witty, 8, triumphant winner.[19]

The Brochos Bee was simultaneously an entertaining method to obtain a better command of Jewish blessings and a Judaization of a popular American educational pastime. Competition was a means to elevate all contestants. Boys in the Intermediate Division were trained to answer questions with cleverer questions. For instance, when a judge asked for the blessing on applesauce, the youngster atop the podium offered a counter-question: "Home-made or store bought?" To borscht: "With or without potatoes?" Perhaps trickiest of all was pizza. Judges expected the following response: "One slice for a snack or two or three for a full meal?" More confounding still was Kellogg's Crispix, but merciful Brochos Bee organizers left that rice-corn combination food off competition blessing lists.[20] This sort of cultural coalescence was the hallmark of a particular brand of Orthodox Judaism in the United States. Torah Umesorah provided support and services to all types of Orthodox day schools, but its administration and rabbinic leadership identified with the Orthodox Right.[21]

This religious group avoided affiliation and interaction with the non-Orthodox and non-Jewish realms. Take for instance Rabbi Yaakov Feitman's description of "baseball syndrome" in a Torah Umesorah magazine. The writer lamented how "baseball, that most American of pastimes, recurs again and again in American Jewish literature as a metaphor of Americanization—and, in the process, de-Judaization."[22] Yet the Orthodox Right did incorporate aspects of American culture, so long as its adherents could reinforce its steady need to remain apart from it. The Brochos Bee was proof. It was patterned after an American game but intended just for Jews. Despite this Orthodox parents and educators liked that the Brochos Bee seemed to unite all varieties of Orthodox young people and promoted advanced knowledge of Jewish law. The more moderate Modern Orthodox did not usually agree with this insular stance but found the Brachos Bee sufficiently acceptable. The Modern Orthodox competed with the children of the so-called Yeshiva world. The rare ecumenical opportunity convinced Orthodox Jews that they could duel alone, away from non-Jews and other non-Jewish influences. Its focus on Jewish literacy and good-natured competition for elementary- and middle school–aged girls and boys (in separate divisions) was deemed too wholesome to resist.

In 1972 Rabbi Price expanded the competition beyond New York, and dug deeper into Torah Umesorah's nonprofit coffers to award prizes like tape recorders and wristwatches. The "out-of-towners" fared well against the Gothamites. Finalists for the second year's championships hailed from Milwaukee, Montreal, New Orleans, and San Diego.[23] The competition grew, and Brochos Bee preparation became a taken-for-granted part of the day school curriculum for many schools by the close of the decade.[24] The following year's event included more than four hundred schools. Torah Umesorah leaders congratulated themselves for a contest that had "evoked widespread interest and admiration."[25] San Diego's participation was something of an aberration. Most West Coast schools were located too far away to compete in the New York–based competition. In 1975 Los Angeles's Hillel Hebrew Academy and Emek Hebrew Academy hosted their own Brochos Bee contest amid considerable fanfare. The Emek match was judged by Israel's chief rabbi, Ovadia Yosef. Rabbi Yosef quizzed the children on basic blessings and made sure the pupils knew the "historical roots and spiritual concepts involved."[26]

The craze was soon formalized in the West. In May 1977 Rabbi Eliezer Wenger and Torah Umesorah formalized the West Coast section of its National

Brochos Bee enterprise. While serving as a teacher at New England Hebrew Academy in Boston (both Wenger and Hebrew Academy were affiliated with Chabad), Wenger had become enchanted with the Brochos Bee idea. After relocating to San Francisco, Wenger convinced Torah Umesorah to migrate the blessing bee westward. He recruited schools from Arizona, California, and Oregon.[27] He also published his popular two-volume *Brachos Study Guide* to level the playing field and encourage youngsters to memorize their blessings. Along with an NCSY blessing book, Wenger's textbooks became the go-to manuals for the Torah Umesorah competition.[28] Withal, Wenger published nine editions of the guidebook from 1978 to 1991.[29] The blessing books were also very helpful for Orthodox educators. It familiarized the less culturally inculcated youth with kosher cuisine. Wenger recommended that the "teacher should take time to explain about certain foods and if possible to bring a sample to class." The textbooks introduced Jewish children to leading luminaries like Rabbis Shlomo Zalman Auerbach, Moshe Feinstein, and Pinchas Hirschsprung. The author also offered some guidance on how to drum up enthusiasm for the Brochos Bee:

> To maintain the excitement of the Brochos Bee, it is necessary to constantly display pictures of foods on the classroom walls and bulletin boards. An excellent source for beautiful color pictures of fruit and vegetables is your local grocer, supermarket or fruit store. Ask them to save for your use extra display pictures which they obtain from their distributors. These pictures are large, colorful and impressive. Writing to Government agencies, dairy associations and the various food manufacturers can also prove productive.[30]

In its first two years, the West Coast showdown took place in the Bay Area. The competition received considerable attention from Jews and non-Jews. In 1978 San Francisco mayor George Moscone greeted the finalists, praising "their determination to preserve the sturdy traditions of Judaism."[31] His words had a way of validating the youngsters' efforts, confirming their meaningfulness and putting them on par with other competitions they read about or watched on television. The whole pageantry helped convince all those involved that their Brochos Bee was no less American than its spelling bee counterpart.

Wenger emerged as a Brochos Bee pied piper, much to the delight of Dovid Price and Torah Umesorah back in New York. In 1979 Wenger accepted the principalship at a school in Miami Beach. Once settled he founded the Florida division of the Brochos Bee. Wenger believed in the power of blessings. To him it was no mundane religious act borrowed from the American spelling bee. He taught his students—and anyone else who would listen—that the many blessings recited by observant Jews remind them to be grateful for food and all other forms of sustenance. "I think if more people realized these things and were thankful," Wenger told a Fort Lauderdale newspaperman, "they'd lead better lives."[32] In Florida Wenger followed the same successful model he had executed on the West Coast. In May 1982 Miami Beach mayor Norman Ciment—Torah Umesorah happily reported that Ciment was the "only Shomer Shabbos [Sabbath observant] mayor in the United States"—attended the final round of the Florida Brochos Bee. In his introductory remarks Mayor Ciment extolled Wenger and the other program organizers for starting a competition that "reinforces emphasis on those ideals and ethics which give religion its true meaning, teaching holiness and humanity."[33] In other words the Brochos Bee was just as Jewish as it was an American-styled game.

In 1984 the itinerant Wenger moved to Cincinnati and formed the Midwest Brochos Bee competition. Also sponsored by Torah Umesorah, Wenger assembled schools from Cleveland, Chicago, Columbus, Detroit, Indianapolis, and Louisville. The Midwest region also provided a testing ground for Torah Umesorah to experiment with computerized sections of the blessing quiz.[34]

Still Wenger—for all his bountiful and boisterous Brochos Bee pride—could not compete with Philadelphia's rabbinic firepower. In the 1980s the local Torah Academy was the premier training ground for Brochos Bee champions among the five hundred schools and four thousand boys and girls who faced off in the annual contest. Back then Torah Academy served a wide range of Orthodox children, never pushing too hard on "divisive" issues like Zionism or coeducation, at least in the younger grades. In 1981 Ahron Shlomo Svei won the Brochos Bee's Senior Boys Division. He was the son of Rabbi Elya Svei, the head of the Talmudical Yeshiva of Philadelphia—the "Philly Yeshiva"—and a member of the Agudath Israel's Moetzes Gedolei HaTorah. Apparently Svei did not mind the competition and interaction with Modern Orthodox Jews.[35] Two years later Rabbi Svei's younger son, Mayer Simcha, claimed another

Brochos Bee championship for Philadelphia. The youngster memorized more than a thousand blessings for foodstuffs, and other blessings on smelling and seeing things. The junior Svei earned a perfect score on the final exam and outmatched his counterparts in the oral round. "I've had good role models," said the twelve-year-old, whose pastimes included Torah study and basketball. "My brother has been a good influence and my father is a rosh yeshiva, a head rabbi for the Philadelphia yeshiva."[36] In addition to Mayer Simcha Svei, Eliyahu Gold, Torah Academy's Shlomit Zeiger, and Malka Kamenetsky also placed high in their respective division finals. Most of these children were raised in well-known rabbinic households.[37] In 1984 Torah Academy boasted another blessing champ. That year Yehuda Mandelbaum, ten, won the Intermediate Boys Division. Mandelbaum's triumph was far more understated than that of the Svei brothers. "I wasn't too confident because there were so many other kids," explained Mandelbaum, "and I had only two weeks to study while most others had more. I thought I'd come in fifth place, not first."[38]

The Brochos Bee allowed its young contestants to tap into the usual rhetoric of American competition. It boasted bigtime powerhouses and overachieving underdogs, playoffs, and school pride. That Torah Umesorah freighted the Brochos Bee with this American-style culture helped endear the quiz contest to thousands of Orthodox Jews. However, its content and educational purpose transformed the Brochos Bee from a hackneyed American pastime to a religious ritual. In effect the two aspects of the Brochos Bee complemented one another. The sportslike hype that surrounded the nationwide contests and attention paid to the New York–based championship rounds raised awareness and pride for the increasingly more insulated Orthodox Jewish culture in the United States. What is more, those attitudes were reinforced by a burgeoning material culture aimed at youngsters which promoted Orthodox sensibilities in American packaging.

## Gedolim Cards and the Commodification of Rabbi-Saints

In the summer of 1988, Rabbi Mordechai Nissel spotted a novelty item near the cashier's station at a Jewish book store in Baltimore. The opened box revealed a bounty of cellophane-wrapped rabbi cards retailing for just about eighty cents a pack. The fourth-grade teacher was on vacation, almost four hundred miles away from his classroom in the Providence Hebrew Day School. But his mind was on his students, and the cards' clever slogan captivated him: "Collect Full Sets. Trade With Friends, Learn About Torah Leaders." The scheme was a simple one to decode, no talmudic logic needed: Revere rabbinic superstars, not baseball all-stars.[39] Still the message was understated, ensuring that the cultural insularism and coalescence of the hobby were just slightly more aggressive than the Brochos Bee competitions.

Rabbi Nissel was unsure. Could rabbi cards become a denomination of classroom currency, a reward for good behavior and test scores? Surely the Orthodox teacher was unaware that a similar trend was underfoot in Sunday schools, where Christian educators bribed their pupils with "Jesus and Disciples" trading cards.[40] In any case the store manager informed him that the rabbi cards were all the rage in Baltimore, especially among eight- to fifteen-year-old boys. Nissel remained unconvinced. After all the Baltimore Orioles were downright woeful. They had begun that season a dreadful 0–21.[41] The season-long slump was surely enough for local Orthodox youngsters to abandon baseball cards for any alternate card-collecting hobby. But the phenomenon had moved beyond the Chesapeake. Rumor had it that eager boys in other Orthodox hubs had already purchased packs and packs of the Torah Personalities cards, and that its creator, Arthur Shugarman, was planning a larger second series.[42] The out-of-town customer was still incredulous. Then the manager informed the patron that he was authorized to offer a half-price discount to Orthodox day schools. Nissel was sold. He brought a case of cards back to Rhode Island.

Sure enough the first thirty-six-card series produced by the nonprofit Torah Personalities, Inc. sold out in about six months. Partnering with a well-to-do kosher candy distributor, Shugarman sold 400,000 packages in a variety of Orthodox-dense locales.[43] In Miami, for example, the owner of Judaica Enterprises found it "unbelievable how many calls I've been getting about the rabbi cards." He therefore seized on the demand and ordered 288 packs of Shugarman's trading cards.[44] Concomitantly a Judaica dealer in Detroit estimated that among the 10,000 Orthodox Jews in his area, perhaps a little under two-thirds constituted the considerable market for rabbi cards.[45] The principal of a day school in Philadelphia corroborated all of this in terms her young students might have used: "The Gedolim are very popular, very hot."[46]

What accounted for this success? After all, rabbi cards were not an altogether new idea. Shugarman was the first to admit that his product was not the stuff of sheer innovation. "In New York City," he once told an interviewer, the "selling of pictures of rabbis had gone on for some time." Legend had it that a collector known as "Yarmish" had more than 100,000 postcard-sized rabbi images in his Flatbush home.[47] Most children in this Orthodox circle sported more modest collections but aspired to be like Yarmish. According to one report, were someone to investigate

> the six-grade classroom of almost any prominent yeshiva in Brooklyn, Monsey, or any other "yeshivishe" neighborhood at recess-time, he would invariably see groups of boys huddled over desks, bargaining over "the latest Rav Yaakov" or "the Klausenberger [Rebbe] shooting a bow and arrow on Lag B'Omer." In fact, sales have reached such a pitch in one yeshiva that it has introduced price-control on all pictures. The *Menahel* [principal] appraises each picture and sets a price not to be exceeded.[48]

In 1980 the youth division of the Agudath Israel of America produced a thirty-five-card series of "Photocards of Gedolei Yisroel," or the "great ones" of Israel.[49] The set featured black-and-white cards of deceased European-born rabbis, all at one point or another institutionally connected to (twenty-two sat at one point on the "Council of Torah Sages") or politically in sync with the Orthodox Right movement.

Overseas the most fervently righteous in Israel also collected these cards. In the mid-1980s Shmiel Shnitzer's Photo Geula was one of a half-dozen stores in Jerusalem that peddled rabbi photos.[50] In Shnitzer's shop most images were sold for the shekel equivalent of a dollar. Some, though, were slightly more expensive. For a time young yeshiva men paid top dollar for a picture of the Lubavitcher Rebbe until too many copies were produced and flooded the market. The Amshinover Rebbe, who did not approve of his image commercialized in this manner, was perhaps the priciest photograph. Rabbi Avrohom Yitzchok Kohn (i.e., the Toldos Aharon), who strictly forbade the distribution of his portrait, was unavailable at Photo Geula. Instead young boys acquired the Toldos Aharon in "seedier" places like in the back of the yeshiva study halls. Or they might trade. In 1988 the going rate for a Toldos Aharon was a Rabbi Elazar Shach, of the Ponevezh yeshiva, and the Sephardic kabbalist the Baba Sali.[51] Posthumousness also increased the value of a rabbinic photograph. For rabbi-card dealers this was no time to mourn. For instance, when the Lelover Rebbe passed away, the proprietor of Geula Photo "printed up 100 pictures of him right after I heard," and sold out the same day. In some morbid manner the image commodified the deceased. The Lelover Rebbe was transformed into a Jewish saint, not a part of the "lowly" present-day generation. No longer available to offer guidance and wisdom, he was in heaven's hall of fame, in high demand for his immortal place in Jewish tradition.[52]

Arthur Shugarman's genius was to blend the rabbi-picture–collecting hobby with baseball cards. His Torah Personalities cards did not compete with venders and photographers in the rabbi-card markets. Instead his cards joined them. For this reason Shugarman printed cards in 4-by-6-inch format, much bulkier than a standard 2½-by-3½-inch baseball card, meant to fit comfortably in the palms of young collectors. To some this made the rabbi cards appear amateurish, an awkward kind of collectable. Still, Shugarman preferred the Kodak-regulation images, which better resembled the "real photographs" that had "caught on big" in certain Orthodox circles. The rabbi-card entrepreneur credited his success to a blending of Judaism and American consumerism:

> Among the many lessons I have learned from this project, is that we have a responsibility to use the many recent technological advances to our advantage, to enable us to accomplish much more than in the past for furthering Torah causes. As Torah representatives to the world at large, we should never settle on producing our material in any but the best manner possible. You never know when the world (non-religious Jews, as well as non-Jews) may take a look, creating an immeasurable *Kiddush Hashem* [sanctification of God's name]. And then, the subject matter of what we are producing deserves no less than the best.[53]

The gimmick was sufficiently effective to convince one Orthodox educator to purchase the cards for students while otherwise thinking that the "importance placed on baseball cards and players in our society is absolutely asinine." Yet, like baseball cards, Shugarman's rabbi cards featured the essential "statistics" of leading rabbinic luminaries. Birthdates, educational information, and bibliographical details were printed on the back of each trading card. Torah Personalities cards were also blessed with propitious timing. Between 1975 and 1980 the number of "serious" baseball-card collectors rose from 4,000 to 250,000 in the United States. By the close of the decade, three to four million Americans collected sports cards to some degree or another.[54] The exponentially rising interest in the collectables inspired upstarts like Fleer and Upper Deck to more vigorously compete with the longtime standard-bearer, Topps. Shugarman launched Torah Personalities in August 1988, amid the trading-card boom.

For some, the rabbi cards displaced baseball stars. In Baltimore a middle-schooler happily bequeathed his baseball cards to his younger brother, since rabbi cards were "more interesting." Little Yossi Brull accepted his sibling's collection but also became fonder of rabbi cards.[55] Sixteen-year-old Avrohom Rosenberg of Philadelphia grew unimpressed with his submediocre Phillies and its roster full of men of "physical capabilities and nothing great." In contrast, claimed the teenaged Rosenberg, "rabbi cards give us something to look up to." Other boys did not abandon sports cards but treated their rabbi cards with a decided degree of reverence. Children did not flip them or ding the corners. Two youngsters, also of Philadelphia, vowed never to trade rabbi cards for baseball cards, though rumor had it there were "kids who have."[56] Far more often Orthodox children traded endogamously, rabbi card for rabbi card. The editors of *Time* were correct that the "most coveted" card was Rabbi Moshe Feinstein of New York's Lower East Side. His trading-card likeness was unavailable for a one-to-one swap, say, for a Rabbi Ovadia Yosef or a Rabbi Mordechai Gifter card. Interested collectors were prepared to offer two or three rabbis for a Feinstein, who sat comfortably and unquestionably atop the Orthodox rabbinic power rankings.[57]

Shugarman was aware of the fast-growing market for trading cards. He knew it well from a previous life, before he entered the Orthodox fold. As a youngster in Baltimore, Shugarman collected coins, figurines, and stamps, but his truest passion was baseball cards. Hometown hero Brooks Robinson was Shugarman's favorite card to collect. They shared much in common. Both were mild-mannered, dependable men. Robinson used those qualities to become the "Human Vacuum Cleaner," the most dependable third-baseman in professional baseball. At 5'5" Shugarman was in no position to succeed his idol.[58] The idea to fashion sets of rabbi cards had percolated for some time—probably as early as 1982, when, in his late twenties, Shugarman sold his large stash of baseball cards. It was not a prerequisite to enter the "strictly Orthodox" fold. But the decision to unload his collection made it easier to transition to a new environment. Shugarman had replaced Brooks Robinson

הרב משה פיינשטיין,
זצ"ל
ר"מ תפארת ירושלים
(נוא יארק)
מחבר: שו"ת אגרות משה,
דברות משה

*RAV MOSHE FEINSTEIN,*
ZT'L

Rav—Luban ( Russia )
Rosh Yeshiva—Mesivta Tifereth Jerusalem
(New York City)
Chairman of Moetzes Gedolei HaTorah of Agudath Israel
President of Agudath Harabbonim
President of Chinuch Atzmai—Torah Schools

Born in Russia
Nifter in 5746

PHOTO BY ED BERNSTEIN

©1988 Torah Personalities, Inc.     U.S.A.
Sold on condition not to copy.     1-8

הרב יעקב יצחק הלוי רודערמאן,
זצ"ל
ר"מ נר ישראל (באלטימאר)
מחבר: עבודת לוי

*RAV YAAKOV YITZCHOK RUDERMAN,*
ZT'L

Rosh Yeshiva—Yeshivas Ner Israel
(Baltimore)
Member of Moetzes Gedolei HaTorah
of Agudath Israel
Chairman of Vaad Roshei Yeshiva
of Torah Umesorah

Born in Russia
Talmid of Slobodka
Nifter in 5747

PHOTO BY ED BERNSTEIN

©1988 Torah Personalities, Inc.     U.S.A.
Sold on condition not to copy.     1-23

Rabbis Moshe Feinstein and Yaakov Yitzchok Ruderman and their relevant "stats" depicted in the first series (1988) of Torah Personalities trading cards, front and back sides. (Torah Personalities, Inc.)

with Rabbi Yaakov Kamenetsky of Yeshiva Torah Vodaath.[59] Kamenetsky had recently died. And upon the death of Ruderman, the last of a group that also included Rabbi Moshe Feinstein, one observer noted in a private letter to his successor at Ner Israel in Baltimore that "Rav Ruderman was the last of that small coterie of European Torah giants."[60] This, then, reflected Shugarman's good timing. Orthodox Jews in the United States had recognized that they were vulnerable and bereaved. Their children and students could no longer learn from the famed rabbinic leaders. They could, however, interact with and learn about the rabbis on the back of each card. For the collector this was a form of retrieval. For the distributor it was a religious commodification.

Shugarman made the most of this dire moment. The first series of Torah Personalities featured fifteen dead rabbis, and all but two had passed away within the previous decade. Among the twenty-one living rabbis depicted on the cards, most were quite aged and had just a few more years to live. The Baltimore native consulted with local rabbis and some in New York about which rabbis to include in the first trading-card installment. Shugarman insisted that he would consider only color images, thereby excluding scholars from previous centuries. Scholarly output was also a factor. Most of all Shugarman, who still had that "collecting blood," sought out popular rabbinic men.[61] He was satisfied with his initial selection. He had amassed hundreds of extra photos—enough, as it would turn out, to furnish another five series of rabbi cards. Analysis of the first set reveals the bias of the American Orthodox rabbis consulted during the development of the rabbinic roster. Two-thirds of the carded rabbis flourished in the United States, as opposed to Israel. Just three were American-born. And nearly half sat on the Agudath Israel's rabbinic presidium. Still Shugarman believed he had nailed it, offering a wide variety of rabbinical personalities. To be sure Shugarman included images of Hasidic luminaries like the Bostoner Rebbe, the Lubavitcher Rebbe, and the Satmar Rebbe. Luminaries like the Babi Sali and Rabbi Ovadia Yosef fulfilled the Sephardic quota.

Many felt uneasy about injecting Jewish holiness into the collecting enterprise. Yeshiva University undergraduates who did not share the same degree of clericalism lampooned rabbi cards in their annual Purim magazine. A mock advertisement announced the appearance of "Centrist Orthodox Gedolim Cards." Readers were encouraged to "collect both cards."[62] In addition a Reform rabbi in Philadelphia described rabbi cards as "utter nonsense." An

Orthodox clergyman joked that "there's nothing wrong except that it's a form of idolatry."[63] From the opposite perspective an Orthodox woman from Long Island opined that it did not redound well to rabbis to be associated with the athletes and celebrities often depicted on trading cards. In her words, rabbis had been "grouped in together with ugliness, proving beyond a shadow of a doubt the argument against the distribution of these cards."[64] The Torah Personalities operation also betrayed a heightened level of modesty that was connected to the rabbinate. In fact some, like Rabbi Elya Svei of Philadelphia, were reluctant to embrace this cultural coalescence and lend their likenesses to the project but acquiesced after it was impressed on them that the cards carried a certain educational value.[65]

Nonetheless the enthusiasts overmatched the critics. Rabbi Mordechai Gifter of the Telshe Yeshiva in Cleveland did not mind having his likeness appear on a trading card. "I tell you," he said to a reporter, "it's better for Jewish religious school children to play with the pictures of rabbis than to play with the pictures of baseball players."[66] Gifter thus embraced American-Jewish coalescence. To date Torah Personalities Inc. has sold some three million rabbi cards and has been featured on National Public Radio and in *Sports Illustrated.*[67] Shugarman inspired other brands. In the 1990s Torah Cards and Torah Links Cards emerged on the growing market of Orthodox collectables.[68] Like other popular collectables, Torah Personalities cards were traded, sold, and cherished. This righteous commodity, however, doubled as a two-dimensional fragment of tradition that could fit somewhat awkwardly into the palm of a young Jewish child's hand.

## Mitzvah Merchants and Their Made-in-America Toys

In 1994 Barbara Shine founded Double Play Toys in Borough Park. Shine's operation targeted a similar clientele among the Orthodox Right. Back then Shine had to sift through catalogs to identify values-appropriate merchandise. True, there were items like rabbi cards and an impressive number of English- and Yiddish-language children's books. But there was not much in the way of full-fledged toys. Her customers entered Double Play Toys knowing that the store's proprietor had already done much of the work eliminating nonprudish toys.[69] Two decades later Shmuel Lipschitz opened his Wise Buys toy store in Brooklyn's Williamsburg neighborhood. Like Shine, the young entrepreneur set his sights on "kosher" children's playthings. However, Lipschitz did not need to sort through catalogs to identify appropriate children's merchandise for his customers. By 2013 the Orthodox Right had assembled a significant line of products. The children and their parents patronized Lipschitz's store for made-for-Orthodox toys that, as Laura Leibman put it, "reinforce rather than undermine their religious traditions and values."[70] Lipschitz must have realized he was on to something. After just a year his business was booming, in large part due to the fact that half the local Jewish population was under eighteen years old.

Wise Buys and Double Play Toys represent a more recent stage in the Orthodox childhood culture. Much more aggressive than the Brochos Bee and Torah Personalities trading cards, these stores aim to replicate and replace American culture. They are filled with "synthesized" merchandise produced by Orthodox Jews in Brooklyn, Lakewood, and overseas in Israel. Once again this parallels other faith communities. More recently some Christian companies have grown increasingly combative toward "secular" material culture. They believe that the latest products of mainstream children's culture are fully stripped of the educational and moral values of earlier generations of toys and toymakers. Making ample use of militant imagery, these manufacturers have declared a "battle for the toybox."[71]

Like their Christian counterparts, the purveyors of Orthodox children's culture have taken up a more agitated stance toward non-Jewish material culture. No longer merely offering a more religious option, the Orthodox Right has become far more insistent that only its brands are acceptable for cultural consumption. In April 2017, for instance, a Bais Yaakov principal in New York wrote to his parent body to warn of the "latest Disney movies and fads that seem harmless but really do seep into your daughter's mind and soul." He offered the following:

> When we met for the first time, I expressed to you my distaste for television. I explained to you what I think a "yiddeshe shtub" [Jewish home] should look like. Not having a television in your home was #1 on the list. Meaning, that the "ikar'" [essence] in this home should not revolve around sports and TV shows. I was very clear when I said, "these are not the types of families that I am looking for. There are other schools where it is not such a big deal."

I rarely asked, "Do you have a television?" because most parents at that point of the conversation would gladly tell me, "We do not have a television." In addition, I would rather not become a school that makes parents sign a paper, stating that there is no television in the house. Why? Because I want to trust all of you. . . . What I did not ask you then, was whether or not your children watch TV shows and movies on your home computer, an iPad or any other electronic device. I hoped that watching television or movies on these devices would be the same "toeivah," "abomination," as watching on a real TV. I meant that seriously. We are so immune to women and men who are worse than immodest in our surroundings that we do not even flinch anymore.[72]

This head of school could no longer tolerate parents' surrender to popular culture norms. He grieved that his community was satisfied with the borders it had established to stave off the "corruption" of American youth culture. According to him, the families whose daughters attended his elementary school were satisfied with a somewhat permeable barrier to insulate their homes. They found it near-impossible to shield their children any better. "Disney," then, was a concession they would tolerate. With an imagined portrait of a cloistered and more innocent Eastern European Jewish world, the principal upbraided Bais Yaakov parents for their unwillingness to be even more vigilant:

The response is, "it's the way of the world." You are correct. But it is not the way of our world. It is not the way of the world that we want our children to grow up in. We hope they become a source of yiddeshe nachas [Jewish pride] to us and to Klal Yisroel [the Jewish People]. It is certainly not the way of the world of our grandparents and great-grandparents who died al Kiddush Hashem a little over 70 years ago merely for being a Jew.

How can you live a Torah life, if pritzus [perversion] and awful visualizations permeate your home and are seared into the hearts and minds of our children? The answer is, one cannot![73]

Hence the market for Disney-less toys. Yet the intensified pressure among the Orthodox Right to remove foreign influences has not halted attempts to replicate American popular culture. Today the most popular items continue to draw from the typical proven and perfected toys. Deal Spiel is a knockoff of Monopoly. Mitzvah Kinder look a lot like Fisher-Price's Little People but with Hasidic-looking folk. In addition, the Shpielmans are Toys-R-Us–worthy, posable, Orthodox-looking figurines that "promote Jewish values, depicting various traditions within our religion and encouraging acceptance of those differences."[74] Perhaps the most innovative is the Lego-like Binyan Blocks. There's a "Shabbos Table" scene, and another inside a sukkah. Instead of a Batmobile, Death Star, or Turtle Van, Binyan Blocks have Chaverim, Hatzolah, and Shomrim emergency-rescue vehicles.

In some respects, Binyan Blocks was the brainchild of a moment. Rabbi Eli Wolf and his young son sat down to build a shul out of Legos. "After a couple of hours," recalled the Lakewood-trained father, "the shul was completed, but of course the people did not look like real shul people. There was no Torah [scroll] and there were many other things that just did not look right." Wolf recruited a cousin and his friend with finance and manufacturing experience to help him along his quest. The triumvirate hailed from three distinct cohorts of the Orthodox Right, prepared to market a toy that might appeal and unite each of their respective social circles.[75] Binyan Blocks, therefore, was a means to unite sometimes disparate subgroups within the Orthodox Right community.

It was also apparent that Binyan Blocks was eager to provide a more Orthodox substitute for Legos. The Orthodox Right has grown suspicious of more recent iterations of Lego (once viewed as a wholesome and educational children's toy) that include Disney princesses and popular superheroes. "A lot of the Lego themes out there aren't so appropriate for *frum* [religiously observant] kids," explained co-creator Aron Weinberger, invoking a Yiddish word for strictly observant Jews. "We wanted to create Legos that could be used to build the things that are more meaningful to us." According to Weinberger, the Orthodox Right and other religiously conservative families have embraced their idea. On the whole the feedback on Binyan Blocks has been positive: "I've gotten e-mails," explained Weinberger, "from non-Jews asking for our sets because they're very wholesome, without movie themes."[76]

The planning and manufacturing took more than a year. In 2014 Binyan Blocks released several small sets and, most impressive of all, a Large Shul known to its plastic prayer-goers as "Kahal Anshei Binyanim." The toy is meant to socialize young children to adulthood and an Orthodox lifestyle.

In keeping with Agudath Israel–style congregations (as opposed to Modern Orthodox "Young Israel" ones), the understated two-toned synagogue was fashioned in the mold of a basic wooden synagogue. The main portion of the sanctuary is flanked by a limited-seating women's section on the left and a cozy space for traditional text study on the right. On the walls hang posters reminding worshipers that it is forbidden to talk during services and the latest times to commence prayers—both very familiar notices.

The Large Shul also features Orthodox-looking figurines, ten in all: eight behatted gentlemen, representing the spectrum of the Orthodox Right; two bewigged women dressed in long dresses. The female attire—or at least the quirky repercussions—irked at least one customer. "One woman, though, wrote to complain that since the women in our Shabbos scene are wearing skirts, they can't sit down!" recounted Weinberger. "She wanted to know why we discriminate against women. I explained that Orthodox Jews hold women in the highest regard, but for reasons of modesty, the women wear skirts."[77] Most customers, however, were far from perturbed.

To the contrary, the shiny, Jewishly oriented toy bricks confirm for young people that their religious practices are normative—stylish, even. The generic Binyan Blocks characters resemble real-life people who pass by them on the streets; perhaps they look more than a little like their own parents and other family members. In all Binyan Blocks and the rest of the Orthodox toy industry legitimated for young "insiders" a lifestyle that, beyond their neighborhood, is considered an American cultural aberration. To accomplish this Orthodox toymakers and proprietors drew from the very American youth culture they sought to keep from their own impressionable children. This top-down strategy betokens the creative way the Orthodox Right enclave has preserved their traditions, leveraging American popular material culture to construct authentic expressions of their Orthodox faith.

## CHAPTER 6

# YESHIVAT RAMBAM AND THE RISE AND FALL OF A MODERN ORTHODOX IDEA

In the summer of 1990, a group of parents arranged a meeting with the Orthodox Rabbinical Council of Baltimore. Encouraged by a few astute local rabbis, the group of young professionals figured it would make good political sense to inform the local board of rabbis of its intention to form a new day school. In Baltimore's Orthodox community the schools were polarized, leaving the moderates positioned in the "center" without a comfortable educational environment. The parents explained that the new school would stress fidelity to Jewish law, embrace Zionism, offer advanced religious education to girls (and to boys), and teach a healthy share of Western culture. Their plan was earnest and sensible, they reckoned. Yet most of the Baltimore rabbis did not agree, nor did they appreciate that laypeople had approached the rabbinical board to "simply inform them of their plans." The meeting provoked a major disconnect.

Shortly after the Baltimore Rabbinical Council meeting, Rabbi Yirmiyahu Kaganoff of Congregation Darchei Zedek sermonized in opposition to the new school. Its founders, he alleged, "were like the two sons of Aaron who were struck down by God because they did not heed their elders." More than a little dismayed, the parents felt their disappointment hung on the understanding that "we're not espousing radical ideas." Several rabbis did deign to lend their support, but the encouragement did not soften the brunt of communal consternation. It was therefore fitting that the lay leaders named the school "Yeshivat Rambam," or Maimonides Academy, after the medieval scholar who "combined secular knowledge and Torah"—and because "he was sharply criticized by traditionalists during his lifetime."[1]

Despite the antagonism from the Orthodox Right, Yeshivat Rambam rapidly emerged as a symbol of a burgeoning Modern Orthodox community in Baltimore. For postwar Orthodox Jews, schools—rather than synagogues—were viewed as the major ideological centers. Long ago, one acute observer noted the "shift of emphasis" from the synagogue to the day school. The school was the place that stood the best chance of curbing assimilation and imparting Jewish ideals and values to the next generation.[2] Likewise the Baltimore group that had initially discussed the idea of starting a Young Israel–type synagogue turned their attention to a day school.[3]

For a short period Yeshivat Rambam accomplished a lot. The enthusiasm exhibited by lay leaders and students mirrored the sort of excitement displayed by that earlier cohort of Modern Orthodox young people back in the 1960s. Yet Rambam's precipitous rise was matched by its eventual and sudden fall. The school closed its doors in 2011. Some blamed the economics, noting that a wedge school was simply unsustainable given the costs of an impressive campus and the need to accommodate remedial and enrichment students. Others pointed fingers at the Orthodox Right and the local Jewish philanthropic organizations for their lack of support. Both claims are valid but overlook other vital considerations.

During its short and mercurial lifespan, Yeshivat Rambam, an institutional child of the 1990s, represented a religious openness that was no longer in vogue within many segments of American religion. The Orthodox Jews who purchased rabbi cards and promoted cultural insularism did not find Rambam's mission compelling or religiously authentic. Situated in Baltimore, a conservative religious stronghold, the day school had persevered and gained a near-immediate foothold. Its leaders were young women and men driven by the Modern Orthodox Judaism that came into focus in the 1960s. They drew on this religious spirit to push against a well-entrenched and unwelcoming religious ethos made even stronger by the rise of the Orthodox Right. By 1990 this enclave made up 40 percent of American Orthodoxy's 500,000 women and men.[4] But under the crush of other unsupportive factors, Baltimore's Modern Orthodox youth revival was finally overmatched by the rigid religious ethos. Other likeminded Modern Orthodox day schools elsewhere in Chicago, Cleveland, and New York survived similar oppositional forces. In Baltimore, however, Modern Orthodox Jews faced a more aggressive and antagonistic religious culture than most. The tale of Yeshivat Rambam features rival forms of religious authenticity and Orthodox youth cultures: the Modern Orthodox's bottom-up versus the Orthodox Right's top-down approach. In the background of these confrontations was the looming presence of an American religious ethos that helped determine the outcome of these important cultural battles.

## Orthodox Judaism in Catholic Baltimore

In the mid-nineteenth century, newly settled German Jews had exerted a "strong Orthodox influence" in Baltimore.[5] At the turn of the twentieth century, Orthodox Jews recalled their "great and lasting influence on the Jewish community of Baltimore."[6] Their "piety and upright character have left a lasting impress upon the community."[7] In June 1989 it was simply dubbed a "Baltimore tradition" that cultivated an ecclesiasticism and rigidness that often stood in the way of moderation and religious change.[8] Among the dominant Catholic population in Baltimore, this was standard fare. Despite an earlier spring of righteous republicanism (the first American bishop, after all, was democratically elected), Baltimore's Catholics by the mid-1800s had Romanized and adopted a hierarchical ministry that encouraged traditionalism and devotion to the religious stylings of Europe.[9] They placed much value on religious traditions and the sacred words of the pope and his cardinals and bishops. Moreover, local Catholic clerics demanded that religious and lay leaders honor the Baltimore priestship with a Vatican-type veneration.[10] Of course there existed significant Jewish and Christian forces in Baltimore that did not adhere to this top-down ecclesiastical formation and sported more liberal features in their religious sphere. Still the overwhelming religious culture in the area supported the traditional Catholic model of religious authority and conservativism.[11]

Baltimore's Orthodox community matured within this ecclesiastical culture. Or, in the words of the most recent historians of Baltimore's Jews: "the continued viability of Orthodoxy, even among Jews who felt strong pressure to conform to the manners and mores of the larger society, was facilitated by the traditional tone of Baltimore's culture."[12] This was none too different from the osmosis processes of other American Jewish communities, as each absorbed broader indigenous religious attitudes. From its earliest iteration as the Dutch-controlled New Amsterdam, New York City, for example, was a relative haven for religious tolerance and representative of a "religious experi-ence [that] was powerfully collective, rooted in joining with others to share rit-ual, belief, and practice."[13] This quality of cosmopolitanism provoked Gotham Judaism to follow in kind. In Philadelphia the Jewish community imbibed the local spirit of anticlericalism. In the 1850s a traveler to the city wrote that there were few rabbis of notable standing; the one "man of knowledge" was rather suppressed by the lay leadership's "Quaker-like" sensibilities.[14] Many years later Rabbi Bernard Levinthal, the so-called chief rabbi of Philadelphia, broke that trend, but he proved to be rather anomalous. "He did not develop," concluded one historian, "another generation of local orthodox leadership."[15]

Baltimore's Jewishly overrepresented Orthodox enclave reinforced this rigid and ecclesiastical-abiding culture. The local Orthodox community defied national demographic trends. In 1968 a full third of Jews in the area identified as Orthodox; more than any other religious movement and a much higher per-centage than the national average. In the highly Orthodox-concentrated Lower Park Heights neighborhood, more than half of Jews affiliated with this branch of Judaism.[16] Furthermore, the strong rabbinical infrastructure perpetuated a conservative current within Baltimore's Orthodox community. This had much to do with Ner Israel Rabbinical College, a traditional yeshiva that hosted hun-dreds of young men who spent their days poring over Talmud tomes and rab-binical codes. Rabbi Yaakov Yitzchok Ruderman founded the yeshiva in the autumn of 1933, convinced by Levinthal that Baltimore's ecclesiasticism would support his efforts, unlike the case of an earlier and much-maligned attempt in Cleveland.[17] The local Jewish newspaper hailed Ruderman as "represent[ing] the best tradition of Yeshiva spirit" and opined that "Baltimore Jewry ought to be fully conscious of the occasion and ought to be alive to the part that a Yeshiva in our midst, if properly supported, will elevate the whole tone of the ethical educational and religious life of our community."[18] After some initial pushback Levinthal proved correct, and Ruderman benefited from Baltimore-styled clericalism.[19] The Orthodox Union, for instance, was fearful of any community organizing that did not involve Ner Israel's rabbinic leaders.[20] In line with the strong Catholic clericalism in the region, Ner Israel's rabbinic elites towered above all other rabbinical forces in the Baltimore community:

> The three most influential Orthodox rabbis in Baltimore are closely tied
> to Ner Israel: Rabbi Yaakov Weinberg is Ner Israel's Rosh Yeshiva, in

effect its president, dean and spiritual leader. Rabbi Herman Neuberger is the executive vice president; and Rabbi Moshe Heinemann gave up his full-time faculty position at the yeshiva to become the rabbi of the Agudath Israel congregation in 1981.[21]

To be sure Ner Israel was far from the most insular yeshiva in the United States.[22] Its students often enrolled in evening college programs at Loyola College in Baltimore, and later at Johns Hopkins University, an arrangement formalized and blessed by Ner Israel's administration.[23] This ensured that among the many Ner Israel students who settled permanently in Baltimore were professionals and businessmen, as well as teachers and rabbis.[24] In addition the school's rabbinical leaders engaged some of the more moderate Orthodox through NCSY.[25] Yet these stances were far from the Modern Orthodox position. Ner Israel and other Orthodox institutions in Baltimore opposed items on the Modern Orthodox agenda, such as a widened interest in non-Jewish wisdom and culture, and a belief in the tenets of Religious Zionism. In the 1970s, for example, students at the local girls' high school were routinely discouraged from attending the Zionist programs held at the local Bnei Akiva Religious Zionist youth movement chapter. In fact on one occasion a girl was informed that her election as student-council president was contingent on her dropping out of a Zionist club.[26] Ner Israel's Rabbi Yaakov Weinberg described Israel Independence Day as a "day of incredible hurt."[27] Later on, in recognition of their zealousness and devotion to one of its leaders, Rabbi Moshe Heinemann, these Orthodox Baltimoreans were dubbed "Heinemoonies" by outsiders.[28]

In the 1980s Baltimore emerged as a bastion of fervent Orthodox Judaism. A fifth of the ninety-three thousand Jews in the city identified as Orthodox.[29] Down from a similar local survey conducted two decades earlier, this Orthodox/non-Orthodox ratio was still much higher than in all other American Jewish locales.[30] Moreover in 1986 researchers found that "Baltimore is the first Jewish community where data show a resurgence of Orthodoxy among the young."[31] Local leaders figured that about two hundred Orthodox families settled in their area each year. A large portion of these were "returnees" to Orthodox Judaism: secularly raised Jews who later in life adopted Orthodoxy, and usually a rightward brand of that faith. Baltimore offered affordable housing and amenities: restaurants, schools, and twenty-four Orthodox synagogues.

All these were very accessible and put to good use, for those tradition-bound Jews who tended to cluster together. About half of the Orthodox lived in the Park Heights corridor, while another quarter resided in the adjacent Mount Washington and Greenspring neighborhoods.

Commentators tended to highlight one aspect of Orthodox Jewish life in Baltimore: Ner Israel, located somewhat apart from the major Orthodox drag, on Mount Wilson Lane on the western edge of Pikesville. "Families move here so their sons can attend the yeshivah," explained reporters. "Many graduates settle here, and they in turn establish roots and raise large families here."[32] Large families, indeed. Baltimore's Jews enrolled about three thousand girls and boys in Jewish day schools. Most of these children attended institutions like Ner Israel High School, Talmudical Academy, and Torah Institute (for boys), and Bais Yaakov (for girls). In their homes and in their schools, these youngsters were reared to avoid American culture. One woman ensconced in the Ner Israel community confessed that, in the late 1980s, she had "borrowed a TV a few years ago and [her] kids covered their eyes when a lingerie commercial came on," in line with the Orthodox Right's trend toward insularism in the final decades of the century. "As for films, the entertainment is not worth the price of my hearing certain words," she explained. All of this was summed up by Neuberger: "In a society where drugs and teenage pregnancies are rampant, to create an island where all this is taboo is an extraordinary happening."[33]

## Modern Orthodox Revivalism

In November 1989 thirteen young couples—most in their early thirties—met to discuss school options for their small children. Roslyn (Roz) and Aaron Goldberg led the grassroots endeavor. The Goldbergs were emblematic of the general and growing cohort that fashioned Yeshivat Rambam and its Modern Orthodox ideology. Both were professionals, an audiologist and physician, respectively. Nearly all of this group held graduate or professional degrees. They also represented a curious confluence of Baltimore natives and newcomers. A Baltimorean, Aaron had graduated from the Talmudical Academy in 1975 and gained much from his education there. Yet he was more than a little chagrined by the school's "move to the right." For him, Rambam was a corrective. Roz hailed from Chicago. There, schools like Hillel Torah and

Ida Crown Jewish Academy bred an "intellectually competitive" atmosphere, and embraced Jewish and non-Jewish knowledge, available to girls and boys.[34] That was proof enough for her that Modern Orthodox Judaism could be a viable, authentic expression in Baltimore. She and other newcomers to the city, claimed Goldberg, "couldn't understand why there wasn't [this type of Modern Orthodox] school here."[35] Her Windy City upbringing convinced Goldberg that nearby Beth Tfiloh was not acceptable to her Modern Orthodox sensibilities. In the mid-1980s Orthodox accommodationists at Beth Tfiloh Congregation launched a high school: a pluralistic "community school" that catered to Orthodox Jews but primarily recruited from non-Orthodox homes. There was a push early on to develop the Beth Tfiloh high school more narrowly as an Orthodox day school, but the effort was thwarted. The close mingling with other sectors of the Jewish enclave was too thorny for many among the more moderate sort of Orthodox Jews in Baltimore.[36]

This sort of frustration-cum-proactiveness was symbolic of that important youth-revivalist trend within American Jewish history. Back in the 1960s YU's Mighty Mites were part of this animated Modern Orthodox spirit. Two decades later the same youthful religious enthusiasm emerged in Baltimore in response to the more-powerful-than-ever Orthodox Right.[37] Before this effort other Orthodox Jews had expressed frustration but elected to send their children to the Hebrew Academy in Silver Spring, a Washington, DC, suburb some forty-five minutes away from Baltimore. These families probably agreed with the assessment of one disenchanted Orthodox Baltimorean who edited the local Jewish paper. He explained the religious disorientation that occurred from moving from the Modern Orthodoxy of Teaneck, New Jersey, to Baltimore:

> Then I moved to Baltimore, 18 years ago, and, as I sometimes tell people, only half in jest, the closest form of Orthodox I was perceived of here was Greek Orthodox.
>
> That's because the standard of Orthodoxy in this community is not Yeshiva University but rather Ner Israel Rabbinical College, one of the world's largest and most respected yeshivas, and a bastion in its own right of the Agudath Israel movement.
>
> That movement puts a premium on a yeshiva education, is generally passive when it comes to the State of Israel, maintains a tradi-

tional view of women's roles and is distrustful of modernity, including secular universities.[38]

In 1991 a busload of more than thirty Baltimore children—most of them Beth Tfiloh defectors—trekked to relatively nearby Silver Spring.[39] Two years earlier one couple had migrated south from New York so that the husband might pursue a fellowship in medicine. Their eldest child was one of those Silver Spring commuters. Not at all happy about the schooling conditions in Baltimore, the Spieglers planned to relocate to the Washington, DC, area if a Baltimore school could not materialize.[40] To do this the young Modern Orthodox revivalists needed to break some long-held local rules.

Lay leaders took up the cause, because the Modern Orthodox rabbinic elites would not. Baltimore's polarizing religious character did not bode well for Orthodox moderates who felt obligated to defer to the Orthodox Right. For example, few Orthodox rabbis participated in interdenominational organizations. Different from other Orthodox communities—particularly those beyond New York—Baltimore's Orthodox rabbis were loath to act out "against the Orthodox doctrine to be a member of a body that is steering the public away from true religion."[41] In the late-1980s a "centrist-leaning" Orthodox rabbi admitted that he and his colleagues oftentimes "require legitimacy from Ner Israel" and "constantly look over their shoulders" for reassurance from the Orthodox Right. "The yeshiva," offered another likeminded clergyman, "keeps everyone in check."[42] Those who disobeyed faced considerable consequences.

Rambam's lay founders showed little compunction about following these ecclesiastical guidelines. It was altogether possible that more than a few of them were plainly unaware of Baltimore's conservative religious standards. About half of the board of trustees had moved to Baltimore in the 1980s. Despite local expectations, the group did not include a single rabbi within its ranks.[43] The Modern Orthodox revivalists also trumpeted a more eclectic set of values than the lion's share of Baltimore's Orthodox. In the earliest stages of the school's development, its organizers felt compelled to justify the authenticity of their enterprise, that it was consonant with the American Orthodox ideologies of Yeshiva University. The Modern Orthodox flagship guided the Goldbergs and the other lay organizers. The day school's leaders also connected with the heads of two recent school startups in Toronto (Yeshivat Or Chaim and Ulpanat Orot) and one in Cleveland (Bet Sefer Mizrachi).[44] These

The earliest photograph of Yeshiva Rambam students was shot in September 1990, before the school secured a rental space at Ner Tamid Greenspring Valley Congregation. (Photo by Norbert Bertling/Courtesy of the *Baltimore Jewish Times*)

centrist schools inspired a mission that advocated "religious Zionism, a synthesis of Torah and Halachah with the secular world, and community involvement provided within a warm, nurturing environment where Halachah is the ultimate guide and the practice of Orthodoxy permeates."[45] In contrast the head of Baltimore's all-boys school described Talmudical Academy as "neutral on Zionism," and that "families may handle the subject as they wish."[46] One longtime Baltimorean opined that "the only hope for religious Zionists in this city is to have a school that supports Zionism and a love of Israel."[47]

To achieve educational equity between girls and boys, Yeshivat Rambam also promoted limited coeducation. In its initial formulation the school was supposed to mix girls and boys until fifth grade. From sixth grade onward Rambam anticipated that it would separate the sexes in Jewish classes.[48] Save for Beth Tfiloh, Baltimore's Orthodox day schools were either all male or all female. Beth Tfiloh hosted mixed dances and other close-quarters coed programs, something that scored poorly on the Modern Orthodox authenticity meter in those days. With more than a modicum of intended prudishness, Rambam wanted no part in the latter sort of activities, which promoted a level of physical intimacy the school considered a violation of traditional Jewish practice.

Rambam also embraced female leadership. Roz Goldberg assumed the presidency and led a cohort of four other male board officers. Even more off the Baltimore pace, Rambam tapped Dr. Rita Shloush as its founding principal. A half-generation older than her lay leaders—she was forty—Shloush was the only female among a pool of twenty candidates.[49] Her relative youth, PhD, and staunch Zionism endeared her to the Baltimore group. Shloush was also armed with considerable experience and polish. The outgoing interim headmaster of Atlanta's Greenfield Hebrew Academy boasted eighteen years of educational service and a sophisticated professionalism that blended well with Shloush's "bubbly, girlish charm."[50] Nonetheless the new principal was not a rabbi, nor was she a man. This was, therefore, entirely out of character in a town where even the girls' school was directed by a male principal.[51]

All of this resonated with the wave of young Orthodox moderates who, for some reason or another, found themselves in Baltimore:

> Dr. Aaron Tokayer and his wife Reva represent the new breed of young couples moving to town, particularly from the New York area, with a Yeshiva University philosophy of centrist Orthodoxy. They have lived in Baltimore a year and the oldest of their three children is only five. Dr. Tokayer said he and his wife found a "void" when they explored the existing day schools.[52]

More parents agreed. A series of focus groups and parlor meetings evolved into more elaborate recruitment gatherings. Numbers were critical, but in these early stages Yeshivat Rambam aspired to serve as a wedge school intended to fit between Beth Tfiloh and the Orthodox Right's schools, catering to a modest cluster of Modern Orthodox families who sought a vibrant space between the two poles of Baltimore Orthodox Judaism. All told fifty-five students enrolled in September 1991, enough to populate classes from kindergarten to third grade. The plan was to increase one grade level each year. Careful to remain understated, Rambam secured a few classrooms in the facilities of Ner Tamid Greenspring Valley Congregation. The school rented the synagogue space since it was affordable, but it certainly helped that it was also beyond the immediate detection of the Orthodox Right and its Park Heights enclave.

To accomplish all this, the school needed to raise $300,000. Most of these funds were required to guarantee salaries for Shloush and eight teachers. Baltimore's Jewish federation offered some financial support, but the bulk was handled by parents and grandparents. In addition the middle-class parent body—composed of professionals, not businesspeople—managed to afford the $4,000 tuition price tag.[53] Somehow all this worked out. "We're meeting with success," Roz Goldberg explained, "because we're not only appealing to potential parents for the school, but to everyone in the community who believes that a school like Yeshivat Rambam is a necessity for the Baltimore Jewish community."[54]

## The Rise

In October 1991 Yeshivat Rambam held its first annual banquet fundraiser.[55] A local reporter noted several details of the dinner but dedicated more lines to the student choir, "dressed in blue and white, march[ing] down the center aisle singing their hearts out."[56] Most memorable was the debut of "Rambam Family Tree," a song adapted from Tom Chapin's popular 1988 song of a similar name. Singalongs and other wholesome public relations were standard fare in Yeshivat Rambam's early goings.[57] Moreover the school song subtly reinforced the school's pride in standing for a brand of Orthodox Judaism that migrated to Baltimore from other locales and stood apart from the indigenous religious attitude:

> Yes, we came from many places
> Yet, we see so many traces
> Of all the love and learning
> Handed down *mi-dor li-dor.*
> You've given us a new school
> Where Torah is the first rule
> We will fulfill the promise
> And go on to do much more.[58]

Communal support manifested itself in numbers. In 1992 Rambam added a fourth grade. This, and a few more children to increase the ranks of the other grades, doubled the school's size to about 120 students (educated by 16 full- and part-time teachers).[59] The lay leaders had much to do with the growth. "There is a tremendous amount of parental involvement at the school," said Goldberg, to explain Rambam's early success and financial fortitude. Routinely parents drove and chaperoned field trips, hosted fundraising events, and handled some custodial labors.[60] Two years later Rambam boasted an enrollment of 160 and anticipated that it would reach the 200-student mark in the following year.[61]

Much had changed since Rambam first took shape. With a touch of over-statement, the local Jewish press described Baltimore in messianic terms as a "promised land" for Modern Orthodox Jews. It represented a confluence of affordability and ideology. Unhappy with the schooling options in St. Louis, one physician turned down a high-paying position in Chicago for a more modest salary at Johns Hopkins so that his children would attend Yeshivat Rambam.[62] Young families were drawn to Rambam, in large part due to the school's knack for public relations. Often the local press—Jewish and otherwise—promoted the young students' involvement in federation fundraisers, art contests, international Zionist competitions, and the PTA's public lectures and forums. Rambam presented itself as fostering a nurturing environment, and as a school that aspired toward professional and academic excellence to boot. Teachers played catch with students during recess, and administrators formed relationships with Johns Hopkins University and other top intellectual centers. The children eagerly arrived at school each morning, and when they could not, offered Shloush, "parents keep telling me how much students hate to miss school."[63]

Families also appreciated the Modern Orthodox educational program. As the school matured and grades advanced, Rambam separated boys and girls for Jewish classes from sixth grade onward, just as it had envisioned at its inception. In time the school held student-led dramatic performances, formed sports teams, and launched other extracurricular programs. The substance of these classes and activities probably did not deviate too much from the local alternative schooling options to the "right" or the "left." The Modern Orthodox school distinguished itself in other ways. For instance, Rambam made much ado over Israel Independence Day, with daylong programs and

In 1995 the ambitious leaders of Yeshivat Rambam purchased the Har Sinai Congregation synagogue building
and seventeen-acre campus. (Avraham Bank)

festivities. Much momentum was derived from Rambam's Zionist agenda. On
one notable occasion Dr. Shloush's husband, Rabbi Eliahu Shloush, arranged
for the Ashkenazic chief rabbi of Israel to take a "diplomatic detour" to the
Upper Park Heights home of Rambam parents for a public lecture, prior to his
meeting with President George Bush in nearby Washington, DC.[64] In addition
the school featured a very strong community-service component. Finally, its
leaders tried their best to be avant-garde, joining organizations like Jewish
Electronic Networking at the start of the digital age.

In short order the school outgrew its rented space. In 1995 Rambam
agreed to purchase Har Sinai Congregation's capacious campus for four
million dollars. Much too large for its student population, the new facility
was intended to accommodate anticipated growth. The acquisition symbolized an important change in perspective. Once viewed as a modest attempt
to create a wedge school for a subgroup of Baltimore's Orthodox Jews, the
forward-thinking Yeshivat Rambam now aspired to develop into a much more
integral institution that carried the potential to become a "major force in both
moderating and modifying our Baltimore Orthodox community."[65] The aim
of the school accordingly underwent some considerable degree of change.
Not just a wedge school, Rambam envisioned itself as the flagship of a more
solidified Modern Orthodoxy in Baltimore. Significantly, the purchase moved
the school from the more innocuous Greenspring area to the entrenched Park
Heights neighborhood, in the heart of Baltimore's Orthodox community. It

was therefore positioned as a more apparent challenge to the Orthodox status quo.[66] A few years after acquiring the real estate, the chairman of the school's board looked forward to cultivating a "community institution."[67]

In 1997 Rambam announced the opening of a high school.[68] The decision to advance into the secondary-school ranks was not without concern. Some lay leaders advised against it, fearing that the costs of more specialized courses in these advanced grades was too much for the young school to absorb. Others, mostly from outside Rambam's circle, believed that the values the school sought to impact could be properly instilled in the younger grades and that its students could then, with appropriate religious accommodations, find a place in other local schools.[69] Each time Rambam's young lay leaders turned down these offers, particularly any and all attempts to "broker a combination of Yeshivat Rambam's High School and the Beth Tfiloh Community High School." For the Rambam leadership theirs was "not simply a Jewish day school with a Judaic and secular curriculum that can be accommodated." Rather Rambam was a "way of life."[70] It was especially frustrating to these individuals to listen to appeals for consolidation because their school was "redundant," a term they interpreted as less than necessary. In one communication a lay leader explained that "Yeshivat Rambam, as you know, satisfied a need and established its place among the Jewish day schools in Baltimore as providing a centrist Orthodox education, which we, our parent body and supporters recognize as a necessary institution. We would obviously take issue with the notion that it is a redundant institution."[71]

The high school went on as planned, but not without considerable attrition. To be sure the excitement for the growth was noticeable, even to casual observers. "The enthusiasm and spiraling enrollment of this young dynamic orthodox day school, excelling in high ideals for all students," reported a local newspaper, "was indeed impressive!"[72] Yet many of the founding families relented and enrolled their children in the proven Beth Tfiloh High School. Amid all this, in October 1998, Roz Goldberg announced that she would step down as president, to be replaced by Harry Kozlovsky.[73] Nonetheless the school moved forward, though for a time weakened by the shakeups in leadership and learners.

Rambam persevered, recognizing that it still required affiliations and partnerships to lend the school legitimacy. The school obtained dual-accreditation from Middle States Association of Colleges and Schools and the statewide

Association of Independent Schools of Maryland. Just two other private schools in the area boasted these credentials.[74] Later the school joined with YU and other likeminded day schools to form the short-lived Association of Modern Orthodox Day Schools and Yeshiva High Schools. In New York, some two hundred miles from his native Baltimore, new president Harry Kozlovsky told the delegates at the conference that in their presence he did not feel so "lonely."[75]

Individual accolades also helped. A goodly number of Rambam graduates enrolled in YU, but another portion matriculated into leading universities. Its students outpaced peers at much larger schools on advanced-placement examinations and other metrics. In November 2000 Rita Shloush became the first woman to receive the coveted Jerusalem Prize for Educational Excellence.[76] Along with the students and young lay leaders who supported the school, Shloush was the most recognizable figure in the Rambam family. The school carefully consulted a few rabbinic leaders and employed rabbis to teach some of its Jewish studies classes, especially for the older students. Still, that Rambam's head of school was female remained a major statement in a male-dominated Orthodox community.[77] Shloush's award, then, was an important source of legitimization, even after ten years of growth. Five years later the US Department of Education ranked Rambam among the fifty best private schools in the nation. Shloush described the accolade as an "affirmation that we are reaching success and striving for excellence." The founding principal of a now four-hundred-student day school recalled that Rambam was "created to fill a niche in the community, and we're accomplishing that. When someone walks into our building, they can feel the pulse of the school."[78] All the happy commotion surrounding Rambam, it was believed, lent the school and its community ample amounts of authenticity currency on the Jewish and American scenes.

## The Challenges

Much less detectable, though, were significant internal and external challenges that threatened the school. None by itself was insurmountable. Taken together though, these forces helped decide the ongoing tug-of-war between the Modern Orthodox revivalists and Baltimore's dominant conservative Orthodox culture. In December 2001 sixty-one members of the Rambam choir were slated to perform at the annual Jewish Food & Life Expo. The choir had become Rambam's poster children, ambassadors to all sectors of the local Jewish community. It was therefore an all-too-familiar sight to see the elementary school students in their tucked-in red polo shirts harmonizing a set of traditional, playful, and Zionistic songs. However, the invitation to perform at the Ner Israel–controlled Etz Chaim Center for Jewish Studies event was something new—and exciting. But then it was cancelled. Rabbi Heinemann ruled that the youngsters were subject to the same proscription against female public singing to which adults were obligated according to Jewish law.[79] "If it's wrong for older people to [sing together], then it's wrong for younger people to do it," explained Heinemann. "It may be that [Yeshivat Rambam's] rabbinic guidance allows the mixed choirs, but our tradition is that we do not allow it."[80] The rabbinic ruling was a blow to morale and the school's tentative hold on religious authenticity. "I feel a little disappointed about it, and we'd been practicing for a long time," said one eight-year-old girl. To assuage those hurt feelings, the principal wrote to parents, explaining that "our choir performances always adhere to recognized halachic standards and are in keeping with our school's ideology." Yet Heinemann's decision reminded Baltimore's Modern Orthodox that it was still far from the dominant local position.[81]

In fact several forces did—or should have—indicated to Rambam's leaders that their institution still stood on a most precarious foundation. First, the Modern Orthodox planks to which Yeshivat Rambam subscribed were far from steady in the late 1980s and 1990s. Time and again Shloush and lay leaders invoked Yeshiva University's Torah u-Madda philosophy—a synthesis of Jewish and Western wisdom—and the scholars who scaffolded that point of view.[82] But Modern Orthodox Judaism and its flagship school were in flux from the moment Rambam took off. YU was "under siege." Members of the rabbinical faculty, claimed students, decried President Norman Lamm and his Torah u-Madda ideology as "treif," or unkosher.[83] This of course was the same Rabbi Lamm who had led the Jewish Center in New York City and helped inspire that earlier revival of American Orthodoxy. Hardly the most militant rabbis in YU's ranks, several faculty members attempted to convince the Baltimore school to separate boys and girls for all subjects, a more extreme position than the one its founders had considered at the outset.[84] A panel of three leading YU rabbis—Yosef Blau, Yaakov Neuburger, and Mordechai Willig—responded that "in principle, gender separation is recommended at grade 5 for

both Jewish and general studies subjects."[85] The school did not heed the rec-
ommendation until much later, and for altogether different reasons. Rambam
continued to champion a commitment to a form of coeducation that ensured
"equal access to Judaism for girls," a Modern Orthodox vision that they hoped
still retained a good amount of religious currency. However, without a firm
ideological center to which to tether itself, Rambam and Baltimore's Modern
Orthodox community lacked much-needed support.

Second, the procurement of the Har Sinai building exposed crucial financial insecurities.[86] In its earliest years as a wedge school, Rambam managed
with a million-dollar budget that paid for rent, educational resources, two
administrators, and twenty-three full- and part-time teachers. Tuitions covered about 80 percent of these costs, while the rest was drawn from modest
fundraising and funds from the local Jewish federation. The move to a larger
facility represented the school's evolution into a community school, intended
to cultivate Modern Orthodoxy in Baltimore rather than to just sustain it.
Upon the purchase of the new building, Rambam engaged in a massive
four-million-dollar fundraising campaign. This proved far too burdensome
for the middle-class professionals who comprised the Rambam constituency,
as did the effort to reach a six-hundred-student enrollment goal. The federation offered some help but not nearly enough to achieve financial solvency.[87]

Third, Rambam struggled to develop the next generation of lay leaders.
Throughout its lifespan, the founding lay members tended to the many needs
of the school, a matter that took a toll on Rambam's revivalist spirits. No
doubt part of the trouble was the limitation of Modern Orthodox growth
within Baltimore's Orthodox Right stronghold. Another was this community's attrition due to migration to Israel, catalyzed in some measure by the
school's strong Zionism.[88] In the 1990s it was common for Rambam to "lose"
a dozen students to *aliyah* in a given year. In May 2000 a Baltimore Jewish
weekly featured an *aliyah*-bound family that credited its impending journey
to their Modern Orthodox community and the school that had nurtured its
children in a Zionist milieu. It certainly helped that Joyce and Richard Levitas
had the support of more than a dozen other Orthodox Baltimoreans who had
settled in Israel, and that their ten-year-old, Tali, would reunite with her "best
friend" who, together with her family, had several years earlier departed Baltimore and Yeshivat Rambam for Israel.[89] In a small but nonetheless significant way, the Zionist emigration from Baltimore withdrew some of the most

committed families from the Rambam constellation. All told these forces exposed crucial weaknesses in the Rambam enterprise.

## The Fall

In March 2008 Rambam announced that it planned to transition to all single-sex classes. The decision was motivated in part by the findings of a consultant that there were four hundred students whose families "may have enrolled at Yeshivat Rambam, had the school been single-sex." Fewer and fewer Orthodox Jews now viewed Modern Orthodoxy's planks as religiously authentic. They were quite taken by the more powerful and indigenous Orthodox Right. From 1999 to 2010 the number of Orthodox households in Baltimore spiked from six thousand to ten thousand. However, most of these families preferred a more rigid brand of Jewish education than Rambam offered.[90] School leaders reckoned that they had no choice. The cost of operating a large campus was too much. The deficits ran too deep. "We haven't changed our philosophy," defended Seth Rotenberg, who had recently assumed the presidency after Harry Kozlovsky stepped down from the helm. "We plan to keep our Zionist philosophy and our ability to recognize God in a secular world."[91] Student leaders voiced displeasure but understood that compromise was necessary in a school that billed itself as "one big family."[92]

Concomitantly Rambam had transitioned from a young and revivalist form of leadership to a rabbinic kind that was in concert with Baltimore's religious environment. Later in 2009 the school lost its matriarch. Rita Shloush retired as head of school. In a letter addressed to the school's parent body, Shloush offered a reflection on Rambam's accomplishments and then explained that "now that Yeshivat Rambam is entering the age of adulthood, it is time for me to move on."[93] Adulthood meant a new leadership structure. On good terms Roz Goldberg and Harry Kozlovsky ceased active involvement, moves that represented an unraveling of the tight original leadership circle. After a short stint at the helm, Rotenberg also resigned as the school's third president. He passed the reins to a final group of Rambam's founders to help lead the way. In addition Rambam tapped Rabbi Shmuel Silber to serve as the school's rabbinic head.[94] Silber was new to Baltimore and more sympathetic to the Orthodox Right than the few rabbis who had encouraged Rambam's founders.[95] Under his leadership at Rambam, the school mandated a far stricter dress code and more closely matched the image—particularly in the case of female students—of the youngsters who attended Baltimore's more religiously conservative Orthodox schools. In fact girls and boys were instructed to use separate staircases while shuttling from classroom to classroom. Silber's designation as a rabbinic leader stood in marked contrast to the lay-driven beginnings of Yeshivat Rambam and in better line with the "rightists" Rambam sought to attract.

The plan did not work. Despite these modifications Rambam was still viewed as a Modern Orthodox school that featured aspects—Religious Zionism, for example—which rendered it inauthentic to the more religiously conservative population of Baltimore's Orthodox community. A clever attempt to swap campuses with a growing all-girls school to downgrade operational expenses also proved insufficient.[96] Then America's "Great Recession" exposed the school's financial shortcomings. In January 2011 school leaders announced that it would close its too-costly high school.[97] Rambam's constituency grieved over the decision to reduce its educational scope. This group recognized that it was always the school's goal to support a Modern Orthodox "idea," an environment that would nurture its youth throughout childhood and adolescence. This is how one recent graduate expressed her dismay:

> I am a 2006 Yeshivat Rambam of Baltimore High School graduate. It has been almost five years since I graduated but I will wear my Red Storm pin on my bag for as long as I can, as I struggle with the closing of my high school. It is very difficult to sit in classes in my master's program at Yeshiva University pondering the future of Jewish education while the place that imbued me with so much of who I am today prepares to close its high school, leaving my 13-year old sister and so many others to search for a new place to stand.[98]

Several months later it became all-too-apparent that institutional amputations could not remedy the financial trauma. In May the school decided to close. Observers stressed that "it is no exaggeration that, for the families and anyone connected to Yeshivat Rambam, the earth moved this week."[99] The announcement represented more than the end of a school. For the self-appointed prognosticators, the Modern Orthodoxy in Baltimore was "done." One local disenchanted Modern Orthodox rabbi interpreted the changing climate as reason enough to retire, sensing that his mission and ideology in Baltimore were severely "diminished."[100] The community was no longer a magnet for middle-of-the-road Orthodox families. "Many families have already left Baltimore or plan on doing so in the near future," averred one Rambam parent. "We have already heard of young families who originally intended to move here now changing their plans and looking for alternative communities. Once an attractive option, Baltimore will cease to be on the list of young professionals seeking a warm, thriving community that approximates their beliefs."[101] Shortly thereafter a new generation of Modern Orthodox revivalists indicated their intention to open a replacement school. Far less ambitious and not jaded by the demise of its predecessor, Ohr Chadash (literally, "New Light") rescued many orphaned day school students.[102]

The elegies that emanated from the communal mourning struck a common chord. The women and men, girls and boys, who counted themselves part of a bygone Rambam family shared a sentiment of surrender. They felt overpowered by the crush of the Orthodox Right and a variety of other forces that weighed on their youthful, Camelot-like Modern Orthodox mission. Now living in Israel, Roz Goldberg offered her pithy perspective: "It was more than a school. It was a philosophy that permeated so many of our lives. We worked very hard to create those feelings, and it was difficult. But today when you look at the kids who came out of Rambam, so many found their education beneficial." She understood that Yeshivat Rambam fired the Modern Orthodox impulses of more than just its students and graduates. "I think the parents of Rambam loved it," said Goldberg.[103] In the end the school could not remain rooted in the local religiously inhospitable soil. The local, deep-rooted religious ethos supported a clericalism that did not redound to the Modern Orthodox mission or its values. Yeshivat Rambam, then, was an "idea" that emerged and vanished in a curious moment and in a particular location, amid competing impulses within American Orthodoxy.

# PART 3

# PROTECTING ORTHODOX MALE SPACE

# CHAPTER 7

# FINDING A *FRUM* FORM OF FRATERNIZING AND THE DYNAMICS OF ORTHODOX MASCULINITY

IN 1935 YESHIVA COLLEGE students arranged a dance at the Peter Stuyvesant Hotel on New York's Upper West Side. It was a poorly attended affair, the first and last of its kind.[1] The dance was very much out of character for the all-male Orthodox school. It was not that Yeshiva men were unaccustomed to dancing and other activities that at this time were token expressions of virility and boyishness. To the contrary, the YC undergraduates socialized with their girlfriends at mixers held in Young Israel synagogues, such as the annual "Matzo Fund Dance."[2] Likewise it was well known that their counterparts at Hebrew Theological College in Chicago enjoyed youthful "American traditions" like weekend dances.[3] In this respect these Orthodox young people honored Jewish law's proscription against physical contact between unmarried women and men in the breach.[4] It was not particularly pious, but it was a practice that many Orthodox Jews lived with. As one writer once remarked, "Social dancing represents Young Israel's only compromise with orthodox Judaism."[5]

Yet it was quite another thing for Yeshiva College to sponsor the event, even if it was quite a distance away from the Upper Manhattan campus. Orthodox interpretation of Halakhah prohibits physical contact between women and men before marriage. The Orthodox school championed fidelity to Jewish law, to engender a *frum*, or religiously observant, atmosphere. It could ill afford this sort of institutional laxity while vigilant European-trained rabbis watched, ready to pounce on Yeshiva's perceived religious shortcomings. Yeshiva replaced the underattended dance with an on-campus evening social that excluded dancing but featured entertainment and all the trappings needed for young Orthodox women and men to mingle like other American college students. For decades the annual affair betokened an enduring tension at the Orthodox school. To be sure the college's relative openness to the liberal arts made it distinct from other *yeshivot* in the United States.[6] But other aspects, the college hoped, would parallel traditional types of Jewish education. For instance, YC aspired to nurture the very same cultural forces inherent in all-male Orthodox schools of higher Jewish learning. Back in Lithuania and other parts of Eastern Europe, just a small minority of Jewish men possessed the background and inclination to study Talmud.[7] It takes years to master and develop the stamina to study these folios of tersely written, punctuationless Judeo-Aramaic. Its topics are litigious yet most rewarding to a relatively small group of scholars and students of Jewish torts, ritual purity, lifecycles, and temple sacrifices. Still, the idealized image of pale and frail Torah scholars migrated to the United States and made a deep impression.[8] The perseverance and diligence required to master these texts represented a non-negotiable feature of Orthodox masculinity, as was obedience, inculcated by older male teachers who possessed Torah knowledge.[9] The yeshiva was intended as a male space to incubate this paradigm. The presence of women at an all-male yeshiva campus, therefore, represented an interruption in the cultivation of this kind of Orthodox maleness.

The experience at Yeshiva College aligns with the definition of masculinity offered by the sociologist Michael Kimmel. To him maleness is much more than the body. It stands for all the interactions relating to male culture, especially, wrote Kimmel, how protectors of manhood have sought to keep others from "dominating" men and "infiltrating" male spaces.[10] In the post–World War II period, religious leaders—especially tradition-bound Protestants—espoused a virile and manly type of rhetoric to invigorate their listeners and stomp out the "soft" Communist attitudes deemed so repugnant during the Cold War.[11] For example, Reverend Billy Graham preached an image of Jesus as "every inch a 'He-man.'" Hoping to toughen up the American man with certain images of masculinity, Graham contended that "Christ was probably the strongest man physically that ever lived. He could have been a star athlete on any team. He was a real man with His strong shoulders [and] squarish jaw."[12] All in all, sermonized America's most well-known minister, the "virtues of manhood are raised to the highest in the life of one who is surrendered to Christ."[13]

Other factors besides Cold War politics mediated the turn toward a more aggressive form of masculinity.[14] Graham and likeminded ministers who adopted this sometimes crude language intended to fortify the boundaries of an under-siege male religious space by resisting others—women, but also different "kinds" of men, usually defined by class or race—who sought to infiltrate it. Like Orthodox Jews, some conservative religionists warned that openness to certain mild feminist causes was bound to lead to a cascading "slippery slope" away from "Christian belief."[15] The revival of the strenuous masculine Christian culture so popular around the turn of the twentieth century also hailed family values and traditional gender roles for men and women—primarily, "earners" and "homemakers," respectively. Hostilities toward feminism were therefore animated by a dual concern for status-quo religion and a feeling that men's spaces were under siege. Perhaps the most colorful example is the case of the Promise Keepers, an Evangelical organization founded by a college football coach in 1990. The group is determined to resist changes to "sacred male space" but is often interpreted as militantly antifeminist.[16] Promise Keepers' programs and literary output intend to rally men to protect the values linked to "Biblical Manhood," like fatherhood and chastity. The Promise Keepers therefore furnished exclusively male spaces for their followers out of fear that feminism and other egalitarian forces threatened to corrupt portions and qualities of religion they maintained as sacred.

For the Orthodox, masculine culture manifested itself in traditionally male spaces. Feminism, then, was not merely a case of religious neophobia and proverbial "slippery slopes." Orthodox men interpreted feminism and a changing American milieu as affronts to these realms and became determined to defend them. The final chapters of this book examine these arenas—the yeshiva and synagogue, in particular—to understand Orthodox Judaism's negotiation with changing notions of gender in American life and its own engagement with a reawakened, religiously conscious masculine spirit in the United States. These webs of encounters and experiences helped bring about considerable tension on the path toward religious authenticity. The need for gender isolation confounded many generations of Yeshiva College students who desired the experiences available to students at other American colleges, where it was far more typical for undergraduates to mix and mingle. Trying his best to put his finger on the problem, one Yeshiva College student affirmed that the "issue of coeducation has always evoked more emotion than logic."[17]

The same was true at other faith-based colleges. On these campuses administrators and faculty leaders struggled to maintain social order and modesty. Conservative Christianity was not equipped with the legal-ritual formulations that proscribed many forms of physical coeducational inter-action. Still it shunned such behavior. Christian colleges were encouraged by a new spirit of "neo-orthodoxy" that had abandoned the manly styled YMCA and so-called muscular Christianity in favor of a less-fleshy, more God-centered faith.[18] Yet steps to curtail this behavior were met with resistance from undergraduates and complaints that college leaders were no longer in line with culturally approved conduct on campuses. Their protracted strug-gle to adapt their religious climate to American norms represents the uneasy challenges of calibrating authentic American religious expressions. For its part Yeshiva College charted its own unique path toward a reconciliation of this rather touchy subject. This chapter, then, explores the sometimes painful struggle of Orthodox Judaism to negotiate the tensions between the Ortho-dox male space and liberal American culture. The long-drawn-out tensions at Yeshiva College demonstrate the elusiveness of American authenticity and its mediating powers to reach a satisfying middle ground, especially when the experiences and episodes threatened the integrity of some of the most easily identifiable spatial structures of tradition-bound religion.

## Collegiate Manliness and Faith-Based Campuses

In 1928 President Bernard Revel founded Yeshiva College, encouraging stu-dents and faculty to participate in a creative blending of Judaism and liberal culture.[19] In the earliest years Revel was the most vocal and prominent voice on the value he described, somewhat nebulously, as "synthesis."[20] Time and again Revel defended his school's Orthodox character on the basis that leading scholars like Moses Maimonides had performed similar types of "harmoni-ous blending."[21] His students seized on Revel's words and conjured up more practical applications than philosophical ones. For these young men it was very important to find time to form athletic teams and debate clubs, establish student newspapers, and host socials. In these activities Yeshiva men con-ducted themselves with the heightened degree of reverence one might expect at a faith-based school as opposed to more liberal universities. The under-graduate newspaper, for example, did not often cross a line to rail against the administration, as their peers at nearby City College and Columbia were all too accustomed to do.[22]

Synthesis was far trickier when it came to establishing a set of rules for Orthodox young men and their female friends. Other Orthodox institutions faced the same challenge. In New York several Orthodox high schools "countenanced" the infusion of organized athletics on their premises—even if it broke up the long day of study—but their leaders drew a firm line when sporting events brought male students into contact with young women (as when cheerleaders were in attendance).[23] Yet it was not just the halakhic rules prohibiting physical contact that dictated this path. Orthodox Judaism's notion of masculinity was at odds with the general conception of maleness in the United States, perhaps even more than among its Protestant counterparts. The heroics of Orthodox bookishness—for that matter, American Jewry's "gentler, less aggressive manhood"—simply did not resonate with other men in the United States who felt tremendous pressure in the interwar years to prove they were not "weak" and incapable of providing for their families in a depressed economic climate.[24] President Charles Eliot of Harvard, for instance, told members of the New England Society that "nowadays a scholar is not a recluse, or a weakling incapable of the strenuous pursuits. . . . Not a bookworm," the Harvard man of the early twentieth century possessed a "strenuously tough and alert body."[25] Universities became arenas for young men to demonstrate that vigor, particularly on the dance floor—much to the chagrin of Christian clerics.[26] New rules of conduct trending across American college campuses allowed for this. For example, Columbia and Barnard Colleges lifted the ban on the turkey trot, and the administrations at the universities of Illinois, Wisconsin, and Iowa no longer prohibited the tango.[27] In these more relaxed and unsupervised social settings, young men sought to prove their manliness on the dance floor.[28]

Yeshiva College, more than most, struggled mightily with coed culture. But the Orthodox college was not alone in grappling with this kind of commotion. Other faith-based schools encountered conflict over courtship ethics, especially as the average age of the student body dropped to the early twenties.[29] In the 1930s the pressure placed on young people to mingle often caused a state of "pandemonium" at John Brown University in Arkansas.[30] Faith-based colleges could not adopt the loose supervision standards of nonreligious college campuses. This was one area—in addition to the study of science and evolution—where American religion could not accommodate modern impulses. In 1945 the heads of Bob Jones College in Tennessee boasted to their board members that "in eighteen years we have never sent home one girl in shame and disgrace to her mother."[31] Young women and men dated at the school, but they did so under the watch of scrupulous chaperones. To increase surveillance, Bob Jones encouraged students to take ample advantage of the official "date room."[32] In Boston, Gordon College maintained a looser stance on dating than John Brown but was still far more restrictive than other colleges. For example, Gordon mandated a curfew for female students. The young women who desired to stay out past 10:30 PM were required to sign a "social agreement." Late curfews were strictly enforced for dormitory residents, particularly after "College functions held on school nights."[33] The nondenominational Christian school also sought to better regulate relationships in their more advanced stages, using policy language that focused on the young man's (note the preponderance of the pronoun "his") behavior and requirements:

> Since Gordon College is co-educational in character, it is to be expected that student romances will not be entirely foreign to the life of the College. That abiding Christian friendships might be encouraged and temporary emotional excesses avoided, it is required that resident students shall not announce their engagements to one another during the school year and that a student who marries during his College course shall withdraw from school for at least a year. A Senior however, may announce his engagement during his last semester in the College, and Veterans may petition to be exempted from the general requirement concerning marriage if circumstances warrant.[34]

All told the leaders of these sorts of institutions were fearful of compromising their religious values on the altar of modern campus culture. For these schools, then, it was crucial to strike a balance between liberal education and conservative traditionalism, oftentimes erring on the side of the latter. More acutely, Yeshiva College's leaders worried about collegiate behavior on campus, but they grew even more nervous over protecting their male space. The masculine ideals valued at Yeshiva could not survive, its rabbinic heads believed, if its campus was pierced by the presence of young women.

# Class Nite and the Social Limits of a Once-a-Year Mixer

In March 1938 Yeshiva collegians figured out a solution to the vexing problem: Class Nite.[35] The once-a-year event, full of musical and dramatic productions, was a means to inject a "new and wholesome spirit." It also offered a chance for students at the all-male college to behave like other undergraduates and bring along their dates who, reportedly, made their presence known with their "embarrassing giggles."[36] The affair sold hundreds of tickets, always purchased in pairs. The 1940 Class Nite, for instance, drew a record 1,200 guests to the Yeshiva campus, while the college population numbered only 150 students.[37] Audiences enjoyed an original musical production performed by the Dramatics Society and four other class productions. A panel of faculty members served as judges and awarded prizes to the superior class skit.

The situation was far from remedied, however. For more than a decade, Yeshiva students and faculty fiercely debated the propriety of the coed event at a men's college. For their part student organizers branded Class Nite a harmless—or not-too-harmful—break from the most acceptable forms of Orthodox social norms. By and large students and faculty looked forward to Class Nite as a once-a-year respite from the usual Orthodox forms of male space.[38] For this reason, though, proper religious conduct at the mixer was not entirely out of mind. The administration and students demanded that all acts be conducted with proper religious reverence, and only a touch of subversiveness was tolerated. On one occasion students complained that a few Class Nite performances "proved to be in questionable good taste, at least for Yeshiva men, and reacted unfavorably with some members of the audience." All were well aware that similar sorts of productions "would have passed unnoticed in a presentation of the student body of almost any other college" but did not pass the requisite level of "dignity and responsibility" expected on Yeshiva's campus.[39]

Then it stopped. In 1944 the newly appointed president, Rabbi Samuel Belkin, shut down Class Nite. For him the social event was far too much. It broke too sharply from the daily routine of Orthodox all-male schools. Opposition ensued. Quick to invoke the legacy of the late Bernard Revel, student leaders protested that Belkin was guilty of an "abandonment of the ideal of synthesis, or at least an abandonment of it in that guise in which it has appeared since the foundation of the college." They demanded that Belkin reinstate Class Nite, or at least explain his transgression against the "synthesis ideal."[40] Belkin did just that. He told the undergraduate resistance that Class Nite was not an "activity revealing or reflecting the personality of the traditional Yeshiva man."[41] Belkin drew a distinction between the religious alchemy performed in the classroom and coed events. The former, he believed, just as his late predecessor had, did not undermine the religious integrity of his Orthodox school. Earlier iterations of tradition-abiding Jews had encouraged study of Jewish and non-Jewish texts. To his mind, though, there were no acceptable precedents to authenticate gender-mingling at an Orthodox yeshiva. In Belkin's view students were welcome to court young women off campus and attend mixers at more appropriate venues. However, warned Belkin, students could not host such affairs on campus, where they would be totally out of keeping with the masculine Orthodox culture that a traditional yeshiva aimed to promote.

Lingering anxieties festered and confused matters. In 1947 Belkin restored Class Nite in response to student disappointment that Yeshiva's head had failed to comprehend that so much of the collegiate experience hinged on the social and inseparable aspects of campus life. However, to protect the masculine yeshiva atmosphere, the event was moved to the cafeteria, out of sight of the nearby study hall. Students applauded the turnabout but were puzzled: "We can bring guests to mixers. But the search for synthesis, even in this case, still continues."[42] Then Belkin changed his mind again. He decreed that "shows, smokers, faculty mixers, or any other form of get-together are henceforth considered objectionable, if female guests or if the parents of the students are to be invited." In a bout of righteous indignation, student leaders dispatched a delegation to speak with the president. The students complained that YC undergraduates could not be told to lead their lives as a farce: maintaining connections to females outside of Yeshiva and then abandoning those relationships when stepping inside. Refusing to consider themselves "irresponsible" or "willful creators of dissent," the students called for the YC administration to recognize them as trustworthy "mature individuals" capable of being at the same time good Yeshiva men and socially modern gentlemen.[43] It worked, and Class Nite resumed.[44]

But coed mixer advocates failed to defeat the opposition altogether. In February 1950 YC student council president Henry Keller held a meeting in his dorm room to decide whether student government would sponsor Class Nite.[45] A Long Island native, Keller was a "very earnest student" with "lofty ambitions." A member of the French club and the debate team, this student leader was most "incline[d] scholastically to Talmud."[46] Keller represented a minority faction that deeply deplored fraternizing on campus grounds.[47] Before the vote Keller threatened to resign from his post if the event remained coed. As it turned out the zealous young man cast the deciding vote against an "open Class Nite." The matter did not end there, however. Under student protest, Keller agreed to a revote. In this second tallying student council decided 8–4 in favor of a social "with outside guests attending."[48] True to his word Keller promptly resigned, as the event was "out of keeping with the ideals and traditions of Torah-Judaism in general, and Yeshiva in particular."[49]

For a two-week period the students vociferously argued the merits of a coeducational social, "the like of which has rarely been seen at Yeshiva." The faculty also got involved. On one occasion Rabbi Joseph B. Soloveitchik and Rabbi Yeruchim Gorelick faced off outside the study hall. As one student recalled many years later, Soloveitchik took the side of those who wanted the affair, explaining that it was better for his students to meet eligible young women under the watchful eye of faculty chaperones.[50] It was not, he surmised, too much of a break from the masculine yeshiva environment. Soloveitchik did not feel that the social was tantamount to a forfeiture of Yeshiva's Orthodox character. In contrast the much more religiously rigid Gorelick condemned the event as scandalous and religiously inauthentic.[51] Most students aligned themselves with Soloveitchik and lamented Gorelick's position as "most depressing." In a final student-wide vote, Class Nite won by a tally of 156–43.[52] However, Class Nite was not held that year or ever again. Sensing the haunting tensions around campus, Belkin canceled the social. Students could no longer argue that Class Nite represented a once-a-year break from traditional yeshiva culture. Rather Class Nite had turned into a months-long distraction for students to debate the merits of American-style fraternizing instead of concentrating on their schoolwork and Talmud studies. The event had stretched well beyond its one-evening allowance and invaded the space and culture of Yeshiva College. The experiment, it seemed, had failed.

# The "Sexual Revolution" and the Preservation of Orthodox Male Space

In December 1960 the Yeshiva College student newspaper polled students on their religious punctiliousness. Sixty percent of those surveyed admitted—despite Jewish law's proscription against it—to having regular "physical contact with girls." In response to the startling figure, the editors lamented that a "majority of the Yeshiva boys apparently have not the slightest appreciation of what Orthodox Judaism fully entails."[53] The exposé disrupted a decade-long agreement, however unofficial, to avoid the subject on Yeshiva's campus. Perhaps this was unavoidable. Back in the 1940s YC graduated about sixty to seventy students per year. In the mid-1950s the student population began to swell. The numbers spiked well into the hundreds, as young men attempted to find religious exemptions to dodge the draft during the Vietnam War and public school graduates expressed greater interest in Yeshiva.[54] Yeshiva's administration vowed that the admission of these students would not compromise the religious atmosphere at the school.[55] However, laxity was inevitable and apparent.[56] For example, students in the more religiously advanced programs urged the newcomers to keep away from a recently opened pool hall that threatened to exacerbate the general "apathy to the religious responsibilities which touches upon every aspect of student life both in and out of the university area."[57]

The changed atmosphere was not sudden. The "sexual revolution" of the 1960s was an outgrowth of cultural elements that had developed in previous decades. Yet it was in this period that campuses received oversized attention, forcing college leaders to react in kind.[58] In an earlier epoch the Orthodox had boasted of their community's controlled and measured sexual ethic.[59] The 1960s forced Orthodox leaders to assume a different posture, one that was far less tolerant. For example, the National Council of Young Israel, which had once countenanced certain "suspect" behaviors (like social dancing), no longer believed this was acceptable, even if some congregations would not adhere to the new policy.[60] In one instance a rabbi issued a plea to members of Young Israel synagogues to reconsider the way young women and men met and mingled. The writer recommended discrete matchmaking, the kind practiced in a "few Chassidic communities," but not much else. He recognized just how unpopular his position would be among young people who enjoyed their "Saturday night movies" and other fun activities.[61]

Faith-based colleges shared a common concern over the changing sexual morality in the United States. These schools felt more empowered to take a firm stand in the name of "religion" during this postwar period of "Judeo-Christian America."[62] In Skokie, Illinois, Hebrew Theological College purchased a seventeen-acre suburban campus to house its separate men's and women's schools for the Orthodox Jews of Chicago. However, the administration halted plans to move female students to the campus after an uproar from rabbinic faculty members.[63] To counteract the increasingly sexualized atmosphere of the 1960s, Boston's Gordon College banned social dancing. The school's heads warned that any "violations involving dancing or the use of profane language will be referred for disciplinary actions."[64]

Students tended to follow the new rules imposed in school and at home, but with detectable discontent. One suitor wrote to his girlfriend at the Presbyterian-affiliated Hanover College in Indiana that he was "sorry to hear that your mother frowns on the hop."[65] Others were fed up that college campuses no longer seemed conducive to finding a mate. Consider the frustrated tone of an undergraduate letter-writer studying at the Presbyterian-based University of the Ozarks in Arkansas. She was more than a little perturbed that the only undergraduates who seemed to mingle with one another on campus were the so-called steadies. In her words:

This might as well be a non-coed school—as far as dates go anyway. . . . What is wrong with the girl-boy relationship at this college? Why is it that only a select few of the girls in Strong Hall are honored with dates, and most of these are steadies?

If the boys would get rid of the idea that we are snobs, and wouldn't date them even if we were asked, there might be a more pleasant relationship between the two sexes.

It's not that we're man-crazy, but it's just that college women expect to date SOME![66]

Surveillance was also reinforced on faith-based college campuses. More than before Christian colleges urged students to take advantage of the formal mixers and traditions that promoted religious values and chastity.[67] Some students took the formalism in stride and with a sense of humor. A coed at Brigham Young University related that the "most popular practice here at BYU is that if a guy kisses you on a date, you owe an ice cream cone to all your roommates."[68] But more often these events tended to exhaust students. "The biggest majority of us girls," offered one John Brown undergraduate, "would be satisfied to study with our guy in the library, go to church together, or just take a walk."[69] Another frustrated student queried an all-knowing undergraduate advice columnist to see if there was "any place on this campus where you can be alone? My boyfriend and I can't find any place to talk without having ten people around. He doesn't have a car and he's afraid to go into the graveyard after dark, so we can't even go there."[70] At Gordon the sexual tension and formal dating structure provoked the following editorial in the student newspaper:

> Several on the campus have voiced the opinion that the Gordon dating standard is rather immature. If a guy and girl should be seen on campus together twice within a twenty-four-hour period it seems to be taken for granted that they are going steady and ALL FELLOWS take note accordingly—no further comment necessary.[71]

In New York, Yeshiva College encountered the same religious current that sought to protect the campus from the spread of more sexually progressive forces. In their case Yeshiva collegians found increased resistance to any kind of coeducational program. The school imposed heftier dormitory supervision and placed more rules on social events. Yeshiva students reacted to the pressures placed on them to conform to standards which, they understood, were hardly in line with most other collegians. Some students were in favor of more conservative policies to regulate campus socializing. In 1965, for example, a student journalist expressed his disappointment with his peers who flagrantly disregarded Orthodox Judaism's restrictions on "premarital touching." On this the young writer sided with his equally frustrated teachers. "For those as yet ignorant of the matter" he volunteered Yeshiva's rabbinic faculty, who "would be more than willing to explain the details and implications of this law."[72]

Yeshiva leaders were therefore "all in" to defend its sacred male space. The most important factor that raised concern over coed mingling was the

Undergraduates from Yeshiva College and Stern College for Women chat on the men's campus in the 1960s. (Yeshiva University Archives, Public Relations Photo Events Collection)

formation of Stern College for Women. In 1954 Yeshiva University founded the all-women's school in Midtown Manhattan. Soon enough it became all too natural for young women and men enrolled in the same university to consider how they might more formally fraternize.[73] That many Stern College women had a considerable interest in seeing their YC counterparts was beyond question. The women's student newspaper ran a revealing headline that read: "28 Seniors Plan to Teach, Study and Marry."[74] In 1960 15 percent of Stern College students were either married or engaged, even though nearly two-thirds of the student body had not yet turned eighteen years old.[75] Eligible young Stern College undergraduates made the most of their access to YC men. To lampoon the situation, one Milwaukeean published a "recipe" for Yeshiva men to follow as they prepared for dating life:

> 1 lovely Stern maiden
> 1 pound of luck

1 pound of pluck

1 bucket of mathematical skill

1 good-natured dad

2 horsepower of hydraulic pressure

1 Cadillac convertible

2 "My Fair Lady" tickets.[76]

The response to this was twofold. A number of Yeshiva men shared these interests in mingling and had much to recommend to their female companions. One irritated Yeshiva collegian wrote a letter to the Stern College campus newspaper complaining that female students should be more punctilious in observing the "10-minute telephone rule." Referring to the limitations of the dormitory switchboard, this young man was frustrated by this "continuous obstacle." So "formidable" a hurdle, he conceded, "can cause one to lose interest."[77] Others were far less sanguine and redoubled their efforts to protect their uptown male space. Stern collegians, one YC undergraduate explained, attended the Purim holiday festivities on the men's campus, and "week after week they stuff our mailboxes with invitations to various social gatherings."[78] Like the earlier generation of Yeshiva students, this young man was troubled by the increased presence of women uptown and their interference with daily life on campus. Another student complained that "every sports event [is made] into a social." He pleaded with his fellow students to concentrate on their Talmud studies rather than the "number of Stern College students at a fencing match."[79] Others, however, labeled such students "fanatics."[80]

All this concerned the Yeshiva administration. But the school also understood that Stern College provided an outlet to divert coed mingling from their all-male campus to a more "appropriate" venue. It was a solution to preserve the character of that traditional male space. In line with other faith-based schools, Yeshiva monitored the mingling on the Stern College campus, but it did not need to ban it, as the school had done on the men's campus. After all, part of the Orthodox feminine culture was to prepare for marriage. The standards for gendered sites were not the same in Orthodox Judaism. Nonetheless, the sight of young women and men on an all-female Orthodox campus was, to some, jarring. It was peculiar, admitted one undergraduate, "to see boys walking around the school."[81] That changed. Yeshiva students inaugurated the Freshman-Junior Affair. With faculty chaperones to keep matters in order, YC juniors trekked downtown to Stern College to meet their freshmen dates for a "delightful evening" of coffee-sipping, cake-munching, and "lively Hebrew songs."[82] The social quickly became a "tradition" for students. For the young female freshmen, the affair exposed them to life as "college people" and "as cosmopolitan young ladies."[83] For the Yeshiva men, the supervised event protected the modesty of the undergraduate culture. Just as important, it preserved the cultivation of masculine behavior at Yeshiva College. For the Orthodox school, therefore, it made good sense that social events should take place on the women's campus in Midtown Manhattan, some 150 blocks from where Yeshiva men studied and learned in authentically Orthodox conditions.

## The Dean's Reception Affair

The Stern College campus did not solve matters. In February 1966 controversy over fraternization once again erupted at Yeshiva College, an affair that was remembered as "famous in Orthodox circles" for years to come. The commotion centered on the Dean's Reception, a scaled-down replacement for the erstwhile Class Nite social. Compared to other college campus events, the Dean's Reception was a "mild, drab affair, with nonalcoholic punch."[84] Despite the dearth of pomp and circumstance, Yeshiva College students looked forward to the Dean's Reception, describing it as the "social highlight of the year."[85] With significant reluctance, the YC student council canceled the event as a "favor" to Rabbi Soloveitchik, the most respected rabbinic figure on campus. The event had caused much consternation among students; "slander" and "warring" had spun discussion about the social out of control.[86]

More than a dozen years earlier, Soloveitchik had adopted a more relaxed stance toward these sorts of socials. Informed of his earlier position, some students wondered how "after 20 years the Rav suddenly awoke to the realization that a Dean's Reception is improper or out of place."[87] If Soloveitchik's position had changed, so had the conditions at Yeshiva College. By the 1960s the student profile at Yeshiva was more complex. Whereas Soloveitchik had once thought it helpful for young women and men to court one another by more socially conventional means, he held no such faith in the later generation of Yeshiva undergraduates. Some students felt betrayed by Soloveitchik's newfound "closemindedness." They wondered aloud why he had joined with "right-wing faculty members" to denounce the event "on the grounds that it was inappropriate for a school of religious education."[88] This group did not speak for the entire student body, however. For instance, the student newspaper congratulated Soloveitchik for settling the debate over coeducation on the men's campus. "The firm leadership of the Rav in this matter," an editorial read, "has put an end, for a while, to the growing rift among students concerning the propriety of the Dean's Reception."[89] Another student agreed, suggesting that those in favor of the Dean's Reception overestimated the "sexual behavior of Orthodox Jewish youth."[90]

The Dean's Reception affair added to the exacerbated tensions at Yeshiva College. That same year, Rabbi Irving Greenberg publicly called on Orthodox rabbis to "promulgate a new value system . . . about sex."[91] Coming from a Harvard-educated PhD and charismatic teacher, Greenberg's words were potent and, to many on campus, undermined the prevailing Orthodox sentiment.[92] His interview published in the student paper touched the very sensitive nerve of traditional yeshiva comportment. In turn Greenberg's provocative statements compelled vociferous responses from the Yeshiva rabbinic faculty. The most public criticisms were levied by two of Soloveitchik's relatives, both members of the Yeshiva rabbinic faculty. His brother, Rabbi Ahron Soloveichik (he spelled his surname slightly differently), decried Greenberg's statements as "lustful" and "parasitic." For the younger Soloveichik, any deviation from the traditional Jewish approach to sex and marriage represented a move away from his cardinal planks of Torah-minded "devotion." Soloveitchik's son-in-law also got involved. Rabbi Aharon Lichtenstein called Greenberg at best "irresponsible." At worst, claimed Lichtenstein, Greenberg had given the impression that an Orthodox rabbi was "advocating premarital sexual relations."[93]

In addition Lichtenstein offered a very public objection to the Dean's Reception. Several days after his father-in-law's call to end the social, Lichtenstein interrupted his daily Talmud lecture to discuss recent events.[94] He admitted that the mixer on its own was not in violation of Jewish law. Yet, he argued, it was still beyond the acceptable boundaries of an Orthodox yeshiva. It broadcasted a message that "life in general is to be governed by secular values and worldly considerations."[95] Jewish law promoted a sexual ethic and moral behavior. Any conduct that betrayed those values was trouble, even if chapter and verse were uncitable. The spiritual consequences of the Dean's Reception, then, were too much for an Orthodox men's school to bear. In light of the sexualized 1960s, the mixer was, to Lichtenstein and most of his rabbinic colleagues, decidedly an inauthentic religious experience at an Orthodox yeshiva.

The vociferous debate had drastic consequences. In 1967 the Dean's Reception was reincarnated once again as the "Student Council Reception."[96] Tellingly, the end-of-year event was restricted to male students, which did not at all pose a threat to the insular yeshiva environment. In fact the administration took special precautions to ensure that no young women attended. All dormitory entrances were locked, and the elevators were shut off. "When confronted with these unexpected conditions," it was reported, "some students were amused but many others were insulted." The student newspaper spoke up for many among the student body who felt infantilized by the Yeshiva administration:

> There are just as many young women present on any Sunday as there were on the evening of the Reception, yet no "special regulations" are necessary. If the administration wishes to ban females from the campus, let them issue an edict to that effect. If not, we respectfully request that they do not embarrass us further by arbitrary regulations.[97]

This satisfied some but did not resolve the whole issue. Three years later one Yeshiva collegian wrote a letter to the editor of the campus newspaper to complain that zealous students had torn down dozens of posters he had hung in the dormitories. The posters, advertising a coed social organized by a "Jewish youth organization," were deemed inappropriate for Yeshiva's standards and were therefore replaced with alternative signs inviting students to "lectures to be given by rabbis."[98] In the following year students published a provocative editorial—with political implications—entitled "Sexual Apartheid." In it the undergraduate journalists openly disagreed with unnamed rabbinic faculty members who "believe that coeducation would be detrimental to the religious attitudes among students." In the students' words: "The mythical stereotypes and misconceptions about the typical YU boy and the Sternlie would cease. A member of the opposite sex would be viewed as someone more human and intellectual than just a Saturday night diversion."[99]

The unevenness of this religious tug-of-war revealed the specific concern of those opposed to Orthodox fraternizing. Amid all the raging debate over the preservation of Yeshiva College's masculine culture, the school made it easier for young Orthodox women and men to socialize on the Stern College campus. In Midtown the rules were not all that relaxed, but the attitude was substantially different. In March 1966 the young women released the results of an "unofficial survey at YC" that showed that "many boys are willing to spend Shabbos here and would pay for meals at Stern College instead of at YU."[100] Orthodox collegians had a few other organized outlets for social gatherings off-campus. From time to time they met as volunteers for Yeshiva's Torah Leadership Seminar or NCSY.[101] In 1960 Yeshiva College joined Yavneh, an organization that offered Orthodox undergraduate women and men opportunities to meet religiously likeminded young people.[102] In fact Rabbi Lichtenstein supported Yavneh and other off-campus coed ventures. The common denominator was that these forums were removed from the yeshiva setting, in places where intermingling would be acceptable. In contrast Yeshiva College was meant, like other Orthodox *yeshivot*, to provide a sacred male space to breed a particular kind of Orthodox man. Anything that detracted from this rendered the experience, even in American climes, altogether inauthentic.

## CHAPTER 8

# RABBI JOSEPH B. SOLOVEITCHIK AND THE UNORTHODOX OPTICS OF WOMEN'S TALMUD STUDY

In January 1953 the chairman of a New York day school's education committee wrote to Rabbi Joseph B. Soloveitchik. Leonard Rosenfeld wished to obtain Soloveitchik's position on teaching girls Talmud, often called *gemara*, the essential digest of Judaism's oral traditions and rabbinic legislations. The topic was a concerning one for the parents and teachers of the Hebrew Institute of Long Island. On the one hand, among the Orthodox, Talmud was reserved for boys. It was the essential text used by young men studying in yeshiva. No other sacred text better reflected the insular masculine world of Orthodox Judaism. Not at all a simple discipline, Talmud learning requires many years of practice to navigate the many folios of cryptic Judeo-Aramaic and its accompanying commentaries. Much in the same manner that Theodore Roosevelt spoke about sport or wilderness experiences to define manliness, Orthodox men drew from the "strenuousness" of Talmud study to shape their religious identities.[1] On the other hand, the day school understood that Orthodox Judaism had—however gradually—expanded the girls' curriculum. In the early twentieth century Sarah Schenirer had launched the Bais Yaakov movement in Krakow, which exposed girls to Jewish subjects previously unknown to Orthodox women. With much support from the politically resourceful Agudath Israel, Bais Yaakov achieved an authentic station in hundreds of Orthodox enclaves throughout Europe.[2] Perhaps Talmud learning could be an antidote for what community leaders perceived as religious malaise and intellectual boredom among the Orthodox girls of Far Rockaway. Rosenfeld's committee was at a stalemate, so they petitioned this leading Orthodox rabbi to help steer the day school toward a resolution.

Soloveitchik's opinion was already well known. Since the 1940s both girls and boys at his Maimonides School in Boston had studied Talmud.[3] He was also the leading rabbinic figure at Yeshiva University in New York—he commuted each week—and advised several local schools on this educational matter. For Soloveitchik mixing younger girls and boys did not pose the same problem that it did at Yeshiva College, where controversy seemed to erupt regularly over the propriety of young women and men meeting and greeting one another.[4] Moreover he was unconcerned with the emasculation of the traditionally male Talmud curriculum during these early, unripe ages. Notwithstanding this and despite his well-known opinion, Soloveitchik was reluctant to issue a formal decision unless Rosenfeld and the school administration agreed that his "recommendations will be followed." He explained his reservations in rather strident tones:

> The reason for my reluctance to engage in this controversial issue is the unique stand taken by many of our Jews on matters of Law and tradition. We have reached a stage at which party lines and political ideologies influence our halakhic thinking to the extent that people cannot rise above partisan issues to the level of Halakhah-objectivity. Some are in a perennial quest for "liberalization" of the Law and its subordination to the majority opinion of a political legislative body, while others would like to see the Halakhah fossilized and completely shut out of life. I am not inclined to give any of these factions an opportunity for nonsensical debates.[5]

The committee assented to those terms by a vote of 9–6. In turn Soloveitchik confirmed that for him Talmud education for girls was not just "permissible"—it was an "absolute imperative." Those who "discriminated" against girls by not offering Talmud had, to his mind, "contributed greatly to the deterioration and downfall of traditional Judaism."[6] Soloveitchik acknowledged that the matter was controversial. Orthodox girls did not study Talmud. Boys learned Talmud, extensively if not exclusively. According to Rabbi Yitzchok Hutner of Yeshiva Chaim Berlin in Brooklyn, a "boy must strive to encompass the totality of Torah knowledge." As the basic digest of rabbinic legal and exegetic thought, this meant intensive doses of Talmud. Hutner's words were freighted with images of exhausting labor and male strenuous activity. His description of the female role in Torah study was much different. "The girl must learn Torah only as a means to acquire her Jewish personality," explained Hutner. Other texts were more suitable and less intellectually challenging than Talmud for this more modest educational mission.[7] But Soloveitchik did not view Talmud education in gendered terms. Instead he argued that a knowledgeable Jew must be Talmud-literate. Girls just as much as boys. For him Talmud was the foundation—the pathway to the "inner halls"—of Jewish identity and thought. Soloveitchik averred that blocking access to the depths of Jewish literacy threatened to turn away young people from the text-based faith of Orthodox Judaism.

Nonetheless Soloveitchik was cognizant that his position might be perceived as inauthentic, despite the currents of change in advanced women's education in the United States. Others contended that women's Talmud study was an attempt to replicate Orthodox male spaces. This was not just a neophobic claim of heterodox behavior. The very image of women engaged in Talmud learning could devalue the all-men's yeshiva experience. Soloveitchik's hesitations with Rosenfeld also reflected Soloveitchik's understanding about how others might construe his decision as a nod toward egalitarianism: an "inauthentic" spirit, it was alleged, that guided the non-Orthodox Jewish movements. Other faiths also struggled to decouple their efforts for women from certain "feminist heresies." In the post–Vatican II era, Catholic leaders worked hard to separate a desire to support women's leadership from other feminist initiatives. For instance, many American Catholic clerics advocated for women to be a part of the lay ministry.[8] They also listened carefully to Catholic women who urged the Church to back the Equal Rights Amendment (ERA) in the 1970s and early 1980s. However, Catholics feared that aligning with this agenda would also appear as tacit approval of other feminist causes, like abortion and birth control, which they deemed irreconcilable with their faith.[9] In the end the political link was too much for Catholics to formally advocate for the ERA. The same was true of other Christian fundamentalists who concluded that the ERA was tied to feminist agitations that, in their view, threatened the survival of the traditional family and the male-dominated workplace.[10] In the Orthodox Jewish context, Soloveitchik's challenge was to convince others—including some of his otherwise devoted followers—that women's Talmud study and feminism had nothing in common.

It cannot be overstated that feminism was a very real concern for Orthodox Jews. The movement mounted campaigns to change rituals that Halakhah, in its most traditional reading, designated exclusively for men, such as leading prayers and counting for a worship quorum. Activists like historian Paula Hyman simultaneously congratulated Conservative Judaism for reforms to elevate women and accused Orthodox Judaism of a misguided allegiance to traditional Jewish law and an incorrigibleness that was out of line with the "established Jewish community."[11] Overwhelmed by feelings of cultural besiegement, many Orthodox women and men deflected anything that might be associated with feminism and the "slippery slope" toward major reform of Jewish law.

This included women's Talmud study, an activity that did not violate ritual but certainly encroached on traditional Orthodox male space. Consider a heated exchange during the panel "The Orthodox Jewish Woman and the New Feminism" at an Orthodox Union convention in November 1974. In response to one female panelist's call for an "upgrading of the scholastic program in Jewish women's schools," another woman educator protested, attributing this and other "problems troubling contemporary women to pagan and anti-Jewish influences in Western civilization which degrade [a woman] as a sex object and deny her the dignity and individuality to which she has every right."[12] Steadfastly certain that Talmud education was essential for men and women, Soloveitchik could not accept the explicit cries of feminism or the implicit fears of emasculation. Rescued from these associations, women's Talmud study stood a chance to achieve religious authenticity. But like the experiences of other American faith groups, disentangling acceptable change in tradition-bound religion and gender politics was a formidable challenge to overcome. The quest for authenticity in the case of women's Talmud, then, was mediated by the resistance to feminism and concern for the preservation of male sacred space in America's tradition-bound religious communities.

# Rabbi Soloveitchik, Day Schools, and the
# Women's Talmud Cause

In August 1932 Joseph and Tonya Soloveitchik and their young daughter, Atarah, arrived in New York.[13] Their journey had been arduous, to say the least. Their travels from Europe to the United States—by way of Liverpool, England—were strenuous and full of political maneuvering to obtain the necessary paperwork. Soloveitchik's rabbinical credentials permitted the young family to bypass the strict American immigration quotas.[14] His initial days in the United States were little better. The Hebrew Theological College in Chicago, the institution that had arranged for Soloveitchik's immigration papers, informed the twenty-nine-year-old scholar that, due to the financial impairments wrought by the Great Depression, it could no longer guarantee his salary.[15]

Boston rescued the Soloveitchiks. In short order the lay leaders of the Beth Hamidrash Hagadol invited him to serve as "Chief Rabbi of Boston."[16] The title fit Soloveitchik's high ambitions. Within months of his arrival and with the aid of an interpreter—his English would vastly improve in the years to come—the rabbinic-scion-cum-Berlin-PhD-philosopher declared his intentions to elevate Jewish education in the United States for both male and female students. He wished to "give our generation of growing boys and girls an all-embracing, well-balanced educational development."[17] This was not an altogether new rabbinic concern. Earlier in the century Rabbis Shlomo Yosef Zevin and Yisrael Meir Kagan issued pleas to improve Jewish education for girls.[18] What is more, Soloveitchik was joined by other Orthodox Jews in the United States who described girls' education as a "field which had also been grossly neglected in America."[19] But no one before the newly minted Bostoner had supported Talmud education for girls. After all the Talmud (Sotah 20a) looked askance at women opening its tomes.

Five years after their arrival, the Soloveitchiks' vision—Dr. Tonya Soloveitchik was a partner in forming this institution—took shape as the Maimonides School. Founded in 1937, Maimonides taught Talmud to girls alongside boys. Other Orthodox day schools in New York introduced Talmud to girls as well. In Upper Manhattan the coeducational Yeshiva Rabbi Moshe Soloveichik taught Talmud to girls and boys. In 1956 eighth-grader Klara Shermanberg "gloried" in her exposure to Talmud and devoted teachers, remarking that she

A female student learning Talmud in the 1950s at Yeshiva Rabbi Moshe Soloveichik in Manhattan. (Religious Zionists of America)

was the envy of her friends enrolled in other Orthodox day schools.[20] Owing to its close ties to Soloveitchik, the coeducational Ramaz School on New York's Upper East Side chose to keep boys and girls together in Talmud classes.[21] In the 1960s school leaders grappling with how to increase the hours of daily Talmud study rejected any plans that might have solved the scheduling challenge for boys but did not keep up the pace for their female counterparts.[22] Ramaz solved the problem a few years later, at least for the most able students. The school launched an Honors Talmud Program for boys and girls under the tutelage of Yeshiva University's Rabbi Yehuda Parnes.[23] At some point in the 1950s, YU's Central Yeshiva High School in Manhattan instituted a mandatory requirement in Mishnah (the foundational text of the Talmud) and offered a Talmud elective.[24] Yeshiva's other girls' high school, this one in Brooklyn, also scheduled a Mishnah class. Each year the best student won the Edith Weiss Memorial Award for Excellence in Mishnah. The Brooklyn branch also offered Talmud, a subject taught in the 1950s by Rabbi Baruch Rabinowitz.[25] One of his best pupils was Miss Shirley Sonnenfeld, described by her teenage peers as "Central's Hebrew sage." She was known to quote "from any Talmud page."[26] More than a decade later, several schools in the Bronx merged to form SAR

Academy. Its leaders—particularly Rabbi Irving Greenberg, who had been inspired by Soloveitchik when Greenberg had lived in Boston and saw Maimonides School up close—demanded Talmud education for girls. In all these instances the schools' messages reflected the need to leverage Talmud study to elevate Jewish identity and knowledge for boys and girls rather than to mirror feminist causes and break down the barriers of traditional male spaces.

These schools were encouraged by Soloveitchik's support, especially as tradition-bound varieties of postwar American faiths reinforced masculine ideals.[27] Orthodox Judaism was no exception. In this period, for instance, most Orthodox congregations abided by the letter of Jewish law, adopting firmer guidelines on separate seating in the synagogue.[28] In November 1954 Soloveitchik himself took a very hardline approach. He ruled that a worshiper remain home and miss the shofar blasts rather than pray in a synagogue that sat women and men together.[29] Past generations of the American Orthodox rabbinate had also insisted on similar positions. It was not until the mid-twentieth century that Orthodox laypeople felt so compelled to listen, partially due to the reinvigorated sense of maleness overwhelming American religion at that time. However, Soloveitchik was convinced that Talmud was different. Its presence in the girls' curriculum had to do with education and preservation of Jewish identity, and therefore transcended religious gender norms.

Few followed. Fear of blurring gender boundaries informed curricular decisions at several Orthodox schools. In most Orthodox settings, as Hutner and Bais Yaakov advocates had prescribed, girls learned the Pentateuch and "practical religious knowledge" while their male counterparts "stud[ied] Mishnah and Talmud."[30] Consider the case of the Hebrew Institute of Long Island, the Far Rockaway day school mentioned earlier that had solicited Soloveitchik's position and pledged to follow it without exception. Despite this, the school's administration did not adhere to Soloveitchik's decision. To the Long Island head of school, the need to better Jewishly educate Orthodox girls came up short against the need to maintain separate curricula for the sexes. The latter need was too strong and compelling to accommodate the former. "The principal of the school," recalled a memoirist many years later, "thought it was forbidden to teach the girls Talmud." Basing his decision on the edicts of other prominent scholars, like Rabbi Moshe Feinstein, the head of school "invalidated the board's decision."[31]

Other day schools also met resistance, which persuaded them to side with the more traditional Orthodox position. For example, the Yeshivah of Flatbush on principle wished to offer thorough Torah study to its male and female students but struggled over how best to accomplish this goal. In the early 1950s, in the first years of its high school program, the Brooklyn high school taught Talmud to boys and girls together.[32] A few years later, however, students were split based on sex, no doubt to appease more conservative families and faculty members who preferred more inflexible separation. Girls still received a Talmud education but not at the most "advanced" level, which was made available just to gifted young men. Thus the highest forms of—and most sacred spaces for—rabbinic scholarship were still reserved for males, as it always had been. By the end of the decade, Yeshivah of Flatbush decided to end girls' Talmud study after sophomore year and instead focus on "Jewish philosophy," a field of Jewish learning that was less linked to *yeshivot* and male spaces.[33] The vacillation betokened the religious tension in this community, its dual commitment to traditionalism and the progressive modern spirit. Time and again the Flatbush school could not separate its educational goal from the perception that it was surrendering to egalitarian impulses that threatened the persistence of tradition-bound religion in the United States.

All this troubled Soloveitchik and likeminded Orthodox leaders. The defeat on Long Island was a probably painful blow. On that occasion Soloveitchik had worried about subversiveness and negotiated a promise that his word would carry the decision without interference. He had underestimated the reaction to challenging the status quo and sharing the "male" curriculum with girls. In the late 1950s Torah Umesorah adopted aggressive positions to discourage day schools from teaching girls Talmud, fearing that the blurring of gender-separate curricula was too closely aligned with American egalitarian sensibilities.[34] In January 1965 the Agudath Israel published a checklist to "help parents rate the institutions that seek to provide a Torah education for their children." One item in the field of "Curriculum" read: "The boys' curriculum leads to, and emphasizes *Gemorah*, and the girls' curriculum excludes it."[35] Still most resistors of women's Talmud learning just avoided polemic altogether. They saw no need to pick a fight. There were plenty of schools that offered just the right dosage of Torah education that fit their needs, sans Talmud. By 1964 there existed twenty-five Bais Yaakov schools in the United States, with a total enrollment that surpassed five thousand girls.[36] For these Orthodox families, the all-girls schools' emphasis on Bible, Halakhah, and Jewish philosophy had widened the scope of female Orthodox education just enough. All this stood in the way of mainstreaming girls' Talmud studies in the immediate postwar era. It was only on the rarest of occasions in the 1950s and 1960s that writers in popular Orthodox periodicals broached the subject of a boys-styled "Yeshiva High School for girls."[37] Most Orthodox educators could not fathom how a "yeshiva," designated as a men's space, could ever be reassigned to a female domain. Nonetheless Soloveitchik and others pressed forward. Soloveitchik's support of women's Talmud studies remained unequivocal as the movement struggled to overcome the deleterious accusations of "egalitarianism," which were motivated by the very real impression that women were emasculating the conditions of Talmud learning.

## The Stern Talmud Lecture

One of the most important sites for women's Talmud study was YU's Stern College for Women.[38] In the 1950s Stern College emerged with the promise of elevating higher education for Orthodox women in all fields and disciplines, above and beyond what was offered to girls in day schools. No longer adolescents and in their own female spaces, mature young women, Soloveitchik and others hoped, would refine their Talmud studies and prove the importance of this educational venture. It took time. In the realm of Jewish studies, the school's first academic catalogs listed four different levels of courses in "Talmudic Literature," but these were classes without the same depth offered in the Talmud courses at Yeshiva College.[39] A decade later members of the Stern College faculty sought Soloveitchik's guidance on whether to add a more substantive Talmud class to the curriculum. Notes from that meeting record that "Rabbi Soloveitchik strongly favored giving the girls a class in Gemara (as an elective) to acquaint them with the process of Halakhah and Torah she-Ba'al Peh [Oral Law, i.e., Talmud]. He recommended tractates that would offer a religious experience—such as Mo'ed, etc."[40] In response Stern College added an "advanced level" Talmud class taught by Rabbi Melech Schachter. Outside of this more formal setting, some of Yeshiva's top rabbinic scholars traveled from time to time to Stern College's Midtown Manhattan campus to lecture and maintain a presence.[41] A few Stern undergraduates also periodically trekked uptown to attend Soloveitchik's public lectures.[42]

Stern College redoubled its efforts in the late 1970s. A new generation of teachers and scholars wanted more for their female students. Just as youth-conscious as he had been in his Jewish Center career, the newly inaugurated YU president Norman Lamm named Karen Bacon—Stern College's 1964 valedictorian—dean of the school. Other new appointments, including Rabbis Saul Berman, Jacob Rabinowitz, and Haym Soloveitchik, also enhanced the Jewish studies offerings at the school.[43] Berman was chairman of the Department of Jewish Studies. He promised to expand the Talmud curriculum aided by "constant consultation" with Rabbi Soloveitchik and his son, Haym Soloveitchik.[44] All in all, asserted Berman, the new personalities at Stern College reflected a "renewed dedication to the ideals and purpose . . . of YU."[45] By this time American women had gained unprecedented access to higher education.[46] It therefore made good sense, boasted Stern College officials, that the "nation's only institution of higher education for women under Jewish auspices has developed a setting and structure for learning that has been unavailable to women until the present."[47]

Yet it would prove even more difficult to uncouple women's Talmud study from feminist impulses and the perception that it was an affront to Orthodox male space. Jews held a disproportionate role in the concurrent feminist awakening, and many of these women tied their feminist agenda to their religious identities.[48] Their activism made immediate inroads. In 1972 Reform Judaism started to ordain women, and there was significant stirring within Conservative circles to do the same.[49] The "moderate women's liberationists" at Stern College also agitated for change, claiming that the "image of a female who must make do with less than her male counterpart is long outdated."[50] Taking stock of all this, many within the Orthodox enclave viewed feminism as the most potent threat to the Jewish family and traditional religious life. Orthodox rabbis blasted feminist-advocated ritual reforms, and they also attacked changes to educational and cultural norms. The Orthodox Right warned its wives and daughters against "seek[ing] acceptance in a man's world." Intellectually curious women, wrote Rabbi Nisson Wolpin, often did this "for the wrong reasons." The "search can become tragic," wrote Wolpin in an Agudath Israel magazine, as they were risking a "de-feminization" and the abandonment of their families.[51] Rabbi Shlomo Wolbe also sensed much unease among young Orthodox women and cautioned them about comparing their religious studies with those of their future husbands. On one occasion

On October 11, 1977, Rabbi Joseph B. Soloveitchik (center) delivered the inaugural lecture for Stern College for Women's Beit Midrash program. The administrators pictured to the right of Soloveitchik are President Norman Lamm, Dean Karen Bacon, and Rabbi Saul J. Berman. (Yeshiva University Archives, Public Relations Photo Events Collection)

he told a group of Bais Yaakov students in Israel that they ought not compare their learning with the male "yeshiva" experience. "Even if she knows a lot," said Wolbe about the disgruntled Orthodox woman, "she will never reach the ankles of her husband when it comes to the wisdom and depths of Torah."[52]

In contrast, the Modern Orthodox separated religious designations and ritual innovation from educational initiatives. Soloveitchik led the way. For instance, he was on record for his staunch opposition to ordaining women.[53] Perhaps some, fearing a mangled message, might have anticipated that he would tone down his push for women's Talmud study. But then again his mission was education-driven, not based in feminism. Stern College relied on Soloveitchik's vision to negotiate the boundaries of Orthodox authenticity. School leaders also anticipated that a more robust Talmud track could attract Orthodox students looking for advanced Talmud education and reinforce that brand of Orthodox Judaism. In the school's first two decades, about three-quarters of Stern College students hailed from outside New York and arrived at the Manhattan-based college with limited levels of Jewish education. Stern College drew from YU's New York–based girls' high schools, but the bulk of the local Orthodox young women preferred the tuition-free Queens and Brooklyn Colleges.[54] An enhanced Talmud program, YU administrators supposed, might draw day school graduates with elevated Jewish studies backgrounds and raise the profile of their school.

Rabbi Saul Berman was at the forefront of the charge. In March 1977 he delivered a major lecture on women's Torah study.[55] Around the same time he wrote to Stern College students, alerting them about preparations for the new Talmud program under Soloveitchik's guidance.[56] Berman echoed Soloveitchik's sentiments, that Talmud education had nothing to do with feminism, no matter how it appeared to others. Reflecting this, he made efforts to ensure that other aspects of Stern College, like the dress code, remained modest, feminine, and aligned with an "orthodox manner."[57] For Berman this meant outlawing "sleeveless or capsleeve clothing; shorts or other garb of immodest length; and blue jeans."[58] The more conservative dress code would mollify concerns of feminism. For their part the Orthodox students applauded the widened Talmud curriculum, even if they were none too keen about the harsher dress code.[59] The editor of the campus newspaper described it as a "daring venture, for it opens new options to women that have never before been approached by normative *halakha*." Accounting for more than just herself, the student journalist wrote that the "proposal is commendable in every respect, and the general reaction among the student body has been a mixture of surprise and delight."[60] YU inaugurated the Stern College Beit Midrash on October 11, 1977. On that occasion Soloveitchik himself delivered a Talmud discourse to fifty female undergraduates. The bulk of the lecture did not address the moment and its importance to his decades-long mission to advance women's Talmud study. Soloveitchik waited until the end to tackle that point. He confirmed his "complete support." In closing, said Soloveitchik, "If you have problems come to me, I'll fight your battles."[61] Clearly Soloveitchik and his followers anticipated that others would confuse their intentions and label Talmud study an inauthentic and religiously inappropriate activity for Orthodox women. Soloveitchik was still determined to convince them to the contrary.

# The Awkward Optics of Women's Talmud Study

The reaction to Soloveitchik and the Stern Beit Midrash was mixed. Many within the Orthodox Right's circle read about the event in the pages of a Yiddish newspaper, where they learned that Stern College students intended to study Talmud with the same vigorous "intensity" as men in traditional yeshiva settings.[62] Much later Berman recalled that several prominent New York rabbis considered issuing a ban on Stern College. The comments of Yeshiva Chaim Berlin's Rabbi Aharon Schechter, recorded six months after the Stern College lecture, reflect the attitude of his superior, Rabbi Hutner, and many others within this fold: "There are religious modernists who are rightists in their own camp. And what do these rightists say? They establish a young women's Beis Medrash. I mean, are we crazy!"[63] However, Soloveitchik's standing and his intimate involvement in the Talmud initiative convinced them to back down.[64] In contrast to the Orthodox Right, most Jewish weeklies seized on the moment, praising Soloveitchik's path-breaking enterprise.[65] It also galvanized others to trumpet Soloveitchik's cause and follow suit.[66] In 1979 Rabbi David Silber founded the Drisha Institute for adult female learners on the grounds that it was "preposterous that women who are advancing in all other fields should be held back when it comes to Jewish studies."[67] The Manhattan-based institute scheduled classes at convenient times for young mothers, and the school welcomed the occasional sleeping baby in the corridor adjacent to the formal study hall. Outside New York, adult women had fewer resources but still tried their best to cultivate learning opportunities. For instance, in Silver Spring, Maryland, one woman wrote about a weekly learning group. "At present, we learn for over two hours and usually have about 20 women regularly attending the class," she explained.[68] Just as important, this same woman also lamented the existence of "negative forces that play upon us and our families from without."

Several Orthodox day schools were inspired to implement Talmud classes for girls. The Frisch School in New Jersey incorporated it into its curriculum and invited Soloveitchik to teach and observe. This is how the school yearbook recalled a concluding assembly that afternoon, which featured Soloveitchik's visit and the principal's telling remarks on that occasion:

> Paraphrasing Rashi's question on Exodus 18:1, Rabbi [Menahem] Meier asked "what did rebbe [Rabbi Soloveitchik], the aristocrat of spirit and

intellect, revered and loved by his disciples, hear to bring him to Frisch?" Two possibilities were advanced: 1) The Frisch School, based upon a world view promulgated by the Rav [Rabbi Soloveitchik] and with Jewish studies faculty consisting predominantly of the Rav's disciples, is in reality an extension of the Rav's contribution to the American Jewish scene; 2) the concept of teenage boys and girls committing themselves daily to the noble and ennobling act of Talmud Torah, and thereby to God and Israel, is uplifting to the Rav.[69]

But the attitude among many day school educators was far from sanguine. A few started to teach girls Talmud in the mid-1980s, but most others resisted. School principals offered several reasons. They claimed there was a lack of support among parents and students who could not rally behind an educational program that appeared too much like the feminism they were taught to avoid. One principal predicted that the whole women's Talmud effort "will almost certainly disappear." He also blamed the overwhelming stock of educators trained in Orthodox centers that disapproved of Soloveitchik's position.[70] They adhered to rabbinic authorities like Rabbi Yaakov Weinberg of Ner Israel in Baltimore, who once told a group of teachers that it was prohibited, and even the "girls themselves have the instinct and the feeling that it is wrong, and most do not take it seriously." Educators could not teach girls Talmud, trumpeted Weinberg, even if that meant, due to economic reasons and class sizes, "that boys never see a Gemara" either.[71] Overall the pessimistic principal opined that his rabbinic faculty's efforts to teach Talmud to girls—if they agreed to it—was rather uninspired. "They don't really teach the girls Talmud like the boys. They will take a line or two from the Talmud and then switch into commentaries which are not Talmudic. The more right wing teachers won't teach the girls, so I do it."[72]

This amounted to a lack of curricular consistency throughout Modern Orthodox day schools. In Yeshivah of Flatbush, for example, Talmud was exclusively offered to honors-level female students.[73] For the rest, "while the boys are having a double period of Talmud, the girls are given one period of Halacha and one period of dance."[74] The separation between male and female forms of educational spaces was obvious. The all-girls Shulamith School in Brooklyn debated the matter throughout the 1980s. At one point the conflicted faculty struck a compromise. The school added an optional Talmud class before the official start of the school day. Then Shulamith instituted an elective course for seniors, but mollified its constituencies by designating it a more generic "Oral Law" class rather than Talmud. The course's near-hundred-page packet was extensive and focused squarely on the question of women's Torah study.[75] In 1981 Chicago's Ida Crown Jewish Academy started a girls Talmud track, but the school observed little traction among female students.[76] Communities in Detroit, Long Island, and St. Louis debated the matter but ultimately decided against teaching Talmud to girls. The subject was not much broached in locales like Atlanta, Los Angeles, and Seattle. One prominent educator recognized all this and called for Soloveitchik and other leaders to come up with a set of official guidelines to retain some of the dwindling momentum.[77]

Interest also waned at Stern College. Two years after Soloveitchik's lecture, Stern College undergraduates still showed far greater interest in "concentrating their learning in Tanach [Bible] and other areas." The Beit Midrash Program was "eventually dissolved." Owing to the Talmud tug-of-war in the day schools, Stern College students complained that they lacked the "learning skills in Talmudic material and the teaching of those skills is not systematically addressed in these content-important classes."[78] The program reopened a few years later, with modest results. In the autumn of 1984, "only six women joined the Stern Beit Midrash under the tutelage of Rabbi Moshe Kahn."[79] The new Stern College Talmud teacher described the rigor of the program this way: "The level of the class is comparable to any Gemara shiur [lecture] where the participants have not had much previous experience but are serious and motivated."[80] The lack of Talmud background among Stern College students and the dearth of undergraduates interested in the program represented the decades-long challenge to redeem women's Talmud study from unorthodox attitudes. For many the image of girls and women studying Talmud still did not appear as a valid expression of Orthodox Judaism. There was still a maleness attached to it, no matter how much Soloveitchik tried to reverse the perception.

The decline of women's Talmud study had much to do with inauspicious timing. In October 1983 the Jewish Theological Seminary faculty voted 34–8 to allow women into the Conservative movement's flagship rabbinical program.[81] At least one prominent Conservative rabbi linked women's ordination with Stern College's recently established Talmud program. "Noteworthy and admirable," affirmed Rabbi Harold Schulweis, "is the decision of the Orthodox Stern College for Women in New York to introduce intensive courses in

Talmudic studies for women, a course of studies introduced by none other than Rabbi J. B. Soloveitchik who offered its introductory Talmudic shiur."[82] The link with the non-Orthodox movement and the feminist attitudes that informed recent religious reforms rendered the authenticity of women's Talmud all the less credible. Yet there were still more damaging associations. The Orthodox feminist activist Blu Greenberg used Talmud learning to justify women's Orthodox ordination. "Young women now study rabbinic studies as never before," she declared in 1984, "at their own institutions of higher learning. I foresee the day, in my lifetime, when there will be the ordination of women given in the Orthodox community."[83] The opposition took notice. Writing in an Agudath Israel magazine, a self-described "Monsey housewife" who made sure to express her "indebtedness" to her husband for accumulating the "sources on which this article is based," seized on this particular connection. The author criticized women who study the male curriculum: "Unfortunately, some women who have learned 'some' Torah become arrogant, and their Torah knowledge serves to corrupt their character. Such women are definitely misusing their knowledge, for the purpose of Torah learning is to improve character, to make a person more humble and sincere."[84]

The languished state of feminism in the 1980s was a second factor that impaired these endeavors. In 1982 the Equal Rights Amendment that guaranteed legal gender parity failed a series of state ratifications. Despite their triumphs in the 1970s, feminists were branded "antifamily." Hugely empowered conservative pundits lashed out against liberal politicians who "do not want to help families meet the increasing costs of raising children."[85] Most successful women's activists in this period achieved their victories with understated language, and beyond media detection. Those who decided to employ forceful feminist rhetoric usually struggled against the strong rightist cultural currents.[86]

Finally, the 1980s proved a precarious moment for Modern Orthodox leadership. Soloveitchik was physically limited. Students recalled the "heartbreak" of watching their mentor "struggle to board an airplane, enter and leave a car" and require the support of "two students to help him walk across Amsterdam Avenue" toward his lecture room on YU's campus.[87] During these years various factions within Modern Orthodox Judaism sometimes put forward competing views, each claiming Soloveitchik's support.[88] He was in no position to rebut or clarify. In 1985 Soloveitchik retired from Yeshiva and the public scene. His absence within the Modern Orthodox orbit had much to do with a communal crisis of self-confidence. After all, as a sign of ultimate respect his students often referred to Soloveitchik as the "Rav," or "the rabbi." For many Modern Orthodox Jews, he was the singular and peerless rabbinic figure in their religious orbit. As one rabbinic leader put it: "The question will be, 'What did the Rav say and when did he say it.'"[89] In the mid-1980s a Modern Orthodox rabbi expressed distress that his colleagues "collapse into miserable surrender" against the outcries of "so-called right-wing Orthodox groups."[90] No doubt Soloveitchik would not have supported every initiative. But he also worried about many of his students who, he believed, disregarded his viewpoints. "My ideas are too radical for them. If they could find another one, it would be alright."[91] To be sure, some carried on his mission for women's Torah education. Amid Soloveitchik's worsening health, Saul Berman continued to champion women's Talmud study.[92] Likewise, Haym Soloveitchik repeated his father's "educational considerations" on women's Talmud.[93] Rabbi Aharon Lichtenstein, Soloveitchik's son-in-law, by then living in Israel, was also a staunch proponent of women's Talmud learning.[94] Nonetheless Soloveitchik's decline and departure weakened the movement. One YU-affiliated Orthodox rabbi, speaking before a large audience at a Long Island synagogue, called the entire women's Talmud movement into question, reminding his listeners that Rabbi Soloveitchik's was very much the minority opinion.[95] Rather than surrender Soloveitchik's position, some just revised it. In October 1987 one of Soloveitchik's leading disciples told a large gathering of Orthodox educators that a full and intensive Talmud curriculum for women, on the level of their male counterparts, was "alien" to Orthodox Judaism.[96] This point of view did not precisely represent Soloveitchik's attitude. However, it did help authenticate Soloveitchik and his more "acceptable" positions among the rest of Orthodox Judaism.[97]

## In the Wake of the Rav

Women's Talmud study never did gain the sturdiest of footholds in Soloveitchik's lifetime. Most Orthodox Jews viewed and designated its supporters feminist-inclined outsiders trespassing on male space. That changed in the subsequent decade, thanks in large measure to a different sort of Talmud-education campaign in Israel. There, women—primarily American-born—claimed ownership of this movement and generated credibility for the authentic image of female teachers and students of Talmud.[98] In 1977 Rabbi Chaim Brovender and Malka Bina founded Michlelet Bruria, the first Israeli institution that offered Talmud study to women. In Israel there was state-mandated space for their efforts. The Israeli government required two years of military service for women. Young women could be exempt from the military for community service or religious study. A year or two of Talmud learning therefore fit neatly into Israeli women's pathways to adulthood.

Proponents of women's Talmud in Israel could also point to respected female scholars and educators as symbolic exemplars of their cause.[99] These women, unlike any of their American counterparts, boasted impeccable credentials and confidence. In contrast to Rabbi Soloveitchik, this cadre of Israeli educators embraced the lingering gender tension and sought to shift the perception of Talmud learning. First and foremost was the outstanding scholar Nehama Leibowitz, who focused mostly on Bible scholarship but who was also a supporter of the women's Talmud enterprise.[100] A private but undaunted figure, Leibowitz was, according to one account, "perhaps one of the few female Torah scholars in the world who can cause a lecture full of men to rise in deference when she enters." Bina was a similarly erudite figure who eschewed the polemics that typically followed Orthodox "women's issues." She also enjoyed considerable rabbinic support. "They see that I am doing it for the right reasons, and if there is somebody who doesn't agree with me, so what. We have a long tradition of differing opinions."[101] The rabbinic elite did not interpret her initiatives as a challenge to Orthodox male space. In the late-1980s Bina established Matan for adult women to engage in intensive Talmud study.[102] Her efforts were celebrated as "pioneering" and patently Orthodox in Israel and in the United States.[103] Around this time Chana Henkin founded Nishmat, a school with a similar purpose. A few years later Michlelet Bruria morphed into Midreshet Lindenbaum, and boasted a very strong faculty that included elite women scholars and housed 120 young women in a well-stocked talmudic study hall.

The success of the Israeli women's Talmud movement owed much to the notion of "dualism of space."[104] In Israel women's Talmud centers did their business quietly, describing their work as a "quiet revolution." In most of these schools, men (except for teachers) were not allowed or strongly discouraged from entering women's Talmud spaces.[105] Furthermore, Bina and others strived for acceptance, not dominance. Therefore it did not matter much to them that the vast majority of Orthodox families did not feel compelled to send their daughters to these Israeli schools. They were content that most tolerated or ignored the developments of women's advanced Torah study. Bina, Henkin, and likeminded educators earned this ideological truce because theirs was an insulated feminine space: by women, for women. This quality of their work ensured that just a few agitators had much concern that the intellectual activity buzzing within these spaces was in fact traditionally male Talmud study.

The achievement was all too apparent. Scores of American-born women enrolled in Lindenbaum, most often during a gap year between high school and college. In turn graduates of Brovender's seminary and other similar institutions (there were about thirty schools by 2012) brought this invigorated spirit back with them to the United States. The impact was substantial. Learning from the Israeli schools, the new American efforts sought to install female role models as the feminine icons of the initiatives. In 1992 Rabbi Silber's Drisha Institute claimed two hundred female students, forty of whom registered as fulltime learners. Silber's school also launched a much-publicized "scholars" program that featured its most accomplished alumnae.[106] In Boston, Ma'ayan, a new women's Torah initiative, gained a popular following, particularly among those interested in studying Talmud with Soloveitchik's daughter, Atarah Twersky.[107] In 1996 Esther Krauss, who had decades earlier unsuccessfully tried to establish girls' Talmud study at a school in St. Louis, opened an all-girls day school that offered ample opportunities for Talmud study.[108]

Likewise, teachers and students at Stern College obtained the foothold for which earlier, no-less-encouraging leaders had hoped. Once women's Talmud study was authenticated by forces beyond the entangled American religious environment, more and more undergraduates enrolled in Talmud courses. In February 2000 Stern College announced the opening of its Graduate Program for Women in Advanced Talmudic Studies with generous stipends. YU officials explained that the program was part of the Orthodox university's longtime commitment to advanced women's Talmud study, one that owed much to Soloveitchik's determination.[109] They were right. But more than that, Orthodox women's Talmud study was empowered by a new generation of women's Talmud learners and scholars who, by bypassing the challenges posed by an indigenous American culture, decoupled their movement from attitudes and expressions that posed a threat to the tradition-bound faith of Orthodox Judaism.

# CHAPTER 9

# WOMEN'S PRAYER GROUPS VERSUS SYNAGOGUE JUDAISM

IN DECEMBER 1977 A frustrated band of Orthodox women in Los Angeles wrote a lengthy letter to Blu Greenberg. About a year earlier Greenberg had penned an essay on Orthodox women, the first major literary enterprise in a pathbreaking career. Though they had never sought her counsel before or encountered her in person, this small group looked up to Greenberg as a mentor. The Los Angeles women bemoaned an inescapable feeling that they each served a "spectator role in the synagogue." Their hope was not to infiltrate male sacred space but to create one of their own. Greenberg's musings on the subject therefore resonated with them, and her antidote appeared reasonable enough: to establish women's prayer groups, "as a way of encouraging the involvement of women in prayer." This arrangement, wrote Greenberg, "means women actually leading prayer, being called to and reading the Torah, and so on."[1]

Her correspondents needed more than that. Surely, they reckoned, a "women's minyan"—"minyan" denotes a formal prayer service with at least ten men—could not function the same as a male quorum; the women needed guidance on how to adjust and to keep within the boundaries of Jewish law. In addition the "majority of the members of the group believe it is imperative to have the sanction of an Orthodox rabbi in order to attract a greater number of women and to make us feel more comfortable about it." The letter-writers reported that local traditional-leaning clergymen had offered "many hostile remarks." Most disappointing, they confessed, was Rabbi Moshe Meiselman, someone the group had thought might be more understanding than most. After all, Meiselman worked at the recently established modern-leaning Yeshiva University of Los Angeles, held a PhD from MIT, and, perhaps most impressive of all, was a nephew of Rabbi Joseph B. Soloveitchik. Moreover the group had heard the most marvelous reviews of his ongoing "Women in Jewish Thought" course.

Meiselman provided some helpful suggestions. He advised the women to omit certain sections of the prayer—in Yiddish, *davening*—that were reserved for a normative quorum of men.[2] But Meiselman warned that such a women's service would be a "religiously inferior type of worship as opposed to participation in a halakhically-constituted minyan." Departing their meeting with Meiselman, the Los Angeles women were overwhelmed by a "feeling of general depression." Unsure of where to turn next, they queried Greenberg whether there might be "other religious authorities who may have more liberal views." Greenberg, they presumed, had better experiences than the kind they had endured with Rabbi Meiselman and the rest of Los Angeles's Orthodox rabbinate.[3]

Greenberg could not offer much help. At that moment just a few Orthodox rabbis had signed on to support women's prayer groups, and that backing was limited. This disappointed the hundreds of advocates who could not comprehend the objections. After all, the leaders of women's prayer upheld some of the basic implicit tenets of "Orthodox" authenticity. They eschewed feminism and sought rabbinic approval for their ritual innovation, one they believed fit well within the parameters of Jewish law. Their clear intentions to leave the synagogue space alone was enough, so they thought, to separate the women's prayer cause from non-Orthodox, feminist-inspired ritual changes to create gender parity in the same religious spaces. Despite this the women's prayer group episode has been understood by historians as part of Orthodox Judaism's decades-long battle with feminism.[4] Accordingly scholars have paid closer attention to the prayer groups' opponents who often branded it that way. The demonization of prayer groups as "feminist" was meant to convince coreligionists that female worship was beyond the pale of Orthodox Judaism and to transform otherwise Orthodox insiders into outsiders. Historians have taken this rhetoric at face value, interpreting these historical experiences as part of Judaism's encounter with women's liberation instead of studying how detractors of women's prayer were animated by an aggressive defense of Orthodox male sacred space. Both forces paralleled broader trends in the American religious experience and played pivotal roles in this episode in Orthodox Jewish life.

Many within the prayer groups' ranks were day school–educated Orthodox Jewish women who understood their efforts as part of a continuum that had commenced with advanced Jewish studies for women. Prayer groups furnished separate female spaces that mirrored traditional worship as much as possible. From their perspective there was little difference between a Bais Yaakov homeroom and their monthly gatherings in a member's home.[5] Their miscalculation was similar to the experiences of Rabbi Soloveitchik and others who had misjudged the importance of male space in Orthodox Jewish life. Many within the Orthodox establishment shunned women's prayer out of fear of its impact on traditional, male-dominated synagogue turf. Others turned women's prayer away, dubbing it a "slippery slope" to more "feminist" initiatives. Their arguments rarely centered on any explicit violation of Jewish law. The challenge to the women's prayer movement was therefore to overcome the overwhelming perception that its advocates were trespassing on male space. The caution and consternation that had impeded these women in the late 1970s did more than just continue into the subsequent decade. It intensified, festered, and proved near-insurmountable. In the process the debates over women's prayer groups reinforced Orthodox men's need to preserve male space and to convince the mainstream Orthodox women that any threats to such spaces were inherently and religiously inauthentic. Prayer groups were therefore consigned to the "anti-religious" sphere known as feminism.

## The Beginning of Women's Prayer

In 1972 Rabbi Shlomo Riskin permitted a women's prayer and Torah reading on Simhat Torah at Lincoln Square Synagogue in New York City, despite the outcry from other Manhattan rabbis.[6] Given the centrality of prayer in Jewish life and of Torah reading on that holiday, the Upper West Side women were eager to tap into the religious ethos of the occasion. As he later recalled, Riskin responded to the congregants' request with a careful analysis of how the ritual would maintain a commitment to Halakhah. To demarcate women's prayer and Torah reading from an official quorum-style prayer, Riskin demanded the elimination of the *kaddish* prayer and other responsive portions of the service. These were central elements of Orthodox prayer, and omission threatened to render the prayer groups' services second-rate rituals. The challenge was to retain enough of the traditional prayers and their forms. Prayer groups accomplished this, and not with just a modicum of creativity. For instance, prayer groups could not recite the "communal" *Shemoneh Esrei* directly after its members prayed the "silent" or "individual" rendition of that prayer. Only a minyan could do that. Instead, the prayer leader—the "hazanit"—waited for all the other members of the group to conclude their respective *Shemoneh Esrei* prayers, and then she recited hers, aloud and in song. Similarly, prayer groups summoned women to recite a blessing before they received a formal *aliyah*. Rather than recite a minyan-required blessing on the Torah portion, the women offered the blessing on Torah study, which varied just slightly from the more typical ritual.[7] Pedantic as these matters might seem, straddling Halakhah and ritual innovation was crucially important to these Modern Orthodox women.

Riskin's congregation continued to host women's prayer groups on Simhat Torah and other occasions, at least once in the synagogue's main sanctuary.[8] Besides Lincoln Square a few other New York–based groups met monthly for prayer and Torah reading throughout the 1970s, but without much fanfare.[9] Their muted activities were the result of the lack of public support for their cause. The small clusters of interested parties had heard rumors, "stray bits of information that such-and-such a rabbi in this city or such-and-such a group in another city has found halachic evidence for a women's minyan." Riskin claimed Rabbi Joseph B. Soloveitchik's support, but the latter never issued a public decision on the matter.[10] In a private responsum to a rabbi in Brooklyn, Rabbi Moshe Feinstein ruled that a scaled-back prayer group was theoretically acceptable, but he doubted that any cohort of women interested in such a ritual would undertake this initiative for the "sake of heaven."[11]

A similar situation could be found in Baltimore. In 1974 Israel's chief rabbi, Shlomo Goren, wrote a private letter to Aaron Siegman of Baltimore. Siegman had written to Israel's top Ashkenazic authority on behalf of ten or so women who wished to form a formal women's prayer group. For Goren the twelfth-century Tosafists (Eruvin 96a) had offered an "opening for women to pray among themselves as a minyan." He therefore ruled: "It is not within our power to prevent [these women] or forbid them from forming a minyan among themselves."[12] Unlike all other rabbinic sponsors at that time—clandestine and otherwise—Goren permitted all the trimmings of a formal prayer quorum: responsive recitations, the *kaddish* prayer, and formal *aliyot*. The small but formidable circle of Baltimore women cherished the confidential and lenient—in their words, "radical"—ruling. In fact when word finally did spread in the early 1980s about the Goren responsum, the leaders of the Baltimore group—who knew the high stakes in the ecclesiastically charged Maryland area—made it clear to their counterparts that the decision "was, and continues to be, strictly for the private use of the Baltimore Women's Minyan."[13]

However, Halakhah was more than just jurisprudence. Halakhic change had to pass an authenticity test. It was therefore near-impossible for women's prayer groups to obtain a public and positive ruling. In February 1976 the Women's Minyan of St. Louis was denied space in Bais Abraham Congregation, where many of the thirty founding members prayed on a regular basis. To be sure, this group of Washington University–affiliated women called their operation a "minyan" and performed some of the rituals that other prayer groups omitted. For this reason Rabbi Simcha Krauss of the local Young Israel told the group that he too could not "sponsor a minyan of that sort."[14] The same was the case for Rabbi Yaakov Weinberg of Baltimore's Ner Israel Rabbinical College, who visited St. Louis in November 1977 and met with the Women's Minyan but could not offer the group his blessing.[15]

On New York's Upper West Side, the leaders of the nascent Kol Nashim wrote to twenty modern-thinking Orthodox rabbis to collect their positions and gain some support for their prayer group.[16] In one instance a Chicago-based rabbi responded that he did not have the time to offer the "serious attention and considerable time which the subject deserved" but hoped that he might "receive copies of replies of other rabbis"—a response that "disappointed" the women, who were already quite "nervous" about their religious project.[17]

Their concern emerged out of the realization that this middle-of-the-road position was less than agreeable to people on both ends of the "women's issues" spectrum. It was neither an authentic religious expression of Orthodox Judaism nor was it authentically—or for that matter, openly—in line with the Jewish feminist cause. In Boston, Rachelle Isserow recalled the experiences of her group of "knowledgeable university women" who had a women's prayer service that "carefully [followed] Halachic guidelines." Some of the more progressive participants were "dismayed" by the circumspection of the enterprise: "Since when do revolutionaries ask for guidelines to define the limits of their rebellion?" On the other hand, wrote Isserow, "many Young Israel people are shocked and amused that Orthodox women, some bordering on middle age, would feel the need to participate in such new-fangled thrill-seeking nonsense. They are convinced that the lack of precedence is enough to classify the service as non-halachic. And besides, why can't all women be satisfied with things as they are?"[18]

The narrow appeal of women's prayer groups was evident. Shortly after his confrontation with the Los Angeles women, Meiselman produced a book on women and Jewish law. In it he objected to the "supposedly technically correct" halakhic maneuverings of women's prayer groups. The author condemned these gatherings—particularly those that involved *aliyot*, for venturing into the uncharted and precarious religious space, "creating the fallacious impression" that these prayer meetings were "in full accordance with all the details of strict halakhic observance."[19] They were, to Meiselman, very much inauthentic religious experiences.

The same was true of the other side. On the prayer groups' leftward flank, Blu Greenberg eventually made it clear that she, too, could not align with the prayer group leaders:

> Women's Tefilla groups are being careful not to call themselves minyonim, not to say certain prayers in their groups which evoke God's kingship and require a minyon for recitation.
>
> I imagine that something is happening in heaven. God on the Kingly throne hears Jews all over the world calling his name. And then he says, "Why do women deny my kingship?" It's not a simple question of what does God want. But it's strange that these women can't say certain things, it's strange that there is an active leaving out of women from the spiritual congregation.[20]

Most of all Greenberg objected to the separatist character of these groups. It wasn't in line with the feminism she championed. To her it made far more sense to educate and identify opportunities for women in prayer within the general context of the service—with women and men participating. Another Jewish feminist with traditional leanings wrote that she was "opposed to women's prayer groups and women's minyanim because I am against segregation. As I see it, women's prayer groups are a revival—more sophisticated, but still a revival—of the weibershe shul."[21] This egalitarian principle was in keeping with the spirit of feminism that carried much support throughout the 1960s and 1970s.[22] Greenberg recognized that her vision for women and Orthodox

Judaism was not shared by those involved in single-sex prayer. In her 1981 book on women and Judaism, she made it apparent that she found the latter's method unfulfilling:

> A word is in order here about women's minyanim as a solution to the problem of peripheral status. A women's minyan does have considerable value, for in it a woman can acquire skills she otherwise would have no opportunity to develop: leading prayer, reading the Torah, even acquiring a familiarity with the order of *tefilot* that men routinely develop. Individual communities ought to help women to form prayer groups. . . . [However,] a women's minyan is an interim solution at best. A totally separatist solution is not what the covenantal community is all about. Moreover, a separate minyan will continue to be satisfying only for a small number of women. For the majority, full access will have to come within a range of a full community. A synagogue naturally is a place that strengthens family, not divides it.[23]

Women's prayer nonetheless persevered, at least momentarily. The women's prayer group movement gained modest momentum, despite the lack of public support. For example, several Stern College students journeyed uptown to the West Side to participate in women's Simhat Torah prayer groups.[24] In 1981 an observer noted that "there has been significant growth of women's Minyanim gathering together on a regular basis to share the experience of Tefilla."[25] A year later New York City councilwoman Susan Alter made headlines when she established the first prayer group in Brooklyn, and eventually donated a Torah scroll to that assembly of women.[26] In truth women's prayer continued to develop, in large part because most groups avoided words like "minyan," terms freighted with maleness and masculine religious space. To that very point the participants' goal was to create an all-women's domain for religious experience that did not infringe on or compete with the traditional men's synagogue space. All this generated a sense of optimism.

## Obtaining Some Religious Authenticity

But at the outset of the 1980s, women's prayer practitioners still operated along the fringes of Orthodox Judaism, unable to obtain the level of religious currency to enter the mainstream. The leaders of the movement recognized the challenges they faced while linked to feminism. In Cleveland a Federation-sponsored poll of Orthodox Jews found that fewer than 30 percent of men felt "positively" about the shifting roles of women.[27] There existed a kind of nervousness to raise the issue. The editor of an Orthodox Union magazine offered that the "status of women in Orthodox Judaism" is "one of the most important issues," but "speaking out on this issue is very hazardous."[28] Most tended to heed this advice, trying their best to avoid the matters of feminism, gender, and women's roles in Judaism. To be sure, some younger voices disagreed. One Manhattan woman described feminism's impact on her Upper West Side Orthodox cohort, particularly in light of the "Jewish family." She acknowledged that a "concentration of professional Jewish women in the upper 20s are single, and a lot of religious men can't deal with it." She was in the minority, however. Another young Orthodox woman, this one hailing from Long Island, agreed that feminist forces had "challenged Jewish family patterns" but did not reach Orthodox religion and ritual. "I don't think women have much more of a role in the Jewish community. The power lies in shuls and organizations, which men control."[29]

Most Orthodox women seemed to accept the boundaries between male and female spaces, at least outwardly. Those who deigned to take up the issue frequently voiced support for the status quo and condemned feminist sensibilities. For instance, Yehudis Perlow figured that domestic responsibilities were more than sufficient to satisfy Orthodox women. On par with other religiously conservative faith groups and not at all in line with other sectors of American Judaism, Perlow told a reportedly large crowd in Great Neck that "traditional or normative Judaism has always permitted and even encouraged self-fulfillment for women."[30] All this, so long as women remained homemakers and kept out of the male-controlled synagogue. This sentiment was agreeable to many other Orthodox Jews. Perhaps the same Long Island women who had listened to Perlow's descriptions of feminine domesticity were reportedly "not very receptive" to the Orthodox feminist champion, Blu Greenberg, when she spoke at the congregation a few years later about enlarging the scope of women's roles in the synagogue.[31] In nearby Plainview the local Young Israel elected a woman to its board, but one who made it clear she was uninterested in invading male space, like "dancing with the Torah on Simchat Torah."[32] The head of the RCA told a reporter that "the Orthodox woman by and large is very satisfied with her role within the Jewish community."[33]

Orthodox Judaism's posturing away from feminism was a calculated maneuver. In the United States the feminist movement was at a nadir. In response to the women's ordination debates within the Conservative movement, a leading Orthodox woman dismissed any Orthodox female interest in the rabbinate and the feminist cause, as Jewish women were far too busy "conducting the religious services in her home."[34] Women's prayer groups accepted all this, to a degree. Susan Alter, Rivka Haut, and other women's prayer leaders eschewed any kind of "feminist"—the "F-word"—designation. Haut, especially, was very careful of this. She and her husband, Rabbi Irwin Haut, were highly Jewishly educated and committed Modern Orthodox moderates.[35] Haut and others feared its social implications and the potential alienation from their friends and local Orthodox institutions.[36] Rather than champion an egalitarian cause, they sought to create new space that women could control. Haut would often shrug and explain that she and her colleagues did not take their cues from feminism or Conservative Judaism. In the 1950s the Conservative movement responded to calls to include women in worship by counting them as equals among their male counterparts.[37] "I can't help what it looks like," Haut once explained. "If we wanted that we could go to Conservative shuls."[38] The Orthodox Right paid attention—then called these "reassuring words"—but did not fully believe Haut.[39] Despite their claims to the contrary, Haut and other prayer group proponents could not counter allegations that their ritual resembled that of Conservative Judaism or was inspired by feminist doctrine.

Part of the problem was a miscalculation. Modern Orthodox women's middle-of-the-road strategy had helped elevate women's Talmud study. The modestly enlarged learning opportunities recently available signaled new worship prospects to prayer groups. In fact the well-educated prayer-group members often engaged in Torah study at worship meetings.[40] One supporter urged women to form prayer groups and "press forward with demands for a full Torah, Talmud and advanced Jewish education of the same high standards available to men."[41] The creation of female learning and prayer spaces, they figured, offered women genuine opportunities for religious development—the standard religious touchstones their male counterparts had—that did not encroach on traditional male space.

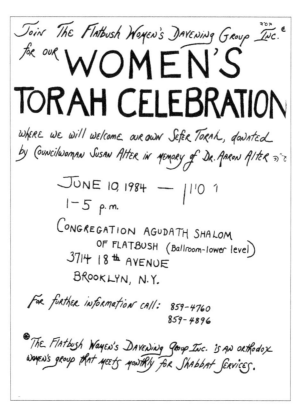

A flyer promoting a special Torah scroll dedication at the
Flatbush Women's Prayer (or in Yiddish, "Davening")
Group in June 1984. (Sheryl Haut)

However, the two were not the same, at least in perception. First, women's
Talmud study enjoyed the adamant and vocal support of Rabbi Soloveitchik, even as it, too, struggled to gain a foothold within the arena of Modern
Orthodox education.[42] Second, women's Talmud study did not interfere with
the synagogue, the very site where Orthodox leaders had defended against
changes championed by Reform and then Conservative Judaism: mixed seating, increased participation by women in the worship, and the ordination of
female rabbis and cantors. These religious reforms blurred gender boundaries.
In response Orthodox Judaism was bent on protecting the maleness of the synagogue and religious worship. It was not sufficient that men dominated their
own Orthodox prayer space; they were compelled to control it for women,
as well. Orthodox Jews viewed their strict defense of synagogue norms as a

noble protection of tradition. The president of the RCA offered the following differentiation between Talmud and prayer in a platform he articulated in the 1980s: "Torah study for women—yes. Coopting of our most able men and women for communal leadership—yes. Maintaining the traditional sanctity of the synagogue—most emphatically yes."[43]

Owing to this, the prayer groups' rhetorical gestures and dismissals of feminist leanings and religious inauthenticities did not make up for the threat that women's prayer posed to Orthodox male space. In 1982 the Agudath Ha-Rabbonim banned women's prayer on the grounds that it was a ritual imposter, a danger to male-dominated Orthodox prayer.[44] The rabbinical group charged that a "daughter of Israel may not participate in such worthless ceremonies that are totally contrary to Halacha" and threatened to "take the strictest measures to prevent such 'Prayers.'"[45] The Agudath Ha-Rabbonim's short declaration offered nothing on how prayer groups violated the specifics of Halakhah but focused entirely on devaluing feminine attempts to model traditionally male-dominated rituals.

## Mainstreaming Women's Prayer

Women's prayer groups continued, despite the backlash. In the main, the Orthodox rabbinate continued to balk at requests for public encouragement. Prayer groups, therefore, were compelled to turn inward for moral support. Two events in Teaneck, New Jersey, underscore this point. In June 1983 the so-called Task Force on Jewish Women hosted the conference "Women, Prayer and Tradition." The purpose of the gathering was to offer workshops to novices on "How to Start a Women's Tefilah" and to bring together some of the stalwarts of the fourteen or so prayer groups to consider how to generate a more unified movement.[46] Six months later a local Jewish newspaper published a lengthy report on Teaneck's women's prayer group. The group had started two years earlier, encouraged by the efforts of likeminded women in Manhattan and Brooklyn, and set into motion by the arrival of a veteran and liturgically capable member of the Riverdale cohort.[47] The Teaneck prayer group met monthly, attracting about sixty women, sometimes more than a hundred on the occasion of a bat mitzvah, engagement, or another notable lifecycle moment. The worshipers tended to fill the professional ranks of teachers, librarians, and social workers—women possessing advanced degrees and high levels of Jewish education. The group met in homes, within a few blocks of the local congregation where most of the women and their families typically prayed on the Sabbath. Just like the others, the Teaneck group made clear that theirs was a movement committed to "rational modern Orthodoxy" and not at all in line with feminism. The Teaneck women also banned masculine cues and costumes: no prayer shawls or yarmulkes. While the group did not set it as a requirement, married women covered their heads in the usual feminine Orthodox fashion.[48]

This, though, was not enough for the detractors, most of them, in this case, women defending traditional male and female Orthodox spaces. The attacks on the women worshipers decried their prayer services as inauthentic and therefore non-Orthodox. Some claimed that "my grandmother didn't do it, and she was a wonderful woman." Another Teaneck woman questioned why her neighbors were so eager to enter men's spaces. In Teaneck and in other large Modern Orthodox hubs, prayer group founders spoke about the importance of moving past the female position as "passive observers" in Orthodox prayer. They reflected on the spiritual thrill of touching and chanting from a Torah scroll and leading the prayer service, however limiting that ritual was from a halakhic point of view. But, as it did for the outspoken Anne Senter, this struck an uncomfortable nerve for many who were all too satisfied with their Sabbath and holiday routines, inside and outside the synagogue:

> I do not feel inferior because I sit on the women's side of the Mechitza. And when the wind-chill factor is -2° or it is raining hard outside and my husband and sons have to walk to the synagogue because it is the Sabbath, I am very happy that I can fulfill my religious obligations at home. When the aroma of the "chulent" that I prepare fills my home and my family gathers around the Sabbath table which my daughter set and we eat the challah which my children and I baked, and my family sings "Eishet Chayil"—then I am truly fulfilled as a Jewish wife and mother. And don't let anyone put that job down—it is a foundation stone without which Judaism cannot survive.[49]

Others offered much of the same, claiming that the only way to overcome the breach of tradition was to obtain the sanction of major rabbinic authorities, an achievement that earlier advocates had failed to secure. Judith

Rosenbaum—apparently uninformed or untrusting of the hushed rabbinic sanctions of the 1970s—offered the following:

> Throughout the ages, in G-d fearing Jewish communities, whenever radical change was sought or needed, there was one way and one way only in which it was done—with the approval of the Gedoley Hador. Only the foremost giants of the generation had the authority and the wisdom to institute change. Even these sages, when themselves faced with major decisions, consulted with and sought the approval of their peers. Have the members of the Women's Tefillah consulted directly with today's Gedoley Hador, such as Rav Moshe Feinstein or Rav Joseph B. Soloveitchik?"[50]

Prayer group leaders recognized the dilemma. Their grassroots initiative could not develop in a more natural, consensus-minded fashion. Truth to tell, some still fought back, standing their ground as Orthodox insiders and entitled to engage in a mode of religious practice that betokened their education and upbringing. "However delicious it may be to snuggle under the covers when husbands and sons have to brave zero temperatures," responded a Teaneck woman to Senter, "the feeling pales by comparison to the satisfaction that comes from knowing one has fulfilled a religious obligation—albeit one which was undertaken voluntarily."[51] Moreover, opponents understood prayer groups' efforts as an attempt to sabotage the male-dominated synagogue. Recall that Modern Orthodox male sacred space had already endured a blow from women's Talmud study and was under siege from more religiously fundamentalist circles that boasted a more confident spirit of Old World traditionalism.[52]

The sustainability of women's prayer therefore relied on the unlikely support of the Orthodox rabbinate and their synagogues. It required some sort of formal incorporation into the Modern Orthodox mainstream. When asked, YU President Norman Lamm balked at the invitation to endorse.[53] So did the National Council of Young Israel.[54] Yet it made the most sense for women's prayer groups to seek out the approval of an organization of congregational rabbis. For the Modern Orthodox, this was the Rabbinical Council of America. The RCA boasted a membership of a thousand rabbinic members. Almost two-thirds of the organization held positions in congregations and were in a position to bring about change.[55] There was some initial hope. Shortly after the

Teaneck affair, outgoing RCA president Rabbi Gilbert Klaperman beseeched his colleagues to decide on the matter of "women's davening groups." Klaperman urged those in power to "provide a halachically valid guide for those who want and/or need it."[56]

## Rabbi Louis Bernstein and the Feminist Heresy

Klaperman's call was heeded, but not in the way he had in mind. In May 1984 the RCA elected Rabbi Louis Bernstein as its president—his second stint in that position. He was a moderate and respected Modern Orthodox clergyman. A very busy man, Bernstein served for many decades at the pulpit of the Young Israel of Windsor Park in Queens, New York. He taught at Yeshiva University and held high positions in Religious Zionist circles and other Orthodox organizations. Born in 1927, Bernstein was old enough to recall the old guard that had struggled to establish Orthodox Judaism in the United States and to keep it religiously level-headed. Once elected, Bernstein announced that it was "time for the center of the Orthodox religious movement to assert itself and fulfill its role of guiding a delicate course between extremes of both left and right in religious Judaism."[57] Evidently Bernstein believed there was more work to be done on his supposed left flank. As one insider put it: "Rabbi Bernstein is more extreme than his predecessor where women's rights are concerned and that, had there been a different constellation of authority, the RCA's attitudes and responses might have been very different."[58] According to one observer, Bernstein had "singled out women joining for prayer to be the central issue confronting American Orthodoxy."[59]

On his return to the top of the RCA's hierarchy, Bernstein engaged in a public debate with prayer group defenders. Time and again he characterized the innovation as an attempt to form a "minyan," and its perpetrators as feminists. On some occasions Bernstein announced that his crusade was on par with other formative Orthodox battles, such as the mid-century battles with Conservative Judaism over the *mehitzah*. "We heard the same argument on mixed pews," he declared, "and fortunately, so many stood their ground."[60] He conflated egalitarianism with female-only spaces. But by aligning those causes, Bernstein reignited the comparisons between women's prayer and the Conservative movement, women rabbis, and feminists, all believed to be the most trenchant threats to Orthodox Judaism. Bernstein and Rabbi Irwin

Haut (Rivka Haut's learned husband) traded a half-dozen vituperative letters in the pages of the Brooklyn-based *Jewish Press*, arguing over the halakhic propriety of women's prayer and the usefulness of the rabbinic leaders who supposedly supported it.[61] The gist of Haut's letters called on Bernstein to vouch for the piety of his wife and her prayer group compatriots, and to press Bernstein to rubberstamp their efforts as religiously legitimate. Bernstein outright refused.

The undaunted Bernstein also met the controversy head on and in person. In November 1984 he participated in a debate with Rabbi Avi Weiss, one of the few staunch rabbinic advocates of women's prayer. At Weiss's liberal-minded Hebrew Institute of Riverdale, Bernstein dubbed the movement a "passing trend" and refused to place the matter on the RCA agenda for discussion. Rehearsing many of Haut's arguments in the newspapers, Weiss demanded Bernstein reconsider his stance, imploring him to recognize that the issue was not about halakhic change or liberal culture. "[The] women who want this experience," said Weiss, "are not looking for shortcuts." Bernstein did not back down. In response to an audience member's question on who should determine whether women's prayer deserved consideration, the RCA president quipped: "When I ask halachic questions, I ask them to halachic experts. When I want to know about cooking, I ask my wife."[62] The response reportedly caused quite a stir, reminding all in attendance of Bernstein's attempt to consign Orthodox women to a very specified feminine space.

Soon enough, though, Bernstein raised the issue at an RCA executive meeting, but not before "stacking the deck," as he was later accused.[63] After departing Weiss's synagogue, Bernstein asked five young and influential rabbinic faculty members of YU's Rabbi Isaac Elchanan Theological Seminary (RIETS) to rule on the permissibility of women's prayer groups. Rabbis Nisson Alpert, Abba Bronspigel, Yehuda Parnes, Hershel Schachter, and Mordechai Willig were all noted scholars and disciples of leading luminaries of the past generation, including Soloveitchik and Feinstein. Later on Bernstein admitted that he had "an idea of their position" before he posted the query.[64] The so-called RIETS Five outlawed prayer groups on the grounds that "these practices are intended to emulate the ways of the gentiles, since these customs are derived from the feminist movement."[65] Their responsum also referred to women's "minyanim," a deliberate decision to imply the women's encroachment on Orthodox men's space. Like earlier attacks on prayer groups, this responsum did not offer many traditional rabbinic sources from the Talmud and codes, a fact pointed out by several critics.[66]

The YU rabbis argued that Orthodox women should defer to the status quo. Prayer group practitioners, in the words of one member of the RIETS Five, Rabbi Abba Bronspigel, were "denying themselves real *minyanim*." He and the others believed that wherever there existed regular services—ones led by men—then "women cannot create their own."[67] The decision may well have been influenced by certain knowledge that the local Washington Heights prayer group went, in the words of its founder, "a little further" than others. Like the cohorts in Baltimore and St. Louis, the Upper Manhattan group headed by Freda Birnbaum recited some passages usually reserved for a traditional quorum of men. Nonetheless, several critics rebuked the rabbis for supplying a dearth of citations from Talmud and codes to enforce their prohibition. Even more were dismayed that the YU scholars refused to meet with prayer group leaders before issuing their responsum. "A lot of us know these women and know what's going on in our Orthodox communities," explained one of the writers, Rabbi Yehuda Parnes. "We're very familiar with their attitudes, so there's no point in hearing them out again."[68] A mimeographed copy of the responsum made the rounds before its more official debut in the RCA rabbinic journal in May 1985. In the meantime prayer group leaders "attempted to meet with Rabbi [Hershel] Schachter before publication of his more elaborate article, to discuss the matter with him." Rivka Haut reported that "he was too busy."[69]

The going got tougher. The Bernstein affair instantly mobilized advocates of women's prayer. In short order they established the Women's Tefillah Network, started a regular newsletter, and organized conferences in New York and Israel.[70] They continued to challenge Bernstein throughout his presidential tenure. One year after he had posed his halakhic quandary to the RIETS Five, Bernstein confessed to the RCA membership that "anybody who dares scorn the fury of the ladies is tempting a fate as least worse than hell."[71] Still, Bernstein and other opponents had thwarted the movement's momentum, branding the women leaders extremists and Orthodox outsiders, despite their intensive Orthodox upbringings. The network's sporadically published newsletters were routinely filled with despondence. "We in Montreal are still meeting but having problems with declining numbers," wrote Norma Joseph to her so-called Tefillah Friends. "This month we will study Ruth and try to blend more study into our regular meetings. It is helpful to get the newsletter and feel a part of something larger. If anyone has had similar problems and worked out successful solutions, we'd love to hear from you."[72] Most poignant, prayer group leaders worried that there was a paucity of youth involved in their cause. Naomi Doron and her teenage daughter, Gitty, told a journalist that her male teachers did their very best to dissuade them from these innovations. Likewise Shulamith School for Girls in Brooklyn wrote a letter to parents declaring that "Shulamith is committed to the unity of the Jewish people and does not subscribe to factions or splinter groups." Mrs. Doron added that girls "get interested in boys and learn boys are not so interested in girls who learn [and pray] so much."[73]

For the balance of the 1980s, reports on prayer groups in the Jewish media underscored their role in facilitating religious experience for a very small, niche Orthodox group. Prayer groups were inconspicuously "flourishing in secret gardens" and "davening in the dark."[74] Those, though, were kind descriptions. Despite their efforts to straddle a middle ground and boast an authentic halakhic spirit, women's prayer groups had lost much in their struggle. No doubt much of the problem was the dearth of rabbinical support. Bernstein and the RIETS responsum had caused considerable commotion. Several months after it was issued, the RCA's executive committee debated the matter and resolved "that the opinion of the five Roshei Yeshiva was not the official opinion of the RCA regarding this matter; [and] that the RCA has to date not taken any official position regarding the Halachic admissibility of women's T'filot."[75] Yet its existence convinced several leaders, like Rabbi Kenneth Auman of the Young Israel of Flatbush in Brooklyn, to renege on earlier commitments to support the women's efforts.[76] The lion's share of Modern Orthodox rabbis remained cool to the notion of women's prayer, and incorrigible about the prospects of inviting their rituals into the synagogue.

The point was that prayer groups could not overcome their opponents' charge that their efforts were somehow less than authentic by American Orthodox measures. It did not matter all that much that prayer groups had plenty of halakhic sources for support and that their rivals were in short supply of the same. In this context prayer group advocates overestimated—or oversimplified—the role of formal Halakhah in determining the borderlines of Orthodox Judaism, as well as their standing as Orthodox insiders. More important was the threat to Orthodox male space. Their efforts to downplay feminism and other Orthodox taboos fell short.[77] From Jerusalem the Jewish philosopher Eliezer Berkovits commented on the struggle that "there may be a great deal of Orthodoxy around. Unfortunately, there is only very little halachic Judaism."[78] The women's prayer movement languished because it failed to gain traction as an authentic religious expression. Their efforts posed too great a threat to Orthodox male space. In retaliation they were labeled a heresy because Orthodox Judaism was much more than a commitment to the basics of Jewish law.

# CONCLUSION

In the final stages of writing this book, I shared some of its ideas of authenticity and religious culture with my students. I explained to this group of undergraduates enrolled in an Orthodox Jewish college that we ought to understand authenticity as a set of experiences informed by a myriad of indigenous forces. I also shared Rabbi Leonard Gewirtz's sentiments, quoted in the opening pages of this book, about Yom Kippur, animated by the "soul-stirring cry of repentance." Instantly one student offered that this was also the message of a well-known song, "Deaf Man in a Shteeble." The song was first performed in the 1980s by the folksy Jewish musician Yossi Toiv, also known as "Country Yossi." Several groups have covered it since then. Eager to see how the discussion would progress from here, I entreated the young man to elaborate.

The stirring song describes a momentous Yom Kippur eve in a small town. The all-important Kol Nidrei service is delayed because of a tardy cantor. Also absent is his deaf father, who regularly attends synagogue, even though he cannot hear his son's chants and melodies. Suddenly the cantor barrels into the synagogue sanctuary, ready to lead the prayers with unsurpassed power, but not before "he wipes away a tear." His spirited prayers break the hearts of the other worshipers and ignite their souls, though they are unaware that the cantor's performance was inspired by tragic circumstances. Here's the punchline:

> And when he finished davening,
> The rabbi asked to tell
> What was it he was thinking of
> That made him sing so well.
> "Well you knew my dad was deaf," he said,
> "Last night he passed away.
> It's the first time that my father's
> Heard me pray."

Most students agreed that Country's Yossi's "Deaf Man" was a tear-jerker, a song that elicits powerful religious feelings that authentically express Yom Kippur's atonement-seeking experience. Yet one young man remained incredulous. He informed the rest of us that Country Yossi's song was far from original. In 1975 David Geddes composed "The Blind Man in the Bleachers." Shortly thereafter the single was made famous when it was covered by country singer Kenny Starr. In this version it is a backup football player who leads a second-half comeback after learning that his blind father has passed away. After the victory the coach asks the boy "what was it he was thinkin' of that made him play so well." In response the hero athlete explains:

> "You knew my dad was blind," he said,
> "Tonight he passed away.
> It's the first time that my father's seen me play."

Our class struggled over this revelation. On the one hand, "Deaf Man in a Shteeble" is not authentically Jewish, at least in the way that a certain group of historians and scholars understand the term. Its heartstring-tugging message is drawn from a popular American country-music song. Its origins are far from Jewish. On the other hand, the adaptation strikes deep into its audience's hearts. I confess that I have listened to the song nearly a hundred times, often with welled-up tears. It resonates as something deeply religious, tapping into the mystique of death and the relationships between parents and children. After a lively conversation, the class decided to contact and query Country Yossi on the matter. Would he defend his song as authentic? He did. "The song has overtones of mysticism, religion, love and profound emotion," he responded. "Those are the ingredients for a musical classic."[1] His argument also jibes with the thesis of this book: In religious terms, authenticity has much more to do with lived experiences than a confirmation of originality or fidelity to an ancient tradition.

Authenticity is a contested idea. For instance, a small number among the Orthodox Right have raised their concerns over the "propriety" of popular balladeers like Country Yossi and Uncle Moishy.[2] Their overt attempts at cultural "coalescence" were deemed more harmful than helpful. Accordingly, these pages have made a case for the dynamics of religious authenticity, how it is experienced and mediated by a variety of ever-changing cultural forces. To illustrate it is useful to return to Passover peanut oil, or at least its afterlife in the kosher kitchen. In 1997 the Star-K issued Passover certification for quinoa.[3] Toward the end of the 1990s, more and more Jewish chefs and kitchen connoisseurs discovered that they could do much with quinoa, a grainlike crop with edible seeds. These women and men therefore applauded the Baltimore-based kosher certifying agency. Before long though, controversies reminiscent of the Passover peanut oil debates appeared annually in the Jewish press, always a few weeks before the springtime holiday. For one Orthodox woman a 2008 rumor that several *kashrut* agencies had considered whether to "ban quinoa [had] just sent [her] over the edge."[4] In 2012 a kosher supermarket in Brooklyn "placed *all* quinoa in the *kitniyot* section" of its store, enraging customers who had freely eaten quinoa on Passover for the past several years.[5] One year later the Orthodox Union's leading authority in *kashrut* told a reporter that he could not "certify quinoa." Rabbi Menachem Genack's reasoning echoed the same cautious refrain that Orthodox Jews had voiced ever since the more stringent Hungarian Jewish folkway made its way to the United States. "It's a disputed food," explained Genack, "so we can't hold an opinion, and we don't certify it. Those who rely on the OU for *kashrut* just won't have quinoa on Passover."[6] In other words it was a less-than-authentic Passover ingredient for many American Orthodox Jews and therefore unacceptable, no matter how much the rabbinic logic tilted in the other direction. When it came to food, lenient positions did not seem to catch on. For instance, a Chicago-based *kashrut* administrator vented some frustration over how "many people would rather not consume items that need an article such as this to explain why it is acceptable to eat."[7]

Not everyone agreed to abide by the Hungarian-style status quo, especially those who still clung to the Lithuanian rabbinic culture that had once thrived in American Orthodoxy. "Rav Moshe Feinstein said we weren't to add on to the rules of *kitniyot*, so I don't know why anyone would," offered a representative of another *kashrut* organization, referring to Feinstein's peanut oil responsum. "And what's more telling of this ridiculous debate," concluded the exasperated *kashrut* administrator, "is that quinoa is a seed not a legume."[8] Of course that upset *kashrut* supervisor was correct. However, he underestimated the importance of authenticity in determining religious observance, even when common sense and precedents were on his side. Inexplicably, renewed agitation made a difference. Despite the fall of peanut oil from Passover grocery shelves, the Lithuanian folkway made a comeback of sorts. In 2014 the Orthodox Union listed quinoa in its Passover-approved directory.[9]

The recent revival of the Lithuanian folkway in American Orthodox Judaism is a reminder of the dynamic nature of authenticity in religious life. The constant shifting in the lived religious experience of American tradition-bound faiths proves that authenticity is a moving target. It also challenges the prevailing assumption that Orthodox Judaism has moved "rightward" in a one-dimensional path. It may be too soon to properly understand all the American forces that have helped retain quinoa as an acceptable Passover ingredient. However, we can be confident that there is more to it than religious declension and the lingering responses of "modernity," as the Jacob Katz school might posit.

Moreover, religious and cultural change ensures that authenticity has remained elusive. Take for example a public controversy in New York, long after bat mitzvah was commonplace in Gotham. On January 21, 1997, sixty-two members of the Vaad Harabonim of Queens met at a Forest Hills restaurant. The group convened in response to a query submitted by the principal of the Yeshiva of Central Queens (YCQ). Rabbi Aaron Brander and members of the school's parent body were deeply concerned about the contents of a bat mitzvah invitation circulating among seventh graders. The note invited the girl's friends to join her at a prayer group where the young lady would be "called to the Torah to read." By this time Orthodox Jews in Queens had grown comfortable with many types of bat mitzvah ceremonies. However, a women's prayer group was certainly not one of them. Parents asked the YCQ head of school whether their daughters were permitted to attend this quasi-halakhic service. Prayer groups, as we have seen, had garnered significant attention in the prior decade. Brander savvily submitted the question to the local rabbinical council.[10] In response the Queens rabbis banned the event as a violation of "authentic Judaism"—a condemnation of the prayer group, not bat mitzvah altogether.

The twelve-year-old girl's rabbi defended the practice. Rabbi Simcha Krauss of the Young Israel of Hillcrest lectured the Vaad that there was nothing wrong with the ritual, so long as the women's group omitted all parts of prayer that could be recited only among a minyan of at least ten men. He had apparently come around to women's prayer after declining to support it while in St. Louis during the 1970s. Whatever the case, Krauss's remarks in the 1990s paralleled one side of the debate from the 1980s. His detractors mirrored the other side of the argument. Rabbi Fabian Schonfeld and other rabbis explained that they preferred the more stringent position penned more than a decade earlier by the five leading YU scholars. The Vaad politely implied to Krauss that he was outranked. Then they voted on the matter a final time. Twelve members of the Vaad left the room to avoid implication. Most of those remaining sided against women's prayer groups and the girl's bat mitzvah.[11]

The Orthodox Right blamed the whole matter on feminism and used the affair to call other religious practices into question. "This is what happens when you let women learn Talmud," said one rabbi at the Forest Hills meeting.[12] He interpreted both as an affront to Orthodox male sacred space. In fact the Queens episode became a much broader attempt to reclaim this space. Covering a host of rituals and religious habits, Rabbi Aryeh Ginzberg called on all "Torah Jews" to reconsider their stance on "women's issues" and resist those who "trample over Mesoras Yisroel [Jewish tradition] at every turn."[13] Ensuing events helped justify their conflations. A week after the Vaad issued its statement, the nascent Jewish Orthodox Feminist Alliance (JOFA) held its first public meeting, which featured several sessions on women's Torah study, lifecycle rituals, and prayer groups. The organizers had published a modest number of conference programs, figuring that at most only a few hundred would attend the liberal Orthodox group's convention. Instead seven hundred women and men gathered at the New York conference, spurred by the rabbinical condemnations and invigorated by Blu Greenberg's hope for a more egalitarian Orthodox Judaism.[14] To delegitimize JOFA's efforts as inauthentic, Orthodox leaders explained that Greenberg and her colleagues "have made common cause with Reform, Conservative, and Reconstructionist feminists."[15]

The entire commotion conflated bat mitzvah, women's Talmud study, and prayer groups all at once. It also questioned the propriety of introducing debatable ideas into a day school and challenging the status quo youth culture. On their own each of these rituals and practices had achieved varying levels of religious authenticity. By the late 1990s most Orthodox Jews considered bat mitzvah authentically Orthodox. Women's Talmud and prayer groups trailed behind. The new religious conditions and cultural forces reopened earlier conversations, challenging the authenticity of reasonably established Orthodox practices. To protect bat mitzvah and "normative" Orthodox practices, two Modern Orthodox scholars produced a 114-page article that separated the

One week after the Queens Vaad banned a girl's bat mitzvah celebration in 1997, more than seven hundred women and men turned out for the inaugural conference of the Jewish Orthodox Feminist Alliance. (Jewish Orthodox Feminist Alliance)

girls' rite of passage from prayer groups on halakhic grounds. More than that, Rabbis Aryeh and Dov Frimer urged Orthodox Jews to understand that the latter ritual was "not authentically Jewish."[16] The word "authentic" appeared many times in their much-discussed essay. For example, by excusing themselves from regular Orthodox Sabbath services, prayer groups participants, they alleged, were "actively and deliberately opting for the inauthentic in place of the authentic."[17] In 2013 the same writers deployed similar strategies to defend "normative" Orthodoxy against a new generation of avowedly feminist Jewish women and men in search of more egalitarian modes of halakhically acceptable prayer. Their solution was a so-called partnership minyan, services that empower women to lead select portions of the worship.[18] The Frimers determined that this was "unacceptable" from an Orthodox point of view.[19]

In response Rabbi Heshie Billet of Long Island refused to concede the role of authenticity to determine the contours of Orthodox faith. To him it was wrong to dismiss rituals that could be justified by Jewish law, even if he himself did not subscribe to them. "This is not a non-Orthodox venture," wrote the former RCA president of quasi-egalitarian services. "We should not lose sight of the fact that, while the people involved in these minyanim may be mistaken, they are primarily Orthodox Jews committed to halakhic Judaism." Concluded Billet: "They deserve to be seriously critiqued but not delegitimized."[20] But in fact this is how American Orthodoxy has developed and negotiated its borderlines. Like other tradition-bound faiths, Orthodox Judaism is in tension with the cultural forces that surround it. This is the stuff of religious authenticity.

# NOTES

## Introduction

1. See Sidney E. Mead, "Denominationalism: The Shape of Protestantism in America," *Church History* 23 (December 1954): 291–320.
2. Leonard B. Gewirtz, *The Authentic Jew and His Judaism: An Analysis of the Basic Concepts of the Jewish Religion* (New York: Bloch, 1961), 59.
3. Ibid., 9.
4. Ibid., 21.
5. See Charles Lindholm, *Culture and Authenticity* (Oxford: Blackwell, 2007), 8–11. Lionel Trilling traced "sincerity," an adjunct of authenticity, to the fifteenth century and the rise of a less "personal" Protestant faith. See Lionel Trilling, *Sincerity and Authenticity* (Cambridge, MA: Harvard University, 1972). For a survey on the social and philosophical conceptions of authenticity, see Charles Lindholm, "The Rise of Expressive Authenticity," *Anthropological Quarterly* 86 (Spring 2013): 361–95.
6. Ronald Weed, "Jean-Jacques Rousseau on Civil Religion: Freedom of the Individual, Toleration, and the Price of Mass Authenticity," in *Civil Religion in Political Thought*, ed. Ronald Weed and John von Heyking (Washington, DC: Catholic University of America Press, 2010), 145–66.
7. Hermann Schwab, *The History of Orthodox Jewry in Germany* (London: Mitre Press, 1950), 11.
8. See Charles Guignon, "Authenticity and the Question of Being," in *Heidegger, Authenticity and the Self: Themes from Division Two of Being and Time*, ed. Denis McManus (London: Routledge, 2015), 8–20.
9. See Eliezer Berkovits, *With God in Hell: Judaism in the Ghettos and Death-camps* (New York: Sanhedrin Press, 1979), 61–77.
10. See, for example, Herman Wouk, *This Is My God* (Garden City, NJ: Doubleday, 1959), 235–45.
11. S. N. Eisenstadt, "Post-Traditional Societies and the Continuity and Reconstruction of Tradition," *Daedalus* 102 (Winter 1973): 20.
12. Eric Hobsbawm, "Introduction: Inventing Traditions," in *The Inventions of Tradition*, ed. Eric Hobsbawm and Terrance Ranger (Cambridge: Cambridge University Press, 1983), 1. See also Richard Handler and Jocelyn Linnekin,

"Tradition, Genuine or Spurious," *Journal of American Folklore* 97 (July–September 1984): 273–90.

13. See Clifford Geertz, *The Interpretation of Cultures: Selected Essays* (New York: Basic Books, 1973), 127.

14. See Dimitrios Theodossopoulos, "Laying Claim to Authenticity: Five Anthropological Dilemmas," *Anthropological Quarterly* 86 (Spring 2013): 337–60.

15. See Timothy Matovina, "Remapping American Catholicism," *U.S. Catholic Historian* 28 (Fall 2010): 31–72.

16. See Arnold M. Eisen, "Constructing the Usable Past: The Idea of 'Tradition' in Twentieth-Century American Judaism," in *Uses of Tradition: Jewish Continuity in the Modern Era*, ed. Jack Wertheimer (New York: Jewish Theological Seminary of America, 1992), 429–61.

17. Regina Bendix, *In Search of Authenticity: The Formations of Folklore Studies* (Madison: University of Wisconsin Press, 1997), 13–14.

18. Ibid., 198.

19. See Iddo Tavory, *Summoned: Identification and Religious Life in a Jewish Neighborhood* (Chicago: University of Chicago Press, 2016), 1–19.

20. Gewirtz, *The Authentic Jew and His Judaism*, 8.

21. See Robert A. Orsi, *Between Heaven and Earth: The Religious Worlds People Make and the Scholars Who Study Them* (Princeton, NJ: Princeton University Press, 2005), 5.

22. See Wade Clark Roof, *A Generation of Seekers: The Spiritual Journeys of the Baby Boom Generation* (San Francisco: HarperSanFrancisco, 1993), 250.

23. Reinhold Niebuhr, "Varieties of Religious Revival," *New Republic* (June 6, 1955): 14.

24. See Paul Hutchinson, "Have We a 'New' Religion?" *Life* 38 (April 11, 1955): 139.

25. See, for example, David Ellenson, *Tradition in Transition: Orthodoxy, Halakhah, and the Boundaries of Modern Jewish Identity* (Lanham, MD: University Press of America, 1989), 1–5.

26. See Gary Phillip Zola, *Isaac Harby of Charleston, 1788–1828: Jewish Reformer and Intellectual* (Tuscaloosa: University of Alabama Press, 1994), 112–49.

27. Isaac Harby, *A Discourse, Delivered in Charleston, (S.C.) on the 21st of Nov. 1825, before the Reformed Society of Israelites, for Promoting True Principles of Judaism According to Its Purity and Spirit, on Their First Anniversary* (Charleston, SC: A. E. Miller, 1825), 6.

28. Ibid.

29. See L. C. Moise, *Biography of Isaac Harby: With an Account of the Reformed Society of Israelites of Charleston, S.C., 1824–1833* (Macon, GA: Central Conference of America Rabbis, 1931), 91–97.

30. Jacob Mordecai, "Remarks on Harby's Discourse Delivered in Charleston (S.C.) on the 21st day of Nov. 1825 Before the Reformed Society of Israelites on

their First Anniversary by a Congregationalist of Richmond, Virginia, January 1826," Transcribed by Gary P. Zola, SC- 8422, 1–3, American Jewish Archives, Cincinnati, OH.

31. See Naomi W. Cohen, *Encounter with Emancipation: The German Jews in the United States, 1830–1914* (Philadelphia: Jewish Publication Society of America, 1984), 176–80.

32. Harby, *A Discourse*, 27.

33. See Emily Bingham, *Mordecai: An Early American Family* (New York: Hill and Wang, 2003), 147–53.

34. Mordecai, "Remarks on Harby's Discourse."

35. See Thomas D. Hamm, *The Transformation of American Quakerism: Orthodox Friends, 1800–1907* (Bloomington: Indiana University Press, 1988), 15–20.

36. See Michael W. Casey, *The Battle Over Hermeneutics in the Stone-Campbell Movement, 1800–1870* (Lewiston, NY: Edwin Mellen Press, 1998), 97–151.

37. See Jay P. Dolan, *In Search of an American Catholicism: A History of Religion and Culture in Tension* (Oxford: Oxford University Press, 2002), 54–55.

38. Nation O. Hatch, *The Democratization of American Christianity* (New Haven, CT: Yale University Press, 1989), 65.

39. See David Hackett Fischer, *Liberty and Freedom: A Visual History of America's Founding Ideas* (Oxford: Oxford University Press, 2005), 213–20.

40. Mordecai Noah, "Jewish Converts," *New York National Advocate* (October 18, 1825): 2.

41. See Jacob Katz, "Orthodoxy in Historical Perspective," in *Studies in Contemporary Jewry*, vol. 2, ed. Peter Y. Medding (Bloomington: Indiana University Press, 1986), 3–17; Rachel Manekin, "Orthodox Jewry in Kraków at the Turn of the Twentieth Century," *Polin* 23 (2011): 165–98; Moshe Samet, "The Beginnings of Orthodoxy," *Modern Judaism* 8 (October 1988): 249–69; and Michael K. Silber, "The Emergence of Ultra-Orthodoxy: The Invention of a Tradition," in *Uses of Tradition*, 23–84.

42. See Jacob Katz, *With My Own Eyes: The Autobiography of a Historian*, trans. Ann Brenner and Zipora Brody (Hanover, NH: Brandeis University Press, 1995), 78–79, 92–93.

43. Mordechai Breuer, *Modernity within Tradition: The Social History of Orthodox Jewry in Imperial Germany*, trans. Elizabeth Petuchowski (New York: Columbia University Press, 1992), 31–38.

44. See Yosef Salmon, *Do Not Provoke Providence: Orthodoxy in the Grip of Nationalism*, trans. Joel A. Linsider (Boston: Academic Studies Press, 2014), 85–86.

45. On Müller and his viewpoint, see Eric J. Sharpe, *Comparative Religion: A History* (London: Duckworth, 1975), 35–46. See also Richard B. Miller, *Casuistry and Modern Ethics: A Poetics of Practical Reasoning* (Chicago: University of Chicago Press, 1996), 212.

46. See Ari L. Goldman, *The Search for God at Harvard* (New York: Random House, 1991), 33.

47. See Moshe Davis, *The Emergence of Conservative Judaism: The Historical School in Nineteenth-Century America* (Philadelphia: Jewish Publication Society of America, 1963), 283–310. For a fuller treatment of the relevant primary sources, see Moshe Davis, *Yahadut Amerika Be-Hitpathutah* (New York: Jewish Theological Seminary of America, 1951), 291–319.

48. See Zev Eleff, *Who Rules the Synagogue? Religious Authority and the Formation of American Judaism* (Oxford: Oxford University Press, 2016), 129–63.

49. See Mark A. Noll, "The Image of the United States as a Biblical Nation, 1776–1865," in *The Bible in America: Essays in Cultural History*, ed. Nathan O. Hatch and Mark A. Noll (New York: Oxford University Press, 1982), 39–58.

50. See Jonathan D. Sarna and Nahum M. Sarna, "Jewish Bible Scholarship and Translations in the United States," in *The Bible and Bibles in America*, ed. Ernest S. Frerichs (Atlanta, GA: Scholars Press, 1988), 83–116.

51. M. M. Noah, "Restoration of the Jews," *Occident* (April 1845): 34.

52. See, for example, Robert Liberles, "Champion of Orthodoxy: The Emergence of Samson Raphael Hirsch as Religious Leader," *AJS Review* 6 (1981): 43–60.

53. See Breuer, *Modernity within Tradition*, 83.

54. See Jonathan D. Sarna, "The Debate over Mixed Seating in the American Synagogue," in *The American Synagogue: A Sanctuary Transformed*, ed. Jack Wertheimer (Cambridge: Cambridge University Press, 1988), 363–94.

55. "What Can Be Done?" *Occident* (December 1852): 417. Emphasis in the original.

56. Jacob Ezekiel, "Zion Collegiate Association," *Israelite* (March 30, 1855): 301. Emphasis in the original.

57. "Pseudo-Judaism," *Jewish Messenger* (April 7, 1865): 116.

58. "American Judaism," *Jewish Messenger* (February 22, 1867): 4.

59. See "The Rebuilding of the Temple," *Charleston Daily Courier* (March 20, 1841): 2. Emphasis in the original.

60. "Rev. Mr. Rosenfeld's Address," *Occident* (May 1847): 79.

61. See Jacob R. Marcus, *The American Jewish Woman: A Documentary History* (New York: Ktav, 1981), 101.

62. See James P. Byrd, *Sacred Scripture, Sacred War: The Bible and the American Revolution* (Oxford: Oxford University Press, 2013), 1–14.

63. On this, see Nathan O. Hatch, "Mormon and Methodist: Popular Religion in the Crucible of the Free Market," *Journal of Mormon History* 20 (1994): 24–44.

64. Sidney E. Mead, *The Lively Experiment: The Shaping of Christianity in America* (New York: Harper & Row, 1963), 108–15.

65. See Jan Shipps, *Mormonism: The Story of a New Religious Tradition* (Urbana:

University of Illinois Press, 1985), 46–48; and John T. McGreevy, *Catholicism and American Freedom: A History* (New York: Norton, 2003), 25–37.

66. Bernard Illowy, "An Oration at the Dedication of the Cincinnati Jewish Hospital," *Israelite* (March 30, 1866): 308.

67. M. J. Raphall, *Constancy of Israel: A Discourse Delivered before the Congregation Shearit Israel, Charleston S.C.* (Charleston: Edward C. Councell, 1850), 17.

68. On these concepts in American religious life, see Richard L. Bushman, *The Refinement of America: Persons, Houses, Cities* (New York: Knopf, 1992), 313–52.

69. See Lance J. Sussman, "Isaac Leeser and the Protestantization of American Judaism," *American Jewish Archives Journal* 38 (April 1986): 1–21.

70. See Arthur Kiron, "Golden Ages, Promised Lands: The Victorian Rabbinic Humanism of Sabato Morais" (PhD diss., Columbia University, 1999), 47.

71. See Joseph L. Blau and Salo W. Baron, *The Jews of the United States, 1790–1840*, vol. 2 (New York: Columbia University Press, 1963), 447–49.

72. L.D., "Parties—Keep Peace," *Asmonean* (August 4, 1854): 125. Lilienthal often wrote under the pseudonym "L.D." See David Philipson, *Max Lilienthal: American Rabbi* (New York: Bloch Publishing, 1915), 57.

73. "The Demands of the Times," *Occident* (October 1844): 313–14.

74. "A Protestant Jewish Church," *Occident* (April 28, 1859): 26.

75. See William R. Hutchison, *Religious Pluralism in America: The Contentious History of a Founding Ideal* (New Haven, CT: Yale University Press, 2003), 11–24.

76. See Nathan M. Kaganoff, "A Historic Document," *Tradition* 7 (Winter 1965): 122.

77. See Shari Rabin, *Jews on the Frontier: Religion and Mobility in Nineteenth-Century America* (New York: NYU Press, 2017), 97–99.

78. See Allan Tarshish, "The Board of Delegates of American Israelites (1859–1878)," *Publications of the American Jewish Historical Society* 49 (September 1959): 30.

79. Minutes of Congregation Beth Ahabah, October 31, 1867, MS-298, AJA.

80. Isaac M. Wise, "Reply," *Israelite* (March 30, 1855): 301.

81. "The Theory, the Practice, the People," *American Israelite* (November 27, 1885): 4.

82. "The American Israelite," *American Israelite* (September 3, 1886): 4.

83. See Alan Silverstein, *Alternatives to Assimilation: The Response of Reform Judaism to American Culture, 1840–1930* (Hanover, NH: Brandeis University Press, 1994), 48–49; and Jeffrey S. Gurock, "The Orthodox Synagogue," in *The American Synagogue*, 43–44.

84. Benjamin F. Peixotto to Isaac Leeser, November 16, 1859, SC-9474, AJA.

85. Patrick, "The Jewish Pulpit," *Jewish Messenger* (October 29, 1869): 1.

86. See Mark A. Noll, *America's God: From Jonathan Edwards to Abraham Lincoln* (Oxford: Oxford University Press, 2002), 22–45.

87. See Louis Menand, *The Metaphysical Club: A Story of Ideas in America* (New York: Farrar, Straus and Giroux, 2001), 49–69.

88. K.H., "1869 and Judaism," *Jewish Messenger* (January 21, 1870): 4.

89. K. Kohler, *Studies, Addresses, and Personal Papers* (New York: Bloch, 1931), 201.

90. Quoted in "Religious Attitude of the Jews," *Jewish Messenger* (August 1, 1879): 2.

91. See Naomi W. Cohen, "The Challenges of Darwinism and Biblical Criticism to American Judaism," *Modern Judaism* 4 (May 1984): 121–57.

92. "The Old Synagogue Service," *Universalist Quarterly* 12 (October 1875): 498.

93. See Israel Goldstein, *A Century of Judaism in New York: B'nai Jeshurun, 1825–1925, New York's Oldest Ashkenazic Congregation* (New York: Congregation B'nai Jeshurun, 1930), 153.

94. "Leeser's Pulpit," *Jewish Messenger* (April 10, 1885): 4.

95. "Editor's Historical Record," *Harper's* 57 (July 1878): 315.

96. Experientia Docet, "The Forty-Fourth Street Synagogue," *American Hebrew* (September 3, 1880): 32.

97. Phil Point, "Positive Judaism," *American Israelite* (September 22, 1876): 5.

98. Congregation Anshe Amunim Minutes, July 7, 1872, MF-216, AJA.

99. For population figures, see Jonathan D. Sarna, *American Judaism: A History* (New Haven, CT: Yale University Press, 2004), 375.

100. See Adam S. Ferziger, *Beyond Sectarianism: The Realignment of American Orthodox Judaism* (Detroit, MI: Wayne State University Press, 2015), 4–7; Jeffrey S. Gurock, "Resisters and Accommodators: Varieties of Orthodox Rabbis in America, 1886–1983," *American Jewish Archives Journal* 35 (November 1983): 100–187; Samuel C. Heilman, "The Many Faces of Orthodoxy, Part I," *Modern Judaism* 2 (February 1982): 23–51; and Chaim I. Waxman, *Social Change and Halakhic Evolution in American Orthodoxy* (Oxford: Littman Library, 2017).

101. See Waxman, *Social Change and Halakhic Evolution*, 4.

102. See Samuel C. Heilman, *Sliding to the Right: The Contest for the Future of American Jewish Orthodoxy* (Berkeley: University of California Press, 2006), 15–61.

103. See Henry Illoway, *The Controversial Letters and the Casuistic Decisions of the Late Rabbi Bernard Illowy Ph.D.* (Berlin: M. Poppelauer, 1914), 28–29.

104. See, for example, Adam S. Ferziger, "Hungarian Separatist Orthodoxy and the Migration of Its Legacy to America: The Greenwald-Hirschenson Debate," *JQR* 105 (Spring 2015): 250–83.

105. See Menachem Keren-Kratz, "The Contemporary Study of Orthodoxy:

Challenging the One-Dimensional Paradigm," *Tradition* 49 (Winter 2016): 24–52. See also Avi Sagi, "Orthodoxy as a Problem," in *Orthodox Judaism: New Perspectives*, ed. Yosef Salmon, Aviezer Ravitzky, and Adam S. Ferziger (Jerusalem: Magnes Press, 2006), 21–53.

106. See Robert Orsi, "Everyday Miracles: The Study of Lived Religion," in *Lived Religion in America: Toward a History of Practice*, ed. David D. Hall (Princeton, NJ: Princeton University Press, 1997), 3–21.

107. For a notable exception, see Gil Graff, "Giving Voice to 'Torah-True Judaism' in the U.S., 1922–39: Leo Jung and the Legacy of the *Rabbinerseminar*," *Modern Judaism* 34 (May 2014): 167–87.

108. See, for example, David L. Moore, *That Dream Shall Have a Name: Native Americans Rewriting America* (Lincoln: University of Nebraska Press, 2013), 365–77.

109. See Timo Müller, "The Uses of Authenticity: Hemingway and the Literary Field, 1926–1936," *Journal of Modern Literature* 33 (Fall 2009): 28–42; and Jeffrey B. Ferguson, *The Sage of Sugar Hill: George S. Schuyler and the Harlem Renaissance* (New Haven, CT: Yale University Press, 2005), 245–53.

110. See Miles Orvell, *The Real Thing: Imitation and Authenticity in American Culture, 1880–1940* (Chapel Hill: University of North Carolina Press, 1989), 33–39; and Mary McAleer Balkun, *The American Counterfeit: Authenticity and Identity in American Literature and Culture* (Tuscaloosa: University of Alabama Press, 2006), 1–17.

111. See, for example, Joseph A. Varacalli, *The Catholic Experience in America* (Westport, CT: Greenwood, 2006). To a certain extent, the American entanglement between religion and authenticity began in the nineteenth century. See, for example, Pamela E. Klassen, "The Robes of Womanhood: Dress and Authenticity among African American Methodist Women in the Nineteenth Century," *Religion and American Culture* 14 (Winter 2004): 39–82.

112. Leslie Woodcock Tentler, *Catholics and Contraception: An American History* (Ithaca, NY: Cornell University Press, 2004), 279.

113. See Marc B. Shapiro, *Changing the Immutable: How Orthodox Judaism Rewrites Its History* (Oxford: Littman Library, 2015), 1–55.

114. See Zev Eleff, "American Orthodoxy's Lukewarm Embrace of the Hirschian Legacy, 1850–1939," *Tradition* 45 (Fall 2012): 35–53; and Zev Eleff, "A Far-Flung Fraternity in a Fertile Desert: The Emergence of Rabbinic Scholarship in America, 1887–1926," *Modern Judaism* 34 (October 2014): 353–69.

115. See, for example, Emanuel Rackman, "A Challenge to Orthodoxy," *Judaism* 18 (Spring 1969): 46.

116. See "The Orthodox and Others," *Jewish Advocate* (December 10, 1964): A2.

117. See Charles S. Liebman, "Orthodox Judaism Today," *Midstream* 25 (August/September 1979): 22.

118. See "Entering Our Third Year," *Jewish Observer* 3 (December 1965): 3.

119. Norman Lamm, "The Need for Tradition," *Tradition* 1 (Fall 1958): 11. Emphasis mine.

120. See Carol Brzozowski, "The New Orthodoxy," *Sun Sentinel* (July 24, 1987): 1.

121. See Michael A. Meyer, *Response to Modernity: A History of the Reform Movement in Judaism* (Oxford: Oxford University Press, 1988), 225–63; and Michael R. Cohen, *The Birth of Conservative Judaism: Solomon Schechter's Disciples and the Creation of an American Religious Movement* (New York: Columbia University Press, 2012), 1–14. On Jewish identity and authenticity, see Stuart Z. Charmé, "Alterity, Authenticity, and Jewish Identity," *Shofar* 16 (Spring 1998): 42–62. See also Stuart Z. Charmé, "Varieties of Authenticity in Contemporary Jewish Identity," *Jewish Social Studies* 6 (Winter 2000): 133–55; and Ken Koltun-Fromm, *Imagining Jewish Authenticity: Vision and Text in American Jewish Thought* (Bloomington: Indiana University Press, 2015).

122. See Bernard Bailyn, *Atlantic History: Concept and Contours* (Cambridge, MA: Harvard University Press, 2005), 1–56; and Daniel T. Rodgers, *Atlantic Crossings: Social Politics in a Progressive Age* (Cambridge, MA: Harvard University Press, 1998), 33–75.

123. See Tamar El-Or, *Educated and Ignorant: Ultraorthodox Jewish Women and Their World*, trans. Haim Watzman (Boulder, CO: Lynne Rienner, 1994), 65–66.

124. Riv-Ellen Prell, *Fighting to Become Americans: Assimilation and the Trouble Between Jewish Women and Jewish Men* (Boston: Beacon Press, 2000), 4.

125. Pamela S. Nadell, *Women Who Would be Rabbis: A History of Women's Ordination, 1889–1985* (Boston: Beacon Press, 1998), xii–xiii.

126. See Karla Goldman, *Beyond the Synagogue Gallery: Finding a Place for Women in American Judaism* (Cambridge, MA: Harvard University Press, 2000), 84, 131; and Sarna, "The Debate over Mixed Seating in the American Synagogue," 368.

127. See Goldman, *Beyond the Synagogue Gallery*, 172–99.

128. See, for example, Deborah Grand Golomb, "The 1893 Congress of Jewish Women: Evolution or Revolution in American Jewish Women's History?" *American Jewish History* 70 (September 1980): 52–67; and David Kaufman, *Shul with a Pool: The "Synagogue-Center" in American Jewish History* (Hanover, NH: Brandeis University Press, 1999), 76–82.

129. See Ann Braude, "Women's History *Is* American Religious History," in *Retelling U.S. Religious History*, ed. Thomas A. Tweed (Berkeley: University of California Press, 1997), 87–107.

130. For an exception, see Jeffrey S. Gurock, *Judaism's Encounter with American Sports* (Bloomington: University of Indiana Press, 2005).

131. See Clifford Putney, *Muscular Christianity: Manhood and Sports in Protestant America, 1880-1920* (Cambridge, MA: Harvard University Press, 2001), 33-39.
132. See Michael S. Kimmel, *Manhood in America: A Cultural History* (Oxford: Oxford University Press, 2006), 6.
133. Sarah Imhoff, *Masculinity and the Making of American Judaism* (Bloomington: Indiana University Press, 2017).
134. Yehuda Turetsky and Chaim I. Waxman, "Sliding to the Left? Contemporary American Modern Orthodoxy," *Modern Judaism* 31 (May 2011): 119-41.

## Chapter 1. Battling Foodways and Halakhic Folkways: The Case of Passover Peanut Oil

1. Sidney Roth, "Reminiscence of Passover as Celebrated on the Lower East Side of New York," SC-10468, AJA.
2. See Barbara Kirshenblatt-Gimblett, "Kitchen Judaism," in *Getting Comfortable in New York: The American Jewish Home, 1880-1950*, ed. Susan L. Braunstein and Jenna Weissman Joselit (New York: Jewish Museum, 1990), 93.
3. See Shaul Stampfer, "The Geographic Background of East European Jewish Migration to the United States before World War I," in *Migration Across Time and Nations: Population Mobility in Historical Context*, ed. Ira A. Glazier and Luigi de Rosa (New York: Holmes & Meir, 1986), 220-30. See also Simon Kuznets, "Immigration of Russian Jews to the United States," *Perspectives in American History* 9 (1975): 35-124.
4. See Mordechai Zalkin, "Lithuanian Jewry and the Concept of 'East European Jewry,'" *Polin* 25 (2013): 57-70; and Salmon, *Do Not Provoke Providence*, 115-59.
5. "Piskei Halakhah: *Kitniyot*," in *The Daf Hakashrus, 1992-1997*, ed. Yosef Grossman (New York: Orthodox Union, 1998), 18. For the Conservative movement's position on peanut oil during Passover, see Ben Zion Bergman, "A New Look at Peanuts—From the Ground Up," *Proceedings of the Committee on Jewish Law and Standards of the Conservative Movement, 1986-1990* (New York: Rabbinical Assembly, 2001), 269-72.
6. Haym Soloveitchik, "Migration, Acculturation, and the New Role of Texts in the Haredi World," in *Accounting for Fundamentalisms: The Dynamic Character of Movements*, ed. Martin E. Marty and R. Scott Appleby (Chicago: University of Chicago Press, 1994), 212; and Haym Soloveitchik, "Rupture and Reconstruction: The Transformation of Contemporary Orthodoxy," *Tradition* 28 (Summer 1994): 86. See also Heilman, *Sliding to the Right*, 127-39.
7. Soloveitchik, "Migration, Acculturation, and the New Role of Texts in the Haredi World," 201.
8. See David Hackett Fischer, *Albion's Seed: Four British Folkways in America* (New York: Oxford University Press, 1989), 7-11.

9.  See Joseph P. Chinnici, *Living Stones: The History and Structure of Catholic Spiritual Life in the United States* (New York: MacMillan, 1989), 35–85.

10. See Moses Rischin, *The Promised City: New York Jews, 1870–1914* (Cambridge, MA: Harvard University Press, 1962), 76–94.

11. Zevi Hirsch Masliansky, *Sermons*, trans. Edward Herbert (New York: Hebrew Publishing Company, 1926), 203. In the 1940s Eliezer Berkovits complained that Orthodox Jews in the United States and England were still reluctant to discard their Continental European identities and embrace "Minhag America" and "Minhag Britanya." While this book argues that Orthodox Jews acculturated to certain indigenous religious norms, it is still very interesting that this religious group refused by and large to adopt an unabashedly "American" set of customs, as they had done in Europe. See Eliezer Berkovits, *Between Yesterday and Tomorrow* (Oxford: East and West Library, 1945), 120–21.

12. Hasia R. Diner, *Hungering for America: Italian, Irish, and Jewish Foodways in the Age of Migration* (Cambridge, MA: Harvard University Press, 2001), 202.

13. See Silber, "The Emergence of Ultra-Orthodoxy: The Invention of a Tradition," 23–84; and Adam S. Ferziger, *Exclusion and Hierarchy: Orthodoxy, Nonobservance, and the Emergence of Modern Jewish Identity* (Philadelphia: University of Pennsylvania Press, 2005), 186–92.

14. See Jonathan D. Sarna, "How Matzah Became Square: Manischewitz and the Development of Machine-Made Matzah in the United States," in *Chosen Capital: The Jewish Encounter with American Capitalism*, ed. Rebecca Kobrin (New Brunswick, NJ: Rutgers University Press, 2012), 272–88.

15. There are a number of terms used for "peanuts" in the responsa literature. For Hebrew and Yiddish terms, see "She'elot un Teshuvot," *Yiddishe Shprakh* 33 (1974): 80.

16. See Dovid Zaklikowski, *Kosher Investigator: How Rabbi Berel (Bernard) Levy Built the OK and Transformed the World of Kosher Supervision* (New York: Hasidic Archives, 2017), 260.

17. "Pea-Nut," *Harper's Weekly* (July 16, 1870): 449.

18. Andrew F. Smith, *Peanuts: The Illustrious History of the Goober Pea* (Urbana: University of Illinois Press, 2002), 68–70.

19. Ibid., 101–7.

20. Harold J. Clay, *Marketing Peanuts and Peanut Products* (Washington, DC: United States Department of Agriculture, 1941), 97.

21. "Prolific Peanuts: 'Mr. Peanut' Grows Up, Becomes Symbol of Huge Industry," *Literary Digest* (March 6, 1937): 42; and "Planters Hi-Hat Peanut Oil," *Hapardes* 10 (April 1936): 40. Planters' peanut-oil line was initially certified by Rabbi Hersh Kohn.

22. For example, see "Planters Hi-Hat Peanut Oil," *American Hebrew* (May 7, 1937): It is probable that Rokeach also commenced production of peanut oil

in 1936. See "Rokeach's Kosher and Pure Products for Passover," *Hapardes* 10 (April 1936): 46.

23. Moses Maimonides, *Mishneh Torah*, Laws of Hametz u-Matzah 5:1.

24. See Marc J. Rosenstein, "Legumes on Passover," *CCAR Journal* 22 (Spring 1975): 33.

25. Yitzhak ben Yosef, *Sefer Mitzvot Katan*, no. 222.

26. Yisrael Ta-Shma, *Minhag Ashkenaz ha-Kadmon* (Jerusalem: Hebrew University Magnes Press, 1992), 271–82. See also Alfred S. Cohen, "*Kitniyot* in Halachic Literature, Past and Present," *Journal of Halacha and Contemporary Society* 6 (Fall 1983): 65–77.

27. The majority opinion recorded in the Talmud (Pesahim 114b) implies that one should not refrain from *kitniyot* on Passover.

28. See Moses Isserles's gloss on Joseph Caro, *Shulhan Arukh, Orah Hayyim* 453:1.

29. For a fuller treatment of the history of this stringency, see Shlomo Yosef Zevin, *Ha-Mo'adim Bi-Halakhah*, vol. 2 (Jerusalem: Mekhon Ha-Talmud Ha-Yerushalmi Ha-Shalem, 1980), 305–12. Zevin also discussed the rabbinic assumption that the oils and juices extracted from *kitniyot* receive the same stringent status as actual *kitniyot*. See also Hayyim Hezkiyahu Medini, *Sdei Hemed*, vol. 8 (Bnei Brak: Beit Ha-Sofer, 1962), 233–40.

30. Jacob Katz offered a similar theory in what he called "ritual instinct." See Jacob Katz, *Goy shel Shabbat* (Jerusalem: Zalman Shazar, 1984), 179–80. On "rabbinic intuition," see Haym Soloveitchik, "Law and Change: The Medieval Ashkenazic Example," *AJS Review* 12 (Autumn 1987): 220–21.

31. See Jacob Katz, *Divine Law in Human Hands: Case Studies in Halakhic Flexibility* (Jerusalem: Magnes Press, 1998), 429–31. See also Moshe Leiter, "Issur *Kitniyot* bi-Pesah," *Ha-Darom* 15 (Nissan 1962): 59–67. Some earlier tradition-minded rabbinic scholars like Rabbi Zvi Ashkenazi (the "Hakham Zvi") also considered abolishing the *kitniyot* custom but understood the gravity of the practice and relented. See Yaakov Emden, *Mor u-Ketziah Ha-Shalem*, ed. Avraham Yaakov Bombakh and Yaakov Yosef Schacter (Jerusalem: Makhon Yerushalayim, 1996), 428.

32. *Samuel Adler, 1809–1857: His Years in Germany*, trans. Agnes Goldman Sanborn, 21, MS-423, Samuel Adler Papers, American Jewish Archives.

33. See Seymour Siegel, "The War of the *Kitniyot* (Legumes)," in *Perspectives on Jews and Judaism: Essays in Honor of Wolfe Kelman*, ed. Arthur A. Chiel (New York: Rabbinical Assembly, 1978), 383–93.

34. See Hagi Ben-Artzi, *He-Hadash Yitkadesh: Ha-Rav Kook Ki-Posek Mi-Hadesh* (Tel Aviv: Yedi'ot Aharonot, 2010), 119–50; and Neirah Gotel, *Innovation in Tradition: The Halakhic-Philosophical Teachings of Rabbi Kook* (Jerusalem: Magnes Press, 2005), 25–35.

35. Mildred Grosberg Bellin, *The Jewish Cook Book: According to the Jewish Dietary Laws* (New York: Bloch, 1941), 360.
36. *46 Oyfanim far Besere Peyseh Maykholim* (Suffolk, VA: Planters Edible Oil Co., 1948), 1. For another prominent example, see Carole B. Balin, "'Good to the Last Night': The Proliferation of the Maxwell House Haggadah," in *My People's Passover Haggadah: Traditional Texts, Modern Commentaries*, vol. 1, ed. Lawrence A. Hoffman and David Arnow (Woodstock, NY: Jewish Lights Publishing, 2008), 85–90.
37. Thousands of Hungarian Jews settled in America during the nineteenth century but identified with their German coreligionists rather than maintaining a distinct culture in the New World. See Robert Perlman, *Bridging Three Worlds: Hungarian-Jewish Americans, 1848–1914* (Amherst: University of Massachusetts Press, 1991), 253–55.
38. Smith, *Peanuts*, 66–68.
39. Moshe Feinstein, *Iggerot Moshe*, vol. 5 (New York: Noble Book Press, 1973), 370–71. One rabbinic scholar's extensive list of foods considered *kitniyot* makes no mention of peanuts. See Shmuel Burstein, *Ma'adanei Shmuel* (Petrikov, 1908), 333–35. On numerous occasions, Eastern European Jews asked permission from leading rabbis to eat *kitniyot* during years of famine. For example, see "Rusland," *Ha-Magid* (March 25, 1868): 100.
40. Yitzhak Elhanan ben Israel Isser Spektor, *Be'er Yitzhak* (Jerusalem, 1970), 24a–25b.
41. For a contemporaneous account of Spektor's influence on American émigrés, see "The Last Gaon in Russia," *Reform Advocate* (March 28, 1896): 116–17. See also Kimmy Caplan, *Orthodoxy in the New World: Immigrant Rabbis and Preaching in America (1881–1924)* (Jerusalem: Zalman Shazar, 2002), 72–74. Rabbinic authorities from Germany also ruled leniently on peanut oil. For this, see David Zvi Hoffman, *Melamed Le-Ho'el*, vol. 1 (Frankfurt: Hermon, 1926), 106. In addition to his own decision, Hoffman also testified to the lenient position of Rabbi Samson Raphael Hirsch.
42. Yosef Eliyahu Henkin, "Piskei Halakhot bi-Inyanim Shonim," *Am ha-Torah* 10 (1979): 6. See also Yosef Eliyahu Henkin, *She'elot u-Teshuvot Gevurot Eliyahu*, vol. 1 (Lakewood, NJ: Mahon ha-Rav Henkin, 2013), 242.
43. Eitam Henkin, "'Mara De-Atra shel America,'" *Yeshurun* 20 (2008): 126–39.
44. "Shemen shel Peanuts," *Hapardes* 8 (March 1935): 14–15. He also offered a similar leniency regarding poppyseed oil. See Yehudah Leib Graubart, *Havalim Ba-Ne'imim*, vol. 1 (Petrikov: Shmuel Pinski, 1901), 168–69.
45. "Shemen shel Peanuts," 15.
46. "Shemen shel Peanuts Le-Pesah," *Hapardes* 9 (March 1936): 7. See also "She'elot ha-Netzuhim le-Pesah," *Hapardes* 13 (April 1939): 7. For Pardes's

supervision of Rokeach products, see "I. Rokeach & Sons, Inc.," *Hapardes* 6 (April 1932): 1.

47. Morris Max, "Report of Kashrut Commission," *Proceedings of the Twelfth Annual Convention of the Rabbinical Council of America* (1948): 57. It is therefore curious that one writer claimed that Rabbi Joseph B. Soloveitchik, the leading authority within this organization and a scion from an Eastern European rabbinic family, did not personally approve most cooking oils for Passover. See Moshe Meiselman, "The Rav, Feminism and Public Policy: An Insider's Overview," *Tradition* 33 (Summer 1999): 12.

48. See, for example, *Kosher for Passover Product Directory* (New York: Union of Orthodox Jewish Congregations of America, 1966), 10.

49. See *Passover Guide* (Chicago: Chicago Rabbinical Council, 1954), 5.

50. Joseph Hager, "Passover Laws and Customs," *Light* 25 (April 1959): 20.

51. Ruth Jacobs, "Passover Suggestion from Planters Oil," *Jewish Advocate* (March 25, 1965): 5.

52. See "Kosher Le-Pasah," *Jewish Advocate* (March 31, 1960): A9; and "Planter's [sic] Peanut Oil," *Jewish Advocate* (March 24, 1960): A11.

53. See "For Passover Enjoyment," *Jewish Exponent* (March 18, 1955): 20.

54. "New Planters Jewish Recipe Book," *Jewish Advocate* (March 20, 1969): A1. The publication was first distributed in 1967.

55. *5 Great Cuisines with Planters Peanut Oil* (New York: Standard Brands Inc., 1967), 21.

56. "Oy Va-Voy al Avdan Ish Kasher Ha-Rav Yaakov Goldman Einenu," *Hamaor* 47 (April–May 1994): 26.

57. See "Ha-Shas He-Hadash shel Ozer Ha-Sefarim," *Hamaor* 28 (March–April 1977): 32.

58. Feinstein, *Iggerot Moshe*, vol. 5, 370–71.

59. See Emanuel Rackman, "Halachic Progress: Rabbi Moshe Feinstein's Igrot Moshe on Even Ha-Ezer," *Judaism* 13 (Summer 1964): 365; and Simha Elberg, "Rav Moshe," *Hapardes* 39 (February 1965): 2.

60. Aaron Kirschenbaum, "Rabbi Moshe Feinstein's Responsa: A Major Halachic Event," *Judaism* 15 (Summer 1966): 369. For another understanding that dates Feinstein's emergence as American Orthodoxy's preeminent halakhist to the 1970s, see Adam Mintz, "A Chapter in American Orthodoxy: The Eruvin in Brooklyn," *Hakirah* 14 (Winter 2012): 21–59.

61. See Yisrael Hayyim Friedman, *Lekutei Maharyah*, vol. 3 (New York: Avraham Yitzhak Friedman, 1965), 21b; and Moshe Yisrael Feldman, *Lekutei Maharmi: Hilkhot Pesah* (New York: E. Grossman's Publishing House, n.d.), 8a. See other sources listed in Gavriel Zinner, *Nitei Gavriel: Hilkhot Pesah*, vol. 2 (Jerusalem: Cong. Nitei Gavriel, 2002), 205. On the relatively cordial relationship between

Hasidim and Mitnagdim in Hungary, see Michael K. Silber, "The Limits of Rapprochement: The Anatomy of an Anti-Hasidic Controversy in Hungary," *Studia Judaica* 3 (1994): 124–47.

62. See letter published in Ephraim Yosef Dov Ashkenazi, *Haggadah shel Pesah im Peirush Divrei Yo'el* (Brooklyn, NY: Jerusalem Book Store Inc., 1984), 18.

63. "Le-Afrushei Me-Issurra," *Tal Talpiyot* 22 (Nissan 1913): 196. See also Yitzhak Ze'ev Kahane, "Hashpa'ot Hitzoniyot be-Halakhot Pesah," *La-Mo'ed* 3 (1946): 89–90.

64. See Avraham lev Trutzer, Responsum no. 134, *Tal Talpiyot* 22 (Adar 1913): 155; and Yitzhak Lemberger, Responsum no. 145, *Tal Talpiyot* 22 (Nissan 1913): 166.

65. See Zvi Lebovitch, "Bi-Inyan Gezerot *Kitniyot* Bi-Pesah," *Hachaim* 1 (April 1922): 13–14; and Yitzhak Zvi Lebovitch, "Bi-Inyan Gezerot *Kitniyot* Bi-Pesah u-be-Sha'ar Yom Tov," *Hachaim* 1 (June 1922): 36–37.

66. See Yehuda Lev Tsirelson, *Atzi Ha-Livanon* (Klausenburg: Avraham Koyfman, 1922), 15–16; Hillel Posek, *Divrei Hillel*, vol. 1 (Sinaia: Jacob Wider, 1925), 13a–15a; and Hillel Posek, Letter to the Editor, *Beit Va'ad Le-Hakhamim* 7 (Tishrei 1928): 50–51. See also Nissan Telushkin, "Minei Peirot She-Dineiheim Meyuhadim," *Or Hamizrach* 1 (Elul 1954): 20.

67. See Yaakov Shlomo Aryeh Rubenfeld, "Bi-Inyan Akhilat Shemen Zayit bi-Pesah, u-Birur Da'at Maran Heitev Lev," *Kovetz Beis Vaad L'chachumim* (Nissan 2011): 130–42.

68. See Jerome R. Mintz, *Hasidic People: A Place in the New World* (Cambridge, MA: Harvard University Press, 1992), 27–42.

69. See Solomon Poll, *The Hasidic Community of Williamsburg: A Study in the Sociology of Religion* (New York: Free Press, 1962), 29; and Samuel C. Heilman, *Who Will Lead Us? The Story of Five Hasidic Dynasties in America* (Berkeley: University of California Press, 2017), 152–209.

70. Moshe David Tendler, *Responsa of Rav Moshe Feinstein: Care of the Critically Ill* (Hoboken, NJ: Ktav, 1996), 18. For one of the most strident oppositions to Feinstein's rulings, see Yom Tov Schwartz, *Ma'aneh Le-Iggerot* (New York, 1973), 3–25.

71. See Yehezkel Roth, *Kuntres Lekutei Halakhot al Hilkhot Hag ha-Pesah* (Borough Park, NY: Beit Midrash Kahal Yirei Hashem, 1982), 21.

72. On Steif, see George Kranzler, *Hasidic Williamsburg: A Contemporary American Hasidic Community* (Northvale, NJ: Jason Aaronson Inc., 1995), 160. In Budapest, Steif's rabbinic journal, *Hachaim*, affirmed the stringent position toward peanut oil. See "Bi-Inyan Gezerot *Kitniyot* Bi-Pesah u-be-Sha'ar Yom Tov," 37.

73. See Yitzhak Yaakov Weiss, *She'elot u-Teshuvot Minhat Yitzhak*, vol. 3 (Jerusalem, 1973), 240–41; and Yitzhak Yaakov Weiss, *She'elot u-Teshuvot Minhat Yitzhak*, vol. 4 (Jerusalem, 1975), 248.

74. See Zvi Hersh Kohn, "Bi-Din Devash Devorim Mekhasemet," *Hamaor* 6 (April 1956): 6–7; Aharon Shuchatowitz, "Bi-Davar Devash Devorim," *Hamaor* 6 (May 1956): 14–15; and Natan Leizer, "Min Dagan o Min *Kitniyot*," *Hamaor* 7 (March 1957): 20.

75. See *The Kosher Directory: Passover Edition* (New York: Union of Orthodox Congregations of America, 1985), 19.

76. Shimon D. Eider, *A Summary of Halachos of Pesach* (Lakewood, NJ 1977), 14.

77. Avrohom Blumenkrantz, *The Laws of Pesach: A Digest* (Far Rockaway, NY: A. Blumenkrantz, 1981), 16.

78. See "A Passover Recipe from the Passover Oil," *Jewish Press* (March 25, 1971): 10; "A Passover Recipe from the Passover Oil," *Jewish Exponent* (March 18, 1977): 56; and "A Passover Recipe from the Passover Oil," *Jewish Advocate* (April 13, 1978): A5.

79. Later and fully unrelated to the above, the reputation of the "OK" and its administrator declined. See Timothy D. Lytton, *Kosher: Private Regulation in the Age of Industrial Food* (Cambridge, MA: Harvard University Press, 2013), 70–71.

80. Bernard Levy, "Keeping Kosher: The OK Symbol of Kashrut," *Jewish Home-maker* (February–March 1978): 19. See also David Kraemer, *Jewish Eating and Identity Through the Ages* (New York: Routledge, 2007), 148.

81. See Paul Boyer, "The Evangelical Resurgence in the 1970s: American Protestantism," in *Rightward Bound: Making America Conservative in the 1970s*, ed. Bruce J. Schulman and Julian E. Zelizer (Cambridge, MA: Harvard University Press, 2008), 34–35.

82. See Darren Dochuk, *From Bible Belt to Sunbelt: Plain Folk Religion, Grassroots Politicians, and the Rise of Evangelical Conservatism* (New York: Norton, 2011), 326–61. One writer who noticed the Hungarian Orthodox Jews' emergence at an early date offered a different explanation: "They are sustained by the aristocratic feeling of belonging to 'the saving remnant.' With the growing appreciation in the sixties of the exotic and the nonconformist, they and others no longer view their basic posture as being somehow 'un-American.'" See Jacob Agus, "Jerusalem in America," in *The Religion of the Republic*, ed. Elwyn A. Smith (Philadelphia: Fortress Press, 1971), 107.

83. See George M. Marsden, *Fundamentalism and American Culture: The Shaping of Twentieth-Century Evangelicalism, 1870–1925* (New York: Oxford University Press, 1980), 4.

84. Axel R. Schäfer, *Countercultural Conservatives: American Evangelicalism from the Postwar Revival to the New Christian Right* (Madison: University of Wisconsin Press, 2011), 111–12.

85. Ibid., 113.

86. See Hutchison, *Religious Pluralism in America*, 196–218.

87. See also Simha Elberg, "Rav, Admor Hasidi, Rosh Yeshiva—Le-Mi Me-Heim yesh Hashpa'ah?" *Hapardes* 37 (March 1963): 2–3; and William B. Helmreich, *The World of the Yeshiva: An Intimate Portrait of Orthodox Jewry* (New York: Free Press, 1982), 45–46.
88. Egon Mayer, *From Suburb to Shtetl: The Jews of Boro Park* (Philadelphia: Temple University Press, 1979), 72–80.
89. For a very insightful, near-contemporaneous view of the Orthodox turn toward what they perceive as "authentic" forms of lived religion and Meal Mart cuisine, see Martha Meisels, "Flying with People," *Jerusalem Post* (August 12, 1983): B15.
90. See, for example, "Perfect Dessert for Passover," *Jewish Advocate* (April 2, 1981): A6.
91. Abraham B. Hecht, "Campaign to Reduce Price of Kosher for Passover Products Bringing Beneficial Results," *Jewish Press* (April 3, 1981): 49.
92. Martha Meisels, "Kosher Confusion," *Jerusalem Post* (April 5, 1985): A23.
93. Behnam Dayanim, "Fewer Brand Names on Pesach, But More Food in the Pantry," *Jewish Advocate* (April 13, 1989): A6.
94. "Found Some Peanuts," *Boruch Learns His Brochos*, story and song by Shmuel Kunda (Brooklyn, NY: Shmuel Kunda Productions, 1982), audiocassette. See also Shmuel Kunda, *Boruch Learns His Brochos* (Brooklyn, NY: Shmuel Kunda, 2005).
95. Hoffman, *Melamed Le-Ho'el*, vol. 1, 106.
96. Zvi Pesah Frank, *Mira'ei Kodesh*, vol. 2 (Jerusalem: Mekhon Ha-Rav Frank, 1974), 205.
97. Yehoshua Moshe Aaronson, *Yeshu'at Moshe* (Petah Tikva: Y. M. Aaronson, 1967), 173–74.
98. See Katriel Fishel Tsorsh, "Shalosh She'elot," *Halikhot* 37 (Tishrei 1937): 20; and "Le-She'elot Ha-Betanim bi-Pesah," *Halikhot* 38–39 (1968): 23–24. See also Shlomo Hayyim Aviner, *Am Ke-Lavi* (Jerusalem: S. H. Aviner, 1983), 131–33.
99. See Martha Meisels, "Oil Turmoil," *Jerusalem Post* (March 25, 1988): A14. See also Yoel Schwartz, *Kuntres 'Hametz Mashehu': Madrikh Li-Inyani Ha-Kashrut bi-Pesah* (Jerusalem: Davar Yerushalayim, 1988), 59–60.
100. See Yosef Shalom Elyashiv, *Kovetz Teshuvot*, vol. 3 (Jerusalem: Keren Re'em, 2012), 97; and Moshe Turetsky, *Yashiv Moshe* (Gateshead: M. Turetsky, 1989), 59.
101. See Julius Liebb, "Rabbi Feinstein's Illness Remains Undiagnosed," *Jewish Press* (March 22, 1985): 2
102. See Wolfe Kelman, "Moshe Feinstein and Postwar American Orthodoxy," *Survey of Jewish Affairs 1987*, ed. William Frankel (Cranbury, NJ: Associated University Presses, 1988), 173–87.

103. Bill Osey, e-mail message to author, December 12, 2013. Osey is a member and webmaster for the Peanut Pals Collectors Club. See also http://www.sadiesalome.com/recipes/passover-rolls.html (accessed March 13, 2017). Special thanks to longtime Peanut Pals member Sherwin Borsuk for pointing out this online source.

104. The 2001 edition of the Orthodox Union's Passover food guide was the final directory to include peanut oil. See "Products Directory," *Jewish Action* (Passover 2001): 53. See also Avrohom Blumenkrantz, *The Laws of Pesach: A Digest* (Far Rockaway, NY: Bais Medrash Ateres Yisroel, 2001), 24–25.

## Chapter 2. How Bat Mitzvah Became Orthodox

1. "Three B'not Mitzvah to be Honored at Seudah Shlishit this Shabbat Afternoon," *Kehilath Jeshurun Bulletin* 41 (December 15, 1972): 3. A month later, Kehilath Jeshurun celebrated another bat mitzvah in similar fashion. See "Seudah Sh'lishit in Honor of Lisa Kassover," *Kehilath Jeshurun Bulletin* 41 (January 19, 1973): 2. The New York–based synagogue bulletins used in this research were identified using the Yeshiva University Digital Library. Available at http://digital.library.yu.edu/new-york-synagogue-bulletins (accessed March 11, 2019).

2. "Bat Mitzvah," *Kehilath Jeshurun Bulletin* 41 (April 6, 1973): 2.

3. Thirty-seven years later Kagan was appointed a US Supreme Court justice. See Meira Bienstock, "Riskin: Kagan Showed Great Wisdom in Her Youth," *Jerusalem Post* (June 29, 2010): 6. See also Lisa W. Foderaro, "At 12, Kagan Tested Her Faith's Confines," *New York Times* (May 13, 2010): A25, and Kagan's remarks delivered at the November 2014 General Assembly of the Jewish Federations of North America, available online at https://www.youtube.com/watch?v=iIahUJDura4 (accessed January 3, 2019).

4. See, for instance, "Chanukah, 5734," *Lincoln Square Synagogue Bulletin* 8 (January 1974): 4; "News & Notes of L.L.S.," *Lincoln Square Synagogue Bulletin* 8 (Tu B'Shvat 1975): 5; and "Hebrew Education for the Learning Disabled Child," *Lincoln Square Synagogue Bulletin* 11 (Chanukah 1975): 10.

5. Norman Lamm, "Tradition and Innovation," November 2, 1974, Lamm Archives at Yeshiva University, New York, NY.

6. J. David Bleich, "Survey of Recent Halakhic Periodical Literature," *Tradition* 14 (Fall 1973): 126.

7. See Charles S. Liebman, "Orthodoxy in American Jewish Life," *American Jewish Year Book* 66 (1965): 23–25.

8. "Three B'not Mitzvah to be Honored at Seudah Shlishit This Shabbat Afternoon," *Kehilath Jeshurun Bulletin* 41 (December 15, 1972): 3.

9. "Congratulations and Mazel Tov," *Lincoln Square Synagogue Bulletin* 8 (June 1973): 3.

10. See Silber, "The Emergence of Ultra-Orthodoxy," 23–84. See also Gerald J. Blidstein, "From the Home to the Synagogue: On the Innovations of the Post-Talmudic Synagogue," in *Ta Shma: Studies in Judaica in Memory of Israel M. Ta-Shma*, vol. 1, ed. Avraham (Rami) Reiner, Joseph R. Hacker, Moshe Halbertal, Moshe Idel, Ephraim Kanarfogel, and Elchanan Reiner (Alon Shvut: Tevunot Press, 2011), 105–34.

11. Rabin, *Jews on the Frontier*, 53–54.

12. Frederick J. Turner, "The Significance of the Frontier in American History," in *Proceedings of the State Historical Society of Wisconsin at Its Forty-first Annual Meeting* (Madison, WI: Democrat Printing Company, 1894), 80.

13. See Gordon S. Wood, "Evangelical America and Early Mormonism," *New York History* 61 (October 1980): 359–86; and Hatch, *The Democratization of American Christianity*, 59–62. However, Christianity would experience "urban revivals" in the decades surrounding the turn of the twentieth century. See, for example, Thekla Ellen Joiner, *Sin in the City: Chicago and Revivalism, 1880–1920* (Columbia: University of Missouri Press, 2007).

14. See Marshall Sklare, *Conservative Judaism: An American Religious Movement* (Glencoe, IL: Free Press, 1955), 66–82. See also Marshall Sklare and Joseph Greenblum, *Jewish Identity on the Suburban Frontier* (Chicago: University of Chicago Press, 1967), 120–33.

15. See Cohen, *The Birth of Conservative Judaism*, 123–37.

16. Charles S. Liebman, *The Ambivalent American Jew: Politics, Religion, and Family in American Jewish Life* (Philadelphia: Jewish Publication Society of America, 1973), 45–49.

17. See Jeffrey S. Gurock, "The Late Friday Night Orthodox Service: An Exercise in Religious Accommodation," *Jewish Social Studies* 12 (Spring/Summer 2006): 137–56.

18. See Emanuel Feldman, "The Case for 'Out-of-Town,'" *Jewish Observer* 1 (September 1963): 13–20.

19. "Rabbi P. M. Teitz's Speech," *Hamaor* 8 (October–November 1958): 13.

20. See "Speeches Delivered at the Agudath Ha-Rabbonim Convention," *Hamaor* 10 (November–December 1960): 17; and "Agudath Ha-Rabbonim Convention," *Hapardes* 35 (January 1961): 42.

21. Interestingly, for a short while in German Jewish communities, Orthodox congregations hosted some form of bat mitzvah ceremony in synagogues, at the direction of Rabbi Yaakov Ettlinger. On this, see Judith Bleich, "Between East and West: Modernity and Traditionalism in the Writings of Rabbi Yehi'el Ya'akov Weinberg," in *Engaging Modernity: Rabbinic Leaders and the Challenge of the Twentieth Century*, ed. Moshe Z. Sokol (Northvale, NJ: Aronson, 1997), 204, n.81.

22. See Mel Scult, *Judaism Faces the Twentieth Century: A Biography of Mordecai*

M. *Kaplan* (Detroit, MI: Wayne State University Press, 1993), 415, n.31. See also
Jeffrey S. Gurock and Jacob J. Schacter, *A Modern Heretic and a Traditional
Community: Mordecai M. Kaplan, Orthodoxy, and American Judaism* (New
York: Columbia University Press, 1997), 139; and Judith Kaplan Eisenstein, "No
Thunder Sounded, No Lightning Struck," in *Eyewitness to American Jewish
History, vol. IV: 1915–1969*, ed. Azriel Eisenberg (New York: Union of Ameri-
can Hebrew Congregations, 1978), 30–32.

23. See Paula E. Hyman, "The Introduction of Bat Mitzvah in Conservative Juda-
ism in Postwar America," *YIVO Annual* 19 (1990): 133–46; and Regina Stein,
"The Road to Bat Mitzvah in America," in *Women and American Judaism:
Historical Perspectives*, ed. Pamela S. Nadell and Jonathan D. Sarna (Hanover,
NH: Brandeis University Press, 2001), 223–34. See also David Golinkin, "The
Participation of Jewish Women in Public Rituals and Torah Study, 1845–2010,"
in *The Status of Women in Jewish Law: Response* (Jerusalem: Schechter
Institute of Jewish Studies, 2012), 4–7.

24. Aharon Walkin, *Zaken Aharon*, vol. 1 (New York, 1958), 13–14.

25. "On Bat 'Mitzvah' Celebrations," *Hamaor* 8 (December 1958): 19.

26. Hananiah Yom Tov Lipa Deutsch, *Taharat Yom Tov*, vol. 9 (New York, 1959),
40.

27. Eliezer Silver, "On 'Bat Mitzvah' Celebration," *Hamaor* 8 (December 1958): 25.

28. See Yitzhak Isaac Liebes, *Beit Avi*, vol. 2 (New York, 1980), 85–86.

29. Later on, one of Rabbi Feinstein's leading disciples, Rabbi Ephraim Greenblatt,
published a number of responsa in support of bat mitzvah. See, for example,
Ephraim Greenblatt, *Revevot Ephraim*, vol. 1 (Memphis, 1975), 124–25.

30. Moshe Feinstein, *Iggerot Moshe*, vol. 1 (New York: Noble Book Press, 1959),
170.

31. Moshe Feinstein, *Iggerot Moshe*, vol. 4 (New York: Noble Book Press, 1963),
47–48.

32. "A Letter of Protest against the Disrespect to the Honor of Rabbi Moshe Feinstein," *Hamaor* 14 (December 1964): 22. See also S. Deblitsky, "More on the
Prohibition of Artificial Insemination," *Hamaor* 15 (February 1965): 19. Many
of the attacks on Rabbi Feinstein in this period were provoked by his permis-
sive position on artificial insemination. See "A Brief on the Preservation of the
Holiness and Lineage of Israel," *Hamaor* 14 (October–November 1964): 5–20.

33. See Marc B. Shapiro, *Between the Yeshiva World and Modern Orthodoxy:
The Life and Works of Rabbi Jehiel Jacob Weinberg* (Oxford: Littman Library,
1999), 212.

34. Yehiel Yaakov Weinberg, "Is It Permitted to Celebrate Bat Mitzvah?" *Hapardes*
37 (April 1963): 7. Translated in Bleich, "Between East and West," 203. See also
the translation in Shapiro, *Between the Yeshiva World and Modern Orthodoxy*,
212.

35. See "Letters of the Gaon Rabbi Yehiel Yaakov Weinberg, z"l," *Hapardes* 40 (July 1966): 36. For a position in between Rabbi Feinstein and Rabbi Weinberg, see Yosef Eliyahu Henkin, *Gevurot Eliyahu*, vol. 2, ed. Daniel Osher Kleinman (Brooklyn, NY: Mehon Ha-Rav Henkin, 2016), 166. Interestingly, there are important differences in Rabbi Weinberg's treatment of Rabbi Feinstein's position in the former's original *Hapardes* responsum and the version later published in *Seridei Eish*. Rabbi Weinberg deleted a small section in his original essay in which he claimed that he was in full agreement with Rabbi Feinstein. In the later publication of his collected responsa, Rabbi Weinberg reinserted the paragraph in which he puts forward in more adamant terms his agreement with Rabbi Feinstein, perhaps due to the concern raised by Elberg. See Yehiel Yaakov Weinberg, *Seridei Eish*, vol. 3 (Jerusalem: Mosad Ha-Rav Kook, 2003), 297. I thank Marc Shapiro for his e-mail correspondence that helped clarify this discrepancy.

36. See Yitzhak Nissim, "On the Blessing of *Barukh She-Petarani*," *Noam* 7 (1964): 4–5; Erica S. Brown, "The Bat Mitzvah in Jewish Law and Contemporary Practice," in *Jewish Legal Writings by Women*, ed. Micah Halpern and Chana Safrai (Jerusalem: Urim, 1998), 232–58; Alfred S. Cohen, "Celebration of the Bat Mitzvah," *Journal of Halacha and Contemporary Society* 12 (Fall 1986): 5–16; and most recently, Zvi Ryzman, "*Barukh She-Petarani* and Bat Mitzvah," in *Sefer Ratz Ka-Tzvi*, vol. 1 (Jerusalem, 2005), 103–13.

37. Jerome Tov Feinstein, "The Bas Mitzvah Comes to Our Synagogue," *Orthodox Union* (October 1944): 25. See also Jenna Weissman Joselit, *The Wonders of America: Reinventing Jewish Culture 1880–1950* (New York: Hill and Wang, 1995), 128–29.

38. David Horowitz, "The Propagation of Our Eternal Light," *Scroll* (June 1955): 35.

39. See Albert I. Gordon, *Jews in Suburbia* (Boston: Beacon, 1959), 97–98.

40. See Jonathan J. Golden, "From Cooperation to Confrontation: The Rise and Fall of the Synagogue Council of America" (PhD diss., Brandeis University, 2008).

41. See, for instance, "Reject Rabbi Hollander's Proposal!" *National Jewish Post* (February 17, 1956): 16. See also Raphael Medoff, *Building Orthodox Judaism in America: The Life and Legacy of Harold M. Jacobs* (Toronto: CreateSpace, 2015), 142–47.

42. Moses Hyamson to Samuel Rosenblatt, March 10, 1936, Beth T'filoh Congregation Archives, Baltimore, MD.

43. Samuel Rosenblatt, *The Days of My Years: An Autobiography* (New York: Ktav, 1976), 128–30. See other sources cited in Sarna, *American Judaism*, 411 n.35.

44. See Uri Miller to Oscar Z. Fasman, May 2, 1958, Hebrew Theological College Archives, Skokie, IL.

45. Margie Pensak, "Raising the Bar on Bas Mitzvah," *Where What When* 19 (May 2004): 102.
46. "Rabbis Discuss New Ritual for Girls," *Jewish Advocate* (August 16, 1940): 6.
47. Oscar Z. Fasman, "This Friday Night Forum," *Orthodox Union* 11 (February 1944): 6.
48. See Irving Wolin to Oscar Z. Fasman, November 1, 1962, HTC Archives.
49. See Joel Lehrfield, "The Rabbi's Study," *Lincolnwood Jewish Congregation Bulletin* (January/February 2011): 1.
50. The non-Orthodox took notice. See S. Felix Mendelsohn, "The Question Box," *Sentinel* (May 27, 1943): 11.
51. Isadore M. Friedman to Traditional Synagogues of Greater Chicago, January 7, 1963, MS-125.55, Spertus Institute Archives, Chicago, IL.
52. Lillian Krupnick, *Cavalcade of Motherhood* (Chicago: Yeshiva Women, n.d.), 3.
53. "KINS Holds Its First Bat Mitzva on a Saturday Night," *Sentinel* (March 12, 1964): 27. To be clear, KINS held non–Saturday evening bat mitzvah celebrations before 1964. See "Judith Mendelsberg to Mark Her Bat Mitzva Next Friday," *Sentinel* (March 22, 1962): 23.
54. "Merle Warshausky Celebrates Bat Mitzva at Lincolnwood Cong.," *Sentinel* (October 1, 1964): 21.
55. "Greese' Daughter to be Bat Mitzvah," *Sentinel* (November 12, 1964): 29.
56. Curiously, in the 1960s and 1970s, upstart Orthodox synagogues in Chicago either halted bat mitzvah rituals or did not publicize them as Traditional synagogues had done. See, for instance, "Bar Mitzvah Dates," *Or Torah Bulletin* 1 (Shavuot 1979): 5. Bat mitzvah returned in full force to Or Torah in Skokie and other Chicago suburban congregations by the early 1980s.
57. See "Derer Bat Mitzvah," *Southern Israelite* (June 30, 1967): 16.
58. See "Bas Mitzvah," *B'nai B'rith Messenger* (January 7, 1955): 21.
59. Jack Porter, "Differentiating Features of Orthodox, Conservative, and Reform Jewish Groups in Metropolitan Philadelphia," *Jewish Social Studies* 25 (July 1963): 192.
60. See Harriet Ehrlich, *Adas Yeshurun Synagogue Centennial Celebration* (Augusta, GA: Adas Yeshurun, 1991), 32.
61. *B'nai Emunah: Tulsa Oklahoma, 1916–1966* (Tulsa, OK, 1966), 89.
62. Stephen Speisman, "Shaarei Shomayim's First Fifty Years," in *From Generation to Generation: Shaarei Shomayim Congregation—The First Fifty Years* (Toronto: Shaarei Shomayim, 1978), 21.
63. Azriel Eisenberg, *The Bar Mitzvah Treasury* (New York: Behrman House, 1952), 8.
64. Sadie Goulston, "Today I Am a Woman," *Jewish Advocate* (April 10, 1967): A3. See also a number of very interesting sources in Esther Nussbaum, "On the

Bat Mitzvah Celebration: An Annotated Bibliography," *Ten Da'at* 3 (Spring 1989): 33–34.

65. See Rachel Isserow, "Some Thoughts on Women and the Orthodox," *Young Israel Viewpoint* (April 1976): 3. In addition, Atlanta's Orthodox community was similar to that of Boston. For years, Atlanta's leading Orthodox congregation was Beth Jacob, led by Ner Israel–trained rabbi Emanuel Feldman. See Robert A. Cohen, "Everything You Need to Know about Your Bar/Bat Mitzvah," *Southern Israelite* (October 7, 1977): 10.

66. See Dov Sadan, "Bat Mitzvah," *Dat u-Medinah* (Jerusalem, 1949), 59–61; Ovadia Hedaya, *Yaskhil Avdi*, vol. 5 (Jerusalem, 1940), 30; and Meshulam Roth, *Kol Mevaser*, vol. 2 (Jerusalem: Mosad Ha-Rav Kook, 1962), 91; Chanoch Zundel Grossberg, "Se'udat Bat Mitzvah," *Ha-Ma'ayan* 13 (Tevet 1973): 41–42; and Shlomo Aviner, "Bat Mitzvah Celebration," *No'am* 21 (1979): 318–20. See also David El'azaraf, *Imrei David* (Tel Aviv, 1970), 22–24. On bat mitzvah in Israel and the lack of concern of its parallel to Conservative and Reform, see David Ben-Zion Klein and Chanoch Zundel Grossberg, "Bi-Inyan Se'udat Bat Mitzvah," *Ha-Ma'ayan* 13 (Nissan 1973): 69–70. For an important exceptional case, see Eliezer Yehudah Waldenberg, *Tzitz Eliezer*, vol. 18 (Jerusalem, 1990), 59.

67. Ovadiah Yosef, *Responsa Yehaveh Da'at*, vol. 2 (Jerusalem, 1978), 109–12.

68. "Bat Mitzva Ruled Valid by Sephardic Rabbi," *Jewish Week* (October 29, 1982): 2, reporting on the publication of the article by Ovadiah Yosef, "On the Celebration of a Bat Mitzvah, If It Is Considered a *Seudat Mitzvah*," in *Shanah be-Shanah* (1983): 157–61.

69. See Zev Eleff, *Living from Convention to Convention: The History of the NCSY, 1954–1980* (Jersey City, NJ: Ktav, 2009), 85.

70. Blu Greenberg, *How to Run a Traditional Jewish Household* (Northvale, NJ: Aronson, 1983), 277. See also Chana K. Poupko and Devora L. Wohlgelernter, "Women's Liberation—An Orthodox Response," *Tradition* 15 (Spring 1976): 51.

71. Sylvia Barack Fishman, "The Impact of Feminism on American Jewish Life," *American Jewish Year Book* 89 (1989): 45. See also Paula E. Hyman, "Where Do We Go from Here? Feminism and Changing Gender Expectations and Roles in Jewish Communal Life," in *Creating the Jewish Future*, ed. Michael Brown and Bernard Lightman (London: Altamira Press, 1999), 185–98.

72. See Aryeh A. Frimer and Dov I. Frimer, "Women's Prayer Services—Theory and Practice," *Tradition* 32 (Winter 1998): 98, n.168.

73. See Rafael Medoff, "Rav Chesed: The Life and Times of Rabbi Haskel Lookstein," in *Rav Chesed: Essays in Honor of Rabbi Dr. Haskel Lookstein*, vol. 2, ed. Rafael Medoff (Jersey City, NJ: Ktav, 2009), 418–19.

74. Reuven P. Bulka, *The RCA Lifecycle Madrikh* (New York: Rabbinical Council of America, 1995), 63–67. For other varieties of bat mitzvah rituals, see Joel B.

Wolowelsky, "Bat Mitzvah Celebrations," in *Traditions and Celebrations for the Bat Mitzvah*, ed. Ora Wiskind-Elper (Jerusalem: Urim, 2003), 84–89.

75. Pinchas Stolper to Yonah Geller, June 5, 1986, Box 33, Folder 2, I-66, American Jewish Historical Society, New York, NY. Notwithstanding this case, several Orthodox congregations have, with considerable success, adopted more liberal bat mitzvah rituals; for example, hosting bat mitzvah in a women's prayer group setting. See, for instance, Harold M. Simansky, "In Newton's Modern Orthodox Shul Women Have Greater Role," *Jewish Advocate* (July 12, 1990): 1. Women's prayer groups are the subject of Chapter 9.

# Chapter 3. Basketball Politics, Yarmulke Wars, and the Dynamics of Halakhic Change

1. See Shlomo Rapoport, *History of the Ida Crown Jewish Academy, 1942–1992* (Chicago: Ida Crown Jewish Academy, 1992).
2. "Senior Varsity," *Holomateinu* (1981): 89.
3. "Prep Highlights," *Chicago Tribune* (February 25, 1981): D3.
4. Complaint, *Moshe Menora et al. v. Illinois High School Association*, 527 F. Supp. 637 (N.D. Ill. 1981), Box 525, Folder 17, MS I-77, AJHS.
5. Ibid.
6. Leonard C. Mishkin Interview, March 4, 1978, Chicago Jewish Historical Society Oral History Project, Chicago, IL.
7. For a very good survey of the halakhic literature on the yarmulke from ancient to modern times, see Eric Zimmer, "Men's Headcoverings: The Metamorphosis of This Practice," in *Reverence, Righteousness, and Rahamanut: Essays in Memory of Rabbi Dr. Leo Jung*, ed. Jacob J. Schacter (Northvale, NJ: Jason Aronson, 1992), 325–52.
8. Lawrence Grossman, "The Kippah Comes to America," in *Continuity and Change: A Festschrift in Honor of Irving (Yitz) Greenberg's 75th Birthday*, ed. Steven T. Katz and Steven Bayme (Lanham, MD: University Press of America, 2010), 129–49.
9. Harry Steinauer, "Holy Headgear," *Antioch Review* 48 (Winter 1990): 20.
10. On the rise of Jewish identity politics, see Marc Dollinger, *Black Power, Jewish Politics: Reinventing the Alliance in the 1960s* (Waltham, MA: Brandeis University Press, 2018), 7–18.
11. Brenda Putnam to Saul Lieberman, January 24, 1950, Box 2, Folder F, Brenda Putnam Papers, Special Collections Research Center, Syracuse University Press, Syracuse, NY.
12. See Neil Steinberg, *Hatless Jack: The President, the Fedora, and the History of an American Style* (New York: Plume, 2004).
13. See Philip Birnbaum, *A Book of Jewish Concepts* (New York: Hebrew Publishing Co., 1964), 292–93.

14. Grossman, "The Kippah Comes to America," 141–43.
15. Mayer, *From Suburb to Shtetl*, 29.
16. See Solomon Poll, "The Persistence of Tradition: Orthodoxy in America," in *The Ghetto and Beyond: Essays on Jewish Life in America*, ed. Peter I. Rose (New York: Random House, 1969), 128–29.
17. See Joseph Weiss, "Why Wear a Yarmulka?" *Jewish Life* 20 (March–April 1953): 20–26. See also Fay S. Sheldon, "The Yarmulka," *Jewish Life* 20 (September–October 1952): 56–61. On the rise of Orthodox triumphalism, see Zev Eleff, "The Jewish Center, Herman Wouk and the Origins of Orthodox Triumphalism," in *A Century at the Center: Orthodox Judaism and the Jewish Center*, ed. Zev Eleff (New Milford, CT: Toby Press, 2017), 279–99.
18. See Norman Lamm, *The Royal Reach: Discourses on the Jewish Tradition and the World Today* (New York: Philipp Feldheim, 1970), 168.
19. See Sara Yael Hirschhorn, *City on a Hilltop: American Jews and the Israeli Settler Movement* (Cambridge, MA: Harvard University Press, 2017), 22–57.
20. See Jack Simcha Cohen, "In Defense of Covering the Jewish Head," *RCA Sermon Manual* 42 (1984): 197.
21. Norman Lamm, "The New Generation—A Summer View," sermon delivered on June 19, 1971, Lamm Archives.
22. Barbara Tranin, "The Yarmulke: Hear to Stay but Always Changing," *Jewish Exponent* (December 22, 1978): 21.
23. "Doing and Believing: A Roundtable Discussion," *Moment* 3 (September 1978): 41.
24. See, for example, Nadine Brozan, "Manhattan Day School Blends Diversity, Jewish Tradition," *New York Times* (September 26, 1985): C1.
25. See Raphael S. Schwartzman, "The O'Neils," *RCA Sermon Manual* 39 (1981): 80.
26. Complaint, *Moshe Menora et. al v. Illinois High School Association*, 527 F. Supp. 637 (N.D. Ill. 1981).
27. See Respondents' Brief to Petition for a Writ of Certiorari, *Moshe Menora et al. v. Illinois High School Association*, No. 82–830, Box 525, Folder, 18, MS I-77, AJHS.
28. See Frank S. Ravitch, "Religion and the Law in American History," in *The Columbia Guide to Religion in American History*, ed. Paul Harvey and Edward J. Blum (New York: Columbia University Press, 2012), 154–68. See also Leonard W. Levy, *The Establishment Clause: Religion and the First Amendment* (Chapel Hill: University of North Carolina Press, 1994).
29. See Kent Greenwalt, *Does God Belong in Public Schools?* (Princeton, NJ: Princeton University Press, 2005), 13–34; William M. Wiecek, *The Birth of the Modern Constitution: The United States Supreme Court, 1941–1953* (New York: Cambridge University Press, 2006), 211–49; and John P. Forren, "State

and Federal Legal Protection for Peyote Use in the United States," in *Peyote: History, Tradition, Politics, and Conservation*, ed. Beatriz Caiuby Labate and Clanncy Cavnar (Santa Barbara, CA: Praeger, 2016), 85–104.

30. Complaint, *Moshe Menora et al. v. Illinois High School Association*, 527 F. Supp. 637 (N.D. Ill. 1981).

31. See Taylor H. A. Bell, *Sweet Charlie, Dike, Cazzie, and Bobby Joe: High School Basketball in Illinois* (Urbana: University of Illinois Press, 2004), 130.

32. Ibid., 56.

33. See Ronald A. Smith, "Winning and a Theory of Competitive Athletics," in *Sport and the Humanities: A Collection of Original Essays*, ed. William J. Morgan (Knoxville: University of Tennessee, 1980), 44–50.

34. Memorandum Opinion and Order, *Moshe Menora et al. v. Illinois High School Association*, No. 81 C960, 527 F. Supp. 637 (N.D. Ill. 1981), Box 525, Folder, 17, MS I-77, AJHS.

35. Samuel Rabinove, "How—and Why—American Jews have Contended for Religious Freedom: The Requirements and Limits of Civility," *Journal of Law and Religion* 8 (1990): 152.

36. See Morris U. Schappes, *A Documentary History of Jews in the United States, 1654–1875* (New York: Schocken, 1971), 69.

37. See Jonathan D. Sarna, "The Impact of the American Revolution on American Jews," *Modern Judaism* 1 (1981): 154–57.

38. See Edward Eitches, "Maryland's 'Jew Bill,'" *American Jewish Historical Quarterly* 60 (March 1971): 258–79.

39. See, for example, "Church and State," *Israelite* (March 10, 1865): 292.

40. "The Church and Prohibition," *Jewish Exponent* (March 1, 1889): 4.

41. See Jonathan D. Sarna, "Is Judaism Compatible with American Civil Religion? The Problem of Christmas and the 'National Faith,'" in *Religion and the Life of the Nation: American Recoveries*, ed. Rowland A. Sherrill (Urbana: University of Illinois Press, 1990), 152–73.

42. Bernard Drachman, *The Jewish Sabbath Question* (New York, 1915), 8. See also Benjamin Kline Hunnicutt, "The Jewish Sabbath Movement in the Early Twentieth Century," *American Jewish History* 69 (December 1979): 196–225.

43. See Jonathan D. Sarna, "American Jews and Church-State Relations: The Search for 'Equal Footing,'" in *Religion and State in the American Jewish Experience*, ed. Jonathan D. Sarna and David G. Dalin (Notre Dame, IN: University of Notre Dame Press, 1997), 23–29.

44. See George Kellman, "Civic and Political," *American Jewish Year Book* 63 (1962): 176–77.

45. See Saul Bernstein, *The Orthodox Union Story: A Centenary Portrayal* (Northvale, NJ: Jason Aronson, 1997), 204–6.

46. "Rabbi Clarifies U.S. School Aid," *New York Times* (April 30, 1961): 42. See also

Ari Y. Kelman and Janet Bordelon, "The Political Economy of Day Schools," *American Jewish History* 102 (January 2018): 59–84.

47. On Chabad menorahs, see Sue Fishkoff, *The Rebbe's Army: Inside the World of Chabad-Lubavitch* (New York: Schocken, 2003), 285–300.

48. See Stewart Ain, "Crèches, Menorahs Raise Issue of Mixing Government and Religion," *Jewish World* (November 30, 1984): 20.

49. Martin E. Marty, *Church-State Separation in America: The Tradition Nobody Knows* (Washington, DC: People for the American Way, 1984), 2.

50. Martin E. Marty, "The Changing Religious Community," *CCAR Yearbook* 96 (1985): 129.

51. See Martin Goldman, "Varia Americana," *Jewish Law Annual* 8 (1989): 210–20.

52. See, for example, "Yarmulkes OK'd for Basketball Players," *Chicago Tribune* (November 19, 1981): G2; and Thomas Rogers, "Sports World Specials," *New York Times* (November 23, 1981): C2.

53. See Gurock, *Judaism's Encounter with American Sport*, 130–53.

54. Ray Ripton, "Yeshiva Wins Off the Court," *Los Angeles Times* (December 30, 1982): WS9.

55. Jerold Isenberg to Donald K. Robinson, February 12, 1981, Appendix A in Complaint, *Moshe Menora et al. v. Illinois High School Association*, 527 F. Supp. 637 (N.D. Ill. 1981).

56. Donald K. Robinson to Jerold Isenberg, February 18, 1981, Appendix B in Complaint, *Moshe Menora et al. v. Illinois High School Association*, 527 F. Supp. 637 (N.D. Ill. 1981).

57. Quoted in Memorandum Opinion and Order, *Moshe Menora et al. v. Illinois High School Association*, No. 81 C960, 527 F. Supp. 637 (N.D. Ill. 1981).

58. See Tsvi Blanchard to Donald K. Robinson, February 17, 1981, Appendix C in Complaint, *Moshe Menora et al. v. Illinois High School Association*, 527 F. Supp. 637 (N.D. Ill. 1981).

59. See in Appendixes D through H in Complaint, *Moshe Menora et al. v. Illinois High School Association*, 527 F. Supp. 637 (N.D. Ill. 1981).

60. See Grossman, "The Kippah Comes to America," 130.

61. "Yarmulkes OK'd," *Chicago Tribune* (February 24, 1981): E3.

62. Raphael S. Schwartzman, "The Yarmulke Scores," *RCA Sermon Manual* 39 (1981): 144.

63. "Rabbi Hits IHSA on Yarmulke Rule," *Chicago Tribune* (February 28, 1981): 19.

64. Memorandum Opinion and Order, *Moshe Menora et al. v. Illinois High School Association*, No. 81 C960, 527 F. Supp. 637 (N.D. Ill. 1981).

65. On the tensions between American legal rulings and the boundaries of using theology to understand law and precedent, see Winnifred Fallers Sullivan, *The Impossibility of Religious Freedom* (Princeton, NJ: Princeton University Press, 2005), 89–137.

66. Memorandum Opinion and Order, *Moshe Menora et al. v. Illinois High School Association*, No. 81 C960, 527 F. Supp. 637 (N.D. Ill. 1981).

67. Rudolph Unger, "Sport Rule Becomes a Religious Issue," *Chicago Tribune* (July 29, 1982): N2.

68. See Judith M. Mills, "Menora v. Illinois High School Association: Basketball Players' Free Exercise Rights Compromised—Technical Foul," *Wisconsin Law Review* 6 (1983): 1487–1503. On Posner's theory of law, see William Domnarski, *Richard Posner* (New York: Oxford University Press, 2016), 59–95.

69. *Moshe Menora et al. v. Illinois High School Association*, No. 81-2960, 683 F.2d 1030 (7th Cir. 1982), Box 525, Folder, 19, MS I-77, AJHS.

70. Ibid.

71. See Stephen Wermiel, "Scholars Blend Law, Economics," *Wall Street Journal* (December 18, 1984): 64.

72. "High Court Stays Out of Dispute Over Skull Caps," *Daily Dispatch* (January 17, 1983): 14.

73. Sylvia Neil to Tzvi Blanchard and Jerold Isenberg, March 23, 1983, Box 525, Folder 21, MS I-77, AJHS.

74. David A. Grossberg to John G. Poust, January 18, 1983, Box 525, Folder 21, MS I-77, AJHS.

75. Maurice Possley, "Judge OKs Skullcaps for Jewish Athletes," *Chicago Sun-Times* (June 8, 1983): 31.

76. Ibid.

77. Earl Raab, "Nit-Picking," *Northern California Jewish Bulletin* (April 1, 1983): 44.

78. Author interview with Shmuel L. Schuman, January 31, 2018.

## Chapter 4. The Mighty Mites and the Bottom-Up Secret behind Modern Orthodoxy

1. Jonathan Sacks, *Future Tense: Jews, Judaism, and Israel in the Twenty-First Century* (New York: Schocken, 2009), 210.

2. See Zev Eleff, "The Decline of the Rabbinic Sermon," *Jewish Action* 74 (Fall 2013): 44–46.

3. Jonathan Sacks, "Torah Umadda: The Unwritten Chapter," *Le'eylah* 30 (Fall 1990): 10.

4. David Luchins, "In Reply," *Commentator* (December 22, 1966): 6. See also Milton Himmelfarb, "An Unknown Jewish Sect," *Commentary* 33 (January 1962): 66.

5. See Zev Eleff, *Modern Orthodox Judaism: A Documentary History* (Philadelphia: Jewish Publication Society, 2016), 139–67.

6. Irving Greenberg, "A Letter to the Editor," *Jewish Observer* 3 (December 1966): 16.

7. See Rackman, "A Challenge to Orthodoxy," 46.

8. See Norman Lamm, "Modern Orthodoxy's Identity Crisis," *Jewish Life* 36 (May–June 1969): 5–8.
9. See Lamm, *The Royal Reach*, 36.
10. R. Laurence Moore, *Selling God: American Religion in the Marketplace of Culture* (Oxford: Oxford University Press, 1994), 247–50.
11. Kimmy Caplan, "The Ever Dying Denomination: American Jewish Orthodoxy, 1824–1965," in *The Columbia History of Jews and Judaism in America*, ed. Marc Lee Raphael (New York: Columbia University Press, 2008), 181–82.
12. Sklare, *Conservative Judaism*, 42.
13. Nathan Glazer, *American Judaism* (Chicago: University of Chicago Press, 1957), 142.
14. Ralph Pelcovitz, "Hirsch for Our Time," *Jewish Life* 30 (October 1962): 59.
15. See Sydney E. Ahlstrom, *A Religious History of the American People* (New Haven, CT: Yale University Press, 1972), 952.
16. Joseph B. Soloveitchik, "The Lonely Man of Faith," *Tradition* 7 (Summer 1965): 5–67; and Joseph B. Soloveitchik, "Confrontation," *Tradition* 6 (Spring–Summer 1964): 5–29.
17. Moses I. Feuerstein, "The Synagogue's Responsibility for the Rising Generation," in *Speeches and Addresses Given by Rabbis and Religious Lay Leaders at the First World Conference of Ashkenazi and Sephardi Synagogues* (Jerusalem: World Conference of Ashkenazi and Sephardi Synagogues, 1972), 94.
18. Lamm, *The Royal Reach*, 168.
19. Jonathan D. Sarna, "The Late Nineteenth-Century American Jewish Awakening," in *Religious Diversity and American Religious History: Studies in Traditions and Cultures*, ed. Walter H. Conser Jr. and Sumner B. Twiss (Athens: University of Georgia Press, 1997), 8.
20. See Robert Liberles, "Conflict over Reforms: The Case of Congregation Beth Elohim, Charleston, South Carolina," in *The American Synagogue: A Sanctuary Transformed*, 282.
21. See Jonathan D. Sarna, "The Making of an American Jewish Culture," in *When Philadelphia Was the Capital of Jewish America*, ed. Murray Friedman (Philadelphia: Balch Institute Press, 1993), 145–55; and Leah Levitz Fishbane, "On the Road to Renaissance: The Young Men's Hebrew Associations of New York and Philadelphia, 1877–1883," in *Jewish Renaissance and Revival in America: Essays in Memory of Leah Levitz Fishbane*, ed. Eitan P. Fishbane and Jonathan D. Sarna (Waltham, MA: Brandeis University Press, 2011), 47–70.
22. See Zev Eleff, "Debating Orthodox Judaism: A Tale of Two Rabbinical Seminaries," *Jewish Action* 78 (Fall 2017): 51–56.
23. Jonathan D. Sarna, "The Crucial Decade in Jewish Camping," in *A Place of Our Own: The Rise of Reform Jewish Camping—Essays Honoring the Fiftieth*

*Anniversary of Olin-Sang-Ruby Union Institute, Union for Reform Judaism,* in Oconomowoc, Wisconsin, ed. Michael M. Lorge and Gary P. Zola (Tuscaloosa: University of Alabama Press, 2006), 42. On the early history of Ramah, see Shuly Rubin Schwartz, "Camp Ramah: The Early Years, 1947–1952," *Conservative Judaism* 40 (Fall 1987): 12–42.

24. Eleff, *Living from Convention to Convention,* 4. True, the Orthodox-oriented Bnei Akiva organization invited diaspora groups to join a world framework in 1954 and opened up Moshava camps in America. Yet parents enrolled their children in Bnei Akiva more for its political philosophies than its religious character.

25. Joseph Maier and William Spinrad, "Comparison of Religious Beliefs and Practices of Jewish, Catholic and Protestant Students," *Phylon Quarterly* 18 (1958): 355–60.

26. Lawrence Grossman, "American Orthodoxy in the 1950s: The Lean Years," in *Rav Chesed: Essays in Honor of Rabbi Dr. Haskel Lookstein,* vol. 1, ed. Rafael Medoff (Jersey City, NJ: Ktav, 2009), 251–69.

27. See C. Kirk Hadaway, "Denominational Defection: Recent Research on Religious Disaffiliation in America," in *The Mainstream Protestant "Decline": The Presbyterian Pattern,* ed. Milton J. Coalter, John M. Mulder, and Louis B. Weeks (Louisville, KY: Westminster/John Knox Press, 1990), 104.

28. Sally Bachner, "Free the World and Your Ass Will Follow: JFK and Revolutionary Freedom in 1960s Youth Culture," in *The Cambridge Companion to John F. Kennedy,* ed. Andrew Hoberek (Cambridge: Cambridge University Press, 2015), 198.

29. See Joseph H. Lookstein, "Goals for Jewish Education," in *Judaism and the Jewish School: Selected Essays on the Direction and Purpose of Jewish Education,* ed. Judah Pilch and Meir Ben-Horin (New York: Bloch, 1966), 218.

30. Alvin Irwin Schiff, *The Jewish Day School in America* (New York: Jewish Education Committee Press, 1966), 49; and Chaim I. Waxman, "From Institutional Decay to Primary Day: American Orthodox Jewry since World War II," *American Jewish History* 91 (September–December 2003): 412.

31. See Eleff, *Living from Convention to Convention,* 39.

32. M. Herbert Danzger, *Returning to Tradition: The Contemporary Revival of Orthodox Judaism* (New Haven, CT: Yale University Press, 1989), 64.

33. See Benny Kraut, *The Greening of American Orthodox Judaism: Yavneh in the 1960s* (Cincinnati, OH: Hebrew Union College Press, 2011), 20–34.

34. Uriel Zimmer, *The Jewish Adolescent: A Guide for Today's Girl* (Brooklyn, NY: Balshon, 1963), 98–99.

35. See Grossman, "The Kippah Comes to America," 129–49; Edward S. Shapiro, *A Time for Healing: American Jewry since World War II* (Baltimore, MD: Johns Hopkins University Press, 1992), 182.

36. See Michelle Rosenthal, *American Protestants and TV in the 1950s: Responses to a New Medium* (New York: Palgrave, 2007), 20–36.

37. "TV or Not TV," *Jewish Parent* 2 (April 1950): 10.

38. See, for example, Thaddeus R. Murroughs, "The Vision of Children in Relation to TV," *Jewish Parent* 5 (April 1954): 6–11.

39. See Jeffrey Shandler and Elihu Katz, "Broadcasting American Judaism: The Radio and Television Department of JTS," in *Tradition Renewed: A History of the Jewish Theological Seminary*, vol. 2, ed. Jack Wertheimer (New York: Jewish Theological Seminary of America, 1997), 382–85.

40. See Mordecai Simon, "The Chicago Board of Rabbis' Broadcasting Commission," *Conservative Judaism* 39 (Winter 1986–87): 23–27.

41. See Oscar Z. Fasman, "From Eternity to Here," *Hashomer* 1 (June 3, 1954): 1–3.

42. William H. Young and Nancy K. Young, *The 1950s: American Popular Culture Through History* (Westport, CT: Greenwood Press, 2004), 232. See also Martin Halliwell, *American Culture in the 1950s* (Edinburgh: Edinburgh University Press, 2007), 155–57.

43. Vincent Terrace, *Encyclopedia of Television Shows, 1925–2007* (Jefferson, NC: McFarland, 2009), 561.

44. Anne Fadiman, *Ex Libris: Confessions of a Common Reader* (New York: Farrar, Straus & Giroux, 2000), 12.

45. *G.E. College Bowl Guide for the 1963–1964 Season* (New York, 1963), 6.

46. "Yeshiva and Stern to Appear on G.E.'s *College Bowl* TV Show," *Commentator* (February 19, 1963): 1.

47. Irwin Geller, "Coast to Coast Judaism; YU Quiz Kids in TV Debut," *Commentator* (February 19, 1963): 3.

48. "Linn Chooses Starting Team as Bowl Debut Draws Near," *Commentator* (May 8, 1963): 1.

49. Samuel Belkin to Asher Reiss, May 1, 1963, Public Relations Collection, Box 1963–1977, *G.E. College Bowl* Folder, Yeshiva University Archive, New York, NY.

50. "U. of Louisville Seeks 5th Win on 'Quiz Bowl,'" *Richmond News Leader* (May 11, 1963).

51. David Condor, "In the Wake of the News," *Chicago Tribune* (May 7, 1963): C1.

52. "Canarsie Housewife Wins $1,500 on TV Program as She Captains All-Male Team," *Canarsie Courier* (May 16, 1963).

53. Dean Eagle, "Bigger Strike Zone Helping the Pitchers," *Louisville Times* (May 25, 1963).

54. "YU Wins *College Bowl*," *Newark Jewish News* (May 17, 1963).

55. Samuel Belkin to W. M. Sahloff, May 15, 1963, Public Relations Collection, Box 1963–1977, Sports-*G.E. College Bowl* Folder, YU Archives.

56. Gilbert Klaperman to Irving Linn, May 14, 1963, Public Relations Collection, Box 1963–1977, *G.E. College Bowl* Folder, YU Archives.
57. Yaakov Homnick to Samuel Belkin, May 19, 1963, Public Relations Collection, Box 1963–1977, *G.E. College Bowl* Folder, YU Archives.
58. "Rabbi Samuel Adelman," *Intermountain Jewish News* (May 17, 1963).
59. Abraham Kellner to Samuel Belkin, May 12, 1963, Public Relations Collection, Box 1963–1977, *G.E. College Bowl* Folder, YU Archives.
60. Leonard Azneer to David Mirsky, May 16, 1963, Public Relations Collection, Box 1963–1977, *G.E. College Bowl* Folder, YU Archives.
61. Tim Timberlake to Yeshiva University, May 16, 1963, Public Relations Collection, Box 1963–1977, *G.E. College Bowl* Folder, YU Archives.
62. Student Government Organization of Yeshiva of Flatbush H.S. to Yeshiva University *College Bowl* Team, May 13, 1963, Public Relations Collection, Box 1963–1977, *G.E. College Bowl* Folder, YU Archives.
63. George Finkelstein to Sam Hartstein, May 14, 1963, Public Relations Collection, Box 1963–1977, *G.E. College Bowl* Folder, YU Archives.
64. Kenneth B. Keating to Samuel Belkin, May 14, 1963, Public Relations Collection, Box 1963–1977, *G.E. College Bowl* Folder, YU Archives.
65. B. S. Gottlieb to Samuel Belkin, May 16, 1963, Public Relations Collection, Box 1963–1977, *G.E. College Bowl* Folder, YU Archives.
66. Willis W. Jones to Sheldon Fink, May 13, 1963, Public Relations Collection, Box 1963–1977, *G.E. College Bowl* Folder, YU Archives.
67. "YU Wins *College Bowl*," *Newark Jewish News* (May 17, 1963).
68. "Shall We Make Fools of Our Children?" *Detroit Jewish News* (June 14, 1963): 4. On the exclusion of Jews from American colleges, see Leonard Dinnerstein, *Antisemitism in America* (New York: Oxford University Press, 1994), 84.
69. Samuel Schreig, "From Everywhere," *Sentinel* (May 30, 1963): 11.
70. "Shall We Make Fools of Our Children?" 4.
71. Jean Howerton, "City, U. of L. Show Their Pride in *College Bowl* Scholars," *Louisville Courier Journal* (May 13, 1963).
72. Harry Loewy to Irving Linn, May 15, 1963, Public Relations Collection, Box 1963–1977, *G.E. College Bowl* Folder, YU Archives.
73. Irving Linn to Harry Loewy, May 19, 1963, Public Relations Collection, Box 1963–1977, *G.E. College Bowl* Folder, YU Archives.
74. Samuel Gordon, "Bitter Bowl Note," *Louisville Courier Journal* (May 20, 1963).
75. Schreig, "From Everywhere," 11.
76. Arthur Raybin to Sam Hartstein, May 12, 1963, Public Relations Collection, Box 1963–1977, *G.E. College Bowl* Folder, YU Archives.
77. Grossman, "The Kippah Comes to America," 142.
78. Jay Friedman to Samuel Belkin, May 13, 1963, Public Relations Collection, Box 1963–1977, *G.E. College Bowl* Folder, YU Archives.

79. Sam Hartstein to Jay Friedman, May 14, 1963, Public Relations Collection, Box 1963–1977, *G.E. College Bowl* Folder, YU Archives.
80. "Triumphant Yeshiva Putting *College Bowl* Laurels on the Line," *New York Journal-American* (May 14, 1963).
81. Lester Dinoff, "Yeshiva University's '*GE College Bowl*' Team to Face Temple Sunday in Search of Third Straight Win," Yeshiva University Press Release, n.d.
82. Bob Williams, "On the Air," *New York Post* (May 20, 1963).
83. "Yeshiva University *College Bowl* Team to Appear at Ambassador Ball Here," Yeshiva University Press Release (May 1963).
84. "Viva Yeshiva!" *B'nai B'rith Messenger* (May 24, 1963): 24.
85. "Our Canarsie Housewife Ups Winnings to $3,000 on TV's '*GE College Bowl*,'" *Canarsie Courier* (May 23, 1963).
86. Ibid.
87. Irving Linn to Herb Falk, 1969, Public Relations Collection, Box 1963–1977, *G.E. College Bowl* Folder, YU Archives.
88. HILI Student Council to *College Bowl* Team, May 26, 1963, Public Relations Collection, Box 1963–1977, *G.E. College Bowl* Folder, YU Archives.
89. Grade 5 Students of Hillel Day School to Debating Team (*College Bowl*), May 22, 1963, Public Relations Collection, Box 1963–1977, *G.E. College Bowl* Folder, YU Archives.
90. Harold L. Kirkpatrick to Irving Linn, May 24, 1963, Public Relations Collection, Box 1963–1977, Sports-*G.E. College Bowl* Folder, YU Archives.
91. Sam Kochanowitz to Sam Hartstein, May 21, 1963, Public Relations Collection, Box 1963–1977, Sports-*G.E. College Bowl* Folder, YU Archives.
92. Lester Dinoff, "Yeshiva University's '*GE College Bowl*' Team to Face Temple Sunday in Search of Third Straight Win," Yeshiva University Press Release, n.d.
93. "Yeshiva University *College Bowl* Team to Appear at Ambassador Ball Here," Yeshiva University Press Release (May 1963).
94. Gerald Nachman, "Yeshiva Students Prepare for a TV Exam," *New York Post* (May 26, 1963): 6.
95. "Yeshiva University *College Bowl* Team to Appear at Ambassador Ball Here," Yeshiva University Press Release (May 1963).
96. "Temple Wins TV '*College Bowl*,'" *Philadelphia Inquirer* (May 27, 1963); Mark Bricklin, "Temple Wins TV Quiz; Curt Noel Sparks Victory," *Philadelphia Tribune* (June 1, 1963); and "Temple Brains Win TV Test," *Philadelphia Daily News* (May 27, 1963).
97. James W. Hilty, *Temple University: 125 Years of Service to Philadelphia, the Nation, and the World* (Philadelphia: Temple University Press, 2009), 97.
98. "*College Bowl*," *Commentator* (May 27, 1963): 2.
99. Irene Schreiber, "Y.U., We're Proud of You," *Jewish Press* (May 31, 1963).

100. Millard E. Gladfelter to Samuel Belkin, May 28, 1963, Public Relations Collection, Box 1963–1977, *G.E. College Bowl* Folder, YU Archives.

101. John Clearly to Samuel Belkin, May 28, 1963, Public Relations Collection, Box 1963–1977, *G.E. College Bowl* Folder, YU Archives.

102. George Tashman, "Tashman on TV," *Richmond Independent* (May 29, 1963).

103. See "Yeshiva U. *College Bowl* Team at Ambassador Ball Here Sunday," *Detroit Jewish News* (May 24, 1963): 6.

104. Sheldon C. Freedman, "The Stereotype," *Kehillat Israel Bulletin* (May 1963): 1.

105. Irving Linn to Herb Falk (1969), Public Relations Collection, Box 1963–1977, *G.E. College Bowl* Folder, YU Archives, New York. See also "Where Are They Now: YU's 1963 *College Bowl* Team," *YU Alumni Review* (Spring 1978): 20.

# Chapter 5. Mitzvah Merchants and the Creation of an Orthodox Children's Culture

1. See Eliezer Wenger, *Brachos Study Guide*, vol. 1 (Ottawa: B'Ruach HaTorah, 1989), 5.

2. See Sylvia Barack Fishman, *Jewish Life and American Culture* (Albany: State University of New York Press, 2000), 9–13; and Yoel Finkelman, *Strictly Kosher Reading: Popular Literature and the Condition of Contemporary Orthodoxy* (Boston: Academic Studies Press, 2011), 44–54.

3. See Ronald A. Smith, "The Lost Battle for Gentlemanly Sport, 1869–1909," in *The Rock, the Curse and the Hub: A Random History of Boston Sports*, ed. Randy Roberts (Cambridge, MA: Harvard University Press, 2005), 60–77.

4. See Waxman, "From Institutional Decay to Primary Day," 405–21. This binary is not always the case, however. See Jonathan Nelson, "HBO Movies Shut Off by YCSC," *Commentator* (January 7, 1976): 1; and "Club Promotes Modesty as a Lifestyle," *Kol Rambam* (Spring/Summer 2017): 2.

5. See Danzger, *Returning to Tradition*, 71–95.

6. See Lucy Dawidowicz to Milton Himmelfarb, November 4, 1958, Box 21, Folder 38, Marshall Sklare Papers, Robert D. Farber University Archives of Brandeis University, Waltham, MA.

7. See Schiff, *The Jewish Day School in America*, 61–62, 237–39.

8. On Agudath Israel's youth revival, see Joseph Friedenson, "A Concise History of Agudath Israel," in *Yaakov Rosenheim Memorial Anthology* (New York: Orthodox Library, 1968), 61.

9. See Dean M. Kelley, *Why Conservative Churches Are Growing: A Study in Sociology of Religion* (New York: Harper & Row, 1972), 178–79.

10. See Nancy T. Ammerman, "North American Protestant Fundamentalism," in *Fundamentalisms Observed*, vol. 1, ed. Martin E. Marty and R. Scott Appleby (Chicago: University of Chicago Press, 1991), 42–43.

11. See Niebuhr, "Varieties of Religious Revival," 13–16. See also R. Laurence Moore, *Religious Outsiders and the Making of Americans* (New York: Oxford University Press, 1986), 149; and Joel A. Carpenter, *Revive Us Again: The Reawakening of American Fundamentalism* (Oxford: Oxford University Press, 1997), 161–76.

12. See Gary Cross, *Kids' Stuff: Toys and the Changing World of American Childhood* (Cambridge, MA: Harvard University Press, 1997), 188–227.

13. See Mark A. Noll and Ethan R. Sanders, "Evangelicalism in North America," in *Twentieth-Century Global Christianity*, ed. Mary Farrell Bednarowski (Minneapolis: Fortress Press, 2010), 186. See also Moore, *Selling God*, 242–44.

14. Colleen McDannell, *Material Christianity: Religion and Popular Culture in America* (New Haven, CT: Yale University Press, 1995), 52.

15. Melinda Bollar Wagner, *God's Schools: Choice and Compromise in American Society* (New Brunswick, NJ: Rutgers University Press, 1990), 133–40.

16. See "Spelling Bee's Revival," *Journal of Education* 117 (June 4, 1934): 314.

17. See James Maguire, *American Bee: The National Spelling Bee and the Culture of Word Nerds* (Emmaus, PA: Rodale, 2006), 68–86.

18. Shalom Auslander, *Foreskin's Lament: A Memoir* (New York: Riverhead, 2007), 19.

19. Israel Shenker, "Children Abuzz with Answers (and Questions) at Hebrew School Blessing Bee," *New York Times* (March 3, 1976): 40.

20. See ibid.

21. See Doniel Z. Kramer, *The Day Schools and Torah Umesorah* (New York: Yeshiva University Press, 1984), 93–114.

22. Yaakov Feitman, "American Jewish Literature: Beware!" *Jewish Parent* 28 (April 1976): 17.

23. "Brachos Bee Goes National," *Olomeinu* 26 (June 1972): 3.

24. See Meir Belsky, "The Day Schools in the U.S.," *Jewish Observer* 12 (January 1977): 6.

25. "A Blessing to Judaism," *Jewish Parent* 28 (April 1976): 19.

26. "Chief Rabbi Grade School Contest Judge," *B'nai B'rith Messenger* (December 26, 1975): 22.

27. "San Francisco Hosts Visiting Emek Students," *B'nai B'rith Messenger* (May 13, 1977): 29. See also Wenger, *Brachos Study Guide*, 5.

28. See "Blessing Bees Are Scheduled," *Jewish Week* (December 9, 1979): 48.

29. See Wenger, *Brachos Study Guide*, frontmatter.

30. Ibid., 10.

31. "A Salute to Students on Both Coasts," *Olomeinu* 32 (June 1978): 3.

32. See Jim Davis, "Rabbi Discovers Competition Can Become a Mixed 'Brocho,'" *Fort Lauderdale News* (March 12, 1982): 7D.

33. "1982-5742 Brachos Bee Winners," *Olomeinu* 36 (June 1982): 2

34. See "Rabbi Wenger to Coordinate Brochos Bee," *American Israelite* (March 1, 1984): 13. See also "Hebrew Day School to Host Regional Brochos Bee," *American Israelite* (March 29, 1984): 13.

35. See Bruce S. Bobbins, "If You Need a 'Bracha,' Mayer Can Say Them All!" *Jewish Exponent* (July 22, 1983): 21.

36. Ibid.

37. "Students in National Contest," *Jewish Exponent* (May 13, 1983): 51.

38. Bruce S. Bobbins, "Torah Academy Student Wins Brachos Bee," *Jewish Exponent* (May 4, 1984): 8.

39. See Bob Kerr, "Students Value Rabbi Cards," *Providence Journal-Bulletin*, undated newspaper clipping obtained from Laibel Shugarman.

40. "Jesus and Disciples," *Boys' Life* 80 (December 1990): 71. See also Steven Hoskins, "Material Culture," in *Encyclopedia of Christianity in the United States*, vol. 5, ed. George Thomas Kurian and Mark A. Lamport (Lanham, MD: Rowman & Littlefield, 2016), 1433.

41. See Louis Berney, *Tales from the Baltimore Orioles Dugout: A Collection of the Greatest Orioles Stories Ever Told* (New York: Sports Publishing, 2004), 157.

42. See Jean Marbella, "Trading Faces," *Baltimore Sun* (April 13, 1989): 1G.

43. See Herb Drill, "Collecting 'Gedolim'—Famous Orthodox Rabbi Cards," *Jewish Times* (September 21, 1989): 67; and Pete Dobrovitz, "Tradition Meets Trend with Rabbi Cards," *Sports Collector's Digest* (July 7, 1989): 60.

44. Boaz Dvir, "Rabbi Cards," *Jewish Journal* (May 18, 1989): 1B.

45. See Chris Cook, "Trading Rabbis," *Chicago Tribune* (April 23, 1989): D2.

46. Murray Dubin, "Oh Those Rabbis, What Cards!" *Philadelphia Inquirer* (April 25, 1989): A1.

47. Francis X. Clines, "Yeshiva Trading Cards: Rabbis but No Red Sox," *New York Times* (February 28, 1987): L4.

48. "America's Old 'Baseball Cards,'" *Jewish Observer* 18 (March 1985): 46.

49. The idea was attributed to Rabbi Reuvain Grozovsky, the head of Yeshiva Torah Vodaath and the co-rabbinic head of the Agudath Israel. See Hanoch Teller, "Israel's New 'Baseball Cards,'" *Jewish Observer* 17 (September 1984): 35.

50. Andrea King, "Getting into the Rebbe Trade," *Washington Post* (April 6, 1988): B1.

51. Ibid.

52. Clines, "Yeshiva Trading Cards."

53. Chonon Shugarman, "The Cards Are Not for Flipping," *Jewish Observer* 23 (March 1990): 50.

54. See John Bloom, *House of Cards: Baseball Card Collecting and Popular Culture* (Minneapolis: University of Minnesota Press, 1997), 16–27.

55. Marbella, "Trading Faces."

56. Drill, "Collecting 'Gedolim'—Famous Orthodox Rabbi Cards."

57. "Collectibles: Bubble Gum Not Included," *Time* 134 (July 17, 1989): 77.

58. Amir Efrati, "Rabbi Cards Have Found Their Niche," *Sarasota-Manatee Jewish News* (June 16, 2004): 17.

59. See Dobrovitz, "Tradition Meets Trend with Rabbi Cards."

60. Pinchas Stolper to Yaakov Weinberg, July 23, 1987, Box 34, Folder 6, MS I-66, AJHS.

61. Drill, "Collecting 'Gedolim'—Famous Orthodox Rabbi Cards."

62. "Centrist Orthodox Gedolim Cards," *Hamevaser* (Purim 1987): 2.

63. Drill, "Collecting 'Gedolim'—Famous Orthodox Rabbi Cards."

64. Cyrel Levovitz, "Leaders of the Pack," *New York Magazine* 27 (February 14, 1994): 6.

65. Dubin, "Oh Those Rabbis, What Cards!"

66. Ken Pellis, "Forget Babe Ruth, You Can Collect Rabbi Cards," *Palm Beach Post* (June 1, 1990): 60.

67. See Boris Weintraub, "(Rabbi) Card Crazy After All These Years," *Moment* 31 (October 2006): 29; and "It's All Kosher," *Sports Illustrated* 70 (May 22, 1989): 11.

68. See Eric Hubler, "I'll Give You Three Mickey Mantles for a Schneerson," *New York Times* (May 24, 1998): CY7; and Abigail Klein Leichman, "Torah Cards," *Amit Women* 66 (Fall 1993): 29.

69. See Joseph Berger, "A Store Where Toys Must be Kosher," *New York Times* (December 18, 2011): WE3.

70. Laura Arnold Leibman, "Children, Toys, and Judaism," in *The Bloomsbury Reader in Religion and Childhood*, ed. Anna Strhan, Stephen G. Parker, and Susan Ridgely (London: Bloomsbury, 2017), 299–306.

71. Christine M. Quail, "The Battle for the Toybox," in *Christotainment: Selling Jesus through Popular Culture*, ed. Shirley R. Steinberg and Joe L. Kincheloe (Boulder, CO: Westview, 2009), 165–68.

72. A copy of this letter is in the possession of the author.

73. Ibid.

74. See Kristen Clark, "Toy Story," *Forward* (March 28, 2014): 20; and "The Shpielmans Have Arrived Just in Time for Chanukah," *Jewish Link* (December 21, 2017): 48.

75. See "Our Story," on the Binyan Block's website, http://www.binyanblocks.com/about-us (accessed February 6, 2018).

76. "Binyan Blocks," *Mishpacha Junior* 636 (November 23, 2016): 25.

77. Ibid.

## Chapter 6. Yeshivat Rambam and the Rise and Fall of a Modern Orthodox Idea

1. Phil Jacobs, "Finding a Niche," *Baltimore Jewish Times* (September 14, 1990): 22–23. Once Rita Shloush assumed the principalship and under her insistence,

the school referred to itself much more consistently as the Hebraized Yeshivat Rambam. The name was also inspired by the Maimonides School in Brookline, Massachusetts. On this, see Seth Farber, *An American Orthodox Dreamer: Rabbi Joseph B. Soloveitchik and Boston's Maimonides School* (Waltham, MA: Brandeis University Press, 2004).

2. Emanuel Rackman, "From Synagogue Toward Yeshiva: Institutionalized Cult or Congregations of the Learned?" *Commentary* 21 (April 1956): 356.

3. Both ideas were catalyzed by a report that a synagogue in nearby Randallstown was preparing to close. The group petitioned the Randallstown Jews to commit their assets to support a new Orthodox initiative. The petition was unsuccessful.

4. See Eli Lederhendler, *American Jewry: A New History* (Cambridge: Cambridge University Press, 2017), 266–67.

5. Israel Tabak, *Three Worlds: A Jewish Odyssey* (Jerusalem: Gefen, 1988), 177. See also Israel Tabak, "Rabbi Abraham Rice of Baltimore: Pioneer of Orthodox Judaism in America," *Tradition* 7 (Summer 1965): 100–120.

6. Harry Friedenwald, "Rice, Abraham," in *The Jewish Encyclopedia*, vol. 10, ed. Isidore Singer (New York: Funk and Wagnalls, 1905), 405. See also Harry Friedenwald, *Life, Letters and Addresses of Aaron Friedenwald* (Baltimore, MD: Lord Baltimore Press, 1906), 23.

7. Henrietta Szold, "Baltimore," in *The Jewish Encyclopedia*, vol. 2, ed. Isidore Singer (New York: Funk and Wagnalls, 1902), 479.

8. Arthur J. Magida, "The Baltimore Tradition," *Baltimore Jewish Times* (June 9, 1989): 56.

9. See Robert Emmett Curran, "Ambrose Marèchal, the Jesuits, and the Demise of Ecclesial Republicanism in Maryland, 1818–1838," *U.S. Catholic Historian* 26 (Spring 2008): 97–110.

10. See E. Brooks Holifield, *God's Ambassadors: A History of the Christian Clergy in America* (Grand Rapids, MI: Eerdmans, 2007), 134.

11. For instance, in the 1810s Baltimore was the site of the first offshoot of Boston-type Unitarianism to take root outside of the Boston area. See Gary Dorrien, *The Making of American Liberal Theology: Imagining Progressive Religion, 1805–1900* (Louisville, KY: Westminster/John Knox Press, 2001), 28. In the 1840s Reform Jews established the Har Sinai Verein. In the 1860s this congregation chose politics over support of its rabbi. See Bertram W. Korn, *American Jewry and the Civil War* (Philadelphia: Jewish Publication Society of America, 1951), 20–22.

12. See Eric L. Goldstein and Deborah R. Weiner, *On Middle Ground: A History of the Jews of Baltimore* (Baltimore, MD: Johns Hopkins University Press, 2018), 125.

13. Jon Butler, "God, Gotham, and Modernity," *Journal of American History* 103

(June 2016): 32. See also Russell Shorto, *The Island at the Center of the World: The Epic Story of Dutch Manhattan and the Forgotten Colony That Shaped America* (New York: Doubleday, 2004), 95–97.

14. Eleff, *Who Rules the Synagogue?* 70.
15. Robert Tabak, "Orthodox Judaism in Transition," in *Jewish Life in Philadelphia, 1830–1940*, ed. Murray Friedman (Philadelphia: Institute for the Study of Human Issues, 1983), 62.
16. Sidney Hollander, *The Jewish Community of Greater Baltimore: A Population Study* (Baltimore, MD: Associated Jewish Charities of Baltimore, 1968), 71–73.
17. See Dovid Katz, "Mishmeret Ha-Levi: Kiyum li-Dimuto u-Lemishmeret Hayyav shel ha-Ga'on Rebbe Yaakov Yitzhak ha-Levi Ruderman," *Yeshurun* 18 (2006): 163–64.
18. "The Baltimore Yeshiva," *Baltimore Jewish Times* (February 9, 1934): 8.
19. See William B. Helmreich, "Old Wine in New Bottles: Advanced Yeshivot in the United States," *American Jewish History* 69 (December 1979): 244.
20. Saul Bernstein to Irving J. Abramowitz, January 30, 1962, Box 1, Folder 2, MS-144, Jewish Museum of Maryland, Baltimore, MD.
21. "Most Influential Rabbis," *Baltimore Jewish Times* (June 9, 1989): 54.
22. See Ferziger, *Beyond Sectarianism*, 214.
23. See Helmreich, *The World of the Yeshiva*, 228.
24. See Tzvi Dole, "An Inside Look at Ner Israel Rabbinical College," *Baltimore Jewish Times* (November 8, 1991): 66.
25. See Eleff, *Living from Convention to Convention*, 52.
26. Jacobs, "Finding a Niche," 23.
27. Arthur J. Magida and Gary Rosenblatt, "Orthodox Judaism: A Surge to the Right," *Baltimore Jewish Times* (June 9, 1989): 55.
28. Jacobs, "Finding a Niche," 23.
29. Gary A. Tobin, *A Population Study of the Jewish Community of Greater Baltimore* (Baltimore, MD: Associated Jewish Charities and Welfare Fund, 1986), 131.
30. On the "winnowing" of American Orthodox Judaism, see Jeffrey S. Gurock, "The Winnowing of American Orthodoxy," in *Approaches to Modern Judaism*, vol. 2, ed. Marc Lee Raphael (Chico, CA: Scholars Press, 1984), 41–53.
31. Tobin, *A Population Study*, 11.
32. Magida and Rosenblatt, "Orthodox Judaism," 51.
33. Ibid., 59.
34. See Lew Koch, "Keeping Kids Safe from Democracy," *Chicago* 24 (January 1975): 122.
35. Jay Merwin, "Cultural Classroom," *Evening Sun* (February 5, 1992): A10.
36. The Orthodox schools did not get along with Beth Tfiloh High School. In the late 1980s, the right-of-center Talmudical Academy declined an invitation to

compete in a national basketball tournament hosted at Beth Tfiloh. See Daniel Schifrin, "A New Mission," *Baltimore Jewish Times* (June 12, 1992): 36. Related to this, and a decade later, was the very public emergence of the teenage "star" basketball player, Tamir Goodman, and his frustrations with the Talmudical Academy administration. See Jeffrey S. Gurock, "The Crowning of a 'Jewish Jordan': Tamir Goodman, the American Sports Media, and Modern Orthodox Jewry's Fantasy World," in *American Judaism in Popular Culture*, ed. Leonard J. Greenspoon and Ronald A. Simkins (Omaha, NE: Creighton University Press, 2006), 161–73.

37.  See Chaim I. Waxman, "The Haredization of American Orthodox Jewry," *Jerusalem Letter/Viewpoints* 376 (February 15, 1998): 1–5.

38.  Gary Rosenblatt, "'Frum' Here to Modernity," *Baltimore Jewish Times* (October 16, 1992): 10.

39.  Ellen Bernstein, "For Baltimoreans, It's Academy," *Washington Jewish Week* (September 26, 1991): 5.

40.  Merwin, "Cultural Classroom," A10.

41.  See Medoff, *Building Orthodox Judaism in America*, 142–47.

42.  Magida and Rosenblatt, "Orthodox Judaism," 54–57. See also Gary Rosenblatt, "Religious McCarthyism," *Baltimore Jewish Times* (November 22, 1991): 10.

43.  Certainly, Rambam was not anticlerical. Rabbi Zvi Hirsch Weinreb (eventually, a board member) of Shomrei Emunah and Rabbi Ervin Preis of Suburban Orthodox Congregation offered behind-the-scenes support. In the earliest years the latter delivered an important and impassioned High Holiday sermon in support of Rambam before hundreds in his crowded synagogue. It also maintained a cordial line of communication with Rabbi Joseph Baumgarten of Bnai Jacob and Rabbi Ronald Schwartz of Beth Jacob. The lay leaders claimed exclusive authority over their educational project.

44.  Merwin, "Cultural Classroom," A10.

45.  Jacobs, "Finding a Niche," 22.

46.  Merwin, "Cultural Classroom," A10.

47.  Jacobs, "Finding a Niche," 23–24.

48.  Ibid.

49.  Tzvi Dole, "Being Comfortable in Both Worlds," *Baltimore Jewish Times* (May 10, 1991): 33.

50.  Ellen Bernstein, "Educator Rita," *Atlanta Jewish Times* (June 7, 1991): 10. At the time Shloush admitted to some "disappointment" that she was not offered the permanent position but accepted the Baltimore position despite other offers in more firmly entrenched New York–and New Jersey–based schools.

51.  Interestingly, the leftwing Beth Tfiloh's longtime "director of education" is a well-regarded female educator. See Phil Jacobs, "On Top of the Steps: Beth

Tfiloh to Honor Zipora Schorr and the Lessons She's Shared," *Baltimore Jewish Times* (March 5, 1999): 16.

52. Jacobs, "Finding a Niche," 24.
53. Kim Asch, "Melding the Orthodox, Secular Ways," *Owings Mills Times* (April 2, 1992): 1.
54. Jacobs, "Finding a Niche," 24.
55. Actually, organizers held a fundraising dinner before the school opened but the leadership deemed this 1991 affair the inaugural banquet.
56. "My Fair Week; a Lyrical One," *Baltimore Jewish Times* (November 8, 1991): 85.
57. See Sandie Nagel, "Around Town," *Baltimore Jewish Times* (February 21, 1991): 57.
58. Becky (Brooks) Gordon and Susan Rotkovitz, "The Rambam Tree," *Yeshivat Rambam Banquet Journal* (1992): 19.
59. Daniel Schifrin, "Finding Its Place," *Baltimore Jewish Times* (May 15, 1992): 21. See also "Yeshivat Rambam Staff," *Yeshivat Rambam Banquet Journal* (1992): 20–23.
60. See Dan Schifrin, "The Classroom Cash Crunch," *Baltimore Jewish Times* (July 30, 1993): 52.
61. See Lisa S. Goldberg, "A School Grows in Pikesville," *Baltimore Jewish Times* (December 30, 1994): 23.
62. Arthur J. Magida, "Flocking to the New Promised Land," *Baltimore Jewish Times* (September 11, 1992): 18.
63. Schifrin, "Finding Its Place," 21.
64. Jay Merwin, "Rabbi Seeking Zeal for Zionism," *Evening Sun* (March 10, 1992): 1.
65. Harry Kozlovsky to Larry Marder, July 18, 1996. A copy of this letter is in possession of the author.
66. See Edward Gunts, "Historic Har Sinai Votes to Sell Property, Leave City," *Sun* (January 23, 1995): 1B. See also Christine Stutz, "A Perfect Marriage," *Baltimore Jewish Times* (January 19, 1996): 35.
67. Seth Rotenberg, "Message from the Chairman of the Board," *Yeshivat Rambam Banquet Journal* (1999): 18.
68. "Rambam Opening High School," *Owings Mills Times* (February 13, 1997): 9.
69. Laurence A. Marder to Seth Rotenberg, July 8, 1996. A copy of this letter is in possession of the author.
70. Harry Kozlovsky to Larry Marder, July 18, 1996. A copy of this letter is in possession of the author.
71. Seth M. Rotenberg to Laurence A. Marder, July 30, 1996. A copy of this letter is in possession of the author.
72. "Yeshivat Rambam Day School Celebrates Seventh Anniversary, Continuing Growth," *Reisterstown Community Times* (December 10, 1997): 16.

73. "Rambam's Prez Steps Down after Eight Years," *Baltimore Jewish Times* (October 15, 1998): 17.

74. Rona S. Hirsch, "Extra Credit," *Baltimore Jewish Times* (February 5, 1999): 23.

75. E. J. Kessler, "Group Formed to Address Concerns of Modern Orthodox Day Schools," *Forward* (November 5, 1999): 7.

76. "In Recognition," *Jewish Post and Opinion* (December 20, 2000): 4.

77. Rita Shloush and Harry Kozlovsky to Yeshivat Rambam Parents, December 11, 1998. A copy of this letter is in possession of the author.

78. See Phil Jacobs, "Winning Big," *Baltimore Jewish Times* (October 7, 2005): 28.

79. On this, see Mosheh Lichtenstein, "Kol Isha: A Woman's Voice," *Tradition* 46 (Spring 2013): 9–24.

80. Lani Harac, "Sounds of Silence," *Baltimore Jewish Times* (December 14, 2001): 16.

81. Ibid.

82. See, for example, Rita Shloush, "Message from the Principal," *Yeshivat Rambam Banquet Journal* (1993): 14–15.

83. Jonathan Mark, "Yeshiva U's Lamm: A Rabbi Under Siege," *Jewish Week* (August 18, 1989): 2.

84. Rambam lay leaders began this line of communication. See Seth M. Rotenberg to Robert S. Hirt, November 24, 1993. A copy of this letter is in possession of the author.

85. Robert S. Hirt to Rita Shloush, December 13, 1993. A copy of this letter is in possession of the author.

86. See Dan Rodricks, "Striving for Modern Orthodox Middle," *Baltimore Sun* (May 19, 2011): 17.

87. See Lawrence Grossman, "Jewish Communal Affairs," *American Jewish Year Book* 98 (1998): 143.

88. See "Rambam High's Finale," *Baltimore Jewish Times* (January 21, 2011): 42; and Rodricks, "Striving for Modern Orthodox Middle."

89. Gabriella Burman, "Finding Their Way 'Home,'" *Baltimore Jewish Times* (May 5, 2000): 44.

90. See Jacob B. Ukeles, *What Does Your Future Hold? The 2010 Greater Baltimore Jewish Community Study* (Baltimore, MD: Associated, 2011), 44.

91. Rochelle Eisenberg, "Rambam Shifts Gears," *Baltimore Jewish Times* (March 28, 2008): 22–23.

92. Ibid.

93. Rita Shloush to Yeshivat Rambam Parents, November 20, 2008. A copy of this letter is in possession of the author.

94. Barry Nabozny and David Sidransky to Yeshivat Rambam Parents, November 20, 2008. A copy of this letter is in possession of the author.

95. Silber, the recently hired spiritual leader of a large Orthodox synagogue in the Park Heights area, found that his religious views did not line up with a sizable portion of his Suburban Orthodox Congregation. See "Then & Now," *Baltimore Jewish Times* (March 21, 2008): 41–45.
96. "Day School Futures," *Baltimore Jewish Times* (July 9, 2010): 40.
97. Phil Jacobs and Rochelle Eisenberg, "Restructuring to Survive," *Baltimore Jewish Times* (January 21, 2011): 32–33. In fact a number of day schools in Arizona, California, New Jersey, and Pennsylvania, exacerbated by the recent economic recession, were forced to close some sections of their academic program or shut down altogether. See E. B. Solomont, "Philadelphia's Day School Dilemma," *Forward* (August 26, 2011): 12.
98. Mollie R. Sharfman, "Rambam's Final Basket," *Baltimore Jewish Times* (April 8, 2011): 36.
99. "Rambam's Difficult Reality," *Baltimore Jewish Times* (May 13, 2011): 40.
100. Phil Jacobs and Simone Ellin, "Rabbi Landau to Retire," *Baltimore Jewish Times* (June 10, 2011): 19–20.
101. Gary Bauman, "Modern Orthodoxy's Demise," *Baltimore Jewish Times* (May 20, 2011): 17.
102. See Rochelle Eisenberg, "An Option Arises," *Baltimore Jewish Times* (May 20, 2011): 18; and Bernie Hodkin, "A New Light Arises," *Baltimore Jewish Times* (December 2, 2011): 18–19. Beth Tfiloh absorbed a number of the stranded Rambam students. See Rochelle Eisenberg and Phil Jacobs, "Rambam Unfurled," *Baltimore Jewish Times* (May 13, 2011): 30–33.
103. Phil Jacobs, "A Message from Above," *Baltimore Jewish Times* (May 20, 2011): 16.

## Chapter 7. Finding a *Frum* Form of Fraternizing and the Dynamics of Orthodox Masculinity

1. "Senior Class History," *Masmid* (1936): 32.
2. Sylvia Finkelstein, "Leaves from our Branches," *Young Israel Viewpoint* 33 (April 1942): 16.
3. Shmuel I. Feigen, "Beit Midrash Le-Torah bi-Chicago," in *Sefer Ha-Yovel shel Agudat Ha-Morim Ha-Ivrim*, ed. Tzvi Sharfstein (New York: Hebrew Teachers Union, 1944), 285.
4. For the prohibition, see Yosef Caro, *Shulhan Arukh, Even ha-Ezer*, 21:5.
5. David Stein, "Mr. Orthodoxy," *Jewish Forum* 45 (May–June 1962): 13.
6. To counter suggestions that its curriculum placed the school beyond the pale of acceptable forms of Jewish learning, Yeshiva staked its claim to authenticity based on earlier precedents of rabbinic scholars who studied non-Jewish wisdom. See Shnayer Z. Leiman, "Rabbinic Openness to General Culture in the Early Modern Period in Western and Central Europe," in *Judaism's*

*Encounter with Other Cultures: Rejection or Integration?* ed. Jacob J. Schacter (Northvale, NJ: Jason Aronson, 1997), 143–216.

7. See Shaul Stampfer, *Families, Rabbis and Education: Traditional Jewish Society in Nineteenth-Century Eastern Europe* (Oxford: Littman Library, 2010), 190–210.

8. See, for example, Mordecai Schiff, *Ateret Mordekhai* (St. Louis, MO: Moinester Printing Co., 1924), 5–6.

9. See Daniel Boyarin, *Unheroic Conduct: The Rise of Heterosexuality and the Invention of the Jewish Man* (Berkeley: University of California Press, 1997), 153–54.

10. Kimmel, *Manhood in America*, 4–5.

11. See Eric R. Crouse, "Popular Cold Warriors: Conservative Protestants, Communism and Culture in Early Cold War America," *Journal of Religion and Popular Culture* 2 (Fall 2002): 1–12.

12. Ibid., 5.

13. See James Gilbert, *Men in the Middle: Searching for Masculinity in the 1950s* (Chicago: University of Chicago Press, 2005), 130.

14. See also K. A. Cuordileone, *Manhood and American Political Culture in the Cold War* (New York: Routledge, 2005), 81–82.

15. See William Oddie, *What Will Happen to God? Feminism and the Reconstruction of Christian Belief* (San Francisco: Ignatius Press, 1988).

16. See Don Deardorff, "Sacred Male Space: The Promise Keepers as a Community of Resistance," in *The Promise Keepers: Essays on Masculinity and Christianity*, ed. Dane S. Claussen (Jefferson, NC: McFarland & Company, 2000), 76–90.

17. "Sexual Apartheid," *Commentator* (November 24, 1971): 2.

18. See Putney, *Muscular Christianity*, 205–6.

19. See Jacob J. Schacter, "Torah u-Madda Revisited: The Editor's Introduction," *Torah u-Madda Journal* 1 (1990): 1–22.

20. See, for example, Bernard Revel, "The Yeshivah College: A Statement of Aims," *Jewish Forum* 11 (May 1928): 253–55.

21. See Aaron Rakeffet-Rothkoff, "The Semi-Centennial Celebrations of Yeshiva and Yeshiva College," in *Ramaz: School, Community, Scholarship, and Orthodoxy*, ed. Jeffrey S. Gurock (Hoboken: Ktav, 1989), 1–19.

22. Zev Eleff, "Freedom and Responsibility: The First Orthodox College Journalists and Early Yeshiva College Politics, 1935–1941," *American Jewish Archives Journal* 62 (December 2010): 55–88.

23. See Gurock, *Judaism's Encounter with American Sports*, 130–53. Some schools and rabbis even encouraged sports. See Jeffrey S. Gurock, "The Beginnings of Team Torah u-Madda: Sports and the Mission of an Americanized Yeshivah, 1916–1940," *Torah u-Madda Journal* 14 (2006–7): 157–72.

24. See Imhoff, *Masculinity and the Making of American Judaism*, 17; and Kimmel, *Manhood in America*, 127–46.

25. See Alar Lipping, "Charles W. Eliot's Views on Education, Physical Education and Intercollegiate Athletics" (PhD diss., Ohio State University, 1980), 176.

26. See Helen Lefkowitz Horowitz, "The 1960s and the Transformation of Campus Culture," *History of Education Quarterly* 26 (Spring 1986): 16; and Carpenter, *Revive Us Again*, 67–69.

27. See Barbara Miller Solomon, *In the Company of Educated Women: A History of Women and Higher Education in America* (New Haven, CT: Yale University Press, 1985), 101–2, 160.

28. See Kimmel, *Manhood in America*, 127–34; and Paul S. Fass, *The Damned and the Beautiful: American Youth in the 1920s* (New York: Oxford University Press, 1977), 300–306.

29. See Virginia Lieson Brereton, "The Bible Schools and Conservative Evangelical Higher Education, 1880–1940," in *Making Higher Education Christian: The History and Mission of Evangelical Colleges in America*, ed. Joel A. Carpenter and Kenneth W. Shipps (Grand Rapids, MI: Eerdmans, 1987), 110–36.

30. "Rab's Blonde Breaks College Girls' Hearts," *Spizzerinktor* (March 17, 1934): 1. See also Rick Ostrander, *Head, Heart, and Hand: John Brown University and Modern Evangelical Higher Education* (Fayetteville: University of Arkansas Press, 2003), 75–91.

31. John R. Rice, "Editor Visits Bob Jones College," *Sword of the Lord* (June 8, 1945): 5.

32. See Mark Taylor Dalhouse, *An Island in the Lake of Fire: Bob Jones University, Fundamentalism and the Separatist Movement* (Athens: University of Georgia Press, 1996), 143–44.

33. See *Student Handbook* (Boston: Gordon College of Theology and Missions, 1945), 28.

34. See *Gordon College Catalog: 1950–1951* (Boston: Gordon College of Theology and Missions, 1950), 18.

35. "Class Affair Set for Next Tuesday," *Commentator* (March 2, 1938):1. The event was originally scheduled for January 8. See "Classes Present Own Floor Show," *Commentator* (December 15, 1937): 1.

36. James Oddo, "Talent Displayed at Social Affair," *Commentator* (March 23, 1938): 1; and "A Mixer and a Class Nite," *Commentator* (March 1, 1939): 2.

37. "Class Nite All Set for Next Sunday," *Commentator* (February 28, 1940): 1.

38. For a similar phenomenon in American Orthodox life, see Zev Eleff, "Behind the Laughter: The Purim Shpiel Comes to America (and Chicago)," *Chicago Jewish History* 40 (Winter 2016): 4–7.

39. "Class Nite—An Aftermath," *Commentator* (March 15, 1939): 2.

40. "An Open Letter from Y. C. Council to Dr. Belkin," *Commentator* (December 14, 1944): 1.
41. Samuel Belkin, "President Belkin's Prospectus," *Commentator* (January 4, 1945): 1.
42. "Juniors, Sophs Win Class Nite Awards," *Commentator* (May 22, 1947): 1. See also "Class Nite," *Commentator* (May 22, 1947): 2.
43. "An Editorial," *Commentator* (November 6, 1947): 1–2.
44. See "Council to Present Annual Class Nite; Masmid Gets Funds," *Commentator* (March 11, 1948): 1; "Class Nite Plays to Be Performed on Lamport Stage," *Commentator* (March 25, 1948): 1; and "Class Night [*sic*] Set for May 16; Dramatic Society Plans Plays," *Commentator* (May 12, 1949): 1.
45. Keller is known now in more fundamentalist Orthodox circles as Rabbi Chaim Dov Keller, *rosh yeshiva* of Telshe Yeshiva in Chicago. Few are aware of his role, brief as it was, in the history of Yeshiva College. Decades later Rabbi Keller revealed some of his critiques about the outlook and limitations of Yeshiva University and its constituent community. See Chaim Dov Keller, "Where Do You Draw the Line? An Open Letter to Rabbi Norman Lamm," *Yated Ne'eman* (February 20, 2004): 4; Chaim Keller, "A Letter That Should NOT Have Had to Have Been Published," *Jewish Observer* 28 (June 1995): 30–32; and Chaim Dov Keller, "Love of Chiddush for Better and for Worse: What's Wrong with Being Modern?" *Jewish Observer* 27 (May 1994): 6–14.
46. "Seniors," *Masmid* (1950): 32
47. See Menachem Bloch, "Fantasia," *Masmid* (1947): 90.
48. "Keller Tenders Resignation as Open Class Nite Passes," *Commentator* (February 27, 1950): 1.
49. "Students Vote Class Nite, 156–43," *Commentator* (March 12, 1950): 1.
50. On Soloveitchik's views on coeducation, see Farber, *An American Orthodox Dreamer*, 68–87.
51. Interview with Rabbi Zevulun Charlop, November 6, 2010. Rabbi Gorelick's involvement in the opposition is confirmed in a subsequent volume of the yearbook. See "A Drama in Four Acts," *Masmid* (1953): 43.
52. The vote would have been far more competitive, but at the behest of Rabbi Gorelick, dozens of anti–Class Nite students boycotted the polls. See "A Time to Cool Off," *Commentator* (March 12, 1950): 2.
53. "With Malice Toward None: An Editorial," *Commentator* (December 15, 1960): 1–3.
54. The immense growth was due in large part to the motivation of students to enroll in the faith-based school and avoid conscription and the Vietnam War. See Jeffrey S. Gurock, *The Men and Women of Yeshiva: Higher Education, Orthodoxy, and American Judaism* (New York: Columbia University Press, 1988) 185.

55. See "Dr. Belkin Discloses New Admissions Plan," *Commentator* (February 8, 1956): 1.
56. See Bernhard H. Rosenberg, "A Study of the Alumni of the James Striar School (JSS) at Yeshiva University," *Journal of Jewish Education* 61 (Spring 1994): 6–11. JSP was renamed the James Striar School of General Jewish Studies in 1965.
57. "Our Religious Responsibility," *Commentator* (November 5, 1959): 2.
58. See John C. Spurlock, *Youth and Sexuality in the Twentieth-Century United States* (New York: Routledge, 2016), 101–29.
59. See Rachel Gordan, "Alfred Kinsey and the Remaking of Jewish Sexuality in the Wake of the Holocaust," *Jewish Social Studies* 20 (Spring/Summer 2014): 72–99.
60. See Liebman, "Orthodoxy in American Jewish Life," 60–61. For an example of a congregation that maintained social dancing until the 1980s, see *Young Israel of New Rochelle Commemorative Journal* (New Rochelle, NY: Young Israel of New Rochelle, 2008), 31.
61. Gershon Taschman, "A Psychological Appraisal of Traditional and Conventional Courtship," *Young Israel Viewpoint* 51 (November 1960): 20.
62. On this, see Kevin M. Schultz, *Tri-Faith America: How Catholics and Jews Held Postwar America to Its Protestant Promise* (Oxford: Oxford University Press, 2011), 15–67.
63. See Oscar Z. Fasman, "Trends in the American Yeshiva Today," *Tradition* 9 (Fall 1967): 58.
64. See *Student Handbook, 1968–1969* (Boston: Gordon College, 1968), 10–11.
65. Clarence Mast to Judith Moffett, September 15, 1960, MSS-25, Box 6, Folder 3, Duggan Library Archives, Hanover College, Hanover, IN.
66. "Battle of the Sexes Rampages Between Strong and MacLean," *Mountain Eagle* (February 18, 1959): 2.
67. See, for example, Brian Clark and Allison Shelley, "Going Up the Tower," in Vertical File Records (RG 9.4), Special Collections, Buswell Library, Wheaton College, Wheaton, IL.
68. "Dating Practices of the BUY Coed," Item #6, March 1977, FA 1, Box 14, No. 139. L. Tom Perry Special Collections, Brigham Young University, Provo, UT.
69. "Behind the Eight-Ball," *Threefold Advocate* (March 13, 1959): 3.
70. "Asking Imogene," *Threefold Advocate* (November 6, 1963): 4.
71. "Love and Marriage," *Gordon Herald* (November 29, 1955): 2.
72. "A Touchy Problem," *Commentator* (December 2, 1965): 2.
73. See Gurock, *The Men and Women of Yeshiva*, 186–212.
74. "28 Seniors Plan to Teach, Study and Marry," *Observer* (May 29, 1959): 3.
75. "Poll Reveals Stern College Information," *Observer* (November 23, 1960): 1.
76. Arlene Becker, "Miss Arlene's Recipe Column," *In Retrospect* (1957): 18. See also "The Sing Songs," *Observer* (March 1965): 1.

77. "A Male's Critique," *Observer* (January 7, 1965): 2.
78. Neil Koslowe, "The Homecoming Weekend Affair—Whither a Yeshiva Generation," *Commentator* (December 10, 1964): 11.
79. David Ebner, Letter to the Editor, *Commentator* (November 19, 1964): 2.
80. Letter to the Editor, *Commentator* (December 31, 1964): 2.
81. "Diary of a Thespienette," *In Retrospect* (1955–1956): 10. See also Josef E. Fischer, "Stern Women Have Big Shindig; Yeshiva Men Receive Invitations," *Commentator* (December 21, 1955): 3. In 1963 Belkin considered merging Yeshiva College and Stern College. See "For Continued Vitality," *Commentator* (April 4, 1963): 2.
82. "Scrapbook of News Events," *In Retrospect* (1957): 8.
83. "Senior Class History," *Kochaviah* (1961): 56–57.
84. "Dean's Mixer Set May 30," *Commentator* (May 29, 1950): 1.
85. See Donald S. Davis, "Inside and Outside the Classroom," in *My Yeshiva College: 75 Years of Memories*, ed. Menachem Butler and Zev Nagel (New York: Yashar, 2006), 164.
86. "Student Council Cancels Planned Dean's Reception," *Commentator* (February 18, 1966): 1.
87. Joseph I. Berlin, "The Myth," *Commentator* (February 18, 1966): 8.
88. James Yaffe, *The American Jews: Portrait of a Split Personality* (New York: Random House, 1968), 132.
89. "Decision on the Dean's Reception," *Commentator* (February 18, 1966): 2.
90. Mark Steiner, "Thanks," *Commentator* (April 28, 1966): 6.
91. Harold Goldberg, "Dr. Greenberg Discusses Orthodoxy, YU, Viet Nam, & Sex," *Commentator* (April 28, 1966): 10.
92. See David Singer, "Debating Modern Orthodoxy at Yeshiva College: The Greenberg-Lichtenstein Exchange of 1966," *Modern Judaism* 26 (May 2006): 113–26.
93. "Rav Lichtenstein Writes Letter to Dr. Greenberg," *Commentator* (June 2, 1966): 7.
94. The following comments and quotations are all derived from an audio recording of Lichtenstein's lecture, in the possession of the author. See also "YC Holds Dialogue; Problems Explored," *Commentator* (May 12, 1966): 10.
95. Later, Lichtenstein offered a fuller treatment of this view. See Aharon Lichtenstein, "Does Jewish Tradition Recognize an Ethic Independent of Halakha?" in *Modern Jewish Ethics: Theory and Practice*, ed. Marvin Fox (Columbus: Ohio State University Press, 1975), 62–88.
96. See "Dean's Reception—Editorial Opinion," *Commentator* (November 3, 1966): 1–2; and "Deans [sic] Reception—A Response," *Hamevaser* (November 10, 1966): 2.
97. "Restrictions," *Commentator* (April 20, 1967): 2.
98. David Mark, Letter to the Editor, *Commentator* (December 3, 1970): 5.

99. "Sexual Apartheid," *Commentator* (November 24, 1971): 2.

100. "Still Minus a Minyan," *Observer* (March 1, 1966): 2.

101. See Norman Linzer, "Understanding Teenage Behavior," in *Torah Leadership Seminar Bar Mitzvah Yearbook, 1955–'67*, ed. Susan Schaalman (New York: Youth Bureau Community Service Division Yeshiva University, 1967), 51–53; and Eleff, *Living from Convention to Convention*, 41–42.

102. See Kraut, *The Greening of American Orthodox Judaism*, 28–30.

## Chapter 8. Rabbi Joseph B. Soloveitchik and the Unorthodox Optics of Women's Talmud Study

1. Michael S. Kimmel, *The History of Men: Essays in the History of American and British Masculinity* (Albany: State University of New York Press, 2005), 61–72.

2. See Gershon C. Bacon, *The Politics of Tradition: Agudat Yisrael in Poland, 1926–1939* (Jerusalem: Magnus Press, 1996), 166–76.

3. See Farber, *An American Orthodox Dreamer*, 68–87.

4. Ibid., 74–84. On Soloveitchik and separating women and men at Yeshiva College, see chapter 7.

5. Joseph B. Soloveitchik, *Community, Covenant and Commitment: Selected Letters and Communications*, ed. Nathaniel Helfgot (Jersey City, NJ: Ktav, 2005), 82.

6. Ibid., 83. The Chabad movement offers an interesting parallel. On this, see Elite Ben-Yosef, "Literacy and Power: The *Shiyour* as a Site of Subordination and Empowerment for Chabad Women," *Journal of Feminist Studies in Religion* 27 (Spring 2011): 53–74.

7. Isaac Hutner, "What Is Jewish Education?" *Jewish Parent* 8 (December 1956): 20.

8. For a most liberal articulation and push for women in the Catholic ministry, see Father John Pawlikowski, "Let's Ordain Women," *U.S. Catholic* 40 (May 1975): 12–13.

9. See Jay P. Dolan, *The American Catholic Experience: A History from Colonial Times to the Present* (Notre Dame, IN: University of Notre Dame Press, 1992), 439; and Ann Braude, "Women, Christianity, and the Constitution," in *American Christianities: A History of Dominance and Diversity*, ed. Catherine A. Brekus and W. Clark Gilpin (Chapel Hill: University of North Carolina Press, 2011), 473–79.

10. See Donald G. Mathews, "'Spiritual Warfare': Cultural Fundamentalism and the Equal Rights Amendment," *Religion and American Culture* 3 (Summer 1993): 129–54.

11. See Paula Hyman, "Jewish Theology: What's in It for—and Against—Us," *Ms.* 3 (July 1974): 76–79.

12. See "Feminists Debate Views at Orthodox Convention," *Jewish Standard* (December 6, 1974): 6.
13. "Rabbi Is Detained," *Brooklyn Daily Eagle* (August 29, 1932): 11.
14. "Science and Religion Do Not Conflict, Says Dr. Soloveitchik, Head of Boston Orthodox Jews," *Boston Herald* (December 18, 1932): B7.
15. See Oscar Z. Fasman, "After Fifty Years, an Optimist," *American Jewish History* 69 (December 1979): 160.
16. See "Ability of Rabbi Soloveitchik Merits Recognition," *Jewish Advocate* (December 1, 1933): A8. See also Aaron Rakeffet-Rothkoff, "Rabbi Joseph Soloveitchik: The Early Years," *Tradition* 30 (Summer 1996): 193–209.
17. Joseph B. Soloveitchik and Sibyl Soroker, "Rabbi Warns Jews on Education, Advises Blend of Secular Study," *Boston Sunday Advertiser* (December 25, 1932): D5.
18. See Shlomo Yosef Zevin, "Problimah Nishkhaha," *Ha-Modia* (September 9, 1910): 332–33. On Kagan and the 1911 publication on this position, see Binyamin Brown, "Erekh Talmud Torah bi-Mishnat Ha-Hafetz Hayyim u-Piskato bi-Inyan Talmud Torah le-Nashim," *Dinei Yisrael* 24 (2007): 110–12. My appreciation to Rabbi Moshe Kolodny for sharing this valuable essay with me.
19. Nissan J. Mindel, "Merkos L'Inyonei Chinuch and Unity in Jewish Education," *Jewish Spectator* 12 (January 1947): 27.
20. See Klara Shermanberg, "Na'arah Misayemet Mesekhet Shelemah," *Talmid* (1956): 2.
21. Jeffrey S. Gurock, "The Ramaz Version of American Orthodoxy," in *Ramaz: School, Community, Scholarship, and Orthodoxy*, 59. On Ramaz and Soloveitchik, see Aaron Rakeffet-Rothkoff, *The Rav: The World of Rabbi Joseph B. Soloveitchik*, vol. 2 (Hoboken: Ktav, 1999), 67.
22. See Benjamin Brickman to Joseph H. Lookstein, April 17, 1964, Box V, Brickman Folder, Joseph H. Lookstein Papers, YU Archives.
23. Haskel Lookstein to Ramaz Parents, October 17, 1968, Box V, School Correspondence Folder, Joseph H. Lookstein Papers. Interestingly, three decades later Rabbi Parnes left YU to join Touro's Lander College, in part over YU's decision to enhance its women's Talmud program. See Shmuli Singer, "Rabbi Yehuda Parnes to Join Rav Bronspigel at Lander College," *Commentator* (May 22, 2000): 1.
24. See Arthur M. Silver, "May Women Be Taught Bible, Mishnah and Talmud?" *Tradition* 17 (Summer 1978): 80–81.
25. See, for example, "Hebrew Faculty," *Elchanette* (1958): 5.
26. "Seniors," *Elchanette* (1954): 33. See also "Graduates," *Elchanette* (1959): 14.
27. See Crouse, "Popular Cold Warriors," 1–12.
28. Sarna, "The Debate over Mixed Seating in the American Synagogue," 379–86.

29. See Yosef Dov Soloveitchik, "Megen Mener un Froyin Zitzen Tzuzamen in Shul?" *Der Tog* (November 22, 1954): 5.

30. See Joseph Elias, "Boys and Girls Together?" *Jewish Parent* 6 (December 1954): 4. See also Yoju Dovika, "Campus and Jewish Education," *Jewish Life* 35 (May-June 1968): 64.

31. Emanuel Rackman, "Why Not Give New Ideas a Fair Chance?" *Jewish Week* (November 9, 1984): 30. For a broad survey of rabbinical positions on women's Talmud study, see Ilan Fuchs, *Jewish Women's Torah Study: Orthodox Religious Education and Modernity* (New York: Routledge, 2015). On Feinstein's position, see Feinstein, *Iggerot Moshe*, vol. 4, 329.

32. See Elaine Pohl Moore, "An Answer to Jewish Apathy: Thirty Years of Yeshivah of Flatbush," *Jewish Forum* 40 (February 1957): 18–24.

33. Joseph Heimovitz, "A Study of Graduates of the Yeshivah of Flatbush High School" (PhD diss., Yeshiva University, 1979), 26.

34. Schiff, *The Jewish Day School in America*, 198.

35. S. Joseph, "A Check List: How Good Is Your School?" *Jewish Observer* 2 (January 1965): 12.

36. See Leslie Ginsparg, "Defining Bais Yaakov: A Historical Study of Yeshivish Orthodox Girls High School Education in America, 1963–1984" (PhD diss., New York University, 2009), 5.

37. For an exceptional case, see Gershon Taschman, "Yeshiva High School for Girls?" *Jewish Parent* 20 (March 1969): 16–17.

38. See Gurock, *The Men and Women of Yeshiva*, 186–212.

39. See, for example, *Stern College for Women Academic Catalog*, vol. 2 (1955–57) (New York: Yeshiva University, 1955), 38.

40. Meeting Notes, May 18, 1966, Rabbi Gersion Appel Papers, held in the family's private collection. A copy of these meeting notes is in the possession of the author.

41. See, for example, Tamar Feldman, "Rabbi Schachter Stresses Pidyon Shevuyim in Realm of Tzedakah," *Observer* (November 26, 1975): 1.

42. See Ivy Kaufman, "Rav Soloveitchik Explores Human Duality: Logos vs. Inner Divine Force," *Observer* (March 20, 1975): 1.

43. See "Dr. Karen Bacon, SCW Alumna, Appointed Dean," *Observer* (October 27, 1977): 1.

44. See Chaya Kleinerman, "SCW Appointments Announced by Dr. Lamm," *Observer* (November 1, 1976): 1; "Tribute to Professors," *Observer* (May 23, 1984): 4; and "New Dimensions for Jewish Studies," *Inside Yeshiva University* 23 (October 1977): 4.

45. Jacob Rabinowitz and Saul Berman to Stern College for Women Students, January 23, 1978, Box 220, SCW Folder, Public Relations Events Collection, YU Archives. On his earliest efforts to expand women's Torah study, see Saul J.

Berman, "The Status of Women in Halakhic Judaism," *Tradition* 14 (Fall 1973): 5–28.

46. See Solomon, *In the Company of Educated Women*, 203. See also Carol P. Christ, "Toward a Paradigm Shift in the Academy and in Religious Studies," in *The Impact of Feminist Research in the Academy*, ed. Christie Farnham (Bloomington: Indiana University Press, 1991), 62.

47. "Look into Learning: Stern College Beit Midrash Program," Box 1, Folder 6, Stern College for Women Records, YU Archives.

48. See Joyce Antler, "Women's Liberation and Jewish Feminism after 1968: Multiple Pathways to Gender Equality," *American Jewish History* 102 (January 2018): 43–48.

49. See Nadell, *Women Who Would Be Rabbis*, 118–214.

50. See Amy Herskowitz, "Dr. Ross Explores Woman's Role," *Observer* (January 8, 1975): 3; and "SCW—Second Class Women," *Observer* (May 16, 1977): 3. For President Norman Lamm's response to undergraduate feminists at Stern College, see Ellen Cherrick and Sharon Yellin, "Tête-à-Tête with the Head of YU," *Observer* (May 16, 1977): 4.

51. Nisson Wolpin, "Jewish Women in a Torah Society," *Jewish Observer* 10 (November–December 1974): 14.

52. Shlomo Wolbe, *Kuntres Hadrakhah le-Kalot* (Bnei Brak: Or Ha-Hayyim Seminary, 1976), 35.

53. See George Cornell, "Orthodox Rabbi Considered Among World's Greatest Philosophers," *New London Day* (June 24, 1972): 11.

54. See Gurock, *The Men and Women of Yeshiva*, 201–10.

55. See "Stern Pays Tribute to Dr. Belkin Z"l," *Observer* (March 30, 1977): 1.

56. Saul J. Berman to Entering SCW Students, n.d., Box 220, SCW Folder, Public Relations Events Collection, YU Archives.

57. See Rachel Katsman, "Dean Rabinowitz Speaks on the J.S. Dept.," *Observer* (May 16, 1979): 4.

58. Saul J. Berman, "Pro," *Observer* (October 27, 1977): 5.

59. "SCW—Second Class Women," 3.

60. Debbie Silver, "When Opportunity Knocks," *Observer* (May 30, 1977): 2.

61. Saul J. Berman, "Forty Years Later: The Rav's Opening Shiur at the Stern College for Women Beit Midrash," *Lehrhaus* (October 9, 2017). Available at https://www.thelehrhaus.com/commentary/forty-years-later-the-rav%E2%80%99s-opening-shiur-at-the-stern-college-for-women-beit-midrash/ (accessed January 8, 2019). See also "Stern College for Women Introduces Pioneering Bet Midrash Program," Yeshiva University Press Release, n.d., Box 220, SCW Folder, Public Relations Events Collection, YU Archives.

62. "Ha-Rav Soloveitchik Zogt Ershten Gamara Shiur for Meidlakh in Stern College," *Algemeiner Journal* (December 30, 1977): 1.

63. See William B. Helmreich and Aharon Schechter Interview Transcript, April 13, 1978, Mendel Gottesman Library, Yeshiva University, MS-1230.

64. Berman, "Forty Years Later."

65. See, for example, "Talmud Study for Women," *Southern Israelite* (December 30, 1977): 5; "New Strides for Orthodox Women," *Jewish Advocate* (December 29, 1977): 1; and "Half of Entering Class at YU Law School Are Women," *Jewish Post and Opinion* (January 27, 1978): 5.

66. See Shlomo Wahrman, "Mitzvat Talmud Torah bi-Nashim," *Ha-Darom* 46 (Nissan 1978): 58.

67. Soshea Leibler, "Teaching Talmud to Women," *Baltimore Jewish Times* (May 30, 1980): 11.

68. Chani Parness to Blu Greenberg, June 3, 1983, Box 15, Folder 13, Blu Greenberg Papers, Arthur and Elizabeth Schlesinger Library on the History of Women in America, Harvard University, Cambridge, MA.

69. "The Rav Visits Frisch School," *The Frisch School Yearbook* (1977): 41.

70. Margaret Charytan, "The Impact of Religious Day School Education on Modern Orthodox Judaism: A Study of Changes in Seven Modern Orthodox Day Schools and the Impact on Religious Transmission to Students and Their Families" (PhD diss., City University of New York, 1996), 163.

71. *Rav Yaakov Weinberg Talks about Chinuch* (Southfield, MI: Targum Press, 2006), 126.

72. Charytan, "The Impact of Religious Day School Education on Modern Orthodox Judaism," 163.

73. See Farber, *An American Orthodox Dreamer*, 68–87; and Gurock, "The Ramaz Version of American Orthodoxy," 59.

74. See Eleanor Finkelstein, "A Study of Female Role Definitions in a Yeshivah High School (A Jewish Day School)" (PhD diss., New York University, 1980), 78–79.

75. See *Mitzvot Talmud Torah (She'Ba'al Peh) Li-Nashim* (Brooklyn, NY: Shulamith School for Girls, n.d.).

76. In fact, the augmented curriculum was not even mentioned in the yearbook, among other recent innovations. See "Memories," *Ida Crown Jewish Academy Keter* (1981): 58.

77. See Alvin I. Schiff, "The Centrist Torah Educator Faces Critical Ideological and Communal Challenges," *Tradition* 19 (Winter 1981): 282–83.

78. Shoshana Jedwab, "Talmud Torah at Stern College," *Hamevaser* (September 1985): 5.

79. Aviva Ganchrow, "On the Other Side of the Mechitza," *Hamevaser* (November 1984): 6.

80. Ibid.

81. Nadell, *Women Who Would Be Rabbis*, 212.
82. Harold M. Schulweis, "Rabbi Wanted: No Women Need Apply," *Reform Judaism* 12 (Fall 1983): 10.
83. Fran Lunzer, "Two Views on 'Feminism: Is It Good for Jews?'" *Jewish World* (April 20, 1984): 12.
84. Fraida Blau, "Women's Place in Torah Study," *Jewish Observer* 17 (Summer 1984): 19.
85. George Gilder, "An Open Letter to Orrin Hatch," *National Review* 40 (May 13, 1988): 34.
86. See Sara M. Evans, "Feminism in the 1980s: Surviving the Backlash," in *Living in the Eighties*, ed. Gil Troy and Vincent J. Cannato (Oxford: Oxford University Press, 2009), 85–97.
87. See Howard Jachter, "The Rav as an Aging Giant (1983–1985)," in *Mentor of Generations: Reflections on Rabbi Joseph B. Soloveitchik*, ed. Zev Eleff (Jersey City, NJ: Ktav, 2008), 330.
88. See Larry Cohler, "RCA Suspends Orthodox Pre-Nuptial Agreement," *Jewish World* (November 23, 1984): 12–14.
89. Larry Yudelson, "After the Rav: RCA Rabbis Listening for Master's Voice," *Jewish World* (May 29, 1987): 20.
90. See Stewart Ain, "Rabbinical Council President Decries Holier-Than-Thou Attitude of Right Wing," *Jewish World* (March 1, 1984): 14.
91. See Rakeffet-Rothkoff, *The Rav*, 240. See also Levi Yitzhak Ha-Yerushalmi, "Sihah me-Yuhedet im ha-Rav Yosef Dov Soloveitchik," *Ma'ariv* (October 28, 1977): 25.
92. See "ECA Convention III," *Educators Council of America Newsletter* 10 (Winter 1980–1981): 3; Saul Berman, "Our Integral Role in Orthodox World," *Observer* (November 11, 1982): 4; and Diane Feldman, "Berman Replaces Riskin at Lincoln Square," *Observer* (April 11, 1984): 1.
93. Bieler, "A Convention Colloquium on Teaching Talmud to Women," 19.
94. See Aharon Lichtenstein, "Torah Study for Women," *Ten Da'at* 3 (Spring 1989): 7–8.
95. See Melanie B. Shimoff, "Speakers Debate Orthodox Women's Role," *Jewish World* (March 18, 1983): 13.
96. See Jack Bieler, "A Convention Colloquium on Teaching Talmud to Women," *Ten Da'at* 2 (Winter 1988): 20.
97. See Lawrence Kaplan, "Revisionism and the Rav: The Struggle for the Soul of Modern Orthodoxy," *Judaism* 48 (Summer 1999): 290–311.
98. See Tamar El-Or, *Next Year I Will Know More: Literacy and Identity among Young Orthodox Women in Israel*, trans. Haim Watzman (Detroit, MI: Wayne State University Press, 2002), 25–51.

99. See Esti Rosenberg, "The World of Women's Torah Learning—Developments, Directions and Objectives: A Report from the Field," *Tradition* 45 (Spring 2012): 13–36.

100. See Yael Unterman, *Nehama Leibowitz: Teacher and Bible Scholar* (Jerusalem: Urim, 2009), 292.

101. Netty C. Gross, "Studying for Their Own Sake," *Jerusalem Post* (February 5, 1993): A8.

102. Ibid.

103. See Larry Yudelson, "Teaching Talmud—and How to Lead a Jewish Life," *Jewish World* (January 13, 1989): 18–20.

104. See Barbara E. Mann, *Space and Place in Jewish Studies* (New Brunswick, NJ: Rutgers University Press, 2012), 20–21.

105. See Lauren B. Granite, "Tradition as a Modality of Religious Change: Talmud Study in the Lives of Orthodox Jewish Women" (PhD diss., Drew University, 1995), 104

106. See Ari L. Goldman, "Jewish Women's Scholarly Gain," *New York Times* (August 2, 1992): 24 EDUC.

107. See Michelle Boorstein, "Boston's Torah Institute for Women Has Debut," *Jewish Advocate* (October 15, 1992): 1.

108. See Jane Linker, "Learning Experience of a Lifetime," *Jewish Week* (January 7, 2000): 38.

109. See Pinchas Shapiro, "Yeshiva Announces Graduate Program in Jewish Studies for Women," *Commentator* (February 21, 2000): 1.

## Chapter 9. Women's Prayer Groups versus Synagogue Judaism

1. Blu Greenberg, "Feminism: Is It Good for the Jews?" *Hadassah Magazine* 57 (April 1976): 11. See also her coauthored article in that same publication, Blu and Irving Greenberg, "Equality in Judaism," *Hadassah Magazine* 56 (December 1973): 14–15, 36–38.

2. Adinah Lindner, Rae Drazin, and Saureet Hayil to Blu Greenberg, December 31, 1977, Box 15, Folder 2, MC-599, Arthur and Elizabeth Schlesinger Library.

3. Ibid.

4. See, for example, Adam S. Ferziger, "Feminism and Heresy: The Construction of a Jewish Metanarrative," *Journal of the American Academy of Religion* 77 (September 2009): 494–546; and Jeffrey S. Gurock, *Orthodox Jews in America* (Bloomington: Indiana University Press, 2009), 279.

5. See Irwin H. Haut, "The Halacha on Women Minyon," *Jewish Press* (September 21, 1984): 42.

6. Shlomo Riskin, *Listening to God: Inspirational Stories for My Grandchildren* (New Milford, CT: Maggid, 2010), 193–96.

7. See Naomi Doron and Aliza Berger, "Brief Guide to Procedures at a Women's Prayer Service," n.d. A copy of this text is in the possession of the author.

8. See Joseph C. Kaplan, "A Women's Sefer Torah," *Sh'ma* 14 (May 11, 1984): 111–12.

9. See "Prayer," *Lilith* 6 (1979): 46–47.

10. Ibid.

11. Mordecai Tendler to Meir Fund, May 26, 1983. A copy of this document is in the possession of the author. See also Norma Baumel Joseph, " 'Those Self-Assured Women': A Close Reading of Rabbi Moses Feinstein's Responsum," *Nashim* 21 (Spring 2011): 67–87.

12. Shlomo Goren to Aaron Siegman, November 25, 1974. A copy of this document is in the possession of the author.

13. Tovah Jane Eisen, "Baltimore Women's Minyan," *Women's Tefillah Network Newsletter* 1 (June 1984): 5.

14. See James E. Adams, "Orthodox Jewish Women Form Their Own 'Minyan,'" *St. Louis Post-Dispatch* (September 10, 1976): 39. See also "Women's Minyan Formed; Invites New Members," *St. Louis Jewish Light* (May 26, 1976): 9.

15. "Young Israel Slates Thanksgiving Event," *St. Louis Jewish Light* (November 9, 1977): 17.

16. Beverly Worthman to Irving Rosenbaum, November 14, 1977, Beverly Worthman File, HTC Archives.

17. Irving J. Rosenbaum to Beverly Worthman, November 29, 1977; and Beverly Worthman to Irving Rosenbaum, December 5, 1977, Beverly Worthman File, HTC Archives.

18. Isserow, "Some Thoughts on Women and the Orthodox," 4.

19. Moshe Meiselman, *Jewish Women in Jewish Law* (New York: Ktav, 1978), 145. Meiselman explained that his view, more than just his own opinion, accorded with that of his uncle, "my revered teacher, Rabbi Joseph B. Soloveitchik." The nephew reported that Soloveitchik had "told me that he is opposed to such aliyot and has never told any rabbi that they are permitted." See ibid., 197 n.64.

20. "Blu Greenberg: Distinct and Equal," *Jewish World* (November 9, 1979): 7.

21. Trude Weiss-Rosmarin "For Integration, Not Female Segregation," *Jewish Week* (June 28, 1985): 22.

22. See Daniel T. Rodgers, *Age of Fracture* (Cambridge, MA: Harvard University Press, 2011), 144–79.

23. Blu Greenberg, *On Women and Judaism: A View from Tradition* (Philadelphia: Jewish Publication Society of America, 1981), 95–96.

24. See Adina Sullman, "Women's Service Makes a Unique Simchat Torah Experience," *Observer* (November 20, 1978): 5.

25. Saul Berman and Shulamith Magnes, "Orthodoxy Responds to Feminist Ferment," *Response* 12 (Spring 1981): 6.

26. See "Councilwoman Alter Announces First Woman's Minyan in Brooklyn," *Jewish Press* (December 10, 1982): 11.

27. "Divergence of Opinion on Changing Roles of Women," *Cleveland Jewish News* (December 30, 1983): 8.

28. Aryeh Kaplan, "The Editor's View," *Jewish Life* 41 (Spring 1974): 4–5.

29. See Zev Brenner, "The Roving Jewish Eye," *Jewish Press* (November 26, 1982): 4.

30. See Roberta Fields, "Lecture Explores Role of Jewish Women," *Jewish World* (July 25, 1980): 7.

31. See Stewart Ain, "Religious Role of Orthodox Women Is Changing," *Jewish World* (February 11, 1983): 17.

32. See Marta Beri Shapiro, "Women in Synagogues on Long Island," *Jewish World* (April 4, 1980): 17.

33. See Irving Spiegel, "Judaism Is Called Cool to Feminism," *New York Times* (March 6, 1977): 54.

34. Esther Jungreis, "Rebbetzin's Viewpoint," *Jewish Press* (January 18, 1980): 44.

35. See Rebecca Paley, "'Torah Feminists' Pray for Religious Freedoms," *Brooklyn Heights Courier* (March 2, 1996): 4.

36. See Sylvia Barack Fishman, *A Breath of Life: Feminism in the American Jewish Community* (Hanover, NH: Brandeis University Press, 1993), 158–68. For two notable exceptions that link feminism and women's prayer, see Cheryl J. Goldberg, "Should Women's Prayer Groups Be RCA Concern?" *Jewish World* (December 7, 1984): 29; and "Davening with Women," *Jewish World* (November 9, 1979): 7.

37. See Michael Panitz, "Completing a Century: The Rabbinical Assembly Since 1970," in *A Century of Commitment: One Hundred Years of the Rabbinical Assembly*, ed. Robert E. Fierstein (New York: Rabbinical Assembly, 2000), 103–16.

38. See Larry Cohler, "Women's Davening Group Comes into Its Own, Despite Criticism," *Jewish World* (July 13, 1984): 18. For accusations to the contrary, see Dvorah Shurin, "On a Minyan for Women," *Jewish Press* (December 24, 1982): 5.

39. See Yaacov Amitai, "Sanctity and Self Expression," *Jewish Observer* 18 (February 1985): 24.

40. See, for example, "Newly Formed Women's Minyan of St. Louis Conducts Sabbath Services," *St. Louis Jewish Light* (September 15, 1976): 10.

41. See Cohler, "Women's Davening Group," 20.

42. In their public disagreements over women's prayer groups, each side claimed Rabbi Soloveitchik's support. That Modern Orthodox Judaism's leading authority did not make his view on the subject clear (as he had done in the case of women's Talmud study) is important, as made evident in this chapter.

43. Louis Bernstein, "Correction on Rabbi Bernstein's Remarks," *Jewish Press* (July 6, 1984): 40.

44. See "Councilwoman Alter Announces First Women's Minyan in Brooklyn," *Jewish Press* (December 10, 1982): 11. See also Howard N. Wallick, "The Dilemma of the Modern Orthodox Layperson," *Cornerstone* 2 (1997): 89.

45. "Union of Orthodox Rabbis Condemns 'Minyan' of Women," *Jewish Press* (December 24, ,1982): 3.

46. Schedule for "Conference on Women, Prayer and Tradition," June 5, 1983. A copy of this document is in the possession of the author. For an accounting of the existing prayer groups at that time, see "Women's Tefilah Groups," *Women's Tefillah Network Newsletter* 1 (June 1984): 15–17.

47. See Susan Rosenbluth, "Orthodox Women's Tefillah Thriving in Teaneck Area," *Jewish Standard* (January 27, 1984): 3.

48. Ibid., 24.

49. Anne Senter, "Oppose Women's Tefillah," *Jewish Standard* (February 10, 1984): 13.

50. Judith Rosenbaum, "Oppose Women's Tefillah," *Jewish Standard* (February 10, 1984): 3. Despite Riskin's and others' claim that women's prayer had Soloveitchik's endorsement, some charged that the case was otherwise. See Meiselman, *Jewish Women in Jewish Law*, 146, 197, n. 64.

51. Marion Krug, "Members Clarify Women's Tefillah," *Jewish Standard* (February 24, 1984): 11.

52. See "Polarization within Orthodoxy Must Be Solved by Dialogue Not Battle," *Jewish Press* (June 15, 1984): 24.

53. See Israel Miller to Rina Russell, March 19, 1985, in *Duties of the Heart Conference Program* (New York: Women's Tefillah Network, 1985).

54. See "Challenges to the Jewish Family," *Jewish Press* (May 4, 1984): 4.

55. See Judy Siegel Itzkovich, "Controversial Rabbi," *Jerusalem Post* (July 4, 1985): 9.

56. "On Cooperation with Reform, Conservative, Blacks and Women," *Jewish Press* (June 8, 1984): 10B.

57. "Rabbi Louis Bernstein, New President of the RCA," *Jewish Press* (June 8, 1984): 10A.

58. See Alice Shalvi, "The Justice of Orthodox Women's Demands," *Jerusalem Post* (August 7, 1985): 8.

59. Yaakov Jacobs, Letter to the Editor, *Jewish World* (March 1, 1985), 4.

60. Louis Bernstein, "Correction on Rabbi Bernstein's Remarks," *Jewish Press* (July 6, 1984): 40.

61. See, for example, Irwin H. Haut, "Women's Davening Group," *Jewish Press* (August 24, 1984): 18A.

62. See Cheryl J. Goldberg, "Should Women's Prayer Groups Be RCA's Concern?"

*Jewish World* (December 7, 1984): 29–30; and Avraham Weiss, *Women at Prayer: A Halakhic Analysis of Women's Prayer* (Hoboken, NJ: Ktav, 2001), xv, n.3

63. Chaim Casper, Letter to the Editor, *Jewish World* (March 8, 1984): 4.

64. See Larry Cohler, "Orthodox Rabbis' Responsa Condemns Women's Prayer Groups," *Jewish World* (February 15, 1985): 16.

65. "Teshuvah bi-Inyan Nashim bi- Hakefot," *Ha-Darom* 54 (Sivan 1985): 51–53. For a translation, see Eleff, *Modern Orthodox Judaism*, 379. The writer David Singer coined the "RIETS Five" term. See David Singer, "A Failure of Halachic 'Objectivity,'" *Sh'ma* 15 (May 17, 1985): 108.

66. See Michael Chernick, "In Support of Women's Prayer Groups," *Sh'ma* 15 (May 17, 1985): 105–8; and Rachel Adler, "Innovation and Authority: A Feminist Reading of the 'Women's Minyan' Responsum," in *Gender Issues in Jewish Law: Essays and Responsa*, ed. Walter Jacob and Moshe Zemer (New York: Berghahn, 2001), 3–32.

67. See Abba Bronspigel, "Minyanim Meyuhadim Le-Nashim," *Ha-Darom* 54 (Sivan 1985): 51–53.

68. Cohler, "Orthodox Rabbis' Responsa Condemns Women's Prayer Groups," 14.

69. Rivkeh [Rivka] Haut, "From Women: Piety Not Rebellion," *Sh'ma* 15 (May 17, 1985): 111.

70. See Patricia Golan, "Women's Prayer Group Prays for Change," *Jerusalem Post* (July 11, 1985): 5.

71. Louis Bernstein to RCA Members, December 23, 1985, Rabbi Irving Greenberg Papers, Harvard University Archives, Cambridge, MA.

72. Norma Baumel Joseph, "Letters," *Women's Tefillah Newsletter* 1 (August 1985): 4.

73. See Larry Cohler, "Women Debate Response to Attacks on Prayer Groups," *Jewish World* (September 27, 1985): 12–13.

74. See Toby Axelrod, "Women's Prayer Groups: Flourishing Secret Gardens," *Jewish Week* (July 7, 1989): 27; and Miriam Rinn, "Are Women's Prayer Groups Still 'Davening in the Dark'?" *Jewish Standard* (February 9, 1990): 4.

75. See Rabbinical Council of America Executive Committee Minutes, February 27, 1985, Box 6, Rabbi Louis Bernstein Papers, YU Archives.

76. See Rivka Haut, "Women's Prayer Groups and the Orthodox Synagogue," in *Daughters of the King: Women and the Synagogue*, ed. Susan Grossman and Rivka Haut (Philadelphia: Jewish Publication Society, 1992), 156, n.49.

77. It is therefore interesting that the 1990s incarnation of women's prayer groups, led by a new generation of Orthodox women, were more welcoming of the feminist moniker and their position as operating from beyond the mainstream of Orthodox Judaism. See, for example, Laura Shaw-Frank, "A Word from the Editor," *Women's Tefillah Network Newsletter* (June 1997): 1. Actually,

Rivka Haut and others started to turn toward Orthodox "taboos" such as cooperation with Conservative and Reform Jews on religious terms (such as the Women of the Wall's battles at the Western Wall in Jerusalem) in the late 1980s. See Phyllis Chesler, "The Walls Came Tumbling Down," *On the Issues* 11 (1989): 7–11.

78. Eliezer Berkovits, "Women's Prayer Groups," *Jerusalem Post* (September 20, 1985): 18.

# Conclusion

1. Yossi Toiv to Zev Eleff, December 12, 2017. A copy of this e-mail is in the possession of the author.
2. See Nosson Scherman, *Rabbi Scherman on Chinuch: Practical, Perceptive Answers to Contemporary Questions* (Brooklyn, NY: Mesorah Publications, 2017), 352–54.
3. Paul Vitello, "Something Tasty, Healthy, and Perfect for the Seder, Unless," *New York Times* (April 18, 2011): A1.
4. Natasha Rosenstock, "The *Kitniyot* Controversy Hits Home," *Washington Jewish Week* (April 17, 2008): 17.
5. Joni Schockett, "Quinoa Broadens Pesach Menu, but Sparks a Rabbinical Debate," *Jewish Advocate* (March 30, 2012): 16.
6. Chavie Lieber, "Is Quinoa Kosher for Pesach?" *Washington Jewish Week* (March 14, 2013): 48. See also Zushe Yosef Blech, *Kosher Food Production* (Ames, IA: Blackwell, 2008), 360. The same was true of varying grades of meat slaughter and other kosher foodstuff that the postwar Hungarian folkway rejected from their kitchens and supermarkets due to a stringent sense of rabbinic intuition. See Roger Horowitz, *Kosher USA: How Coke Became Kosher and Other Tales of Modern Food* (New York: Columbia University Press, 2016). 163–209.
7. See Sholem Fishbane, "The Kashrus Status of Raw Fish on Pesach," in *CRC Guide to Passover* (Chicago: Chicago Rabbinical Council, 2017), 76.
8. Lieber, "Is Quinoa Kosher for Pesach?"
9. See Hody Nemes, "Quinoa, the Rabbi and the Unfolding Tale of Liberation," *Forward* (April 18, 2014): 1.
10. See Jeff Helmreich, "Rabbinical Supervision," *Jewish World* (January 31, 1997): 3; and Norimitsu Onishi, "Reading the Torah, an Orthodox Women's Group Takes on Tradition," *New York Times* (February 16, 1997): 43.
11. See Elicia Brown, "The Politics of Prayer," *Jewish Week* (January 31, 1997): 14. See also Joseph C. Kaplan, "Bat Mitzvah Celebrations," *Sh'ma* 21 (February 8, 1991): 54–55.
12. Helmreich, "Rabbinical Supervision," 8.
13. Aryeh Z. Ginzberg, Letter to the Editor, *Jewish World* (February 28, 1997): 4.

On the fallout of the Queens affair, see Zev Eleff and Ari Lamm, "The State of the Conversation," *Lehrhaus* (February 28, 2017). Available at https://www .thelehrhaus.com/culture/the-state-of-the-conversation/ (accessed March 6, 2018).

14. See Michelle Berman, "Feminist Orthodoxy," *Jewish Tribune* (February 21, 1997): 3.

15. Pinchos Lipschutz, "'Orthodox Feminism' and Mesorah," *Yated Ne'eman* (February 7, 1997): 31. See also Robert Ephraim, "International Conference on Feminism and Orthodoxy," *Jewish Press* (March 7, 1997): 93.

16. Frimer and Frimer, "Women's Prayer Services," 38. On the defense of bat mitzvah, see ibid., 30–31.

17. Ibid., 42.

18. On partnership minyan, see Tova Hartman, *Feminism Encounters Traditional Judaism: Resistance and Accommodation* (Waltham, MA: Brandeis University Press, 2007), 121–33.

19. See Aryeh A. Frimer and Dov I. Frimer, "Women, *Keri'at Ha-Torah*, and *Aliyyot*," *Tradition* 46 (Winter 2013): 67–238.

20. Heshie Billet, "Partnership Minyanim," *Tradition* 47 (Fall 2014): 93.

# SELECTED BIBLIOGRAPHY

## Archival Sources

American Jewish Archives, Cincinnati, OH

American Jewish Historical Society, New York, NY

Arthur and Elizabeth Schlesinger Library on the History of Women in America, Harvard University, Cambridge, MA

Beth T'filoh Congregation Archives, Baltimore, Maryland

Chicago Jewish Historical Society Oral History Project, Chicago, IL

Duggan Library Archives, Hanover College, Hanover, IN

Harvard University Archives, Cambridge, MA

Hebrew Theological College Archives, Skokie, IL

The Jewish Museum of Maryland, Baltimore, MD

L. Tom Perry Special Collections, Brigham Young University, Provo, UT

Robert D. Farber University Archives of Brandeis University, Waltham, MA

Special Collections, Buswell Library, Wheaton College, Wheaton, IL

Special Collections Research Center, Syracuse University Press, Syracuse, NY

Spertus Institute Archives, Chicago, IL

Yeshiva University Archives, New York, NY

## Primary Source Periodicals

Note: As evidenced in the endnotes, I drew from nearly fifty different English, Hebrew, and Yiddish newspaper titles to conduct the research for this book. I gathered and analyzed many of these valuable primary sources from online repositories. For an up-to-date listing of Jewish periodicals available on the Internet, see the "Union List of Digitized Jewish Historic Newspapers, Periodicals and e-Journals" of the Ohio State University Libraries (https://library.osu.edu/projects/hebrew-lexicon/Jewish-Press.htm). Many general press digitized titles are available via ProQuest and Google Books. I also made ample use of newspapers and journals available at institutional archives.

*Am ha-Torah* (Brooklyn, NY)

*Beit Va'ad Le-Hakhamim* (Satmar, Romania)

*Elchanette* (New York, NY)

*The Frisch School Yearbook* (Paramus, NJ)
*Hachaim* (Uzhhorod, Hungary)
*Ha-Darom* (New York, NY)
*Halikhot* (Tel Aviv, Israel)
*Hamaor* (Brooklyn, NY)
*Hapardes* (Chicago, IL, and New York, NY)
*Hashomer* (Chicago, IL)
*Holomateinu* (Skokie, IL)
*Ida Crown Jewish Academy Keter* (Chicago, IL)
*Kehilath Jeshurun Bulletin* (New York, NY)
*Kehillat Israel Bulletin* (Brookline, MA)
*Kochaviah* (New York, NY)
*Kol Rambam* (Brookline, MA)
*Kovetz Beis Vaad L'chachumim* (Monroe, NY)
*La-Mo'ed* (Jerusalem, Israel)
*Lincoln Square Synagogue Bulletin* (New York, NY)
*Lincolnwood Jewish Congregation Bulletin* (Lincolnwood, IL)
*Noam* (New York, NY)
*Or Hamizrach* (New York, NY)
*Or Torah Bulletin* (Skokie, IL)
*The Scroll* (Brooklyn, NY)
*The Talmid* (New York, NY)
*Tal Talpiyot* (Vác, Hungary)
*Yeshivat Rambam Banquet Journal* (Baltimore, MD)
*Yiddishe Shprakh* (New York, NY)

## Published Primary Sources and Primary Source Collections

*5 Great Cuisines with Planters Peanut Oil*. New York: Standard Brands, 1967.
*46 Oyfanim far Besere Peyseh Maykholim*. Suffolk, VA: Planters Edible Oil Co., 1948.
Aaronson, Yehoshua Moshe. *Yeshu'at Moshe*. Petah Tikva: Y. M. Aaronson, 1967.
"America's Old 'Baseball Cards.'" *Jewish Observer* 18 (March 1985): 46.
Ashkenazi, Ephraim Yosef Dov. *Haggadah shel Pesah im Peirush Divrei Yo'el*. Brooklyn, NY: Jerusalem Book Store Inc., 1984.
Auslander, Shalom. *Foreskin's Lament: A Memoir*. New York: Riverhead, 2007.
Aviner, Shlomo Hayyim. *Am Ke-Lavi*. Jerusalem: S. H. Aviner, 1983.
Bellin, Mildred Grosberg. *The Jewish Cook Book: According to the Jewish Dietary Laws*. New York: Bloch, 1941.
Belsky, Meir. "The Day Schools in the U.S." *Jewish Observer* 12 (January 1977): 5–7.
Berkovits, Eliezer. *Between Yesterday and Tomorrow*. Oxford: East and West Library, 1945.

——. *With God in Hell: Judaism in the Ghettos and Deathcamps*. New York: Sanhedrin Press, 1979.

Berman, Saul J. "The Status of Women in Halakhic Judaism." *Tradition* 14 (Fall
1973): 5–28.

——. "Forty Years Later: The Rav's Opening Shiur at the Stern College for Women
Beit Midrash." *The Lehrhaus* (October 9, 2017).

——, and Shulamith Magnes. "Orthodoxy Responds to Feminist Ferment."
*Response* 12 (Spring 1981): 6.

Bieler, Jack. "A Convention Colloquium on Teaching Talmud to Women." *Ten Da'at*
2 (Winter 1988): 19–20.

Billet, Heshie. "Partnership Minyanim." *Tradition* 47 (Fall 2014): 93.

Birnbaum, Philip. *A Book of Jewish Concepts*. New York: Hebrew Publishing Co.,
1964.

Blau, Fraida. "Women's Place in Torah Study." *Jewish Observer* 17 (Summer 1984):
17–19.

Blau, Joseph L., and Salo W. Baron. *The Jews of the United States, 1790–1840*, vol. 2.
New York: Columbia University Press, 1963.

Blech, Zushe Yosef. *Kosher Food Production*. Ames, IA: Blackwell, 2008.

Bleich, J. David. "Survey of Recent Halakhic Periodical Literature." *Tradition* 14
(Fall 1973): 113–31.

"A Blessing to Judaism." *Jewish Parent* 28 (April 1976): 19.

Blumenkrantz, Avrohom. *The Laws of Pesach: A Digest*. Far Rockaway, NY: A.
Blumenkrantz, 1981.

——. *The Laws of Pesach: A Digest*. Far Rockaway, NY: Bais Medrash Ateres Yisroel, 2001.

"Brachos Bee Goes National." *Olomeinu* 26 (June 1972): 3.

Bulka, Reuven P. *The RCA Lifecycle Madrikh*. New York: Rabbinical Council of
America, 1995.

Burstein, Shmuel. *Ma'adanei Shmuel*. Petrikov, 1908.

Chernick, Michael. "In Support of Women's Prayer Groups." *Sh'ma* 15 (May 17,
1985): 105–8.

Chesler, Phyllis. "The Walls Came Tumbling Down." *On the Issues* 11 (1989): 7–11.

Clay, Harold J. *Marketing Peanuts and Peanut Products*. Washington, DC: United
States Department of Agriculture, 1941.

Cohen, Jack Simcha. "In Defense of Covering the Jewish Head." *RCA Sermon Manual* 42 (1984): 195–98.

"Collectibles: Bubble Gum Not Included." *Time* 134 (July 17, 1989): 77.

Dobrovitz, Pete. "Tradition Meets Trend with Rabbi Cards." *Sports Collector's Digest*
(July 7, 1989): 60.

"Doing and Believing: A Roundtable Discussion." *Moment* 3 (September 1978):
40–44.

Dovika, Yoju. "Campus and Jewish Education." *Jewish Life* 35 (May–June 1968): 64.

Drachman, Bernard. *The Jewish Sabbath Question.* New York, 1915.

"ECA Convention III." *Educators Council of America Newsletter* 10 (Winter 1980–81): 3.

Eider, Shimon D. *A Summary of Halachos of Pesach.* Lakewood, NJ, 1977.

Eisen, Tovah Jane. "Baltimore Women's Minyan." *Women's Tefillah Network Newsletter* 1 (June 1984): 5–6.

Eisenberg, Azriel. *The Bar Mitzvah Treasury.* New York: Behrman House, 1952.

Eisenstein, Judith Kaplan. "No Thunder Sounded, No Lightning Struck." In *Eyewitness to American Jewish History, vol. IV: 1915–1969,* ed. Azriel Eisenberg, 30–32. New York: Union of American Hebrew Congregations, 1978.

El'azaraf, David. *Imrei David.* Tel Aviv, 1970.

Elias, Joseph. "Boys and Girls Together?" *Jewish Parent* 6 (December 1954): 4–6, 20.

Elyashiv, Yosef Shalom. *Kovetz Teshuvot,* vol. 3. Jerusalem: Keren Re'em, 2012.

Emden, Yaakov. *Mor u-Ketziah Ha-Shalem,* ed. Avraham Yaakov Bombakh and Yaakov Yosef Schacter. Jerusalem: Makhon Yerushalayim, 1996.

"Entering Our Third Year." *Jewish Observer* 3 (December 1965): 3–6.

Fasman, Oscar Z. "This Friday Night Forum." *Orthodox Union* 11 (February 1944): 4–7.

———. "Trends in the American Yeshiva Today." *Tradition* 9 (Fall 1967): 48–64.

———. "After Fifty Years, an Optimist." *American Jewish History* 69 (December 1979): 159–73.

Feinstein, Jerome Tov. "The Bas Mitzvah Comes to Our Synagogue." *Orthodox Union* (October 1944): 25.

Feinstein, Moshe. *Iggerot Moshe,* vol. 1. New York: Noble Book Press, 1959.

———. *Iggerot Moshe,* vol. 4. Brooklyn, NY: Noble Book Press, 1963.

———. *Iggerot Moshe,* vol. 5. New York: Noble Book Press, 1973.

Feitman, Yaakov. "American Jewish Literature: Beware!" *Jewish Parent* 28 (April 1976): 15–18.

Feldman, Emanuel. "The Case for 'Out-of-Town.'" *Jewish Observer* 1 (September 1963): 13–20.

Feldman, Moshe Yisrael. *Lekutei Maharmi: Hilkhot Pesah.* New York: E. Grossman's Publishing House, n.d.

Feuerstein, Moses I. "The Synagogue's Responsibility for the Rising Generation." In *Speeches and Addresses Given by Rabbis and Religious Lay Leaders at the First World Conference of Ashkenazi and Sephardi Synagogues,* 92–95. Jerusalem: World Conference of Ashkenazi and Sephardi Synagogues, 1972.

Finkelstein, Sylvia. "Leaves from our Branches." *Young Israel Viewpoint* 33 (April 1942): 16.

Fishbane, Sholem. "The Kashrus Status of Raw Fish on Pesach." In *CRC Guide to Passover,* 76. Chicago: Chicago Rabbinical Council, 2017.

Frank, Zvi Pesah. *Mira'ei Kodesh*, vol. 2. Jerusalem: Mekhon Ha-Rav Frank, 1974.

Friedenwald, Harry. "Rice, Abraham." In *The Jewish Encyclopedia*, vol. 10, ed. Isidore Singer, 405. New York: Funk and Wagnalls, 1905.

———. *Life, Letters and Addresses of Aaron Friedenwald*. Baltimore, MD: Lord Baltimore Press, 1906.

Friedman, Yisrael Hayyim. *Lekutei Maharyah*, vol. 3. New York: Avraham Yitzhak Friedman, 1965.

*G.E. College Bowl Guide for the 1963–1964 Season*. New York, 1963.

Gewirtz, Leonard B. *The Authentic Jew and His Judaism: An Analysis of the Basic Concepts of the Jewish Religion*. New York: Bloch, 1961.

Gilder, George. "An Open Letter to Orrin Hatch." *National Review* 40 (May 13, 1988): 28–34.

Glazer, Nathan. *American Judaism*. Chicago: University of Chicago Press, 1957.

Goldman, Ari L. *The Search for God at Harvard*. New York: Random House, 1991.

*Gordon College Catalog: 1950–1951*. Boston: Gordon College of Theology and Missions, 1950.

Graubart, Yehudah Leib. *Havalim Ba-Ne'imim*, vol. 2. Petrikov: Shmuel Pinski, 1901.

Greenberg, Blu. "Feminism: Is It Good for the Jews?" *Hadassah Magazine* 57 (April 1976): 10–11, 30–34.

———. *On Women and Judaism: A View from Tradition*. Philadelphia: Jewish Publication Society of America, 1981.

———. *How to Run a Traditional Jewish Household*. Northvale, NJ: Aronson, 1983.

———, and Irving Greenberg. "Equality in Judaism." *Hadassah Magazine* 56 (December 1973): 14–15, 36–38.

Greenberg, Irving. "A Letter to the Editor." *Jewish Observer* 3 (December 1966): 13–16.

Greenblatt, Ephraim. *Revevot Ephraim*, vol. 1. Memphis, TN, 1975.

Grossberg, Chanoch Zundel. "Se'udat Bat Mitzvah." *Ha-Ma'ayan* 13 (Tevet 1973): 41–42.

Hager, Joseph. "Passover Laws and Customs." *The Light* 25 (April 1959): 20.

Harby, Isaac. *A Discourse, Delivered in Charleston, (S.C.) on the 21st of Nov. 1825, before the Reformed Society of Israelites, for Promoting True Principles of Judaism According to Its Purity and Spirit, on Their First Anniversary*. Charleston, SC: A. E. Miller, 1825.

Hartman, Tova. *Feminism Encounters Traditional Judaism: Resistance and Accommodation*. Waltham, MA: Brandeis University Press, 2007.

Haut, Rivkeh [Rivka]. "From Women: Piety Not Rebellion." *Sh'ma* 15 (May 17, 1985): 110–12.

———. "Women's Prayer Groups and the Orthodox Synagogue." In *Daughters of the King: Women and the Synagogue*, ed. Susan Grossman and Rivka Haut, 135–57. Philadelphia: Jewish Publication Society, 1992.

Hedaya, Ovadia. *Yaskhil Avdi*, vol. 5. Jerusalem, 1940.

Henkin, Yosef Eliyahu. *She'elot u-Teshuvot Gevurot Eliyahu*, vol. 1. Lakewood, NJ: Mahon ha-Rav Henkin, 2013.

———. *Gevurot Eliyahu*, vol. 2, ed. Daniel Osher Kleinman. Brooklyn, NY: Mehon Ha-Rav Henkin, 2016.

Himmelfarb, Milton. "An Unknown Jewish Sect." *Commentary* 33 (January 1962): 66–68.

Hoffman, David Zvi. *Melamed Le-Ho'el*, vol. 1. Frankfurt: Hermon, 1926.

Hutchinson, Paul. "Have We a 'New' Religion?" *Life* 38 (April 11, 1955): 138–40.

Hutner, Isaac. "What Is Jewish Education?" *Jewish Parent* 8 (December 1956): 5, 20.

Hyman, Paula. "Jewish Theology: What's in It for—and Against—Us." *Ms.* 3 (July 1974): 76–79.

Illoway, Henry. *The Controversial Letters and the Casuistic Decisions of the Late Rabbi Bernard Illowy Ph.D.* Berlin: M. Poppelauer, 1914.

Isserow, Rachel. "Some Thoughts on Women and the Orthodox." *Young Israel Viewpoint* (April 1976): 3–4, 7.

"It's All Kosher." *Sports Illustrated* 70 (May 22, 1989): 11.

Jachter, Howard. "The Rav as an Aging Giant (1983–1985)." In *Mentor of Generations: Reflections on Rabbi Joseph B. Soloveitchik*, ed. Zev Eleff, 329–33. Jersey City, NJ: Ktav, 2008.

"Jesus and Disciples." *Boys' Life* 80 (December 1990): 71.

Joseph, Norma Baumel. "Letters." *Women's Tefillah Newsletter* 1 (August 1985): 4.

Joseph, S. "A Check List: How Good Is Your School?" *Jewish Observer* 2 (January 1965): 12–13.

Kaganoff, Nathan M. "A Historic Document." *Tradition* 7 (Winter 1965): 121–23.

Kaplan, Aryeh. "The Editor's View." *Jewish Life* 41 (Spring 1974): 2–5.

Kaplan, Joseph C. "A Women's Sefer Torah." *Sh'ma* 14 (May 11, 1984): 111–12.

———. "Bat Mitzvah Celebrations." *Sh'ma* 21 (February 8, 1991): 54–56.

Katz, Jacob. *With My Own Eyes: The Autobiography of a Historian*, trans. Ann Brenner and Zipora Brody. Hanover, NH: Brandeis University Press, 1995.

Keller, Chaim Dov. "Love of Chiddush for Better and for Worse: What's Wrong with Being Modern?" *Jewish Observer* 27 (May 1994): 6–14.

———. [Chaim Keller]. "A Letter That Should NOT Have Had to Have Been Published." *Jewish Observer* 28 (June 1995): 30–32.

Kirschenbaum, Aaron. "Rabbi Moshe Feinstein's Responsa: A Major Halachic Event." *Judaism* 15 (Summer 1966): 364–73.

Klein, David Ben-Zion, and Chanoch Zundel Grossberg. "Bi-Inyan Se'udat Bat Mitzvah." *Ha-Ma'ayan* 13 (Nissan 1973): 69–70.

Koch, Lew. "Keeping Kids Safe from Democracy." *Chicago* 24 (January 1975): 122.

Kohler, Kaufmann. *Studies, Addresses, and Personal Papers*. New York: Bloch, 1931.

*The Kosher Directory: Passover Edition*. New York: Union of Orthodox Congregations of America, 1985.

*Kosher for Passover Product Directory*. New York: Union of Orthodox Jewish Congregations of America, 1966.

Krupnick, Lillian. *Cavalcade of Motherhood*. Chicago: Yeshiva Women, n.d.

Kunda, Shmuel. *Boruch Learns His Brochos*. Brooklyn: Shmuel Kunda, 2005.

Lamm, Norman. "The Need for Tradition." *Tradition* 1 (Fall 1958): 7–12.

———. "Modern Orthodoxy's Identity Crisis." *Jewish Life* 36 (May–June 1969): 5–8.

———. *The Royal Reach: Discourses on the Jewish Tradition and the World Today*. New York: Philipp Feldheim, 1970.

Leichman, Abigail Klein. "Torah Cards." *Amit Women* 66 (Fall 1993): 29–30.

Levovitz, Cyrel. "Leaders of the Pack." *New York Magazine* 27 (February 14, 1994): 6.

Levy, Bernard. "Keeping Kosher: The OK Symbol of Kashrut." *Jewish Homemaker* (February–March 1978): 18–19.

Lichtenstein, Aharon. "Does Jewish Tradition Recognize an Ethic Independent of Halakha?" In *Modern Jewish Ethics: Theory and Practice*, ed. Marvin Fox, 61–88. Columbus: Ohio State University Press, 1975.

———. "Torah Study for Women." *Ten Da'at* 3 (Spring 1989): 7–8.

Liebes, Yitzhak Isaac. *Beit Avi*, vol. 2. New York, 1980.

Lookstein, Joseph H. "Goals for Jewish Education." In *Judaism and the Jewish School: Selected Essays on the Direction and Purpose of Jewish Education*, ed. Judah Pilch and Meir Ben-Horin, 213–19. New York: Bloch, 1966.

Marcus, Jacob R. *The American Jewish Woman: A Documentary History*. New York: Ktav, 1981.

Masliansky, Zevi Hirsch. *Sermons*, trans. Edward Herbert. New York: Hebrew Publishing Company, 1926.

Max, Morris. "Report of Kashrut Commission." *Proceedings of the Twelfth Annual Convention of the Rabbinical Council of America* (1948): 55–59.

Medini, Hayyim Hezkiyahu. *Sdei Hemed*, vol. 8. Bnei Brak: Beit Ha-Sofer, 1962.

Mindel, Nissan J. "Merkos L'Inyonei Chinuch and Unity in Jewish Education." *Jewish Spectator* 12 (January 1947): 27.

*Mitzvot Talmud Torah (She'Ba'al Peh) Li-Nashim*. Brooklyn, NY: Shulamith School for Girls, n.d.

Moise, L. C. *Biography of Isaac Harby: With an Account of the Reformed Society of Israelites of Charleston, S.C., 1824–1833*. Macon, GA: Central Conference of American Rabbis, 1931.

Niebuhr, Reinhold. "Varieties of Religious Revival." *New Republic* (June 6, 1955): 13–16.

"The Old Synagogue Service." *Universalist Quarterly* 12 (October 1875): 497–99.

*Passover Guide*. Chicago: Chicago Rabbinical Council, 1954.

Pawlikowski, John. "Let's Ordain Women." *U.S. Catholic* 40 (May 1975): 12–13.

Pelcovitz, Ralph. "Hirsch for Our Time." *Jewish Life* 30 (October 1962): 55–60.

Pensak, Margie. "Raising the Bar on Bas Mitzvah." *Where What When* 19 (May 2004): 102, 104.

"Piskei Halakhah: *Kitniyot.*" In *The Daf Hakashrus, 1992–1997*, ed. Yosef Grossman, 18. New York: Orthodox Union, 1998.

Posek, Hillel. *Divrei Hillel*, vol. 1. Sinaia: Jacob Wider, 1925.

Poupko, Chana K., and Devora L. Wohlgelernter. "Women's Liberation—An Orthodox Response." *Tradition* 15 (Spring 1976): 45–52.

"Prayer." *Lilith* 6 (1979): 46–47.

Rackman, Emanuel. "From Synagogue Toward Yeshiva: Institutionalized Cult or Congregations of the Learned?" *Commentary* 21 (April 1956): 352–58.

———. "Halachic Progress: Rabbi Moshe Feinstein's Igrot Moshe on Even Ha-Ezer." *Judaism* 13 (Summer 1964): 365–73.

———. "A Challenge to Orthodoxy." *Judaism* 18 (Spring 1969): 143–58.

Rakeffet-Rothkoff, Aaron. *The Rav: The World of Rabbi Joseph B. Soloveitchik*, vol. 2. Hoboken, NJ: Ktav, 1999.

Raphall, Morris J. *Constancy of Israel: A Discourse Delivered before the Congregation Shearit Israel, Charleston S.C.* Charleston, SC: Edward C. Councell, 1850.

Rapoport, Shlomo. *History of the Ida Crown Jewish Academy, 1942–1992*. Chicago: Ida Crown Jewish Academy, 1992.

*Rav Yaakov Weinberg Talks about Chinuch.* Southfield, MI: Targum Press, 2006.

Revel, Bernard. "The Yeshivah College: A Statement of Aims." *Jewish Forum* 11 (May 1928): 253–55.

Riskin, Shlomo. *Listening to God: Inspirational Stories for My Grandchildren.* New Milford, CT: Maggid, 2010.

Rosenblatt, Samuel. *The Days of My Years: An Autobiography.* New York: Ktav, 1976.

Roth, Meshulam. *Kol Mevaser*, vol. 2. Jerusalem: Mosad Ha-Rav Kook, 1962.

Roth, Yehezkel. *Kuntres Lekutei Halakhot al Hilkhot Hag ha-Pesah.* Borough Park, NY: Beit Midrash Kahal Yirei Hashem, 1982.

Ryzman, Zvi. *Sefer Ratz Ka-Tzvi*, vol. 1. Jerusalem, 2005.

Sacks, Jonathan. "Torah Umadda: The Unwritten Chapter." *Le'eylah* 30 (Fall 1990): 10–15.

———. *Future Tense: Jews, Judaism, and Israel in the Twenty-First Century.* New York: Schocken, 2009.

Sadan, Dov. "Bat Mitzvah." *Dat u-Medinah.* Jerusalem, 1949.

"A Salute to Students on Both Coasts." *Olomeinu* 32 (June 1978): 3.

Schappes, Morris U. *A Documentary History of Jews in the United States, 1654–1875.* New York: Schocken, 1971.

Scherman, Nosson. *Rabbi Scherman on Chinuch: Practical, Perceptive Answers to Contemporary Questions.* Brooklyn, NY: Mesorah Publications, 2017.

Schiff, Alvin I. "The Centrist Torah Educator Faces Critical Ideological and Communal Challenges." *Tradition* 19 (Winter 1981): 275–89.

Schiff, Mordecai. *Ateret Mordekhai*. St. Louis, MO: Moinester Printing Co., 1924.

Schulweis, Harold M. "Rabbi Wanted: No Women Need Apply." *Reform Judaism* 12 (Fall 1983): 10–11.

Schwartz, Yoel. *Kuntres 'Hametz Mashehu': Madrikh Li-Inyani Ha-Kashrut bi-Pesah*. Jerusalem: Davar Yerushalayim, 1988.

Schwartz, Yom Tov. *Ma'aneh Le-Iggerot*. New York, 1973.

Schwartzman, Raphael S. "The O'Neils." *RCA Sermon Manual* 39 (1981): 79–84.

———. "The Yarmulke Scores." *RCA Sermon Manual* 39 (1981): 143–45.

Shaw-Frank, Laura. "A Word from the Editor." *Women's Tefillah Network Newsletter* (June 1997): 1.

Sheldon, Fay S. "The Yarmulka." *Jewish Life* 20 (September–October 1952): 56–61.

Shugarman, Chonon. "The Cards Are Not for Flipping." *Jewish Observer* 23 (March 1990): 49–50.

Silver, Arthur M. "May Women Be Taught Bible, Mishnah and Talmud?" *Tradition* 17 (Summer 1978): 74–85.

Singer, David. "A Failure of Halachic 'Objectivity.'" *Sh'ma* 15 (May 17, 1985): 108–10.

Soloveitchik, Joseph B. "Confrontation." *Tradition* 6 (Spring–Summer 1964): 5–29.

———. "The Lonely Man of Faith." *Tradition* 7 (Summer 1965): 5–67.

———. *Community, Covenant and Commitment: Selected Letters and Communications*, ed. Nathaniel Helfgot. Jersey City, NJ: Ktav, 2005.

Spektor, Yitzhak Elhanan ben Israel Isser. *Be'er Yitzhak*. Jerusalem, 1970.

"Spelling Bee's Revival." *Journal of Education* 117 (June 4, 1934): 314.

Stein, David. "Mr. Orthodoxy." *Jewish Forum* 45 (May–June 1962): 13, 42.

*Stern College for Women Academic Catalog*, vol. 2 (1955–57). New York: Yeshiva University, 1955.

*Student Handbook*. Boston: Gordon College of Theology and Missions, 1945.

*Student Handbook, 1968–1969*. Boston: Gordon College, 1968.

Tabak, Israel. "Rabbi Abraham Rice of Baltimore: Pioneer of Orthodox Judaism in America." *Tradition* 7 (Summer 1965): 100–120.

———. *Three Worlds: A Jewish Odyssey*. Jerusalem: Gefen, 1988.

Taschman, Gershon. "A Psychological Appraisal of Traditional and Conventional Courtship." *Young Israel Viewpoint* 51 (November 1960): 20–24.

———. "Yeshiva High School for Girls?" *Jewish Parent* 20 (March 1969): 16–17.

Teller, Hanoch. "Israel's New 'Baseball Cards.'" *Jewish Observer* 17 (September 1984): 33–35.

Tsirelson, Yehuda Lev. *Atzi Ha-Livanon*. Klausenburg: Avraham Koyfman, 1922.

Turetsky, Moshe. *Yashiv Moshe*. Gateshead: M. Turetsky, 1989.

"TV or Not TV." *Jewish Parent* 2 (April 1950): 10–12.

Waldenberg, Eliezer Yehudah. *Tzitz Eliezer*, vol. 18. Jerusalem, 1990.

Walkin, Aharon. *Zaken Aharon*, vol. 1. New York, 1958.

Wallick, Howard N. "The Dilemma of the Modern Orthodox Layperson." *Cornerstone* 2 (1997): 87–91.

Weinberg, Yehiel Yaakov. *Seridei Eish*, vol. 3. Jerusalem: Mosad Ha-Rav Kook, 2003.

Weintraub, Boris. "(Rabbi) Card Crazy After All These Years." *Moment* 31 (October 2006): 29, 66.

Weiss, Avraham. *Women at Prayer: A Halakhic Analysis of Women's Prayer*. Hoboken, NJ: Ktav, 2001.

Weiss, Joseph. "Why Wear a Yarmulka?" *Jewish Life* 20 (March–April 1953): 20–26.

Weiss, Yitzhak Yaakov. *Sheelot u-Teshuvot Minhat Yitzhak*, vol. 3. Jerusalem, 1973.

———. *Sheelot u-Teshuvot Minhat Yitzhak*, vol. 4. Jerusalem, 1975.

Wenger, Eliezer. *Brachos Study Guide*, vol. 1. Ottawa: B'Ruach HaTorah, 1989.

Wolbe, Shlomo. *Kuntres Hadrakhah le-Kalot*. Bnei Brak: Or Ha-Hayyim Seminary, 1976.

Wolpin, Nisson. "Jewish Women in a Torah Society." *Jewish Observer* 10 (November–December 1974): 12–18.

"Women's Tefilah Groups." *Women's Tefillah Network Newsletter* 1 (June 1984): 15–17.

Wouk, Herman. *This Is My God*. Garden City, NJ: Doubleday, 1959.

Yosef, Ovadiah. *Responsa Yehaveh Daat*, vol. 2. Jerusalem, 1978.

Zimmer, Uriel. *The Jewish Adolescent: A Guide for Today's Girl*. Brooklyn, NY: Balshon, 1963.

## Unpublished Secondary-Source Dissertations and Theses

Charytan, Margaret. "The Impact of Religious Day School Education on Modern Orthodox Judaism: A Study of Changes in Seven Modern Orthodox Day Schools and the Impact on Religious Transmission to Students and Their Families." PhD diss., City University of New York, 1996.

Finkelstein, Eleanor. "A Study of Female Role Definitions in a Yeshivah High School (A Jewish Day School)." PhD diss., New York University, 1980.

Ginsparg, Leslie. "Defining Bais Yaakov: A Historical Study of Yeshivish Orthodox Girls High School Education in America, 1963–1984." PhD diss., New York University, 2009.

Golden, Jonathan J. "From Cooperation to Confrontation: The Rise and Fall of the Synagogue Council of America." PhD diss., Brandeis University, 2008.

Granite, Lauren B. "Tradition as a Modality of Religious Change: Talmud Study in the Lives of Orthodox Jewish Women." PhD diss., Drew University, 1995.

Heimovitz, Joseph. "A Study of Graduates of the Yeshivah of Flatbush High School." PhD diss., Yeshiva University, 1979.

Kiron, Arthur. "Golden Ages, Promised Lands: The Victorian Rabbinic Humanism of Sabato Morais." PhD diss., Columbia University, 1999.

Lipping, Alar. "Charles W. Eliot's Views on Education, Physical Education and Intercollegiate Athletics." PhD diss., Ohio State University, 1980.

## Published Secondary Sources

Adler, Rachel. "Innovation and Authority: A Feminist Reading of the 'Women's Minyan' Responsum." In *Gender Issues in Jewish Law: Essays and Responsa*, ed. Walter Jacob and Moshe Zemer, 3–32. New York: Berghahn, 2001.

Agus, Jacob. "Jerusalem in America." In *The Religion of the Republic*, ed. Elwyn A. Smith, 94–115. Philadelphia: Fortress Press, 1971.

Ahlstrom, Sydney E. *A Religious History of the American People.* New Haven, CT: Yale University Press, 1972.

Ammerman, Nancy T. "North American Protestant Fundamentalism." In *Fundamentalisms Observed*, vol. 1, ed. Martin E. Marty and R. Scott Appleby, 1–65. Chicago: University of Chicago Press, 1991.

Antler, Joyce. "Women's Liberation and Jewish Feminism after 1968: Multiple Pathways to Gender Equality." *American Jewish History* 102 (January 2018): 37–58.

Bachner, Sally. "Free the World and Your Ass Will Follow: JFK and Revolutionary Freedom in 1960s Youth Culture." In *The Cambridge Companion to John F. Kennedy*, ed. Andrew Hoberek, 196–209. Cambridge: Cambridge University Press, 2015.

Bacon, Gershon C. *The Politics of Tradition: Agudat Yisrael in Poland, 1926–1939.* Jerusalem: Magnus Press, 1996.

Bailyn, Bernard. *Atlantic History: Concept and Contours.* Cambridge, MA: Harvard University Press, 2005.

Balin, Carole B. " 'Good to the Last Night': The Proliferation of the Maxwell House Haggadah." In *My People's Passover Haggadah: Traditional Texts, Modern Commentaries*, vol. 1, ed. Lawrence A. Hoffman and David Arnow, 85–90. Woodstock, NY: Jewish Lights, 2008.

Balkun, Mary McAleer. *The American Counterfeit: Authenticity and Identity in American Literature and Culture.* Tuscaloosa: University of Alabama Press, 2006.

Bell, Taylor H. A. *Sweet Charlie, Dike, Cazzie, and Bobby Joe: High School Basketball in Illinois.* Urbana: University of Illinois Press, 2004.

Ben-Artzi, Hagi. *He-Hadash Yitkadesh: Ha-Rav Kook Ki-Posek Mi-Hadesh.* Tel Aviv: Yedi'ot Aharonot, 2010.

Ben-Yosef, Elite. "Literacy and Power: The *Shiyour* as a Site of Subordination and Empowerment for Chabad Women." *Journal of Feminist Studies in Religion* 27 (Spring 2011): 53–74.

Bendix, Regina. *In Search of Authenticity: The Formations of Folklore Studies.* Madison: University of Wisconsin Press, 1997.

Bergman, Ben Zion. "A New Look at Peanuts—From the Ground Up." *Proceedings* of the Committee on Jewish Law and Standards of the Conservative Movement, 1986–1990, 269–72. New York: Rabbinical Assembly, 2001.

Berney, Louis. *Tales from the Baltimore Orioles Dugout: A Collection of the Greatest Orioles Stories Ever Told*. New York: Sports Publishing, 2004.

Bernstein, Saul. *The Orthodox Union Story: A Centenary Portrayal*. Northvale, NJ: Jason Aronson Inc., 1997.

Bingham, Emily. *Mordecai: An Early American Family*. New York: Hill and Wang, 2003.

Bleich, Judith. "Between East and West: Modernity and Traditionalism in the Writings of Rabbi Yehiʼel Yaʼakov Weinberg." In *Engaging Modernity: Rabbinic Leaders and the Challenge of the Twentieth Century*, ed. Moshe Z. Sokol, 169–273. Northvale, NJ: Aronson, 1997.

Blidstein, Gerald J. "From the Home to the Synagogue: On the Innovations of the Post-Talmudic Synagogue." In *Ta Shma: Studies in Judaica in Memory of Israel M. Ta-Shma*, vol. 1, ed. Avraham (Rami) Reiner, Joseph R. Hacker, Moshe Halbertal, Moshe Idel, Ephraim Kanarfogel, and Elchanan Reiner, 105–34. Alon Shvut: Tevunot Press, 2011.

Bloom, John. *House of Cards: Baseball Card Collecting and Popular Culture*. Minneapolis: University of Minnesota Press, 1997.

*B'nai Emunah: Tulsa Oklahoma, 1916–1966*. Tulsa, 1966.

Boyarin, Daniel. *Unheroic Conduct: The Rise of Heterosexuality and the Invention of the Jewish Man*. Berkeley: University of California Press, 1997.

Boyer, Paul. "The Evangelical Resurgence in the 1970s: American Protestantism." In *Rightward Bound: Making America Conservative in the 1970s*, ed. Bruce J. Schulman and Julian E. Zelizer, 29–51. Cambridge, MA: Harvard University Press, 2008.

Braude, Ann. "Women's History *Is* American Religious History." In *Retelling U.S. Religious History*, ed. Thomas A. Tweed, 87–107. Berkeley: University of California Press, 1997.

———. "Women, Christianity, and the Constitution." In *American Christianities: A History of Dominance and Diversity*, ed. Catherine A. Brekus and W. Clark Gilpin, 473–79. Chapel Hill: University of North Carolina Press, 2011.

Brereton, Virginia Lieson. "The Bible Schools and Conservative Evangelical Higher Education, 1880–1940." In *Making Higher Education Christian: The History and Mission of Evangelical Colleges in America*, ed. Joel A. Carpenter and Kenneth W. Shipps, 110–36. Grand Rapids, MI: Eerdmans, 1987.

Breuer, Mordechai. *Modernity within Tradition: The Social History of Orthodox Jewry in Imperial Germany*, trans. Elizabeth Petuchowski. New York: Columbia University Press, 1992.

Brown, Binyamin. "Erekh Talmud Torah bi-Mishnat Ha-Hafetz Hayyim u-Piskato bi-Inyan Talmud Torah le-Nashim." *Dinei Yisrael* 24 (2007): 79–118.

Brown, Erica S. "The Bat Mitzvah in Jewish Law and Contemporary Practice." In *Jewish Legal Writings by Women*, ed. Micah Halpern and Chana Safrai, 232–58. Jerusalem: Urim, 1998.

Bushman, Richard L. *The Refinement of America: Persons, Houses, Cities*. New York: Knopf, 1992.

Butler, Jon. "God, Gotham, and Modernity." *Journal of American History* 103 (June 2016): 19–33.

Byrd, James P. *Sacred Scripture, Sacred War: The Bible and the American Revolution*. Oxford: Oxford University Press, 2013.

Caplan, Kimmy. *Orthodoxy in the New World: Immigrant Rabbis and Preaching in America (1881–1924)*. Jerusalem: Zalman Shazar, 2002.

———. "The Ever Dying Denomination: American Jewish Orthodoxy, 1824–1965." In *The Columbia History of Jews and Judaism in America*, ed. Marc Lee Raphael, 167–88. New York: Columbia University Press, 2008.

Carpenter, Joel A. *Revive Us Again: The Reawakening of American Fundamentalism*. Oxford: Oxford University Press, 1997.

Casey, Michael W. *The Battle Over Hermeneutics in the Stone-Campbell Movement, 1800–1870*. Lewiston, ME: Edwin Mellen Press, 1998.

Charmé, Stuart Z. "Alterity, Authenticity, and Jewish Identity." *Shofar* 16 (Spring 1998): 42–62.

———. "Varieties of Authenticity in Contemporary Jewish Identity." *Jewish Social Studies* 6 (Winter 2000): 133–55.

Chinnici, Joseph P. *Living Stones: The History and Structure of Catholic Spiritual Life in the United States*. New York: MacMillan, 1989.

Christ, Carol P. "Toward a Paradigm Shift in the Academy and in Religious Studies." In *The Impact of Feminist Research in the Academy*, ed. Christie Farnham, 53–76. Bloomington: Indiana University Press, 1991.

Cohen, Alfred S. "*Kitniyot* in Halachic Literature, Past and Present." *Journal of Halacha and Contemporary Society* 6 (Fall 1983): 65–77.

———. "Celebration of the Bat Mitzvah." *Journal of Halacha and Contemporary Society* 12 (Fall 1986): 5–16.

Cohen, Michael R. *The Birth of Conservative Judaism: Solomon Schechter's Disciples and the Creation of an American Religious Movement*. New York: Columbia University Press, 2012.

Cohen, Naomi W. *Encounter with Emancipation: The German Jews in the United States, 1830–1914*. Philadelphia: Jewish Publication Society of America, 1984.

———. "The Challenges of Darwinism and Biblical Criticism to American Judaism." *Modern Judaism* 4 (May 1984): 121–57.

Cross, Gary. *Kids' Stuff: Toys and the Changing World of American Childhood*. Cambridge, MA: Harvard University Press, 1997.

Crouse, Eric R. "Popular Cold Warriors: Conservative Protestants, Communism and Culture in Early Cold War America." *Journal of Religion and Popular Culture* 2 (Fall 2002): 1–12.

Cuordileone, K. A. *Manhood and American Political Culture in the Cold War*. New York: Routledge, 2005.

Curran, Robert Emmett. "Ambrose Marèchal, the Jesuits, and the Demise of Ecclesial Republicanism in Maryland, 1818–1838." *U.S. Catholic Historian* 26 (Spring 2008): 97–110.

Dalhouse, Mark Taylor. *An Island in the Lake of Fire: Bob Jones University, Fundamentalism and the Separatist Movement*. Athens: University of Georgia Press, 1996.

Danzger, M. Herbert. *Returning to Tradition: The Contemporary Revival of Orthodox Judaism*. New Haven, CT: Yale University Press, 1989.

Davis, Donald S. "Inside and Outside the Classroom." In *My Yeshiva College: 75 Years of Memories*, ed. Menachem Butler and Zev Nagel, 163–66. New York: Yashar, 2006.

Davis, Moshe. *Yahadut Amerika Be-Hitpathutah*. New York: Jewish Theological Seminary of America, 1951.

———. *The Emergence of Conservative Judaism: The Historical School in Nineteenth-Century America*. Philadelphia: Jewish Publication Society of America, 1963.

Deardorff, Don. "Sacred Male Space: The Promise Keepers as a Community of Resistance." In *The Promise Keepers: Essays on Masculinity and Christianity*, ed. Dane S. Claussen, 76–90. Jefferson, NC: McFarland, 2000.

Diner, Hasia R. *Hungering for America: Italian, Irish, and Jewish Foodways in the Age of Migration*. Cambridge, MA: Harvard University Press, 2001.

Dochuk, Darren. *From Bible Belt to Sunbelt: Plain Folk Religion, Grassroots Politicians, and the Rise of Evangelical Conservatism*. New York: Norton, 2011.

Dolan, Jay P. *The American Catholic Experience: A History from Colonial Times to the Present*. Notre Dame, IN: University of Notre Dame Press, 1992.

———. *In Search of an American Catholicism: A History of Religion and Culture in Tension*. Oxford: Oxford University Press, 2002.

Dollinger, Marc. *Black Power, Jewish Politics: Reinventing the Alliance in the 1960s*. Waltham, MA: Brandeis University Press, 2018.

Domnarski, William. *Richard Posner*. New York: Oxford University Press, 2016.

Dorrien, Gary. *The Making of American Liberal Theology: Imagining Progressive Religion, 1805–1900*. Louisville, KY: Westminster/John Knox Press, 2001.

Ehrlich, Harriet. *Adas Yeshurun Synagogue Centennial Celebration*. Augusta, GA: Adas Yeshurun, 1991.

Eisen, Arnold M. "Constructing the Usable Past: The Idea of 'Tradition' in Twentieth-Century American Judaism." In *Uses of Tradition: Jewish Continuity in the Modern Era*, ed. Jack Wertheimer, 429–61. New York: Jewish Theological Seminary of America, 1992.

Eisenstadt, S. N. "Post-Traditional Societies and the Continuity and Reconstruction of Tradition." *Daedalus* 102 (Winter 1973): 20.

Eitches, Edward. "Maryland's 'Jew Bill.'" *American Jewish Historical Quarterly* 60
(March 1971): 258–79.

El-Or, Tamar. *Educated and Ignorant: Ultraorthodox Jewish Women and Their
World*, trans. Haim Watzman. Boulder, CO: Lynne Rienner, 1994.

———. *Next Year I Will Know More: Literacy and Identity among Young Orthodox
Women in Israel*, trans. Haim Watzman. Detroit, MI: Wayne State University
Press, 2002.

Eleff, Zev. *Living from Convention to Convention: The History of the NCSY, 1954–
1980.* Jersey City, NJ: Ktav, 2009.

———. "American Orthodoxy's Lukewarm Embrace of the Hirschian Legacy,
1850–1939." *Tradition* 45 (Fall 2012): 35–53.

———. "The Decline of the Rabbinic Sermon." *Jewish Action* 74 (Fall 2013): 44–46.

———. "A Far-Flung Fraternity in a Fertile Desert: The Emergence of Rabbinic
Scholarship in America, 1887–1926." *Modern Judaism* 34 (October 2014):
353–69.

———. "Freedom and Responsibility: The First Orthodox College Journalists and
Early Yeshiva College Politics, 1935–1941." *American Jewish Archives Journal* 62
(December 2010): 55–88.

———. *Modern Orthodox Judaism: A Documentary History.* Philadelphia: Jewish
Publication Society, 2016.

———. *Who Rules the Synagogue? Religious Authority and the Formation of American Judaism.* Oxford: Oxford University Press, 2016.

———. "Behind the Laughter: The Purim Shpiel Comes to America (and Chicago)."
*Chicago Jewish History* 40 (Winter 2016): 4–7.

———. "The Jewish Center, Herman Wouk and the Origins of Orthodox Triumphalism." In *A Century at the Center: Orthodox Judaism and the Jewish Center*,
ed. Zev Eleff, 279–99. New Milford, CT: Toby Press, 2017.

———. "Debating Orthodox Judaism: A Tale of Two Rabbinical Seminaries." *Jewish
Action* 78 (Fall 2017): 51–56.

———, and Ari Lamm. "The State of the Conversation." *Lehrhaus* (February 28, 2017).

Ellenson, David. *Tradition in Transition: Orthodoxy, Halakhah, and the Boundaries
of Modern Jewish Identity.* Lanham, MD: University Press of America, 1989.

Evans, Sara M. "Feminism in the 1980s: Surviving the Backlash." In *Living in the
Eighties*, ed. Gil Troy and Vincent J. Cannato, 85–97. Oxford: Oxford University Press, 2009.

Fadiman, Anne. *Ex Libris: Confessions of a Common Reader.* New York: Farrar,
Straus & Giroux, 2000.

Farber, Seth. *An American Orthodox Dreamer: Rabbi Joseph B. Soloveitchik and
Boston's Maimonides School.* Waltham, MA: Brandeis University Press, 2004.

Fass, Paul S. *The Damned and the Beautiful: American Youth in the 1920s*. New York: Oxford University Press, 1977.

Feigen, Shmuel I. "Beit Midrash Le-Torah bi-Chicago." In *Sefer Ha-Yovel shel Agudat Ha-Morim Ha-Ivrim*, ed. Tzvi Sharfstein, 280–91. New York: Hebrew Teachers Union, 1944.

Ferguson, Jeffrey B. *The Sage of Sugar Hill: George S. Schuyler and the Harlem Renaissance*. New Haven, CT: Yale University Press, 2005.

Ferziger, Adam S. *Exclusion and Hierarchy: Orthodoxy, Nonobservance, and the Emergence of Modern Jewish Identity*. Philadelphia: University of Pennsylvania Press, 2005.

———. "Feminism and Heresy: The Construction of a Jewish Metanarrative." *Journal of the American Academy of Religion* 77 (September 2009): 494–546.

———. *Beyond Sectarianism: The Realignment of American Orthodox Judaism*. Detroit, MI: Wayne State University Press, 2015.

———. "Hungarian Separatist Orthodoxy and the Migration of Its Legacy to America: The Greenwald-Hirschenson Debate." *JQR* 105 (Spring 2015): 250–83.

Finkelman, Yoel. *Strictly Kosher Reading: Popular Literature and the Condition of Contemporary Orthodoxy*. Boston: Academic Studies Press, 2011.

Fischer, David Hackett. *Albion's Seed: Four British Folkways in America*. New York: Oxford University Press, 1989.

———. *Liberty and Freedom: A Visual History of America's Founding Ideas*. Oxford: Oxford University Press, 2005.

Fishbane, Leah Levitz. "On the Road to Renaissance: The Young Men's Hebrew Associations of New York and Philadelphia, 1877–1883." In *Jewish Renaissance and Revival in America: Essays in Memory of Leah Levitz Fishbane*, ed. Eitan P. Fishbane and Jonathan D. Sarna, 47–70. Waltham, MA: Brandeis University Press, 2011.

Fishkoff, Sue. *The Rebbe's Army: Inside the World of Chabad-Lubavitch*. New York: Schocken, 2003.

Fishman, Sylvia Barack. "The Impact of Feminism on American Jewish Life." *American Jewish Year Book* 89 (1989): 3–62.

———. *A Breath of Life: Feminism in the American Jewish Community*. Hanover, NH: Brandeis University Press, 1993.

———. *Jewish Life and American Culture*. Albany: State University of New York Press, 2000.

Forren, John P. "State and Federal Legal Protection for Peyote Use in the United States." In *Peyote: History, Tradition, Politics, and Conservation*, ed. Beatriz Caiuby Labate and Clanncy Cavnar, 85–104. Santa Barbara, CA: Praeger, 2016.

Friedenson, Joseph. "A Concise History of Agudath Israel." In *Yaakov Rosenheim Memorial Anthology*, 1–64. New York: Orthodox Library, 1968.

Frimer, Aryeh A., and Dov I. Frimer. "Women's Prayer Services—Theory and Practice." *Tradition* 32 (Winter 1998): 5–118.

———. "Women, *Keri'at Ha-Torah*, and *Aliyyot.*" *Tradition* 46 (Winter 2013): 67–238.

Fuchs, Ilan. *Jewish Women's Torah Study: Orthodox Religious Education and Modernity.* New York: Routledge, 2015.

Geertz, Clifford. *The Interpretation of Cultures: Selected Essays.* New York: Basic Books, 1973.

Gilbert, James. *Men in the Middle: Searching for Masculinity in the 1950s.* Chicago: University of Chicago Press, 2005.

Goldman, Karla. *Beyond the Synagogue Gallery: Finding a Place for Women in American Judaism.* Cambridge, MA: Harvard University Press, 2000.

Goldman, Martin. "Varia Americana." *Jewish Law Annual* 8 (1989): 210–20.

Goldstein, Eric L., and Deborah R. Weiner. *On Middle Ground: A History of the Jews of Baltimore.* Baltimore, MD: Johns Hopkins University Press, 2018.

Goldstein, Israel. *A Century of Judaism in New York: B'nai Jeshurun, 1825–1925, New York's Oldest Ashkenazic Congregation.* New York: Congregation B'nai Jeshurun, 1930.

Golinkin, David. "The Participation of Jewish Women in Public Rituals and Torah Study, 1845–2010." In *The Status of Women in Jewish Law: Response,* 1–29. Jerusalem: Schechter Institute of Jewish Studies, 2012.

Golomb, Deborah Grand. "The 1893 Congress of Jewish Women: Evolution or Revolution in American Jewish Women's History?" *American Jewish History* 70 (September 1980): 52–67.

Gordan, Rachel. "Alfred Kinsey and the Remaking of Jewish Sexuality in the Wake of the Holocaust." *Jewish Social Studies* 20 (Spring/Summer 2014): 72–99.

Gordon, Albert I. *Jews in Suburbia.* Boston: Beacon, 1959.

Gotel, Neirah. *Innovation in Tradition: The Halakhic-Philosophical Teachings of Rabbi Kook.* Jerusalem: Magnes Press, 2005.

Graff, Gil. "Giving Voice To 'Torah-True Judaism' in the U.S., 1922–39: Leo Jung and the Legacy of the *Rabbinerseminar.*" *Modern Judaism* 34 (May 2014): 167–87.

Greenwalt, Kent. *Does God Belong in Public Schools?* Princeton, NJ: Princeton University Press, 2005.

Grossman, Lawrence. "Jewish Communal Affairs." *American Jewish Year Book* 98 (1998): 109–49.

———. "American Orthodoxy in the 1950s: The Lean Years." In *Rav Chesed: Essays in Honor of Rabbi Dr. Haskel Lookstein,* vol. 1, ed. Rafael Medoff, 251–69. Jersey City, NJ: Ktav, 2009.

———. "The Kippah Comes to America." In *Continuity and Change: A Festschrift in Honor of Irving (Yitz) Greenberg's 75th Birthday,* ed. Steven T. Katz and Steven Bayme, 129–49. Lanham, MD: University Press of America, 2010.

Guignon, Charles. "Authenticity and the Question of Being." In *Heidegger, Authenticity and the Self: Themes from Division Two of Being and Time*, ed. Denis McManus, 8–20. London: Routledge, 2015.

Gurock, Jeffrey S. "Resisters and Accommodators: Varieties of Orthodox Rabbis in America, 1886–1983." *American Jewish Archives Journal* 35 (November 1983), 100–87.

———. "The Winnowing of American Orthodoxy." In *Approaches to Modern Judaism*, vol. 2, ed. Marc Lee Raphael, 41–53. Chico, CA: Scholars Press, 1984.

———. *The Men and Women of Yeshiva: Higher Education, Orthodoxy, and American Judaism*. New York: Columbia University Press, 1988.

———. "The Orthodox Synagogue." In *The American Synagogue: A Sanctuary Transformed*, ed. Jack Wertheimer, 37–84. Cambridge: Cambridge University Press, 1988.

———. "The Ramaz Version of American Orthodoxy." In *Ramaz: School, Community, Scholarship, and Orthodoxy*, ed. Jeffrey S. Gurock, 40–82. Hoboken, NJ: Ktav, 1989.

———. *Judaism's Encounter with American Sports*. Bloomington: Indiana University Press, 2005.

———. "The Crowning of a 'Jewish Jordan': Tamir Goodman, the American Sports Media, and Modern Orthodox Jewry's Fantasy World." In *American Judaism in Popular Culture*, ed. Leonard J. Greenspoon and Ronald A. Simkins, 161–73. Omaha, NE: Creighton University Press, 2006.

———. "The Late Friday Night Orthodox Service: An Exercise in Religious Accommodation." *Jewish Social Studies* 12 (Spring/Summer 2006): 137–56.

———. "The Beginnings of Team Torah u-Madda: Sports and the Mission of an Americanized Yeshivah, 1916–1940." *Torah u-Madda Journal* 14 (2006–7): 157–72.

———. *Orthodox Jews in America*. Bloomington: Indiana University Press, 2009.

———, and Jacob J. Schacter. *A Modern Heretic and a Traditional Community: Mordecai M. Kaplan, Orthodoxy, and American Judaism*. New York: Columbia University Press, 1997.

Hadaway, C. Kirk. "Denominational Defection: Recent Research on Religious Disaffiliation in America." In *The Mainstream Protestant "Decline": The Presbyterian Pattern*, ed. Milton J. Coalter, John M. Mulder, and Louis B. Weeks, 102–21. Louisville, KY: Westminster/John Knox Press, 1990.

Halliwell, Martin. *American Culture in the 1950s*. Edinburgh: Edinburgh University Press, 2007.

Hamm, Thomas D. *The Transformation of American Quakerism: Orthodox Friends, 1800–1907*. Bloomington: Indiana University Press, 1988.

Handler, Richard, and Jocelyn Linnekin. "Tradition, Genuine or Spurious." *Journal of American Folklore* 97 (July–September 1984): 273–90.

Hatch, Nathan O. *The Democratization of American Christianity.* New Haven, CT: Yale University Press, 1989.

——. "Mormon and Methodist: Popular Religion in the Crucible of the Free Market." *Journal of Mormon History* 20 (1994): 24–44.

Heilman, Samuel C. "The Many Faces of Orthodoxy, Part I." *Modern Judaism* 2 (February 1982): 23–51.

——. *Sliding to the Right: The Contest for the Future of American Jewish Orthodoxy.* Berkeley: University of California Press, 2006.

——. *Who Will Lead Us? The Story of Five Hasidic Dynasties in America.* Berkeley: University of California Press, 2017.

Helmreich, William B. "Old Wine in New Bottles: Advanced Yeshivot in the United States." *American Jewish History* 69 (December 1979): 234–56.

——. *The World of the Yeshiva: An Intimate Portrait of Orthodoxy Jewry.* New York: Free Press, 1982.

Henkin, Eitam. " 'Mara De-Atra shel America.' " *Yeshurun* 20 (2008): 126–39.

Hilty, James W. *Temple University: 125 Years of Service to Philadelphia, the Nation, and the World.* Philadelphia: Temple University Press, 2009.

Hirschhorn, Sara Yael. *City on a Hilltop: American Jews and the Israeli Settler Movement.* Cambridge, MA: Harvard University Press, 2017.

Hobsbawm, Eric. "Introduction: Inventing Traditions." In *The Inventions of Tradition,* ed. Eric Hobsbawm and Terrance Ranger, 1–14. Cambridge: Cambridge University Press, 1983.

Holifield, E. Brooks. *God's Ambassadors: A History of the Christian Clergy in America.* Grand Rapids, MI: Eerdmans, 2007.

Hollander, Sidney. *The Jewish Community of Greater Baltimore: A Population Study.* Baltimore, MD: Associated Jewish Charities of Baltimore, 1968.

Horowitz, Helen Lefkowitz. "The 1960s and the Transformation of Campus Culture." *History of Education Quarterly* 26 (Spring 1986): 1–38.

Horowitz, Roger. *Kosher USA: How Coke Became Kosher and Other Tales of Modern Food.* New York: Columbia University Press, 2016.

Hoskins, Steven. "Material Culture." In *Encyclopedia of Christianity in the United States,* vol. 5, ed. George Thomas Kurian and Mark A. Lamport, 1433–34. Lanham, MD: Rowman & Littlefield, 2016.

Hunnicutt, Benjamin Kline. "The Jewish Sabbath Movement in the Early Twentieth Century." *American Jewish History* 69 (December 1979): 196–225.

Hutchison, William R. *Religious Pluralism in America: The Contentious History of a Founding Ideal.* New Haven, CT: Yale University Press, 2003.

Hyman, Paula E. "The Introduction of Bat Mitzvah in Conservative Judaism in Postwar America." *YIVO Annual* 19 (1990): 133–46.

——. "Where Do We Go from Here? Feminism and Changing Gender Expectations and Roles in Jewish Communal Life." In *Creating the Jewish*

*Future*, ed. Michael Brown and Bernard Lightman, 185–98. London: Altamira Press, 1999.

Imhoff, Sarah. *Masculinity and the Making of American Judaism*. Bloomington: Indiana University Press, 2017.

Kaplan, Lawrence. "Revisionism and the Rav: The Struggle for the Soul of Modern Orthodoxy." *Judaism* 48 (Summer 1999): 290–311.

Katz, Dovid. "Mishmeret Ha-Levi: Kiyum li-Dimuto u-Lemishmeret Hayyav shel ha-Ga'on Rebbe Yaakov Yitzhak ha-Levi Ruderman." *Yeshurun* 18 (2006): 134–204.

Joiner, Thekla Ellen. *Sin in the City: Chicago and Revivalism, 1880–1920*. Columbia: University of Missouri Press, 2007.

Joselit, Jenna Weissman. *The Wonders of America: Reinventing Jewish Culture 1880–1950*. New York: Hill and Wang, 1995.

Joseph, Norma Baumel. "'Those Self-Assured Women': A Close Reading of Rabbi Moses Feinstein's Responsum." *Nashim* 21 (Spring 2011): 67–87.

Katz, Jacob. *Goy shel Shabbat*. Jerusalem: Zalman Shazar, 1984.

———. "Orthodoxy in Historical Perspective." *Studies in Contemporary Jewry*, vol. 2, ed. Peter Y. Medding, 3–17. Bloomington: Indiana University Press, 1986.

———. *Divine Law in Human Hands: Case Studies in Halakhic Flexibility*. Jerusalem: Magnes Press, 1998.

Kaufman, David. *Shul with a Pool: The "Synagogue-Center" in American Jewish History*. Hanover, NH: Brandeis University Press, 1999.

Kelley, Dean M. *Why Conservative Churches Are Growing: A Study in Sociology of Religion*. New York: Harper & Row, 1972.

Kellman, George. "Civic and Political." *American Jewish Year Book* 63 (1962): 150–204.

Kelman, Ari Y., and Janet Bordelon. "The Political Economy of Day Schools." *American Jewish History* 102 (January 2018): 59–84.

Kelman, Wolfe. "Moshe Feinstein and Postwar American Orthodoxy." *Survey of Jewish Affairs 1987*, ed. William Frankel, 173–87. Cranbury, NJ: Associated University Presses, 1988.

Keren-Kratz, Menachem. "The Contemporary Study of Orthodoxy: Challenging the One-Dimensional Paradigm." *Tradition* 49 (Winter 2016): 24–52.

Kimmel, Michael S. *The History of Men: Essays in the History of American and British Masculinity*. Albany: State University of New York Press, 2005.

———. *Manhood in America: A Cultural History*. Oxford: Oxford University Press, 2006.

Kirshenblatt-Gimblett, Barbara. "Kitchen Judaism." In *Getting Comfortable in New York: The American Jewish Home, 1880–1950*, ed. Susan L. Braunstein and Jenna Weissman Joselit, 77–105. New York: Jewish Museum, 1990.

Klassen, Pamela E. "The Robes of Womanhood: Dress and Authenticity among

African American Methodist Women in the Nineteenth Century." *Religion and American Culture* 14 (Winter 2004): 39–82.

Koltun-Fromm, Ken. *Imagining Jewish Authenticity: Vision and Text in American Jewish Thought.* Bloomington: Indiana University Press, 2015.

Korn, Bertram W. *American Jewry and the Civil War.* Philadelphia: Jewish Publication Society of America, 1951.

Kraemer, David. *Jewish Eating and Identity Through the Ages.* New York: Routledge, 2007.

Kramer, Doniel Z. *The Day Schools and Torah Umesorah.* New York: Yeshiva University Press, 1984.

Kranzler, George. *Hasidic Williamsburg: A Contemporary American Hasidic Community.* Northvale, NJ: Jason Aaronson Inc., 1995.

Kraut, Benny. *The Greening of American Orthodox Judaism: Yavneh in the 1960s.* Cincinnati, OH: Hebrew Union College Press, 2011.

Kuznets, Simon. "Immigration of Russian Jews to the United States." *Perspectives in American History* 9 (1975): 35–124.

Lederhendler, Eli. *American Jewry: A New History.* Cambridge: Cambridge University Press, 2017.

Leibman, Laura Arnold. "Children, Toys, and Judaism." In *The Bloomsbury Reader in Religion and Childhood*, ed. Anna Strhan, Stephen G. Parker, and Susan Ridgely, 299–306. London: Bloomsbury, 2017.

Leiman, Shnayer Z. "Rabbinic Openness to General Culture in the Early Modern Period in Western and Central Europe." In *Judaism's Encounter with Other Cultures: Rejection or Integration?* ed. Jacob J. Schacter, 143–216. Northvale, NJ: Jason Aronson, 1997.

Levy, Leonard W. *The Establishment Clause: Religion and the First Amendment.* Chapel Hill: University of North Carolina Press, 1994.

Liberles, Robert. "Champion of Orthodoxy: The Emergence of Samson Raphael Hirsch as Religious Leader." *AJS Review* 6 (1981): 43–60.

———. "Conflict over Reforms: The Case of Congregation Beth Elohim, Charleston, South Carolina." In *The American Synagogue: A Sanctuary Transformed*, ed. Jack Wertheimer, 274–96. Cambridge: Cambridge University Press, 1988.

Lichtenstein, Mosheh. "Kol Isha: A Woman's Voice." *Tradition* 46 (Spring 2013): 9–24.

Liebman, Charles S. "Orthodoxy in American Jewish Life." *American Jewish Year Book* 66 (1965): 21–92.

———. *The Ambivalent American Jew: Politics, Religion, and Family in American Jewish Life.* Philadelphia: Jewish Publication Society of America, 1973.

———. "Orthodox Judaism Today." *Midstream* 25 (August/September 1979): 19–26.

———. *Culture and Authenticity.* Oxford: Blackwell, 2007.

———. "The Rise of Expressive Authenticity." *Anthropological Quarterly* 86 (Spring 2013): 361–95.

Linzer, Norman. "Understanding Teenage Behavior." In *Torah Leadership Seminar Bar Mitzvah Yearbook, 1955-'67*, ed. Susan Schaalman, 48–55. New York: Youth Bureau Community Service Division Yeshiva University, 1967.

Lytton, Timothy D. *Kosher: Private Regulation in the Age of Industrial Food*. Cambridge, MA: Harvard University Press, 2013.

Maguire, James. *American Bee: The National Spelling Bee and the Culture of Word Nerds*. Emmaus, PA: Rodale, 2006.

Maier, Joseph, and William Spinrad. "Comparison of Religious Beliefs and Practices of Jewish, Catholic and Protestant Students." *Phylon Quarterly* 18 (1958): 355–60.

Manekin, Rachel. "Orthodox Jewry in Kraków at the Turn of the Twentieth Century." *Polin* 23 (2011): 165–98.

Mann, Barbara E. *Space and Place in Jewish Studies*. New Brunswick, NJ: Rutgers University Press, 2012.

Marsden, George M. *Fundamentalism and American Culture: The Shaping of Twentieth-Century Evangelicalism, 1870–1925*. New York: Oxford University Press, 1980.

Marty, Martin E. *Church-State Separation in America: The Tradition Nobody Knows*. Washington, DC: People for the American Way, 1984.

———. "The Changing Religious Community." *CCAR Yearbook* 96 (1985): 127–31.

Mathews, Donald G. " 'Spiritual Warfare': Cultural Fundamentalism and the Equal Rights Amendment." *Religion and American Culture* 3 (Summer 1993): 129–54.

Matovina, Timothy. "Remapping American Catholicism." *U.S. Catholic Historian* 28 (Fall 2010): 31–72.

Mayer, Egon. *From Suburb to Shtetl: The Jews of Boro Park*. Philadelphia: Temple University Press, 1979.

McDannell, Colleen. *Material Christianity: Religion and Popular Culture in America*. New Haven, CT: Yale University Press, 1995.

McGreevy, John T. *Catholicism and American Freedom: A History*. New York: Norton, 2003.

Mead, Sidney E. "Denominationalism: The Shape of Protestantism in America." *Church History* 23 (December 1954): 291–320.

———. *The Lively Experiment: The Shaping of Christianity in America*. New York: Harper & Row, 1963.

Medoff, Rafael. "Rav Chesed: The Life and Times of Rabbi Haskel Lookstein." In *Rav Chesed: Essays in Honor of Rabbi Dr. Haskel Lookstein*, vol. 2, ed. Rafael Medoff, 367–523. Jersey City, NJ: Ktav, 2009.

———. *Building Orthodox Judaism in America: The Life and Legacy of Harold M. Jacobs*. Toronto: CreateSpace, 2015.

Meiselman, Moshe. *Jewish Women in Jewish Law*. New York: Ktav, 1978.

———. "The Rav, Feminism and Public Policy: An Insider's Overview." *Tradition* 33 (Summer 1999): 5–30.

Menand, Louis. *The Metaphysical Club: A Story of Ideas in America*. New York: Farrar, Straus and Giroux, 2001.

Meyer, Michael A. *Response to Modernity: A History of the Reform Movement in Judaism*. Oxford: Oxford University Press, 1988.

Miller, Richard B. *Casuistry and Modern Ethics: A Poetics of Practical Reasoning*. Chicago: University of Chicago Press, 1996.

Mintz, Adam. "A Chapter in American Orthodoxy: The Eruvin in Brooklyn." *Hakirah* 14 (Winter 2012): 21–59.

Mintz, Jerome R. *Hasidic People: A Place in the New World*. Cambridge, MA: Harvard University Press, 1992.

Moore, David L. *That Dream Shall Have a Name: Native Americans Rewriting America*. Lincoln: University of Nebraska Press, 2013.

Moore, Elaine Pohl. "An Answer to Jewish Apathy: Thirty Years of Yeshivah of Flatbush." *Jewish Forum* 40 (February 1957): 18–24.

Moore, R. Laurence. *Religious Outsiders and the Making of Americans*. New York: Oxford University Press, 1986.

———. *Selling God: American Religion in the Marketplace of Culture*. Oxford: Oxford University Press, 1994.

Müller, Timo. "The Uses of Authenticity: Hemingway and the Literary Field, 1926–1936." *Journal of Modern Literature* 33 (Fall 2009): 28–42.

Murroughs, Thaddeus R. "The Vision of Children in Relation to TV." *Jewish Parent* 5 (April 1954): 6–11.

Nadell, Pamela S. *Women Who Would be Rabbis: A History of Women's Ordination, 1889–1985*. Boston: Beacon Press, 1998.

Noll, Mark A. "The Image of the United States as a Biblical Nation, 1776–1865." In *The Bible in America: Essays in Cultural History*, ed. Nathan O. Hatch and Mark A. Noll, 39–58. New York: Oxford University Press, 1982.

———. *America's God: From Jonathan Edwards to Abraham Lincoln*. Oxford: Oxford University Press, 2002.

———, and Ethan R. Sanders. "Evangelicalism in North America." In *Twentieth-Century Global Christianity*, ed. Mary Farrell Bednarowski, 157–89. Minneapolis, MN: Fortress Press, 2010.

Nussbaum, Esther. "On the Bat Mitzvah Celebration: An Annotated Bibliography." *Ten Da'at* 3 (Spring 1989): 33–34.

Oddie, William. *What Will Happen to God? Feminism and the Reconstruction of Christian Belief*. San Francisco: Ignatius Press, 1988.

Orsi, Robert. "Everyday Miracles: The Study of Lived Religion." In *Lived Religion in America: Toward a History of Practice*, ed. David D. Hall, 3–21. Princeton, NJ: Princeton University Press, 1997.

———. *Between Heaven and Earth: The Religious Worlds People Make and the Scholars Who Study Them*. Princeton, NJ: Princeton University Press, 2005.

Orvell, Miles. *The Real Thing: Imitation and Authenticity in American Culture, 1880–1940*. Chapel Hill: University of North Carolina Press, 1989.

Ostrander, Rick. *Head, Heart, and Hand: John Brown University and Modern Evangelical Higher Education*. Fayetteville: University of Arkansas Press, 2003.

Panitz, Michael. "Completing a Century: The Rabbinical Assembly Since 1970." In *A Century of Commitment: One Hundred Years of the Rabbinical Assembly*, ed. Robert E. Fierstein, 99–170. New York: Rabbinical Assembly, 2000.

Perlman, Robert. *Bridging Three Worlds: Hungarian-Jewish Americans, 1848–1914*. Amherst: University of Massachusetts Press, 1991.

Philipson, David. *Max Lilienthal: American Rabbi*. New York: Bloch Publishing Co., 1915.

Poll, Solomon. *The Hasidic Community of Williamsburg: A Study in the Sociology of Religion*. New York: The Free Press, 1962.

———. "The Persistence of Tradition: Orthodoxy in America." In *The Ghetto and Beyond: Essays on Jewish Life in America*, ed. Peter I. Rose, 118–49. New York: Random House, 1969.

Porter, Jack. "Differentiating Features of Orthodox, Conservative, and Reform Jewish Groups in Metropolitan Philadelphia." *Jewish Social Studies* 25 (July 1963): 186–94.

Prell, Riv-Ellen. *Fighting to Become Americans: Assimilation and the Trouble Between Jewish Women and Jewish Men*. Boston: Beacon Press, 2000.

Putney, Clifford. *Muscular Christianity: Manhood and Sports in Protestant America, 1880–1920*. Cambridge, MA: Harvard University Press, 2001.

Quail, Christine M. "The Battle for the Toybox." In *Christotainment: Selling Jesus through Popular Culture*, ed. Shirley R. Steinberg and Joe L. Kincheloe, 153–86. Boulder, CO: Westview Press, 2009.

Rabin, Shari. *Jews on the Frontier: Religion and Mobility in Nineteenth-Century America*. New York: NYU Press, 2017.

Rabinove, Samuel. "How—and Why—American Jews Have Contended for Religious Freedom: The Requirements and Limits of Civility." *Journal of Law and Religion* 8 (1990): 131–52.

Rakeffet-Rothkoff, Aaron. "The Semi-Centennial Celebrations of Yeshiva and Yeshiva College." In *Ramaz: School, Community, Scholarship and Orthodoxy*, ed. Jeffrey S. Gurock, 1–19. Hoboken, NJ: Ktav, 1989.

———. "Rabbi Joseph Soloveitchik: The Early Years." *Tradition* 30 (Summer 1996): 193–209.

Ravitch, Frank S. "Religion and the Law in American History." In *The Columbia Guide to Religion in American History*, ed. Paul Harvey and Edward J. Blum, 154–68. New York: Columbia University Press, 2012.

Rischin, Moses. *The Promised City: New York Jews, 1870–1914*. Cambridge, MA: Harvard University Press, 1962.

Rodgers, Daniel T. *Atlantic Crossings: Social Politics in a Progressive Age*. Cambridge, MA: Harvard University Press, 1998.

——. *Age of Fracture*. Cambridge, MA: Harvard University Press, 2011.

Roof, Wade Clark. *A Generation of Seekers: The Spiritual Journeys of the Baby Boom Generation*. San Francisco: HarperSanFrancisco, 1993.

Rosenberg, Bernhard H. "A Study of the Alumni of the James Striar School (JSS) at Yeshiva University." *Journal of Jewish Education* 61 (Spring 1994): 6–11.

Rosenberg, Esti. "The World of Women's Torah Learning—Developments, Directions and Objectives: A Report from the Field." *Tradition* 45 (Spring 2012): 13–36.

Rosenstein, Marc J. "Legumes on Passover." *CCAR Journal* 22 (Spring 1975): 32–40.

Rosenthal, Michelle. *American Protestants and TV in the 1950s: Responses to a New Medium*. New York: Palgrave, 2007.

Sagi, Avi. "Orthodoxy as a Problem." In *Orthodox Judaism: New Perspectives*, ed. Yosef Salmon, Aviezer Ravitzky, and Adam S. Ferziger, 21–53. Jerusalem: Magnes Press, 2006.

Salmon, Yosef. *Do Not Provoke Providence: Orthodoxy in the Grip of Nationalism*, trans. Joel A. Linsider. Boston: Academic Studies Press, 2014.

Samet, Moshe. "The Beginnings of Orthodoxy." *Modern Judaism* 8 (October 1988): 249–69.

Sarna, Jonathan D. "The Impact of the American Revolution on American Jews." *Modern Judaism* 1 (1981): 154–57.

——. "The Debate over Mixed Seating in the American Synagogue." In *The American Synagogue: A Sanctuary Transformed*, ed. Jack Wertheimer, 363–94. Cambridge: Cambridge University Press, 1988.

——. "Is Judaism Compatible with American Civil Religion? The Problem of Christmas and the 'National Faith.'" In *Religion and the Life of the Nation: American Recoveries*, ed. Rowland A. Sherrill, 152–73. Urbana: University of Illinois Press, 1990.

——. "The Making of an American Jewish Culture." In *When Philadelphia Was the Capital of Jewish America*, ed. Murray Friedman, 145–55. Philadelphia: Balch Institute Press, 1993.

——. "American Jews and Church-State Relations: The Search for 'Equal Footing.'" In *Religion and State in the American Jewish Experience*, ed. Jonathan D. Sarna and David G. Dalin, 1–38. Notre Dame, IN: University of Notre Dame Press, 1997.

——. "The Late Nineteenth-Century American Jewish Awakening." In *Religious Diversity and American Religious History: Studies in Traditions and Cultures*, ed. Walter H. Conser Jr. and Sumner B. Twiss, 1–25. Athens: University of Georgia Press, 1997.

——. *American Judaism: A History*. New Haven, CT: Yale University Press, 2004.

Sarna, Jonathan D. "The Crucial Decade in Jewish Camping." In *A Place of Our Own: The Rise of Reform Jewish Camping—Essays Honoring the Fiftieth Anniversary of Olin-Sang-Ruby Union Institute, Union for Reform Judaism, in Oconomowoc, Wisconsin*, ed. Michael M. Lorge and Gary P. Zola, 28–51. Tuscaloosa: University of Alabama Press, 2006.

———. "How Matzah Became Square: Manischewitz and the Development of Machine-Made Matzah in the United States." In *Chosen Capital: The Jewish Encounter with American Capitalism*, ed. Rebecca Kobrin, 272–88. New Brunswick, NJ: Rutgers University Press, 2012.

———, and Nahum M. Sarna. "Jewish Bible Scholarship and Translations in the United States." In *The Bible and Bibles in America*, ed. Ernest S. Frerichs, 83–116. Atlanta, GA: Scholars Press, 1988.

Schacter, Jacob J. "Torah u-Madda Revisited: The Editor's Introduction." *Torah u-Madda Journal* 1 (1990): 1–22.

Schäfer, Axel R. *Countercultural Conservatives: American Evangelicalism from the Postwar Revival to the New Christian Right*. Madison: University of Wisconsin Press, 2011.

Schiff, Alvin Irwin. *The Jewish Day School in America*. New York: Jewish Education Committee Press, 1966.

Schultz, Kevin M. *Tri-Faith America: How Catholics and Jews Held Postwar America to Its Protestant Promise*. Oxford: Oxford University Press, 2011.

Schwab, Hermann. *The History of Orthodox Jewry in Germany*. London: Mitre Press, 1950.

Schwartz, Shuly Rubin. "Camp Ramah: The Early Years, 1947–1952." *Conservative Judaism* 40 (Fall 1987): 12–42.

Scult, Mel. *Judaism Faces the Twentieth Century: A Biography of Mordecai M. Kaplan*. Detroit, MI: Wayne State University Press, 1993.

Shandler, Jeffrey, and Elihu Katz. "Broadcasting American Judaism: The Radio and Television Department of JTS." In *Tradition Renewed: A History of the Jewish Theological Seminary*, vol. 2, ed. Jack Wertheimer, 363–401. New York: Jewish Theological Seminary of America, 1997.

Shapiro, Edward S. *A Time for Healing: American Jewry since World War II*. Baltimore, MD: Johns Hopkins University Press, 1992.

Shapiro, Marc B. *Between the Yeshiva World and Modern Orthodoxy: The Life and Works of Rabbi Jehiel Jacob Weinberg*. Oxford: Littman Library, 1999.

———. *Changing the Immutable: How Orthodox Judaism Rewrites Its History*. Oxford: Littman Library, 2015.

Sharpe, Eric J. *Comparative Religion: A History*. London: Duckworth, 1975.

Shipps, Jan. *Mormonism: The Story of a New Religious Tradition*. Urbana: University of Illinois Press, 1985.

Shorto, Russell. *The Island at the Center of the World: The Epic Story of Dutch*

*Manhattan and the Forgotten Colony That Shaped America*. New York: Doubleday, 2004.

Siegel, Seymour. "The War of the *Kitniyot* (Legumes)." In *Perspectives on Jews and Judaism: Essays in Honor of Wolfe Kelman*, ed. Arthur A. Chiel, 383–93. New York: Rabbinical Assembly, 1978.

Silber, Michael K. "The Emergence of Ultra-Orthodoxy: The Invention of a Tradition." In *Uses of Tradition: Jewish Continuity in the Modern Era*, ed. Jack Wertheimer, 23–84. New York: Jewish Theological Seminary of America, 1992.

———. "The Limits of Rapprochement: The Anatomy of an Anti-Hasidic Controversy in Hungary." *Studia Judaica* 3 (1994): 124–47.

Silverstein, Alan. *Alternatives to Assimilation: The Response of Reform Judaism to American Culture, 1840–1930*. Hanover, NH: Brandeis University Press, 1994.

Simon, Mordecai. "The Chicago Board of Rabbis' Broadcasting Commission." *Conservative Judaism* 39 (Winter 1986–87): 23–27.

Singer, David. "Debating Modern Orthodoxy at Yeshiva College: The Greenberg-Lichtenstein Exchange of 1966." *Modern Judaism* 26 (May 2006): 113–26.

Sklare, Marshall. *Conservative Judaism: An American Religious Movement*. Glencoe, IL: Free Press, 1955.

———, and Joseph Greenblum. *Jewish Identity on the Suburban Frontier*. Chicago: University of Chicago Press, 1967.

Smith, Andrew F. *Peanuts: The Illustrious History of the Goober Pea*. Urbana: University of Illinois Press, 2002.

Smith, Ronald A. "Winning and a Theory of Competitive Athletics." In *Sport and the Humanities: A Collection of Original Essays*, ed. William J. Morgan, 44–50. Knoxville: University of Tennessee, 1980.

———. "The Lost Battle for Gentlemanly Sport, 1869–1909." In *The Rock, the Curse and the Hub: A Random History of Boston Sports*, ed. Randy Roberts, 60–77. Cambridge, MA: Harvard University Press, 2005.

Solomon, Barbara Miller. *In the Company of Educated Women: A History of Women and Higher Education in America*. New Haven, CT: Yale University Press, 1985.

Soloveitchik, Haym. "Law and Change: The Medieval Ashkenazic Example." *AJS Review* 12 (Autumn 1987): 205–21.

———. "Migration, Acculturation, and the New Role of Texts in the Haredi World." In *Accounting for Fundamentalisms: The Dynamic Character of Movements*, ed. Martin E. Marty and R. Scott Appleby, 197–235. Chicago: University of Chicago Press, 1994.

———. "Rupture and Reconstruction: The Transformation of Contemporary Orthodoxy." *Tradition* 28 (Summer 1994): 64–130.

Speisman, Stephen. "Shaarei Shomayim's First Fifty Years." In *From Generation to Generation: Shaarei Shomayim Congregation—The First Fifty Years*, 7–26. Toronto: Shaarei Shomayim, 1978.

Spurlock, John C. *Youth and Sexuality in the Twentieth-Century United States*. New York: Routledge, 2016.

Stampfer, Shaul. "The Geographic Background of East European Jewish Migration to the United States before World War I." In *Migration Across Time and Nations: Population Mobility in Historical Context*, ed. Ira A. Glazier and Luigi de Rosa, 220–30. New York: Holmes & Meir, 1986.

———. *Families, Rabbis and Education: Traditional Jewish Society in Nineteenth-Century Eastern Europe*. Oxford: Littman Library, 2010.

Stein, Regina. "The Road to Bat Mitzvah in America." In *Women and American Judaism: Historical Perspectives*, ed. Pamela S. Nadell and Jonathan D. Sarna, 223–34. Hanover, NH: Brandeis University Press, 2001.

Steinauer, Harry. "Holy Headgear." *Antioch Review* 48 (Winter 1990): 4–25.

Steinberg, Neil. *Hatless Jack: The President, the Fedora, and the History of an American Style*. New York: Plume, 2004.

Sullivan, Winnifred Fallers. *The Impossibility of Religious Freedom*. Princeton, NJ: Princeton University Press, 2005.

Sussman, Lance J. "Isaac Leeser and the Protestantization of American Judaism." *American Jewish Archives Journal* 38 (April 1986): 1–21.

Szold, Henrietta. "Baltimore." In *The Jewish Encyclopedia*, vol. 2, ed. Isidore Singer, 478–82. New York: Funk and Wagnalls, 1902.

Ta-Shma, Yisrael. *Minhag Ashkenaz ha-Kadmon*. Jerusalem: Hebrew University Magnes Press, 1992.

Tabak, Robert. "Orthodox Judaism in Transition." In *Jewish Life in Philadelphia, 1830–1940*, ed. Murray Friedman, 48–63. Philadelphia: Institute for the Study of Human Issues, 1983.

Tarshish, Allan. "The Board of Delegates of American Israelites (1859–1878)." *Publications of the American Jewish Historical Society* 49 (September 1959): 16–32.

Tavory, Iddo. *Summoned: Identification and Religious Life in a Jewish Neighborhood*. Chicago: University of Chicago Press, 2016.

Tendler, Moshe David. *Responsa of Rav Moshe Feinstein: Care of the Critically Ill*. Hoboken, NJ: Ktav, 1996.

Tentler, Leslie Woodcock. *Catholics and Contraception: An American History*. Ithaca, NY: Cornell University Press, 2004.

Terrace, Vincent. *Encyclopedia of Television Shows, 1925–2007*. Jefferson, NC: McFarland, 2009.

Theodossopoulos, Dimitrios. "Laying Claim to Authenticity: Five Anthropological Dilemmas." *Anthropological Quarterly* 86 (Spring 2013): 337–60.

Tobin, Gary A. *A Population Study of the Jewish Community of Greater Baltimore*. Baltimore, MD: Associated Jewish Charities and Welfare Fund, 1986.

Trilling, Lionel. *Sincerity and Authenticity*. Cambridge, MA: Harvard University, 1972.

Turetsky, Yehuda, and Chaim I. Waxman. "Sliding to the Left? Contemporary American Modern Orthodoxy." *Modern Judaism* 31 (May 2011): 119–41.

Turner, Frederick J. "The Significance of the Frontier in American History." In *Proceedings of the State Historical Society of Wisconsin at Its Forty-first Annual Meeting*, 79–112. Madison, WI: Democrat Printing, 1894.

Varacalli, Joseph A. *The Catholic Experience in America*. Westport, CT: Greenwood, 2006.

Ukeles, Jacob B. *What Does Your Future Hold? The 2010 Greater Baltimore Jewish Community Study*. Baltimore, MD: Associated, 2011.

Unterman, Yael. *Nehama Leibowitz: Teacher and Bible Scholar*. Jerusalem: Urim, 2009.

Wagner, Melinda Bollar. *God's Schools: Choice and Compromise in American Society*. New Brunswick, NJ: Rutgers University Press, 1990.

Waxman, Chaim I. "The Haredization of American Orthodox Jewry." *Jerusalem Letter/Viewpoints* 376 (February 15, 1998): 1–5.

——. "From Institutional Decay to Primary Day: American Orthodox Jewry since World War II." *American Jewish History* 91 (September–December 2003): 405–21.

——. *Social Change and Halakhic Evolution in American Orthodoxy*. Oxford: Littman Library, 2017.

Weed, Ronald. "Jean-Jacques Rousseau on Civil Religion: Freedom of the Individual, Toleration, and the Price of Mass Authenticity." In *Civil Religion in Political Thought*, ed. Ronald Weed and John von Heyking, 145–66. Washington DC: Catholic University of America Press, 2010.

Wiecek, William M. *The Birth of the Modern Constitution: The United States Supreme Court, 1941–1953*. New York: Cambridge University Press, 2006.

Wolowelsky, Joel B. "Bat Mitzvah Celebrations." In *Traditions and Celebrations for the Bat Mitzvah*, ed. Ora Wiskind-Elper, 84–89. Jerusalem: Urim, 2003.

Wood, Gordon S. "Evangelical America and Early Mormonism." *New York History* 61 (October 1980): 359–86.

Yaffe, James. *The American Jews: Portrait of a Split Personality*. New York: Random House, 1968.

Young, William H., and Nancy K. Young. *The 1950s: American Popular Culture Through History*. Westport, CT: Greenwood Press, 2004.

*Young Israel of New Rochelle Commemorative Journal*. New Rochelle, NY: Young Israel of New Rochelle, 2008.

Zaklikowski, Dovid. *Kosher Investigator: How Rabbi Berel (Bernard) Levy Built the OK and Transformed the World of Kosher Supervision*. New York: Hasidic Archives, 2017.

Zalkin, Mordechai. "Lithuanian Jewry and the Concept of 'East European Jewry.'" *Polin* 25 (2013): 57–70.

Zevin, Shlomo Yosef. *Ha-Mo'adim Bi-Halakhah*, vol. 2. Jerusalem: Mekhon Ha-Talmud Ha-Yerushalmi Ha-Shalem, 1980.

Zimmer, Eric. "Men's Headcoverings: The Metamorphosis of This Practice." In *Reverence, Righteousness, and Rahamanut: Essays in Memory of Rabbi Dr. Leo Jung*, ed. Jacob J. Schacter, 325–52. Northvale, NJ: Jason Aronson, 1992.

Zinner, Gavriel. *Nitei Gavriel: Hilkhot Pesah*, vol. 2. Jerusalem: Cong. Nitei Gavriel, 2002.

Zola, Gary Phillip. *Isaac Harby of Charleston, 1788–1828: Jewish Reformer and Intellectual*. Tuscaloosa: University of Alabama Press, 1994.

# INDEX

Page numbers in *italics* indicate illustrations.

authenticity (*continued*)
  University, founding ethos of, 150–51,
  252n6; Yeshivat Rambam and, 125, 126,
  130, 131, 132, 138, 139, 141, 142
Azneer, J. Leonard, 93–94

*ba'alei teshuva* (returnees), 105, 128
Babi Sali, 118
Bacon, Karen, 174, *176*
Bailyn, Bernard, 22
Bais Yaakov, 56, 105, 120, 121, 129, 165, 171,
  172, 175, 187
Baltimore: bat mitzvah rites in, 56; Beth
  Tfiloh, 56, 130–33, 137, 248–49n36, 249n51,
  252n102; conservative Catholic/Orthodox
  Jewish community in, 126–29, 138, 140;
  high school basketball in, 248–49n36; Ner
  Israel Rabbinical College in, 127–28, 129,
  139, 179, 189; Or Chadash, 143; Unitarianism and Reform Judaism in, 247n11;
  women's prayer groups in, 188–89.
  *See also* Yeshivat Rambam
baseball: Americanization, as metaphor of,
  109; Mighty Mites quiz squad and, 98;
  rabbi cards (Gedolim cards) as alternative
  to baseball cards, 24, 112–19, *117*, 125,
  245n49
basketball: Baltimore, high school basketball
  in, 248–49n36; IHSA ban on wearing
  yarmulkes while playing (*See Menora v.
  Illinois High School Association*)
bat mitzvah rites, 22, 46–61; authentication
  and acceptance of, 59–61, 206–9; bar
  mitzvah compared, 46, 51, 52; confirmation ceremonies versus, 48, 51; first
  example of (1922), 51; as imitation of
  gentiles, 52; innovative practice, rejected
  as, 48, 53, 59; male space of synagogue
  and, 48, 51–52, 53, 56; in New York City
  area, 46–48, *47*, 50–53; in Orthodox frontier (outside NYC Tri-State area), 49–50,
  54–59, 231n56; religious egalitarianism,
  concerns about, 46, 48; in women's prayer
  group settings, 206–9, *208*, 233n75
Baumgarten, Joseph, 249n43
Belkin, Samuel, 92, 93, 95, 97, 153–54, 155
Bellin, Mildred, 36
Bendix, Regina, 3
Berkovits, Eliezer, 85, 202, 220n11
Berman, Saul J., 174, 176, *176*, 177
Bernstein, Louis, 198–200

Beth Tfiloh school, Baltimore, 56, 130–33,
  137, 248–49n36, 249n51, 252n102
biblicism, Orthodox Jewish alignment with,
  9–12, 15–16
Billet, Heshie, 208–9
Bina, Malka, 182, 183
Binyan Blocks, 122–23
Birnbaum, Freda, 200
birth control controversy in Catholicism, 20
Bitterman, Murray, 72
Blanchard, Tsvi, 74
Blau, Yosef, 139–40
blessing bee (Brochos Bee), 24, 104, 107–12
"The Blind Man in the Bleachers" (song), 204
blue laws, campaigns against, 70
B'nai B'rith Youth Organization, 86
Bnei Akiva, 128, 239n24
Board of Delegates of American Israelites, 14
Bob Jones College, 152
Bostoner Rebbe, 118
Brander, Aaron, 206
Braude, Ann, 25
Breuer, Mordechai, 8
Brigham Young University, 158
Brochos Bee (blessing bee), 24, 104, 107–12
Brogan, D. W., 4
Brovender, Chaim, 182
Bruckenstein, Ronald, 67
Brull, Yossi, 116
Burstein, Shmuel, 222n37
Bush, George H. W., 136

Calhoun, John C., 5
Camp Ramah, 86
Campbell, Alexander, 6
Catholicism: American biblicism and, 12;
  authenticity and tradition in, 2; contracep-
  tion controversy in, 20; "Romanization" in
  19th century, 6, 31, 126; television medium
  and, 89; women's leadership and, 167;
  Yeshivat Rambam and Orthodox Jewish
  community in Catholic Baltimore, 126–29
Chabad movement, 258n6
Chapin, Tom, 134
Chicago: bat mitzvah rites in, 50, 57–58;
  Council of Traditional Synagogues of
  Greater Chicago, 57; HTC (Hebrew
  Theological College), 57–58, 147, 157,
  169; Jewish Broadcasting Commission,
  89; Modern Orthodox Jewish education
  in, 129–30; Rabbinical Council of, on

Passover peanut oil, 38. *See also Menora v. Illinois High School Association*
Chicago Rabbinical Council, 38
*Chicago Tribune,* 72
childhood and youth culture in American Orthodox Judaism, 23–24. *See also* alternative Orthodox children's culture; bat mitzvah rites; day schools; *Menora v. Illinois High School Association;* Mighty Mites quiz squad; Yeshivat Rambam
Christian Amendment movement (1860s), 70
Christian fundamentalism/Christian Right. *See* Evangelical Christians
Christianity. *See specific denominations*
Ciment, Norman, 110
Civil War, 16, 32
Clearly, John, 102
coeducation: at faith-based Christian colleges, 151–52, 157–58; Mighty Mites quiz team having woman team leader, 99; at Yeshivat Rambam, 132–33, 135, 138, 139–40, 141, 142. *See also* fraternization at Yeshiva College
Cold War/Communist threat and masculinity, 148, 171
*College Bowl* (TV show). *See* Mighty Mites quiz squad
Combs, Bert, 95
Communist/Cold War threat and masculinity, 148, 171
confirmation rites, 48, 51
Conservative Judaism: authenticity and tradition in, 2; bat mitzvah rites in, 48, 49, 51, 61; cooperation between Orthodox, Conservative, Reform, and Reconstructionist feminists, 207, 269n77; gendered spaces and, 24; late Friday services in, 49; mixed seating in synagogues and, 198; ordination of women and, 174, 193; on Passover peanut oil, 219n5; suburban debates between Reform, Orthodox, and Conservative rabbis, 55; television medium and, 89; women in, 168; women's role in, 193; women's Talmud study in, 179–80; working with Orthodox and Reform Judaism, 21, 55; yarmulke, wearing, 63, 64; youth movements in, 86
Constitutional Convention, 70
consumerism, American, 20, 24, 38, 115
contraception controversy in Catholicism, 20

Council of Traditional Synagogues of Greater Chicago, 57
Country Yossi (Yossi Toiv), 203–4

Davidson, Philip, 95
Davis, Moshe, 9, 10
day schools, 187, 207; alternative Orthodox children's culture and, 104, 105, 109, 112–13; Bais Yaakov, 56, 105, 120, 121, 129, 165, 171, 172, 175, 187; economic recession of 2008–2012 affecting, 252n97; female Talmud study at, 165, 166, 171, 176, 178, 183; government aid for, 71; Mighty Mites quiz squad, support for, 94, 99, 100; Modern Orthodox youth movement and, 85; shift in emphasis from synagogue to, 125; yarmulkes and, 66. *See also* Yeshivat Rambam
"Deaf Man in a Shteeble" (song), 203–4
Deal Spiel, 122
*Detroit Jewish News,* 95
Deutsch, Hananiah Yom Tov Lipa, 52
dietary laws. *See* foodways
Disciples of Christ, 6
Diskind, Hirsch, 56
Disney, 120, 121, 122
Dolgin, Simon, 58
Doron, Naomi and Gitty, 201
Double Play Toys, 119, 120
Drachman, Bernard, 70
Driesch, Hans, 10
Drisha Institute, 177

Earle, Robert, 89
Eck, Diana, 9
*Ed Sullivan Show,* 107
education. *See* day schools; *Menora v. Illinois High School Association;* Mighty Mites quiz squad; women's Talmud study and Joseph Soloveitchik; *specific schools and organizations*
Eider, Shimon, 41
Eisenstadt, Shmuel, 2, 3
Eliot, Charles, 151
Elyashiv, Yosef Shalom, 45
Enlightenment, concept of authenticity in, 1–2
Equal Rights Amendment (ERA), 167, 180
Establishment Clause, First Amendment, 67, 69–70, 71

ethnic group identity in 1970s America, 43, 71–72

Ettlinger, Yaakov, 228n21

European Judaism: American Judaism compared, 2, 7–8, 10, 14–15, 16; authenticity issue and, 20–21; migration of Eastern European Jews to US, 18–20, 22, 31, 220n11. *See also* German Judaism; Hungarian Judaism; Lithuanian Judaism

Evangelical Christians: American frontierism and, 49, 228n13; conservative shift in 1970s, 43; education and youth culture initiatives, 106–7, 113, 120; ERA and feminism, 167–68; Free Exercise Clause, First Amendment cases, 72; religious pluralism and tolerance for, 14

Fadiman, Anne, 90

Fasman, Oscar, 57

Feinstein, Jerome Tov, 54, 57

Feinstein, Moshe: bat mitzvah rites and, 52, 53, 55, 229n32, 230n35; Brochos Bee and, 110; on Passover peanut oil, 38–39, 40–41, 42, 45, 223n60; as rabbi card, 116, *117*, 118; women's prayer groups and, 188; on women's Talmud study, 171; on yarmulke wearing, 65

Feitman, Yaakov, 109

Feldman, Emanuel, 85, 232n65

feminism: cooperation between Orthodox, Conservative, Reform, and Reconstructionist feminists, 207, 269n77; fraternization at Yeshiva College and, 149; JOFA (Jewish Orthodox Feminist Alliance), 207, *208*; masculine space, as threat to, 25–26, 149, 167–68, 192–93; Orthodox Judaism's eschewing of, 193, 207; women's prayer groups and, 186, 187, 190, 192–93, 196, 198, 202, 207, 266n36, 268n77; women's Talmud study and, 167–68, 174–76, 179–80, 207

Ferziger, Adam, 18

Feuerstein, Moses, 85

Fink, Sheldon, *91*, 94, 96–97, 100

Finkelman, Yoel, 104

Finkelstein, Louis, 89

First Amendment: Establishment Clause and separation of church and state under, 67, 69–70, 71; Free Exercise Clause, 67–69, 71–73, 77, 78; government aid to religious schools and, 70; in *Menora v. Illinois*

*High School Association,* 63, 67–72, 77, 78; public displays of religious objects, 71–72

Fisher, David Hackett, 30–31

Fishman, Sylvia, 104

foodways: authenticity and, 30–32, 43, 45, 226n89; "glatt" kosher, 43; "OK" symbol, 41, 225n79; quinoa, Passover certification for, 205–6; *schmaltz* (chicken fat), 29–30, 31, 40; sesame-seed oil in Israel, 35. *See also* Passover peanut oil

fraternization at Yeshiva College, 26, 147–64; Class Nite, debate over (1938–1950s), 153–56; courtship ethics at other faith-based campuses and, 150–52, 157–58; dance at Peter Stuyvesant Hotel (1935), 147–48; Dean's Reception/Student Council Reception (late 1960s), 161–64; masculine space in Orthodox Judaism and, 148–49, 152, 159–60, 161, 164; sexual revolution (from 1960) and, 156–61, *159*

Free Exercise Clause, First Amendment, 67–69, 71–73, 77, 78

Freedman, Sheldon, 102

Friedman, Jay, 97–98

Frimer, Aryeh and Dov, 208

frontierism, concept of, 49–50

games and toys for children. *See* alternative Orthodox children's culture

Ganzfried, Shlomo, *Kitzur Shulhan Arukh,* 65

Geddes, David, 204

Gedolim cards (rabbi cards) as alternative to baseball cards, 24, 112–19, *117*, 125, 245n49

Geertz, Clifford, 2

Geller, Yonah, 61

Genack, Menachem, 205

gendered spaces in American Orthodox Judaism, 23–26. *See also* bat mitzvah rites; feminism; fraternization at Yeshiva College; masculinity and masculine space; women and girls; women's prayer groups; women's Talmud study and Joseph Soloveitchik

*General Electric College Bowl* (TV show). *See* Mighty Mites quiz squad

German Judaism: bat mitzvah and, 228n21; Hirsch, Samson Raphael, and Frankfurt Orthodoxy, 2, 10, 14, 20–21; Hungarian Jews in US self-identifying with, 222n37; Orthodox Judaism in Germany, 2, 8, 9, 10; on Passover peanut oil, 35, 222n41

Gewirtz, Leonard, 1, 3, 203
Gifter, Mordechai, 119
Ginsberg, Aryeh, 207
Gladfelter, Millard, 102
"glatt" kosher, 43
Glazer, Nathan, 84
Gold, Eliyahu, 112
Goldberg, Aharon, 129–30, 131
Goldberg, Roslyn (Roz), 129–30, 131, 133, 134, 135, 137, 141, 143
Goldberger, Henry, 58
Goldman, Karla, 24
Goldman, S. Simcha, 72
Goldman, Yaakov, 38
Goldstein, Leonard, 101
Goodman, Tamir, 249n36
Gordon College, 151, 152, 157, 158
Gorelick, Yeruchim, 155, 255nn51–52
Goren, Shlomo, 188–89
Gottlieb, B. S., 94
Graham, Billy, 148–49
Gratz, Rebecca, 11–12
Graubart, Yehudah Leib (Stashever Rebbe), 37, 222n44
Greenberg, Blu, 180, 185, 186, 190–91, 192, 207
Greenberg, Irving "Yitz," 83, 87, 162, 171
Greenblatt, Ephraim, 229n29
Grozovsky, Reuvain, 245n49
Gurock, Jeffrey, 18

hair, Orthodox women covering, 63, 97, 196
Halakhah in American Orthodox Judaism, 22–23. See also bat mitzvah rites; Passover peanut oil; women's prayer groups; yarmulkes
Halevi, David, 74
Hapardes (rabbinical journal), 33
Harby, Isaac, 5–8
Harlem Renaissance, 20
Hartman, David, 87
Hartstein, Sam, 97, 98
Harvard University, 151
Hasidim: on Passover peanut oil, 38, 40–41; relationship of Hasidim and Mitnagdim in Hungary, 223–24n61
Hatch, Nathan, 7
Haut, Irwin, 193, 198–99
Haut, Rivka, 193, 200, 269n77
Hebrew Theological College (HTC; Skokie, Illinois), 57–58, 147, 157, 169. See also Menora v. Illinois High School Association

Heidegger, Martin, 2
Heilman, Samuel, 18
Heinemann, Moshe, 128
Hemingway, Ernest, 20
Henkin, Chana, 182, 183
Henkin, Yosef Eliyahu, 37
Hicks, Elias, 6
Hirsch, Samson Raphael, and Frankfurt Orthodoxy, 2, 10, 14, 20–21
Hirschsprung, Pinchas, 110
Hobsbawm, Eric, 2, 3
Hoffman, David Zvi, 44, 222n31
Holocaust, 30, 40, 65, 121
Homnick, Yaakov, 93
Hoover, J. Edgar, 107
Hopper, DeWolf, 98
HTC (Hebrew Theological College; Skokie, Illinois), 57–58, 147, 157, 169
Rav Huna, 64
Hungarian Judaism: German self-identification of Hungarian Jews in US, 222n37; influence in US of, 43, 225n82; Orthodox Judaism, development of, 8, 9, 10, 14, 19; Orthodox Right and, 105; Passover peanut oil, quinoa, and other foodways, 31, 35, 37, 39–44, 205, 269n6; relationship of Hasidim and Mitnagdim in Hungary, 223–24n61; yarmulke wearing and, 65, 66
Hutner, Yitzchok, 166–67, 171, 177
Hyamson, Moses, 56
Hyman, Paula, 168

Illinois High School Association (IHSA). See Menora v. Illinois High School Association
Illowy, Bernard, 13, 17, 19
Imhoff, Sarah, 26
Isaacs, Samuel Myer, 11, 17
Isenberg, Jerold, 73
Israel: bat mitzvah rites in, 59, 232n66; Israeli Independence Day, 128, 135–36; peanut oil in, 44–45; rabbi cards (Gedolim cards) in, 114–15; sesame-seed oil in, 35; Six Day War (1967), 65, 85; Women of the Wall battles, 269n77; women's Talmud education campaign in, 181–83
Isserles, Moses, of Krakow, 34
Isserow, Rachelle, 189–90

Jefferson, Thomas, 5
Jehovah's Witnesses, 67–68
Jewish Broadcasting Commission, 89

Orthodox Right: creation of alternative children's culture by, 24, 105–9, 114, 119–23; defined, 23; insularity of, 105, 109, 129; origins and development of, 105; Passover peanut oil and, 39, 45; on popular Jewish balladeers, 204; women's prayer groups and, 193, 207; women's Talmud study and, 174, 177; Yeshivat Rambam and, 125–26, 130, 131, 134, 140, 141, 143

Orthodox Union: bat mitzvah rites and, 57, 60–61; Conservative and Reform Judaism, struggle with, 21; NCSY (National Conference of Synagogue Youth), 87; Ner Israel Rabbinical College, Baltimore, and, 127; on Passover peanut oil, 30, 38, 41, 45, 227n104; on quinoa, 205, 206; women's prayer groups and, 192; women's Talmud study and, 168; on yarmulke wearing, 65

Pardes, Shmuel, 37

Parnes, Yehuda, 170, 199, 200, 259n23

Passover peanut oil, 22, 29–45; abandonment of, in America, 44; American Jewish kitchen, peanut oil in, 32–33, *33*; folkways/foodways and Orthodox authenticity in US, 30–32, 43, 45, 226n89; "Found Some Peanuts" song, 44, 226n94; Hasidim on, 38, 40–41; Hungarian folkways, influence of, 31, 35, 37, 39–44, 205, 269n6; Israeli folkways, influence of, 44–45; *kitniyot* status of, 29, 30, 31, 33–37, *36*, 38, 39, 41, 44, 221n29, 222n39; Lithuanian folkways, influence of, 30, 37–38, 39, 41, 205–6; Orthodox Union on, 30; Planters Edible Oil Company/Planters Peanuts and, 32, *33*, *36*, 38, 41, *42*, 44, 45, 220n21; quinoa controversy compared, 205–6; *schmaltz* (chicken fat), traditional use of, 29–30, 31, 40

*Peanuts* (film), 107

Peixotto, Benjamin, 15–16

Perlow, Yehudis, 192

Philadelphia: anticlericalism of, Jewish community absorbing, 127; bat mitzvah rites in, 58; Brochos Bee in, 111–12, 113; rabbi cards in, 113, 116, 118–19

Planters Edible Oil Company/Planters Peanuts, 32, *33*, *36*, 38, 41, *42*, 44, 45, 220n21

Posner, Richard, 78–79

Poupko, Bernard, 52

Poznanski, Gustavus, 11

prayer groups, female. *See* women's prayer groups

Preis, Ervin, 249n43

Prell, Riv-Ellen, 24

Pressley, Elvis, 88

Price, Dovid, 104, 109, 111

Promise Keepers, 149

Protestantism: authenticity and tradition in, 2; biblicism of, 9–12; conservative turn in 1970s, 43; courtship ethics at faith-based campuses, 150–52, 157–58; muscular Christianity and masculinity in, 25–26, 148–50, 151; television medium, religious groups wrestling with, 88–89. *See also* Evangelical Christians; *specific denominations*

public displays of religious objects, 71–72

Putney, Clifford, 25

Quakers, 6, 127

quinoa, Passover certification for, 205–6

rabbi cards (Gedolim cards) as alternative to baseball cards, 24, 112–19, *117*, 125, 245n49

Rabbinical Council of America (RCA): Agudath Israel on, 21; on bat mitzvah rites, 59, 60; on Passover peanut oil, 38, 45; *Tradition* (journal), 85; on women's prayer groups, 197–201; on women's role in Jewish community, 192–93

Rabin, Shari, 14, 49

Rabinowitz, Baruch, 170

Rabinowitz, Jacob, 174

Rackman, Emanuel, 21, 83, 85

Rambam (Maimonides), 34, 64, 124, 150

Raphall, Morris, 13, 17

Raybin, Arthur, 97

RCA. *See* Rabbinical Council of America

Reconstructionist Judaism: bat mitzvah in, 51; cooperation between Orthodox, Conservative, Reform, and Reconstructionist feminists, 207, 269n77; gendered spaces and, 24

Reform Judaism: American biblicism and, 10, 11, 12; American republicanism and, 6–8, 9, 13–14; authenticity and tradition in, 2; in Baltimore, 247n11; bat mitzvah in, 48, 51, 61; belief and praxis differences from Orthodox Judaism, 10; cooperation between Orthodox, Conservative, Reform, and Reconstructionist feminists,

CPSIA information can be obtained
at www.ICGtesting.com
Printed in the USA
LVHW022350220721
693426LV00012B/1175